D0484216

SIMPLY SACRED

Books by Gary Thomas

Authentic Faith

Devotions for a Sacred Marriage

Devotions for Sacred Parenting

The Glorious Pursuit

Holy Available

Pure Pleasure

Sacred Influence

Sacred Marriage

Sacred Parenting

Sacred Pathways

Thirsting for God

SIMPLY SACRED

GARY THOMAS

BESTSELLING AUTHOR OF *SACRED MARRIAGE*

ZONDERVAN.com/
AUTHORTRACKER
follow your favorite authors

We want to hear from you. Please send your comments about this book to us in care of zreview@zondervan.com. Thank you.

ZONDERVAN

Simply Sacred
Copyright © 2011 by Gary Thomas

This title is also available as a Zondervan ebook.
Visit www.zondervan.com/ebooks.

This title is also available in a Zondervan audio edition.
Visit www.zondervan.fm.

Requests for information should be addressed to:

Zondervan, *Grand Rapids, Michigan 49530*

Library of Congress Cataloging-in-Publication Data

Thomas, Gary (Gary Lee)
      Simply sacred : daily readings / Gary Thomas.
        p. cm.
      ISBN 978-0-310-32968-8 (hardcover, jacketed)
      1. Devotional calendars. I. Title.
    BV4811.T485   2010
    242'.2—dc22   2010024265

Published in association with Yates & Yates, www.yates2.com.

Cover design: Jeff Gifford
Cover illustration: GettyImages®
Interior design: Beth Shagene

Printed in the United States of America

11 12 13 14 15 16 17 18 /DCI/ 24 23 22 21 20 19 18 17 16 15 14 13 12 11 10 9 8 7 6 5 4 3 2 1

To our new home and family,
Second Baptist Church, Houston,
for a welcome unlike any other
and for your partnership in the gospel.

CONTENTS

JANUARY

The beginning of each new year provides an opportunity to reorient our hearts and minds toward that all-important call to seek first God's kingdom and his righteousness (Matthew 6:33). "Seek his kingdom" is an invitation to bask in God's presence — the presence of the magnificent Creator who longs to spend unhurried time with us — and to commit ourselves anew to be his faithful servants. The new year helps us put previous failures behind us as we recommit to the second task — growing in righteousness — by drawing on the strength and resources made available to us through God's great goodness.

WHAT DO YOU SEE?

As our plane ascended out of San Antonio, it passed an enclave of mansions. These homes had to contain at least seven to ten thousand square feet of space apiece, with immaculate lawns and gardens, large pools, and huge garages. But from two thousand feet in the air, it's amazing how small they looked. Another few thousand feet, and they became mere playhouses.

And then it hit me: not a home on this planet looks big to heaven; no house looks huge to God. The things that swell our chests with pride look puny from heaven's perspective.

We can't impress God.

And so I prayed, "Lord, help me to see this world with your eyes. Otherwise I might value what you despise and despise what you value."

It dawned on me that I was praying the prayer of Francis of Assisi's conversion, the prayer that led him ultimately to reject his wealth and kiss the lepers. By aligning ourselves with supernatural vision, we can keep ourselves from slipping into the allure of materialism.

That's what the psalmist experienced when he began envying the arrogant. Perhaps, like me, he had passed some of those ten-thousand-square-foot mansions. He noted that the inhabitants had no particular belief in God and he said what many of us have probably wondered from time to time: "Surely in vain have I kept my heart pure; in vain have I washed my hands in innocence" (Psalm 73:13). But when he entered God's house, his eyes were opened and he understood the riches that surrounded him: "Whom have I in heaven but you? And earth has nothing I desire besides you" (verse 25).

Regaining God's perspective — refocusing our spiritual eyesight — changes *everything*. Will you pause for a moment and consider where your eyesight may be growing dim? Are you blinded to God's daily blessings because you're too focused on financial concerns, health issues, or frustrated relationships? Have you stopped seeing people as important and instead stare wistfully at possessions, power, and pleasure? Stop, refocus, and look at your life and your circumstances from God's perspective. What do you see?

Holy Available, 59–60

January 2

JUST ONE HERO

Even though I love writing books, it sobered me recently when I looked up the books of one of my favorite writers, Elton Trueblood. His works are twice as insightful as my own, and better written. He was more intelligent than I am, wiser, and I believe a more powerful communicator. I'm still challenged by his thoughts. Yet almost all of his books are now out of print, and he died a scant two decades ago.

I'm a fool if I believe it will be any different with me. Though out of obedience I want to serve God as he has called me to serve him, the longest-lasting way I can accomplish this is to pour my time into my family.

A theological truth stands behind this reprioritizing. I get really nervous when I see highly visible Christian leaders talking about a particular anointing or special touch from God—creating what I call "spiritual castes." Scripture lauds just one hero, and that is God himself.

In fact, the Bible goes out of its way to document how even major biblical characters had ugly flaws. Eve fell victim to the deception of the serpent. Abraham got ahead of God's plan and fathered a line of descendants that even today remains at war with Israel. Moses killed an Egyptian and later displeased God so much that he lost the right to enter the Promised Land. King David committed adultery and murder. Peter denied knowing Jesus three times. Paul persecuted the early church.

God does not share his glory with anyone. No one can rival the Creator. Our so-called search for significance is often a dangerous attempt to steal some of God's glory. We may make our lust for recognition sound angelic—wrapping our ambition in kingdom-building terms—but at root it becomes a demonic exercise to use God's gifting in order to make *ourselves* seem important.

Don't be fooled. Don't ignore what really matters as you try to play the one in ten billion odds of being the rare historical figure who is still remembered three centuries later. Embrace your insignificance—it feels very freeing—and let it reestablish your focus. In God's delightful irony, embracing temporal insignificance leads to the greatest eternal significance—deeper relationships in the here and now, and everlasting affirmation from Almighty God in eternity.

Sacred Parenting, 160–61

PRESENCE TRUMPS SINCERITY

Spirituality has become a popular word in our culture, but the highest value many people place on spirituality these days is sincerity. According to the popular view, it doesn't matter what we believe as long as we are sincere about it.

This is *not* the biblical perspective. James 1:27 puts this idea to rest with a dozen words: "Religion that God our Father accepts as pure and faultless is this …" If God finds some religion acceptable, then he must find other religions *unacceptable*. If there is a way that God wants to be loved, then there must be a way he *doesn't* want to be loved. Sincerity alone isn't enough.

Christian spirituality is not a search for spiritual enlightenment, new experiences, or esoteric wisdom. It is rather rooted in a passionate pursuit of, and response to, a spiritual being—God himself. "Christian spirituality," wrote the Whiteheads, "can be described as our consistent efforts to respond to the delights and demands of God's presence in our life."[1] The operative word here is *presence*.

The great Christian writers of the past stressed the importance of living in constant awareness of God's presence. Those who have advanced in the Christian life have learned to develop an almost mystical memory that keeps them attuned to the fact that God is always with them, always ready to whisper his words of challenge, encouragement, affirmation, and loving rebuke. He is always watching, always caring, always hearing.

Perhaps the classic literary work on this aspect of the Christian life is Brother Lawrence's *Practicing the Presence of God*. Lawrence, a humble monk, learned to take special delight in God's continual presence, so that he felt equally close to God peeling potatoes in the kitchen as kneeling at the altar in prayer. He said we should "establish ourselves in the presence of God by continually talking to him," suggesting that it was a "shameful thing" to allow trivial thoughts to break into this spiritual conversation. He urged us to "feed our souls on lofty thoughts of God, and so find great joy in being with him."[2]

How can you make yourself more mindful of God's presence today?

Sacred Marriage, 228–29

THE BEAUTY OF SMALL THINGS

My sister Linda and her husband Dan bought a neglected house on a piece of property with a breathtaking view of the Puget Sound. Dan had done much to capitalize on the picturesque scenery. He is the type who looks at a house and sees not what's there but what *could* be there. As such, he had practically torn the house down and rebuilt it.

We parked in full view of the water and ascended the stairs toward the side door. We could see the backyard, and Graham's eyes lit up at the soccer net; Kelsey jumped at the sight of the swing set. We walked into a kitchen with new cabinets, a tile-counter bar, and a living room with no need for pictures. Windows seemed quite sufficient. I wandered around, looked at the staircase that had been moved (mechanically challenged guys like me can't even imagine how to move a staircase), made my way downstairs, listened to Lisa's dad say, "Wow!" when he saw the master bathroom, and overall felt very impressed with my brother-in-law's work.

My meditations dissolved with an urgent "Uncle Gary, Uncle Gary, come quick!" I turned and spotted Colby, my then three-year-old nephew, jumping up and down. "I want to show you a *spider*. A big hairy spider!"

"Where is he?" I asked.

"Come here! I'll show you."

His sense of wonder made me smile. Here we were, several adults, marveling at the great workmanship of a home remodeler, but Colby had no time for new tile floors, a customized kitchen, or a repositioned staircase. An ordinary spider —the kind you could find in any abandoned warehouse or vacant lot—now *that* was something to get excited about.

May God grant us the grace to become a little more like Colby and celebrate the most simple blessings of life.

Sacred Parenting, 134–35

Awakened to God

Do you wish to become awakened to God in a fresh and powerful way? Saint Bonaventure, a disciple of Francis of Assisi, suggested a grid through which you may "school" yourself to seek God outdoors.

First, consider the *greatness* of creation — mountains, sky, and oceans — which clearly portrays the immensity of the power, wisdom, and goodness of the triune God.

Next, look at the *multitude* of creation — a forest has more plant and animal life than you could examine in a lifetime and shows us how God is capable of doing many things at once. Those who wonder how God can hear so many prayers uttered simultaneously have been out of the forest too long. Martin Luther said that when we remember that Jesus became a man, then we can properly appreciate the sun, the moon, the stars, trees, apples, pears, as we reflect that he is Lord over and the center of all things.[3]

Finally, examine the *beauty* of creation — see the beauty of rocks and their shapes, the beauty of colors and shades, the beauty of individual elements (such as trees), and the beauty of overall composition (such as forests). God's beauty cannot be revealed through one form, but is so vast and infinite it can fill an entire world with wonder.

The outdoors also speaks of God's abundance. Stand barefoot in a desert or on a beach and try to guess how many grains of sand lie under your feet or within your sight or on all the beaches and deserts of the world. We serve a God of plenty, whose mercy and love are inexhaustible.

Creation is nothing less than a sanctuary, a holy place that invites you to prayer. See how you can awaken your soul with creation. As you commute to work or the grocery store, consider driving a few extra blocks or even miles if it means you can pass through a country road. Take an extra moment to look around you and appreciate what God has made. Decide that traveling will be more important to you than reaching the next place.

Make it a worship-filled event.

Sacred Pathways, 52–54

CREATED TO CREATE

I stood on the top of Marye's Heights in Fredricksburg, Virginia, site of a ghastly Civil War battle in 1862, and kept whispering, "What a waste." On this spot, Union troops had foolishly tried to take an impenetrable position, charging uphill in an effort to capture the city. They became nothing more than target practice for the Confederates.

The first wave of the Union assault died in a massacre. Ambrose Everett Burnside, the Union general, ordered another wave. The Confederates cheered their bravery, waited until the soldiers got in range, and then shot every one of them.

Burnside sent yet another wave, with the same result. These lives were thrown away virtually on a fool's errand.

Few things anger me more than wasted life. When I hear about high school kids who drive foolishly and end up dead before their nineteenth birthday, when I read about college students who go on a fatal drinking binge, when I read anything about a preventable loss of life, I feel a profound sadness. Part of this springs from my theological belief that as people created in the image of God, we have a responsibility to create. Whether we build a business, a house, a family, a book, a life (through education or medicine), or whatever else we choose to build, we shouldn't waste our lives, but spend them productively.

Have you ever noticed how our culture lives off other people's acts of creation? Consider how many "awards" shows fill the television schedule — the Grammys, the People's Choice Awards, the MTV Awards, the Golden Globes, the Dove Awards, the Emmys, the list goes on and on — as our culture lives vicariously through the achievements of others.

You were made by God to create. If you don't create in a thoughtful and worshipful manner, you will feel less than human because you are, in fact, acting in a subhuman mode. A life spent in a dead-end, joyless job with evenings spent in front of a television set and weekends spent "passing the time" will feel like hell on earth *because it is*. Don't waste your life! Build something worthwhile through God's creative energy.

Sacred Marriage, 240–41

January 7

A SPLASH OF GLORY

Some years ago, my daughter became seriously ill with pneumonia. At the time of her diagnosis, I felt pretty wiped out myself—but when your kid is sick, you just can't afford the luxury of illness.

The doctor checked Allison into the hospital. After we settled into the room, the nurse came in and then left. A few minutes later, she stopped in again. The third time she came into our room, she paused and looked at me.

"I know you from somewhere," she said.

"Do you go to church?" I asked.

A big smile crossed her face. "You're Gary Thomas! Oh, we love your books. Wait until my husband hears I met Gary Thomas."

We talked as she came in and out of the room, but I never saw her after that night until Allison was discharged five days later. She stopped in just to say hi. The nurse explained that she didn't normally work that floor, but the hospital had been unusually busy on Allison's first night. We chatted for a little while, and then she added, "I think God just knew I needed to meet Gary Thomas."

I didn't remember any particularly significant conversation that had taken place; certainly nothing I would consider "ministry." In fact, I had felt rather ill myself and was preoccupied by thoughts about the implications of my daughter's illness.

"It's not what you said," the nurse explained. "You always had a smile. And you were so calm."

And that's when I felt a splash of God's glory. I caught a glimpse of how his presence—and my being available to him—helps transform not only me but also others around me—even when I don't even realize that it's happening. You might be ill yourself, or looking for a job, or worried about so many transitory things. Even in these seasons, will we make ourselves available to God? That's what prayer, Bible study, worship, fellowship, and similar spiritual disciplines point toward: being available to God. Every moment of this new day provides yet another opportunity for God to make himself known through us.

Holy Available, 169–70

GUARD YOUR HEART

It is difficult to overstate the importance of a heart captured by and settled on the things of God. Proverbs 4:23 reads, "Above all else, guard your heart, for it is the wellspring of life."

Above all else.

When our hearts get led astray, we become blind, deaf, and stupid. We are so made that our passions set our course; they shape who we become. The great nineteenth-century preacher Andrew Murray put it this way: "He that sets his heart upon the loving God will find the living God take possession and fill his heart."[4]

I've seen this happen in a negative way many times. I knew a man who walked in godliness for several decades. Two years after his wife died, I noticed a change in his churchgoing habits. When I asked about it, initially he remained silent but then said he had been doing something that, while it might meet his own needs and desires, "could also advance God's kingdom."

"That's great," I said. "Pretty early for evangelism, though." I could feel his discomfort.

"I'm guessing your evangelism involved a woman," I offered, and he nodded. The meek look told me even more.

"And the reason it started early," I surmised, "is because she actually arrived at your house the night before."

"That's about it," he admitted.

"And this advances God's kingdom how?"

"I think I can be a good influence on her."

"By sleeping with her when the two of you aren't married?"

"You know, sometimes you have to meet someone on their own level before they'll hear the gospel."

"So I need to get drunk with alcoholics before I can share the good news with them?"

My friend eventually came around, but I never expected to hear him, of all people, rationalizing something that he had criticized others for doing while his wife was alive. Did his mind suddenly stop thinking? Did his eyes stop seeing? Did his ears stop hearing?

Yes, yes, and yes—and it all began when his heart was led astray. Guard your heart!

Holy Available, 141–42

EMBRACING EVERY SEASON

A massive theological reality unfolds when we realize that the God of the Old Testament attached himself to a certain people. For thousands of years, loyal adherents worshiped the god of the hills, the god of the valley, or the god of the sea; but the idea that there was a God of Abraham, Isaac, and Jacob—a God of particular people—was something new!

This relationship between God and his people, of course, was anything but easy. Periods of great joy and celebration (witness the love affair of God and his people when Solomon dedicated the temple) alternated with seasons of frustration and anger (when God allowed foreign tyrants to conquer), times of infidelity and apostasy (when Israel chased after other gods), and excruciating seasons of silence (including a four-hundred-year stretch between the Old and New Testaments).

Now take these examples and break them down, thinking of them in a smaller context. There were times of great joy and celebration, frustration and anger, infidelity, and excruciating seasons of silence. Sound like any relationship you know? Your own marriage, for example?

Viewed through this lens, the marriage relationship allows us to experientially identify with God and his relationship with Israel. Has your marriage had periods of great joy and celebration? God can relate to and rejoice with you. Have you perhaps experienced the heartbreaking betrayal of unfaithfulness? Or the frustration of mournful silence? If so, you are not alone—and with these, you have been given the raw materials with which to build a more intimate relationship with God.

Viewing marriage through the lens of God's relationship with his people gives us the opportunity to appreciate marriage in its entirety. Though we'd all love to live in unceasing times of great joy and celebration, it's helpful to know that, while the other seasons may be unpleasant, they still have great value, not least of which is that in them we can grow in intimate understanding of the God who has been loving his bride long before our own marriage began.

God has a long history with his people, cycling through many seasons. It's the same with us and our spouse. Let's use and even learn to appreciate each season to grow toward each other and toward our knowledge of God.

Sacred Marriage, 105–6

GOD-SIGHT

If we see only with human eyes, we will quickly lose hope in the face of our sin and the tragedies of this fallen world. That is why we need God-sight, which does not merely avoid negative thinking but goes far beyond to include seeing the blessings God has in store for his people.

Paul prayed that the eyes of our hearts might be enlightened so that we may know the hope to which God has called us, including "his incomparably great power for us who believe" (Ephesians 1:19). God-sight gives us fresh hope and beautiful glimpses of what is possible through God.

Moses' parents "hid him for three months after he was born, because they saw he was no ordinary child, and they were not afraid of the king's edict" (Hebrews 11:23). Moses' parents opened their minds to a brighter future than that of an indentured slave. You may consider yourself poor or disadvantaged intellectually, but it's unlikely that your child was born into an environment marked by centuries of slavery. Will you see with the eyes of Moses' parents, who believed that God could create and then guide a powerful life—even one born in squalor? Human eyes can be blinded by fear, pessimism, shame, or despair. God-empowered eyes can look past all of that and see "no ordinary" future.

If we look at people only through human eyes, we see little hope (and usually a lot of cynicism). But when we see God standing behind someone and see God in someone, hope becomes more than wishful thinking; it morphs into a wise choice based on the historical reality of God changing people from the inside out.

God-sight gives me the ability to see hope for people when they see none for themselves. God-sight allows me to see a purpose for those trapped in triviality. God-sight helps me to proclaim confidently the availability of God's power to those who define themselves only as helpless victims or addicts. When we cooperate with God as he works to transform us into Christ's image, we can become God's eyes for those too blind to see clearly for themselves.

Holy Available, 65–66

CO-REGENTS

The Bible affirms women in a way that was quite radical for the time in which it was written. The Old Testament stepped outside its cultural milieu to insist that women mirror God's own character and image just as fully as do their male counterparts: "So God created man in his own image, in the image of God he created him; male and female he created them" (Genesis 1:27). Right from the start, we learn that women and men together mirror the image of God. Males, by themselves, are not up to the task; since God is above gender, males alone (or females alone) fail to adequately represent his character and image.

While the apostle Paul does ascribe a certain significance to the man being created first, if you look at the line of creation, females are the culmination! Everything keeps getting more sophisticated, more intricate, until finally a woman appears—and only then does God rest.

Just as tellingly, the admonition to act on this world, shape this world, and even to rule over this world is given to women just as much as it is to men: "God blessed *them* [the man and the woman] and said to *them*, 'Be fruitful and increase in number; fill the earth and subdue it. Rule over the fish of the sea and the birds of the air and over every living creature that moves on the ground'" (Genesis 1:28, emphasis added).

Women are not told to sit passively on the sidelines and cheer for their husbands as the men run the show. On the contrary, from the very beginning, women share God's command for humans to rule, subdue, and manage this earth. They are co-regents.

This truth challenges men to look at women with the same respect, and indeed awe, that is appropriate to someone made in God's image. It challenges women to rise up to their calling as regal agents on earth. Though the Bible does discuss various roles along gender lines in both marriage and church government, overall it consistently elevates women to a place of prominence and significant impact. Our attitude should be the same. Men, do we look at women as God does? Women, do you look at yourself the way God looks at you?

Sacred Influence, 22–23

GOD-CENTERED PARENTS

I returned from a weekend speaking trip late one Sunday evening. Because I hadn't seen my daughter for a couple of days, I got up after less than five hours of sleep to drive her to school. She could have caught a bus, but if I drove her to school, she could sleep in a little later and we could talk on the way.

Or so I thought.

It was a Monday, and my daughter (who is normally the most appreciative of all my children) was in a Monday sort of mood. I couldn't pry a sentence out of her any more than I could lift Mount Everest. She got out of our silent car without so much as a thank you. Normally, Allison is quick to express her thanks—but this was just one of those mid-adolescent days.

If I were a child-centered father, I might immediately feel resentful and start stewing: *I get up after just a few hours of sleep, and this is how she treats me? Well, she won't get that chance again! Next week, I'm sleeping in and then playing golf!* Child-centered parents act nicely toward their children only when their children act nicely toward them. A child-centered parent goes out of her way as long as her children appreciate her sacrifice. A child-centered parent bases his or her actions on the kids' response.

A God-centered parent, on the other hand, acts out of reverence for God. Regardless of how my children treat me, I know that God wills that I move toward my children, get engaged in their lives, offer biblical correction and loving support. Though I adore my daughter, I don't get out of bed after just a few hours of sleep solely out of love for her, but out of reverence for God.

In other words, *our own spiritual quest must drive our parenting*. Unfinished or neglected spiritual business inevitably works its way out through our relationships. We become more demanding, controlling, intolerant, resentful. Our spouses and our children cannot quench the God-given spiritual hunger in our souls. When we neglect God, we ask our marriage and our parenting to become stand-ins for God—something they were never designed to do.

If you've lost your motivation for family life, it's usually because you've become spouse centered or child centered instead of God centered. Only God is perfect, which means any other motivation will be spotty at best. Reorient your motivation around reverence for God.

Sacred Parenting, 20–21

GOD IS IN THE ROOM

I'd like to suggest a motto for Christian family life: "God is in the room."

While God is always there, so often we act and think and behave and speak as if he were not. We fight, we argue, we laugh; we play games, watch movies, make love, and do just about everything without even thinking about the implication that *God is in the room.*

Even though we pray before our common meals, it amazes me how quickly I can slip back into thinking and acting as if the word *Amen* is a kind of curtain that I pull down in front of heaven. I've said my obligatory piece, and now I can carry on as if God has passed over us rather than taken up residence among us.

Think of how differently we might treat our children in those frustrating moments if we responded to them with the knowledge that God is in the room. If we truly believed that the God who designed them and who is passionate about their welfare is literally looking over our shoulders, might we be a little more patient, a little more understanding?

Think of how you might talk with each other, play games together, support each other, and encourage each other differently—perhaps much better—if, as you did it all, you consciously remembered that God is in the room. Our casual compliance with sin is often as much forgetfulness of God as it is rebellion against God.

It's such a simple notion, but it can be so revolutionary: *God is in the room!*

Tell it to yourself every morning, every noontime, every evening: God is in the room.

Tell it to each other every time you're tempted to yell or criticize or ridicule, or even ignore each other: God is in the room.

Tell it to your children throughout the day: God is in the room.

Let's keep telling it to ourselves and to each other until we practice it and live it, until we live and breathe with the blessed remembrance: God is in the room.

Devotions for Sacred Parenting, 9

RETURN TO SPLENDOR

Do you view your eyes as God's servants? Do you look at your hands and feet as holy instruments of the mighty Creator? Do you offer your ears to be constantly in tune with God's instruction? Does your heart beat with God's passion, and your mind think God's thoughts? Is your body a living, breathing center of purposeful passion, pointing toward the risen and reigning Christ who works so powerfully within us?

Are you "holy available" to him?

You've probably heard many sermons and read many books on what you *shouldn't* be and *shouldn't* do. I'd like to paint a portrait of what you can become. Our creator God is eager to splash his glory on you. The apostle Peter promises that "[God's] divine power has given us everything we need for life and godliness" so that we "may participate in the divine nature" (2 Peter 1:3, 4).

God didn't create you *not to do something*; if that had been his goal, he never would have formed you, because if you never existed, you never would have sinned. God made each of us in his image, and he wants us to recapture that image, to surrender to his work in our lives, so that we "will be called oaks of righteousness, a planting of the LORD for the display of his splendor" (Isaiah 61:3).

I pray that you will settle for nothing less than the return of this splendor. Let's explore how faith in Jesus Christ can be radically different from and better than what we are currently experiencing. Christianity as a spiritual journey is not defined merely by what we believe or how we behave, but is marked profoundly by who we are. It is a different type of transformation—a transformation of being, not just allegiance; a transformation of experience, not just confession; a transformation of existence, not just adherence.

It is a return to splendor—for the glory of God.

Holy Available, 19–20

DIVINELY DESIGNED DISILLUSIONMENT

Dave and Dina Horne of Spring Lake, Michigan, have an adorable five-year-old daughter named Emma. I was speaking at their church one Sunday, and Emma, along with about twenty other kids in the children's choir, began the service.

Between the two services, I saw Emma lining up to sing for the second service. "You were fantastic, Emma!" I said. "You guys sounded like stars!" Emma smiled, and without missing a beat, she asked me, "Are you gonna hear the second service too?"

Something in the human heart virtually guarantees that we can never be noticed enough. It's a lust every bit as strong and every bit as destructive as sexual lust—only *this* lust doesn't wait until adolescence to awaken. We're born with this one, and most of us will die with it.

When it's all about me, I can never be noticed enough, appreciated enough, thanked enough, or complimented sufficiently. That's why I believe God has created a divine disillusionment inherent in family life. God allows us to go through three stages as he patiently waits for us to finally throw our contentment and our need to be loved in his direction. God waits as we put our hope in our parents—and we get disappointed. God is patient as we place our hope in a romantic attachment—and we become frustrated. God looks on with forbearance as we throw our hope into intimacy with our children—and then we become tired. All the while he waits for us, quietly whispering, "What you're looking for is *me*. I've been here all along. Put your hope in me."

God has been patient with us as we looked elsewhere—but now let's turn our attention to him. It's time we realize our delight depends on his favor. Our hearts will feel satisfied *only* with his love. It's time we stop blaming our parents and our spouses and our children for not noticing us enough, loving us enough, complimenting us enough, appreciating us enough, and supporting us enough. Instead, let's ask God's forgiveness for not looking to him for soul satisfaction.

Devotions for Sacred Parenting, 141–42

FEAR FACTOR

Friends of ours had two children in Columbine High School during the terrible shooting attack of April 1999. Several other tragic events—largely unreported nationally—assaulted the city over the ensuing months. On top of all this, a disturbed church member started violently harassing my friends' family (both are on staff at a local church) by throwing manure on their car, writing filthy graffiti on their church office windows, slashing their tires, and bashing in their car windows outside their home.

All the tragic events happening in the city, combined with the personal war waged against the family, led my friends' young daughter to say, "I can't take this anymore." They reluctantly agreed to send her to an out-of-state boarding school. After months of research, they chose a highly respected private institution located in Long Island, New York. My friends dropped off this psychologically shaken girl in New York on September 9, 2001.

Forty-eight hours later, terrorists crashed two planes into the World Trade Center.

Most of our children will never face such a traumatic series of events, but even for those of us who live in anonymous towns and face normal coming-of-age challenges, fear for our children is an occupational hazard because the dangers are very real.

Jesus once fell asleep during a storm so fierce that his disciples feared for their lives. Jesus cared enough for his disciples to die for them, yet in this moment of crisis his calm attitude was so steady, so unwavering, that it almost tempts us to believe he didn't care—or to conclude he lived with an absolute trust that many of us lack. In fact, Jesus' confidence in the heavenly Father gave him a fierce freedom that could stare down any storm. He didn't lack concern about his disciples' welfare; he simply felt certain of his Father's providential involvement, concern, and sovereign protection.

May we one day be like Jesus, whose great confidence in the heavenly Father enabled him, even in the midst of a storm, to quietly fall asleep in complete peace, entrusting those he loved to the care of his Father, who never sleeps.

Devotions for Sacred Parenting, 35–37

A Divine Conduit

Manuel (short for Emmanuel) is a severely disabled child, the result of an incestuous relationship and a poorly prescribed drug. One night, his foster mother, Gail, was up late as Manuel suffered repeated seizures. Each seizure destroyed more brain cells, and Gail's tears wet Manuel's black hair as she realized Manuel didn't have many brain cells left to lose.

Exaggerated spastic movements shook Manuel's arms. At first his legs were stiff and rigid, until they, too, began to shake and quiver. Manuel's head flinched and jerked out of control. His left eye alternately closed, then bounced in all directions, while his right eye vibrated. At times, Manuel would choke, or saliva would drip from the left corner of his mouth. As the seizures ended, Manuel's tongue would gently quiver, drawing slightly backward.

Exhausted, frightened, and depleted, Gail began crying uncontrollably. She feared that Manuel would die in her arms, so she pleaded with God, "I haven't had enough time with him. Please, God, don't take him from me now."

Gail "heard" what she believed to be God's response: "Whatever you do for the least of my brothers, you do for me. God is with you. Emmanuel."

"But how can we accomplish such a task?" Gail asked. "Can't you see? I don't know what I'm doing!"

"I will give you enough grace to meet each day's needs."

Gail felt weak, but she then sensed the Spirit of God enveloping the entire room. She became aware of the presence of God in a way she had never known before. With what felt like electricity pouring through her body, Gail slowly lifted her head and opened her eyes. She fully expected to have the child Jesus in her arms instead of Manuel.

"My eyes stopped as I made the full circle," she said. "I gazed at Manuel, and I knew."

Gail and her husband care for a child that many people say has no right to live. Doctors dispute whether the three-and-a-half-year-old boy even knows what's happening around him. But God knows, and Gail and her husband know. Manuel is a conduit funneling a deeper sense of the presence of God into Gail's life.

Ordinary acts of care can become extraordinary acts of worship.

Sacred Pathways, 154–56

THE TASTE OF BITTERNESS

In 1990, a young mother of three pleaded for her life after being confronted by an assailant wearing combat fatigues. "Please don't shoot me," she whimpered. The murderer coldheartedly fired anyway, fatally wounding the woman.

The assailant so poorly covered up her crime that it would have been comical, if not for the tragedy. The Colorado Springs police had her in custody within twenty-four hours. Shortly thereafter, they also arrested the victim's husband after determining that the shooter and the husband had been having an affair.

Sydna Masse lived behind the murdered woman. When Sydna heard about the killing, she responded with (in her own words) hatred and rage. "I had a dead friend and now lived behind three motherless kids," she told me. "I felt I had every right to hate the murderer who caused this." Sydna grew "physically hot" whenever the murderer's name—Jennifer—was mentioned or her picture flashed on television. "For a while I couldn't even read the newspaper articles," she admits.

Jennifer's life sentence did little to diminish Sydna's passion. "That's the thing with hatred and bitterness—it eats you alive. Every time I passed the house, I missed Diane and became angry all over again."

Shortly after Jennifer's sentencing, Sydna began a Bible study that included a chapter on forgiveness. Sydna prayerfully asked God whom she needed to forgive—and in her words, "Jennifer's name came right to my head. I literally did a whiplash and protested, 'No way can I forgive her. She killed my friend! She killed a mother of three!'"

As happens so often with the spiritually earnest, God's persistent conviction outlasted Sydna's reluctance. Sydna finally yielded and wrote a carefully crafted letter to Jennifer, expressing her forgiveness. What happened inside her caught her by surprise. As soon as Sydna dropped the letter into the mail, "a weight lifted. I felt like I was losing twenty pounds. That's when I learned that anger, bitterness, and unforgiveness keeps you from experiencing the depths of joy." Bitterness enslaves, while forgiveness frees.

So what do you want? Consuming anger, or depths of joy?

Authentic Faith, 132

RADICALLY SATISFIED

In a fallen world, love begs to be unleashed—a love supernatural in origin, without limit, a love that perseveres in the face of the deepest hatred or the sharpest pain. It is a love silhouetted in a broken world, framed by human suffering, and illuminated in an explosion of God's presence breaking into a dark cellar.

In a world where suffering is certain, friendship with God frees us from being limited by what we don't have, by what we are suffering, or by what we are enduring. Mature friendship with God reminds us that our existence is much broader than our suffering and difficulty. God doesn't offer us freedom *from* a broken world; instead, he offers us friendship with himself as we walk *through* a fallen world—and those who persevere will find that this friendship is worth so much more than anything this fallen world can offer.

In short, we miss out when we insist on self-absorption, affluence, and ease rather than pursue a deeper walk with God. We miss out on an intimacy heralded by previous blessed generations, a fellowship of labor, suffering, persecution, and selflessness. Of course, it doesn't sound like much fun initially; but those who have walked these solitary roads have left behind a witness that they have reached a glorious, invigorating, soul-satisfying land. These women and men testify to being radically satisfied in God, even though others may scratch their heads as they try to figure out how someone who walks such a hardship-filled road could possibly be happy.

The fact is that in a broken, fallen world, we have only two real choices: mature friendship with God, or radical disillusionment. The new groundwork that needs to be laid is an authentic faith that is based on a God-centered life. Rather than the believer being the sun around whom God, the church, and the world revolves to create a happy, easy, and prosperous life, God becomes the sun around which the believer revolves, a believer who is willing to suffer, even to be persecuted, and lay down his life to build God's kingdom and to serve God's church. This is a radical shift—indeed, the most radical (and freeing) shift known in human experience.

If you find yourself hovering on the precipice of disillusionment, ask yourself: What am I living for really? Friendship with God and service to the King, or a life free from hassle?

Authentic Faith, 12–13

January 20

DIVINE ROMANCE

How do you view God—as master, or as husband?

The startling reality is that God views his people as a husband views his wife: "'In that day,' declares the LORD, 'you will call me "my husband"; you will no longer call me "my master." ... I will betroth you to me forever'" (Hosea 2:16, 19).

Think about the difference between *husband* and *master*—and all that these images conjure up in your mind. God wants us to relate to him with an obedience fueled by love and intimacy, not by self-motivated fear. He desires that we develop a loyalty to a divine-human relationship, not a blind adherence to "principles." A husband harbors a passion toward his wife that is absent in a master toward his slave.

Isaiah uses marital imagery to stress how God rejoices in his people: "As a bridegroom rejoices over his bride, so will your God rejoice over you" (Isaiah 62:5). We live in a world where many people are too busy or preoccupied to notice us. But God *delights* in us. We make his supernatural heart skip a beat.

At times, Jesus himself employed this marital imagery, referring to himself as the "bridegroom" (Matthew 9:15) and to the kingdom of heaven as a "wedding banquet" (Matthew 22:1–14). This picture is carried over into the culmination of earthly history, as the book of Revelation talks about "the wedding of the Lamb" in which "his bride has made herself ready" (Revelation 19:7).

Marital analogies often depict the breakdown of *spiritual* fidelity as well. Jeremiah compares idolatry with adultery: "I gave faithless Israel her certificate of divorce and sent her away because of all her adulteries" (Jeremiah 3:8). Jesus referred to an "adulterous" generation (Mark 8:38) in agonizing over a spiritually unfaithful nation that violated its divine marriage to God.

God did not create marriage merely to give us a pleasant means of repopulating the world and providing a steady societal institution. He planted marriage among humans as yet another signpost pointing to his own eternal, spiritual existence. Marriage has many divine lessons to teach us.

Sacred Marriage, 28–29

GIVE HIM YOURSELF

As I grew up, it seemed that the "giants" of the Christian faith were those who had accomplished great things for God — the inspiring leaders, authors, preachers, and servants. Perhaps they had started movements or led people by the thousands to experience salvation. They had long résumés and in meetings received even longer introductions.

The contemplative life points us in an entirely new direction. All our work may seem absolutely essential to us, but I wonder if that isn't just because we have an inflated view of our own importance? Could all our work be more of an attempt to validate our own existence than an expression of our true love for God?

Contemplatives remind us of a startling fact: Each individual Christian can do one thing that nobody else can, namely, give personal love and affection to God. God can raise up plenty of evangelists, teachers, writers, and witnesses, but only I can give my personal love and affection to God. My spouse, pastor, or coworker can't do this for me. Only I can give God this love, a love that he wants very much.

Imagine that you had six children. Five of them loved you dearly, sent you cards and letters on a regular basis, and made sure you frequently knew of their devotion. The other child left several years before, telling you, "I hate you and never want to see you again. As far as I'm concerned, I don't have any parents." Would the love of the five ever erase the pain you'd feel over the alienation of that one rebellious child? Certainly not.

Amazingly, it's the same with God.

You have something to give God that Rick Warren and Beth Moore can't — your own personal devotion. You are the only person who can give God something that he earnestly desires. M. Basil Pennington described it this way: "I sometimes think that God, as he sees us rushing about in all our doing of good, says to himself: If only they would stop for a few minutes and give me themselves!"[5]

It is up to each of us to love God with holy fervor.

Sacred Pathways, 205–6

AVENUES OF SPIRITUAL REFRESHMENT

People find intimacy with God in various ways: by singing hymns, by dancing, by walking in the woods, by caring for others, and by stimulating their minds through reading inspiring books (among many other activities). Each practice awakens different people to a new sense of spiritual vitality. We all have various spiritual temperaments that prompt us to love God in different ways. Focusing on spiritual temperaments helps us understand how we best relate to God so we can develop new ways of drawing near to him. Scripture tells us that the same God is present from Genesis through Revelation — though people worshiped that one God in many ways: Abraham had a religious bent, building altars everywhere he went. Moses and Elijah revealed an activist's streak in their various confrontations with forces of evil and in their conversations with God. David celebrated God with an enthusiastic style of worship, while his son Solomon expressed his love for God by offering generous sacrifices. Ezekiel and John described loud and colorful images of God, stunning in sensuous brilliance. Mordecai demonstrated his love for God by caring for others, beginning with the orphaned Esther. Mary of Bethany is the classic contemplative, sitting at Jesus' feet.

Within the Christian faith there are many acceptable ways of demonstrating our love for God. Our temperaments will cause us to feel more comfortable in some of these expressions than others — and that is perfectly acceptable to God. In fact, by worshiping God according to the way he made us, we are affirming his work as Creator.

If you find yourself stuck in a worship rut or having a difficult time enjoying your devotions, get creative and explore some additional forms of personal worship. We spend plenty of time shopping for food and clothes; why not spend a little time shopping for avenues of spiritual refreshment?

Sacred Pathways, 18–19, 21

A SEASON OF NECESSARY TRIALS

Time and again, some growing Christian has told me of a gut-wrenching season he or she had to walk through, only to say, "In the end, I'm glad it happened. The fruit it creates far outweighs the pain and angst that come with it."

None of them would have chosen to walk through such a difficult trial, but in hindsight, all of them feel grateful for it. We might label such fire-testing seasons as severe gifts from a loving Father (though we rarely receive them as such at first).

We do not walk easily into maturity; this is why such painful seasons are necessary. At first, Christianity can feel like an intoxicating blend of freedom, joy, exuberance, and newfound discovery. Longtime sins drop off us with relatively little effort. Bible study brings rich rewards; we feel like archaeologists discovering an unexplored cave full of exotic artifacts. Intimacy, tears, and the assurance of God's voice and guidance mark our times of prayer.

Spiritual directors and those familiar with spiritual formation know well this "spiritual infatuation" phase. But just as romantic infatuation is self-centered, so spiritual infatuation tends to be "all about me." While it may seem as though it's all about God, the focus of new believers still remains mostly on how well they are defeating sins, as well as cultivating the new joy and spiritual depth that come from walking with God. They are thrilled with what Christianity has done for them.

Eventually, God asks them—and us—to discard this infatuation and move on to a mature friendship with him. In a true friendship, it's no longer "all about me"; it's about partnering with God to build his kingdom. This means both being "fire tested" and growing in ways that we naturally wouldn't be inclined to grow. This growth can bring searing pain, but it's necessary if we are to become the type of women and men whom God can use. Spiritual maturity leads us to yearn for faithfulness, Christlikeness, and other-centeredness with the same zeal that we used to pursue comfort, affluence, and emotional exuberance.

If it feels like God is stepping back, withholding certain pleasures and allowing certain pains, don't be surprised. This is a season of necessary trials, and the trail has been well trod by brothers and sisters in the faith. The same God who overcame the doubts, frustrations, fears, and even crises of faith of our spiritual ancestors can overcome ours.

Authentic Faith, 9–10

OVERWHELMED WITH AMAZEMENT

As we are made alive in Christ and gain release from what the Bible calls the "corrupting influence" of sin, we become participators in the divine nature (2 Peter 1:4) through the uniting work of the Holy Spirit. A marvelous transformation takes place. Formerly wasted and even pathetic lives can become compelling.

The gospel of Mark captures an extraordinary moment in the life of Jesus: "People were overwhelmed with amazement ... 'He even makes the deaf hear and the mute speak'" (Mark 7:37). What God did through Jesus—physically reclaiming eyesight and hearing and the ability to walk—he now wants to do to us through the Holy Spirit, namely, sensitize our bodies and tune them in to the true realities of life.

Nobody, of course, is going to be "overwhelmed with amazement" merely because we stop doing certain offensive things. I may not be inclined to walk into a place that advertises "live nudes," but do I look at women through the eyes of God? Do I listen to them and hear them as God hears them? Do I think about them as God thinks about them? And do I speak of them as God would have me speak of them? Have I surrendered the members of my body to become servants of the risen and ascended Christ, instruments of his purpose, sanctified through his continuing presence?

A man who refrains from lust but who looks at women with condescension and disrespect is not a godly man. His corruption may be of a different sort from the one who undresses women in his mind, but he certainly can't live a compelling life. Why not? Because he hasn't learned what it is to truly *love*.

When we start blessing others with heavenly splashes of glory—when our eyes begin to see with compassion and our mouths begin to speak words of encouragement; when our hands reach out to heal instead of hurt and our feet take us to places where there is need; when our minds plumb the mysteries of heaven and our hearts open up toward all—then God's splendor breaks forth in a powerful way. When we love as Jesus loved, when we inconvenience ourselves for the glory of God, our Spirit-prompted actions may lead to overwhelming amazement.

Holy Available, 47–48

PERSEVERING FORGIVENESS

The great Protestant Reformer John Calvin has helped me deal with the need to call people to justice and repentance in light of the corresponding call to forgive. He teaches that if the offender remains "deaf to our reproofs," continues to flatter himself, stubbornly resists any admonitions, "or excuses himself by hypocrisy," then "greater severity is to be used toward him." But once the offender repents and "trembles under the sense of his sin," we should immediately respond with grace, mercy, and pardon.[6]

This approach helps me, because it shows that the ancients didn't view forgiveness as the whitewashing of sin. We are to be very clear about the offense and how it offends justice; but when genuine repentance comes, we must be eager and quick to offer forgiveness.

Calvin stresses that we have a special duty to forgive fellow believers: "If we have been injured by the members of the Church, we must not be too rigid and immovable in pardoning the offense." He writes that, while forgiveness is generally urged on us toward all persons, we are "harder than iron" if we are not especially eager to forgive members of God's own family.[7]

In light of a multitude of church fights today, the body of Christ would do well to take these words to heart. For some reason, we seem more reluctant to forgive fellow Christians than non-Christians, and we are often the most reluctant to forgive pastors and Christian leaders. This makes us, in Calvin's words, "harder than iron."

Do you have a neighbor — or maybe a family member or friend — to forgive? Are you allowing a past deed to poison your spiritual life, dampen your witness, and ultimately make you miserable?

Perhaps you've tried to forgive someone, but a new offense, or perhaps a recovered memory, has short-circuited the process. Remember, forgiveness requires perseverance. Press on to complete the work God has given you to do. Consciously apply grace to the offense. Begin interceding for and spiritually blessing the offender. Protect yourself and honor God by embracing the fullness that forgiveness offers.

Authentic Faith, 140–41

FIGHTING PARENTAL DISCOURAGEMENT

How can you fight parental discouragement, the feeling that you're just not up to the task? Charles H. Spurgeon suggested that we gain hope from our redemption:

> The Lord seems to say to us, "What I have done before, I will do again. I have redeemed you, and I will still redeem you. I have brought you from under the hand of the oppressor; I have delivered you from the tongue of the slanderer; I have borne you up under the load of poverty and sustained you under the pains of sickness; and I am able still to do the same. Why, then, do you fear? Why should you be afraid, since already I have again and again redeemed you? Take heart, and be confident, for even to old age and to death itself I will continue to be your strong Redeemer."[8]

If your discouragement stems from perplexity—not knowing what to do—find comfort in God's astonishing work of salvation. If God could figure out how to be just and yet save sinners, then surely he can solve *your* challenges! There never was, nor ever will be, a problem so perplexing that God's guidance can't see you through it.

If you worry about what you lack, financially or in personal abilities, find comfort in God's promise: "He who did not spare his own Son, but gave him up for us all—how will he not also, along with him, graciously give us all things?" (Romans 8:32).

The stakes you face as a parent are much too great to go unnoticed by a God who loves you—and your children—so much that he sent his Son to redeem you. This God watches over you now, the same God who inspired Spurgeon to speak these words more than a hundred years ago and who inspired you to pick up this book to hear his words anew.

God himself has assigned you the task before you. And he is committed to seeing you through.

In the end, that's all we need to know.

Devotions for Sacred Parenting, 13–14

THE DEATH OF COMPLAINING

When my son was three years old, he fell on a fireplace hearth and cut himself just above his left eye. I rushed him to the hospital and stayed with him as the nurses immobilized his arms. As the doctor began putting stitches in Graham's head, I held his hand and almost lost my composure when Graham whimpered, "Please, Daddy, he's hurting me; make him stop! Please, Daddy, don't let him do this, *please*."

Graham felt betrayed. He couldn't understand why the father he had grown to trust was letting a strange man stick a needle in his head. Yet explanations would have done little good. Graham was only three years old and didn't understand what was going on. He just wanted me to protect him, and he felt deeply betrayed because he thought I wasn't.

Now imagine if another man were on the other side of Graham during the stitching, whispering in his ear, "See, Graham, your dad doesn't really love you; otherwise, he wouldn't make you go through all this pain. If you were my son —if you followed me—I wouldn't make you go through this."

That's an accurate picture of what often happens when we go through difficulties. God knows what is best for us, but our spiritual adversary often tempts us with the thought that if God *really* loved us, he would spare us the ordeal. We assume there's an explanation we could understand, and so we resent God for not offering the explanation, never even thinking that perhaps the problem is with our understanding.

At a particularly frustrating time in my life, when I felt as though God had kept me in a hole for eight long years, I found myself continually asking, *God, why are you doing this to me?* Eventually I learned that faith is tested not by how often God answers my prayers in the way I like but by my willingness to continue serving him and thanking him, even when I have no clue as to what he is doing. When I look back on the difficulty of those eight long years, I see their necessity in a new light.

Today, for the good of your soul, put to death all complaining. Rest in God's providence rather than fighting it.

Thirsting for God, 103–6

SUPERNATURAL, NOT SENTIMENTAL, CONCERN

My wife volunteered to work with a weeklong camp that reached out to inner-city children from troubled backgrounds. She soon learned what she was up against. Any romantic notions she might have secretly harbored about the week were quickly dispelled when the trainer taught volunteers how to respond to a kid who is biting you. (Just FYI, rather than pull your arm back—which allows the child's teeth to set—you should push your arm into the child's mouth until the child stops biting. When the arm is pushed in, it's far more difficult to receive a hurtful bite.)

At the end of the camp, I joined my wife for a luncheon given in recognition of the camp workers. One young man received an award for being the most patient in the face of the most abuse. He had been kicked, hit, pummeled, even spit on.

It is important to mention this because some people actually pursue selfless work for selfish reasons. They usually don't last long. That's why Christians who are eager to serve should first do a motivation check. Are you doing this to be loved in return? Are you doing this to save a life? What if the person doesn't want to be saved? What if the addict refuses to quit? What if the crisis pregnancy center client gets pregnant again? Will that make you quit?

Social mercy is based on obedience to God and depends on God's love for his failing children. We cannot maintain or manufacture a false love. Sentimentality won't last you until lunchtime in a real ministry. Nothing short of God's supernatural care and concern will suffice.

But behind this pain is an unparalleled, almost otherworldly pleasure. J. I. Packer once told a class of seminary students, "As you serve the Lord, you hurt. And as you serve the Lord, your hurt, which feels sometimes like a death experience, gives way to a joy which feels like a resurrection experience. The Lord makes it happen."[9]

Let's serve well—for the right reasons with the right motivation.

Authentic Faith, 117–18

SPEAKING *WITH* GOD INSTEAD OF *FOR* GOD

A few days before a preaching engagement, I came across a marvelous passage by R. Somerset Ward that illustrates the human/divine dynamic when God speaks through us. Ward uses the image of fishermen pulling in nets bursting with a catch:

> [A man] turns to his companion and says, "The fishermen have caught a lot of fish today." To his eyes the only important element in the scene he sees is the fisherman. Yet, in reality, the fisherman is only one, and by far the most insignificant, of all the factors that have brought the fish into the boat. The wind, the tide, the warm currents in the sea, all of them mighty and irresistible forces, have had most to do with the result. The fisherman has only cooperated with them. But although his share was so small, it was most necessary. And this may serve as a picture of the work of intercession.[10]

This greatly encouraged me, because I realized that, while people would recognize me as the preacher, I am "only one, and by far the most insignificant, of all the factors that [bring] the fish into the boat." Yet there is nobility in the task, for though my share is "so small, it [is] most necessary." But it is only a small share. Life changes when we live in cooperation with God instead of just working for God.

Imagine meeting a friend for coffee at Starbucks. Let's also imagine that a difficult conversation must take place. It will help more than you know to realize how small (though necessary) a part of the process you really are—when indeed you rely on God. God has given you the words, cultivated the friendship, prepared your coffee-mate's heart, and will set the spiritual climate. You're simply casting a few words, that's all.

Here is the delightful irony: true biblical humility breeds confidence. When we accept the fact that God is already acting, already moving, and already directing the affairs of his world, we can rest in his capability, confident that he has made allowances for our own weaknesses, sin, limitations, and lack of gifting.

You are a part—an important part, to be sure—but only a part. Learn to rest in the providence and active ministry of God.

Holy Available, 83–84

THE GREAT PROBLEM OF CHRISTIAN MINISTRY

How many times have you heard a moving sermon and been almost knocked over by a powerful verse or been given a great new insight—only to lose its effect because you forgot about it soon after it was given? Symbols can help us overcome one of the great difficulties of the Christian life: the problem of a poor memory.

Dietrich Bonhoeffer, the German Christian martyred for standing against Hitler, was fascinated by how his fellow prisoners could come so close to death in an air raid and then forget about it as soon as the danger was past. While allied bombs rocked the prison cells, nonbelieving men would cry out to God for salvation; but as soon as the bombers had passed and the dust settled, the prisoners went back to playing cards and passing time, forgetting all about their supplications to God. Bonhoeffer writes:

> Something that repeatedly puzzles me as well as other people is how quickly we forget about our impressions of a night's bombing. Even a few minutes after the all clear, almost everything that we had just been thinking about seems to vanish into thin air. With Luther a flash of lightning was enough to change the course of his life for years to come. Where is this "memory" today? Is not the loss of this "moral memory" responsible for the ruin of all obligations, of love, marriage, friendship, and loyalty? Nothing sticks fast, nothing holds firm; everything is here today and gone tomorrow. But the good things of life—truth, justice, and beauty—all great accomplishments need time, constancy, and "memory," or they degenerate. The man who feels neither responsibility toward the past nor desire to shape the future is one who "forgets," and I don't know how one can really get at such a person and bring him to his senses. Every word, even if it impresses him for the moment, goes in at one ear and out at the other. What is to be done about him? It is a great problem of Christian ministry.[11]

What are you doing today to hold on to the essential spiritual insights that God entrusts you with? How can we become better stewards of the truth? How can we overcome this "great problem of Christian ministry"? *(Continued tomorrow.)*

Sacred Pathways, 93–94

THE POWER OF SYMBOLS

Symbols have a special power to gain our attention and arouse our thinking. "Speak to the Israelites," God said to Moses, "and say to them: 'Throughout the generations to come you are to make tassels on the corners of your garments, with a blue cord on each tassel. You will have these tassels to look at and so you will remember all the commands of the LORD, that you may obey them and not prostitute yourselves by going after the lusts of your own hearts and eyes. Then you will remember to obey all my commands and will be consecrated to your God'" (Numbers 15:38–40).

I can hear the objections: "But we're saved by faith. We don't need those Old Testament symbols!" While symbols have nothing to do with saving us, they have everything to do with realizing the effects of that salvation on our everyday lives. Just because we're saved doesn't mean we don't need help to live holy lives.

A Christian who has a hard time living out his or her faith while driving, for instance, could hang a symbol—a cross or a fish—on the rearview mirror. (That's certainly preferable to putting a Christian bumper sticker on the back of the car and then driving like a son of perdition!)

A pastor-friend uses a pond near his home as a symbol. As soon as he drives by the pond, he remembers that he is going home and needs to prepare to focus on his wife and children, leaving the cares, worries, and concerns of the church on the north side of the pond. He can pick them back up the next morning when he passes the pond on his way to work.

You can find a symbol to meet virtually every need. Men or women who have failed sexually can wear a cross to remind them of their pledge to remain pure. Others might wear a ring during certain periods of intensive prayer; every time they see the ring, they will be reminded of their prayer. Symbols can become potent ushers of God's presence and reality.

In a spirit of freedom, consider how you can utilize the power of symbols to remind you of precious truths and bedrock commitments. Let's be proactive in taking concrete steps to grow in righteousness, remembering the truth God has called us to embrace.

Sacred Pathways, 94–95

FEBRUARY

What better way to celebrate warm love, both divine and human, than in one of the coldest months of the year? As we soak in God's grace and mercy, we choose to make compassion our own and take joy in caring for loved ones, the unlovely, and the different.

BURYING EXPECTATIONS

"Gary, I kind of locked the keys in the car."

I put down the phone, ready to drive over and bail Lisa out, but when I went to retrieve another set of keys, I noticed the empty hooks where we keep Lisa's car keys. Apparently, Lisa had lost the last set. I had to go through her coats, her pants, her purse, her shoulder bags—anything I could think of—to find a key so I could get her home.

Lisa is a lastborn, and she does lastborn things. She loses stuff. She "forgets" her purse or leaves her wallet at the store. Just the other day she told me, "You know, I haven't seen my Starbucks credit card in three months, but nobody's used it, so I figure it must be lost at home."

She saw the look of horror on my face.

"No big deal," she said. "It'll turn up."

She saw my look of doubt.

"Someday."

I grew up in a household where my mom had enough food, toilet paper, light-bulbs, and batteries stockpiled to last us at least a year. You could have stretched our supply of toilet paper from Seattle to Tacoma. Lisa shops from an entirely different perspective. She buys stuff a day or two (or occasionally a week or two) after we run out. Some mornings, it's milk. Some nights, it's toilet paper. Some afternoons, we're out of keys. But we're usually out of something.

I could read a how-to book that might tell me how to communicate my frustration. Lisa and I could have several talks about being more proactive. Maybe I could draw up charts, or we could try to redivide responsibilities.

Or after two decades of marriage I could just accept that some things will never change, because they won't. I can't expect Lisa to become a different person just because she's married to me—just as she must put up with countless episodes of my own quirks, limitations, and irritating qualities embedded in me as if they were encased in granite. Rather than let little disappointments and minor annoyances steal what is most important, it's healthier to have a spiritual funeral and bury certain expectations. That, sometimes, is what it means to love.

Devotions for Sacred Parenting, 148–49

A LASTING MARK

Todd Beamer's heart no longer beats, his lungs no longer fill with air, his eyes no longer open.

But he is still motivating his children.

Todd died on Flight 93, the plane he and a few other brave souls kept from being employed as a bomb on September 11, 2001. Todd's life may have ended in a Pennsylvania field, but his influence lives on.

Lisa Beamer, Todd's widow, says she has her children look at Todd's picture every day as she tells them that their father was a hero and urges them to aspire to be like him.

William Bennett told the Todd Beamer story to an audience at Hillsdale College, pointing out there is overwhelming proof that the best formula for happy and successful children is a two-parent family. Bennett found even more refreshing, however, another statistic indicating that children who lose a father in the line of duty are indistinguishable from children who grow up in intact two-parent families. According to Bennett, "The moral example doesn't have to be there physically. It can be in the mind and in the heart. As a result of Lisa Beamer saying, 'Be like him,' then, Todd Beamer will be in the minds and hearts of his kids."[1]

Laying down a moral example is like creating a trail in the jungle. Chaos surrounds our kids. They need a mom and a dad to walk before them to show them the way. They need to see how we, overwhelmed by life, find security and hope in a God who is greater than we are, and how we strive to live unselfishly, even sacrificially when need be, to seek first the kingdom of God.

When we model an appropriate fear of the Lord—reverencing him, obeying his Word, walking in his ways—and cultivate a hatred for sin, we construct a spiritual refuge for our children. Proverbs 14:26 tells us, "He who fears the LORD has a secure fortress, and *for his children* it will be a refuge" (emphasis added). That's right—our walking in the fear of God becomes a refuge for our children.

Devotions for Sacred Parenting, 15

AN ACQUIRED LOVE

If you were a male believer around the time of Moses and Joshua, your job was to fight. As the Israelites entered the Promised Land, they were sometimes chastised for their cowardice and lethargy and their refusal to go into battle: "How long will you wait before you begin to take possession of the land that the LORD, the God of your fathers, has given you?" (Joshua 18:3). For a long time, "go into battle" was the rallying cry from God.

Jesus came with a new challenge — a far more difficult one. Someone once asked him to name the single greatest commandment, and Jesus replied with two (see Matthew 22:34 – 40). It isn't enough to love God with all your heart, soul, mind, and strength. If you *really* want to please God, Jesus said, you must also love others.

Marriage can be the gym in which our capacity to experience and express God's love gets strengthened and further developed. To get there, we must realize that human love and divine love aren't two separate oceans, but rather one body of water with many tributaries.

We show our love for God, in part, by loving our spouses well. We can never love somebody "too much." Our typical problem is that we love God too little. The answer is not to dim our love for any particular human, but to expand our heart's response to our Divine Joy.

Marriage creates a climate where this love gets put to the greatest test. The problem is that love must be acquired. Katherine Anne Porter writes, "Love must be learned, and learned again and again; there is no end to it. Hate needs no instruction, but waits only to be provoked."[2]

Love is not a natural response that gushes out of us unbidden. Infatuation sometimes does that — at the beginning of a relationship, at least — but hate is always ready to naturally spring forth, like the "Old Faithful" geyser at Yellowstone National Park. Christian love, on the other hand, must be chased after, aspired to, and practiced. It is hewn out of the daily experiences of routine tasks, practical service, and common conversation. Today, we have the opportunity to do what matters most — grow in our ability to love.

Sacred Marriage, 39–40

BAPTIZING GUILT

One of my favorite biblical phrases for meditation comes from Micah 6:8, where we are told to "love mercy." Micah doesn't tell us to merely "demonstrate" mercy or to "discipline ourselves" toward mercy; he tells us to fall in love with it!

The Hebrew word for this love, 'āhab, is used of a husband toward his wife and appears frequently in Song of Songs. To "love" mercy is to feel enthralled by mercy. A woman or man who loves mercy feels so thankful for the mercy God has shown them that they frequently mention it to others. They will have a childlike awe and wonder: "God has shown me mercy!"

Those who love mercy are not thankful merely for the mercy *they* have received; they also want to show mercy to others. You don't have to convince them to show mercy; they love to show mercy. Mercy is the defining principle of their lives.

Meditating on the wonder of mercy led me to a jaw-dropping truth: God could baptize my guilt, because without guilt there could be no mercy! *God's mercy is more wonderful than our guilt is terrible* ("mercy triumphs over judgment" [James 2:13]). Without acknowledging our own guilt, we would never sense the need for mercy, so we wouldn't appreciate this glorious gift of God. And without the guilt of others, we would never be able to apply mercy. Facing the reality of guilt head-on, unflinching, we open ourselves to the even more beautiful reality of God's mercy.

So turn guilt feelings into a call to worship. Acknowledge your guilt, and then thank God that he has made provision for your guilt. Confess that you have fallen short as a person, but then expend just as much energy worshiping the God who forgives and who will show mercy to you in your failings. And then apply this same mercy to your children, roommates, spouse, or parents. It may sound crazy, but using guilt as a call to adoration can turn guilt into a pathway toward intimacy with God.

Let's use today to fall even further in love with mercy — both for ourselves and for others.

Sacred Parenting, 48–49

An Overflowing Heart

As I walked through Chicago's O'Hare Airport, I fell into what is probably the closest I'll ever come to a true mystical moment. People were everywhere, talking on their cell phones, getting something to eat, typing on their laptops, waiting in line to board. I saw these people as faceless obstacles, making my trip to the next gate complicated and time consuming.

But then, almost as if a shadow passed over me, it was as though I could see them as God sees them — real individuals with real concerns — *and God's heart was beating for every one of them.* I caught a glimpse of how involved God is in every life, even when those lives ignore him.

At that moment, Concourse F of the Chicago airport suddenly morphed into a sanctuary, a holy place of possibility. I didn't see job titles, expensive jewelry, business success, or power; I just saw people — some alienated from God, others knowing him but not relating to him much, still others actively open to hearing his voice. I saw people, without all the trappings — and what defined them beyond anything else was how they relate (or don't relate) to God.

This experience faded by the time I reached the Starbucks just outside the security area, but it shook me up for a good hour. God really does care; God really is involved, even when we don't acknowledge him.

True Christian eyesight is about seeing others with the eyes of God — noticing the unnoticed, not being distracted by what the world considers important, caring about those we once gladly would have looked past. He loves every one of those people who remain faceless and nameless to me.

Without God's eyes, people become invisible to me. The guy shining my shoes at the airport, the woman cleaning my hotel room, the cashier at the grocery store, the police officer directing traffic in the rain — my human heart has little room for the barely seen. Not God's! His heart overflows with concern for their welfare, and he wants to pass on to us this same concern and compassion.

Today, Lord, open our eyes to see people as you see them. Make us aware of who they are before you, and grant us the grace to honor them as you honor them, to treat them as you would have us treat them, to notice them as you would have us notice them, and to love them as you would have us love them.

Holy Available, 61–62

A DIFFERENT NATION

The Bible overflows with verses calling us to reach out to society's disenfranchised. It tells us that God defends the cause of the orphan, widow, and alien (see Deuteronomy 10:18), and that he commanded the Israelites to set aside a portion of their tithes for these three groups (see Deuteronomy 14:28–29). It instructs us to take an active role in defending the cause of the poor: "Speak up for those who cannot speak for themselves, for the rights of all who are destitute. Speak up and judge fairly; defend the rights of the poor and needy" (Proverbs 31:8–9). This means we fulfill our spiritual obligation not simply by doing no harm but by actively getting involved to confront and challenge injustice.

Even business dealings were to take the poor into consideration. Leviticus 23:22 tells the Israelites not to reap the edges of their fields but to leave those for the poor and for the alien. The Israelites were ordered not to return refugee slaves (see Deuteronomy 23:15) and were told they would be cursed if they withheld justice from the alien, the fatherless, or the widow (see Deuteronomy 27:19). Ezekiel forbids the practice of lending money at excessive interest (see Ezekiel 18:8).

Early on, the Old Testament connects our spirituality with our works of kindness. A truly spiritual person is a truly caring person. The book of Proverbs suggests that God's willingness to hear our prayers is tied to our willingness to hear the cry of the poor (see 21:13). If we turn a deaf ear to their cries, God turns a deaf ear to our own prayers. Solomon tells us that "he who oppresses the poor shows contempt for their Maker, but whoever is kind to the needy honors God" (Proverbs 14:31).

We can have perfect church attendance, set records for fasting, have the longest quiet times, listen to the most sermons and praise songs of anyone in our circle of friends, and avoid scandalous sin, but if we miss this part of our religious obligation, namely, social mercy, we miss God entirely.

Authentic Faith, 104–5

LOVING THE TOTALLY OTHER

The beloved disciple John, the apostle of love, could get pretty blunt. "If anyone says, 'I love God,' yet hates his brother, he is a liar," he wrote. "For anyone who does not love his brother, whom he has seen, cannot love God, whom he has not seen. And he has given us this command: Whoever loves God must also love his brother" (1 John 4:20–21).

Your spouse seems so different from you, I know. When you think on one level, she thinks on another. When you're certain this perspective matters most, he brings in another angle entirely. And you ask yourself, "How can I possibly love someone who is so different from me?"

But try asking yourself this one: How could you possibly love *God*? He is spirit, and you are encased in flesh. He is eternal, and you are trapped in time. He is all-holy, perfect, sinless, and you—like me—are steeped in sin. It is far less of a leap for a man to love a woman or for a woman to love a man than it is for either of us to love God.

But it's more than that. God designed marriage to call us out of ourselves and learn to love the "different." Put together in the closest situation imaginable —living side by side, sleeping in the same room, even sharing our bodies with each other—we are forced to respect and appreciate someone radically different from ourselves.

We need to be called out of ourselves because, in truth, we are incomplete. God made us to find our fulfillment in him—the Totally Other. Marriage shows us that we are not all there is. It calls us to give way to another, but also to find joy, happiness, and even ecstasy in another—another who is radically, stubbornly different from us. So unless you're willing to say, "I just can't love God because he is too different from me," don't even contemplate the idea that you can't love your spouse because of radical differences. Perhaps God put these differences there for your benefit. Let's spend time today thinking about what we can learn from these differences instead of resenting them.

Sacred Marriage, 50

LOVING THE UNLOVELY

One of the cruelest remarks I've ever heard came from a man who left his wife for another woman: "The truth is, I've never loved you." The remark is designed to say, "The truth is, I've never found you lovable." But put in a Christian context, it's a confession of the man's utter failure to be a Christian. If he hasn't loved his wife, it is not his wife's fault, but his.

Jesus calls us to love the unlovable—even our enemies!—so a man who says "I've never loved you" is a man saying, "I've never acted like a Christian."

I regularly visit public libraries. One day I was walking toward the computer terminals when the smell of a homeless man became almost overpowering. Out of the corner of my eye, I saw him hunched over a table, his tattered clothes and unkempt hair marking his lack of a permanent address.

I enjoy it when folks tell me how much God has "used" me in their lives, but I shake my head when I think of the gospel missions in most cities dedicated to reaching individuals such as these. It's easy to be "used" when you get to sit in front of a computer in your home and do something you enjoy. It's hardly sacrificial when I'm given well-furnished rooms in hotels and whisked across the country in airplanes.

But we display Christian love in loving those *most* difficult to love, not the easiest. Jesus tells us that when we hold a banquet, we shouldn't invite our friends; they might invite us back and thus repay us. Instead, Jesus said, invite the lame, the paralyzed, the poor, the blind—those who can't pay us back (see Luke 14).

That's what is so difficult about Jesus' call to love others. On one level, it's easy to love God, because God doesn't smell. God doesn't have bad breath. God doesn't reward kindness with evil. God doesn't make berating comments. Loving God is easy in this sense. But to love God through unlovely people? That's the challenge—and that's our call.

Today, think about the one person in your social sphere who is most difficult for you to love; this person may well be God's "angel," a messenger sent to help you become more like Christ.

Sacred Marriage, 40–41

GOD IS NOT SILENT

A woman once approached John Wesley—one of the hardest-working servants of the gospel who ever lived—and said she had a "message from the Lord." She proceeded to chastise Wesley for "laying up treasures on the earth"—a curious message, given that Wesley lived a heroically frugal life, promising to die with less than ten pounds to his name (a promise he kept). This "prophetess" also accused the evangelist of taking his ease (if you pick up his journal, you'll get exhausted just reading about his diligent labor for God's kingdom) and being obsessed with eating and drinking.

I wish I could have seen Wesley as he responded: "I told her, God knew me better; and if he had sent her, he would have sent her with a more proper message."[3]

Accounts like this one—and who among us hasn't been party to a message clearly not from God?—make my instruction on listening for God somewhat controversial. Nevertheless, I maintain that God still speaks.

For me, hearing God's voice is one of the most precious parts of being a disciple. I crave God's insight into my actions and motives. I desire with all my heart to know his particular will for me—not some general direction based on certain principles, but his particular application for my particular need. And I love it when—this is really getting out there—I'm struggling with an issue and God makes everything clear, sometimes even through a dream.

It comes down to this: Should we allow occasional misuse of a clear biblical teaching to steal away the precious reality of hearing from God and being directed by him? I would *never* present a dream or an "inner thought" as direct revelation. The fact is, God's words have sustained me in so many ways that I can't imagine what it would be like to serve a silent God.

God is more than the author of an ancient book. He lives in and guides and builds his church. He is no mute idol. He is the mighty one who spoke this world into existence and even today speaks his wisdom into our chaos. Will we open our ears?

Holy Available, 98–99

I'll Do the Ordering for You

Almost every time we visit Kelsey's favorite restaurant, International House of Pancakes, we see the same three elderly men. If these men aren't in their eighties, they must be in their nineties, and they have to be just about the most pleasant group of men I've ever seen. The waitresses all get a hug, and every diner receives a hearty hello — and they clearly have a deep affection for one another.

As is common with people who are losing their hearing, these men speak loudly. One of these men has a voice roughly equal to a foghorn. "Gimme one of those senior breakfasts," he called out to a waitress a good fifteen feet away — but you could've heard him across the freeway. Kelsey smiled, leaned in close, and whispered, "Daddy?"

"Yeah, honey?"

"When you get to be that old, I'm going to do the ordering for you."

I can't tell you how thrilled I was to hear Kelsey talk about going to IHOP with me when I'm in my eighties. Right now, I go there for her. The food doesn't do much for me, but Kelsey loves it.

Imagining life thirty years from now can help us keep the big picture in view. We can get so busy trying to make sure our children complete their homework, display good manners, not watch too much television, get enough exercise, and eat well that we can forget to enjoy them and relate to them. Kelsey's comment reminded me that building a lifelong relationship with another human being is the most precious aspect of parenting.

May God keep us from ever treating our kids like projects to be improved or monuments to be made. They are people we can enjoy, love, laugh with, and share life's journey together. In the business of educating and equipping, may we keep the relationship paramount.

What are you doing today that will make your child want to spend time with you two decades from now?

Devotions for Sacred Parenting, 52–53

STOP JUDGING AND START LOVING

Cathy once accompanied her daughter, Jamie, on a school trip to Europe. Jamie suffers from obsessive-compulsive disorder (OCD) and was taking prescription medication that sometimes causes a psychotic reaction—which had the unhappy effect of making Jamie even more of an outcast than she already is.

Cathy watched as the other kids on the trip either ignored Jamie or made fun of her. Her gait, her attitude, and the volume of her voice gave cruel kids more than enough fodder for their ridicule. Cathy loved Jamie, but she felt frustrated by her daughter's behavior and the bizarre way the drugs and the OCD interacted in her system. She tried to maintain a positive attitude, but the symptoms of children who face psychotic challenges can wear you down. After months and then years of dealing with it, you can snap.

One day, Cathy reached that limit. To her horror, she heard herself scold Jamie, "Why can't you just be normal?" The words hung in the air long after she had spoken them. Shocked, saddened, and hurt by her own behavior, Cathy realized she had just done the same thing as the kids—faulting Jamie for not being "normal."

Jamie has come a long way since that ninth-grade trip to Europe—but Cathy has come even further. She makes this honest admission: "I learned from this very dark time in my life that my shame and my pettiness had to be revealed in order for me to begin to love Jamie. I was no better than those mean girls on the England trip. I needed to stop judging and to start loving. I had to face the ugly side of my behavior, confess it, and pray for change. I had to realize that I am the broken one in need of fixing, not Jamie."

In fact, every child uniquely stretches us, pushes us, challenges us, and—by God's design—thereby teaches us how to love. Thank God for difficult children!

Devotions for Sacred Parenting, 80–81

"It Was Like He Never Existed"

Ernie had worked for one of the most stable and famous companies in the United States. Until the late 1980s, if you could land a job with this company, you figured you had a job for life. They paid well but demanded a lot out of their workers.

"We gave our lives to the company," Ernie said. "They took care of us, but they expected us to organize our lives around our work. If we ever said no, even once, we'd be taken off the track of promotion and kept in a vocational eddy for the rest of our careers. So we went to work early and stayed late."

One of Ernie's coworkers was a younger man in his late forties who for years worked side by side with Ernie. One morning, the man failed to arrive at work, and Ernie assumed he was sick—until a call came from his wife at 8:30 a.m. with the shocking news that the man had died. His heart had stopped during breakfast.

"They chose his replacement that afternoon," Ernie said, "and the new guy was on the job early the next morning—less than twenty-four hours after his predecessor was pronounced dead."

None of the man's other coworkers attended his funeral; they didn't know his family, so they figured it didn't matter. After his burial, "as far as the company was concerned, it was like he had never existed," Ernie said. "He gave his entire life to the company, coming in early and working late, but the company didn't miss a step—not a single step—once he died. It's terrible to say this, but in a way, the company was less inconvenienced by his death than if he had taken a two-week vacation."

Ernie's words, "It was like he had never existed," still hover over me. I had that talk with Ernie more than a decade ago, but his insight will remain with me for the rest of my life. Many people clamor for our attention, but only a few make room for us in their hearts.

Let's reward those whose affection is genuine and sincere, prioritizing our time toward those who truly matter—our family members and friends—and being willing to take time away from those who won't even miss us when we're gone.

Devotions for Sacred Parenting, 40–41

A QUIETER FULFILLMENT

Marriage, for all of us, is temporary in the light of eternity. The truth is, the relationship Lisa and I have with God will outlive our marriage. Most likely the time will come when either Lisa or I will precede the other into eternity. The remaining spouse will be left alone, no longer married—perhaps even eventually to marry someone else.

For the Christian, marriage is a penultimate rather than an ultimate reality. Because of this, both of us can find even more meaning by pursuing God together and by recognizing that he is the one who alone can fill the spiritual ache in our souls. We can work at making our home life more pleasant and peaceable; we can explore ways to keep sex fresh and fun; we can make superficial changes that will preserve at least the appearance of respect and politeness. But what both of us crave more than anything else is to be intimately close to the God who made us. If *this* relationship is right, we won't make such severe demands on our marriage, asking each other, expecting each other, to compensate for spiritual emptiness.

Marriage is one of many life situations that help me to draw my sense of meaning, purpose, and fulfillment from God. Lisa can't make me happy, at least not in any ultimate sense. Certainly we have some great times together, and she is a wonderful wife, exceeding my dreams—but these great times are sprinkled with (and sometimes seem to get buried in) the demands, challenges, and expectations of paying the bills on time, disciplining children, earning a living, and keeping a house clean. I believe God designed marriage to draw us to himself.

So I guess I'm after a quieter fulfillment, a deeper sense of meaning, a fuller understanding of the purpose behind this intense, one-on-one, lifelong relationship called marriage. As a man who believes his primary meaning comes from his relationship with God, I want to explore how marriage can draw both my spouse and me closer to God.

Sacred Marriage, 23–24

A House of Love

What marks a truly Christian home? Is it the fact that our minivan or SUV pulls out of the driveway every Sunday morning and heads to church? Is it the fact that we have a Bible inside the home? Is it the fact that we pray before meals and at bedtime?

Andrew Murray would say that the true mark of a Christian home is love: "The home is consecrated by the light of Jesus' love resting on the children, the power of His love dwelling in the parents, and the raising of children being made a work of love for Him."[4] "He urges parents, "Try to maintain the rule of love—not merely natural parental love, but love as a principle of action that is carefully cultivated in your family life. Then the children will catch this spirit of love and become your helpers in making your home the reflection of love for which the heavenly Father guides and trains His children."[5]

Charles Spurgeon takes a similar approach:

The best preparation for teaching Christ's lambs is love—love for Jesus and for them ... Where there is no love, there will be no life ... Our object is to create love in the hearts of those we teach, and to foster it where it already exists. But how can we convey the fire if it is not kindled in our own hearts? How can a person promote the flame whose hands are damp and dripping with worldliness and indifference, so that he acts on the child's heart rather as a bucket of water than as a flame of fire?[6]

Both Murray and Spurgeon recognize love as the hallmark of the Christian home. I suspect the apostle John would agree with them. After all, he wrote, "Dear friends, let us love one another, for love comes from God ... Since God so loved us, so we also ought to love one another. No one has ever seen God, but if we love each other, God lives in us and his love is made complete in us (1 John 4:7, 11).

We are born in love, redeemed by love, carried by love, and called to love. May our kids see that our primary motivation, the rule of our lives, the guiding principle in our home, is love—for in that love, they'll see the way of the kingdom and seek to know this love for themselves.

What can we do today—what habits can we cultivate, what lifestyles can we embark on—to make our homes, first and foremost, bastions of love?

Devotions for Sacred Parenting, 86–87

WHAT MAKES GOD HAPPY?

Ask ten people on the street to name their goal in life, and you'll get an amazing variety of answers. For the Christian, Paul couldn't be clearer—his "consuming ambition, the motive force behind all he does,"[7] is *to please God*. But Paul doesn't just say pleasing God is *his* "consuming ambition," he assumes it will be *ours* as well: "*We* make it our goal to please him."

The first purpose in marriage—beyond happiness, sexual expression, the bearing of children, companionship, mutual care and provision, or anything else—is to please God. The challenge, of course, is that this is utterly selfless living; rather than asking, "What will make me happy?" I must ask, "What will make God happy?"

And just in case we don't grasp the concept immediately, Paul underscores it a few verses later: "Those who live should no longer live for themselves but for him who died for them and was raised again" (2 Corinthians 5:15).

I have no other choice as a Christian. I owe it to Jesus Christ to live for him, to make him my consuming passion and the driving force in my life. To do this, I have to die to my own desires daily. I have to crucify the urge that measures every action and decision around what is best for me. Paul eloquently speaks to this fact: "We always carry around in our body the death of Jesus, so that the life of Jesus may also be revealed in our body" (2 Corinthians 4:10).

Just as Jesus went to the cross, so I must go to the cross, always considering myself as carrying around "the death of Jesus." This is required so that *his* new life—his motivations, his purposes, his favor—might dominate everything I do. Every word I say and every action I take is to reflect him and his desires. And that commitment begins in my personal relationships, especially in my marriage. If my marriage contradicts my message, then I have sabotaged the goal of my life: to please Christ and to glorify his Father.

Today, as you talk to your spouse (or others), as you form your thoughts, as you choose how to spend your time, what drives you? Is it whatever makes you "feel" happy, or is it what you think will make *God* happy? "We make it our goal to please him."

Sacred Marriage, 33–34

A DIVINE SET-UP

Have you ever realized that God purposely sets up our lives to reveal his glory? Speaking of one man's healing, Jesus told his disciples, "This happened so that the work of God might be displayed in his life" (John 9:3).

Your limitations can bring glory to God as they provide platforms for him to do something that has no other explanation but God. If I were a naturally gifted writer and a naturally loving husband, you could look at my ministry and say, "What a great guy!" But knowing the truth, you can come to only one conclusion: "What an amazing God, who can use someone like *that!*"

The apostle Paul testifies to this reality this way: "But we have this treasure in jars of clay to show that this all-surpassing power is from God and not from us" (2 Corinthians 4:7). What a joy to work *with* God instead of just *for* God, to see him operate *in spite of* us instead of *because of* us!

Looking at the events of my life through this prism — in particular, the fact that God waited more than four decades to really launch my present career — cut short any sense of pride. On the contrary, it sent me into amazement and appreciation and worship: *God, you've outdone yourself this time. You really pulled it off!*

God wants to do something unique in you too. Austin Farrer, a popular twentieth-century Anglican preacher, wrote, "If God is anywhere more than elsewhere, it is because he works there more richly and more revealingly. He is more present in men than in beasts, in Christians than in pagans, in saints than in Laodiceans."[8]

If it seems there are places and even people where God works "more richly and more revealingly," wouldn't you like to be among them? To experience God is to be transformed by him. Do we not all aspire to become what the early church father Gregory of Nazianzus described as "an [instrument] which the Holy Spirit blows and on which he plays"?[9] God issues that invitation to you. How will you respond?

Holy Available, 25–26, 124

A TRANSFORMED PRESENCE

Without a sense of a powerfully transforming faith, we get stuck on lesser battles and smaller aims. We do this primarily by reducing our faith to a set of intellectual beliefs and a list of forbidden practices. Doctrine is enormously important, as is morality, but by themselves they are not enough.

I wonder what comes to mind when someone mentions the word *holiness*. Does it refer to the words you use or don't use, where you go or don't go on the Internet, how you express or don't express your sexuality? What is a *holy* person? And then ask yourself, can a few prohibitions like this adequately describe the powerful presence of a true man or woman of God?

My problem with those who put so much emphasis on moralism is not that they go too far but that they don't go far enough. They mistake the means for the end. Godly men and women would hardly be likely in today's world to spend their time getting drunk, cussing out inconsiderate drivers, or frittering away their time on salacious Internet searches. But you could never define them by these restraints. On the contrary, they always become known for what they *are*, not for what they *aren't*.

Here's the challenge of a small-minded faith based only on prohibitions: we still sin. If a successful Christian is defined by what she or he doesn't do, we're all in trouble, for "we all stumble in many ways" (James 3:2). Preaching mere moralism is the surest way to tire people out, because in one sense, we're all going to fall short of the ideal; and in another sense, spending our lives trying not to do something is far less than we were created for.

Incarnational spirituality — the living, reigning, and ascended Jesus living through us and transforming us into different people — does not uphold a few rules but rather creates an entirely new person who sees with new eyes, feels with a new heart, hears with renewed ears, and lives with a new passion. It is, I believe, the only life worth living.

Holy Available, 18–19

February 18

THE RIGHT PERSON FOR THE JOB

If you were to ask seminary professors to name the top ten preachers of all time, on the vast majority of those lists would fall the name Charles Haddon Spurgeon (1834-1892). His sermons became so popular that his church had to build a six-thousand-seat facility that could handle the crowds who wanted to hear him every Sunday.

And yet in one sermon Spurgeon made an astonishing confession: "I have been lamenting my unfitness for my work."[10]

Who could imagine that Spurgeon, one of the most successful ever at his position, could feel inadequate for a task at which he clearly excelled?

And yet I meet many involved and capable parents who feel the same way. They think, "Maybe I'm just not up to the task. Parenting asks of me skills and wisdom and energy I just don't possess."

Have you ever been there?

The Great Discourager, Satan, has a way of distracting us with pernicious questions: "Who are *you* to raise a child? What makes you think that *you*, of all people, can be a parent? These children would be better off without you!"

Spurgeon found hope in Isaiah 43:1: "But now, this is what the LORD says —he who created you, O Jacob, he who formed you, O Israel: 'Fear not, for I have redeemed you; I have summoned you by name; you are mine.'"

Spurgeon explains, "I said to myself, 'I am what God created me to be, and I am what He formed me to be. Therefore, I must, after all, be the right man for the place in which He has put me.'"[11]

God not only created you; he created your children. And he chose to place those children in your home. Listen to Spurgeon: "With the bloodstain upon us, we may well cease to fear ... How can we be deserted in the hour of need? We have been bought with too great a price for our Redeemer to let us slip. Therefore, let us march on with confidence."[12]

You are the right person for the job, not because of who you are, but because of Who placed you there—the all-wise Almighty God.

Devotions for Sacred Parenting, 12

A DYNAMIC FORCE

Biblical holiness and personal transformation depend on how present Christ becomes in his followers' lives and how he makes a real difference there. In such a life, Jesus is a genuine reality, a dynamic force, that goes far beyond mere belief. Jesus prayed for his future disciples "that I myself may be in them" (John 17:26). Paul added, "[Christ] is not weak in dealing with you, but is powerful among you" (2 Corinthians 13:3).

Jesus and Paul spoke of people who are benevolently invaded by and radically available to God. This is what the Orthodox Church talks about when it says that Christianity must go beyond Christocentrism to embrace Christification — that is, becoming like Christ, through Christ; in other words, "Christified."

If we don't think about God, pray to God, listen for God's voice, and consciously serve God, by definition we live an ungodly life. We usually think of *ungodly* as being against God, but ungodly can also mean a life that simply ignores God or — out of busyness, indifference, religiosity, or apathy — doesn't tap in to God. In this sense, it is possible to give an *ungodly* sermon that may be theologically accurate. It is possible to lead *ungodly* family devotions that nevertheless focus on spiritual truth. Christianity doesn't address only the ends; it has a lively interest in the means. That's why every healthy, growing believer should experience God every day — his presence, his power, his wisdom.

The early church fathers — as well as the entire Eastern wing of the Christian church — took this reality of personal experience with God so strongly that they often spoke of "deification." Such language (most famously, "God became man that man might become God") understandably causes us evangelicals to choke on our confessions. Reading the church fathers carefully, however, assures us that the best of them didn't teach that we actually become God, but that we should become God*like*. The Godlike quality never becomes our own possession; rather, it is a fruit of the "continuing, uniting work of the Holy Spirit."[13]

Holy Available, 23–24

DIVINE DELIGHT

Experiential Christianity is much more than a human yearning; it is a divine one. Just because I want to experience God isn't enough to make it a noble calling (part of me would also really like the ability to fly). What matters is that God wants to manifest his presence through us by his Spirit, which makes experiential faith a Christian obligation.

Just as an earthly parent takes delight in family resemblance, so our God feels enormous delight when we begin to resemble him in a spiritual sense. This is, in fact, our ultimate glorification: "For those God foreknew he also predestined to be conformed to the likeness of his Son" (Romans 8:29). Such a manifestation calls us to at least some human cooperation (see Philippians 2:12–13; 2 Peter 1:5–9; 1 John 3:3).

Paul warns, "Do not put out the Spirit's fire" (1 Thessalonians 5:19). Many have applied this warning exclusively to the use of the charismatic gifts, but to reduce the Holy Spirit to his gifts alone does not do justice to the reality. Paul teaches that it is possible to reduce the role of the Holy Spirit in our lives, to somehow put out his fire in such a way that God becomes less active, less of a force, and even less of a factor in our daily experience. Paul pleads with the early church, "Don't let this happen!"

But has it happened today?

Evangelicalism has spent the last several decades making the apologetic and historical case for Jesus. We have published books, offered seminars, and filled magazines with the historical claims and compelling intellectual arguments for the Christian faith. Thank God for this important work—but sadly, some of us have neglected the experiential case for the Christian faith, a case that may be even more persuasive with younger generations.

No less a mind than C. S. Lewis warned us of this error. In the conclusion of a talk, the famed apologist for the Christian faith confessed that "we apologists take our lives in our hands and can be saved only by falling back continually from the web of our own arguments ... into the Reality—from Christian apologetics into Christ Himself."[14]

So let's think deeply and study diligently, but let us also live differently, continually open to God and the active force of his dynamic Holy Spirit.

Holy Available, 27–28

WHATEVER GETS YOU THROUGH THE NIGHT

"Sandra" feels ignored by her husband and secretly has occasional regrets about giving up a well-paying job to stay home with her three children, who never seem content. They always want something more. And her husband—don't even get her started talking about his sense of entitlement!

She told me of the evening she had spent with her sister, enjoying a glass of wine as they talked about their families. The conversation stoked the emotional pain, turning a low-burning irritation into a flaming ache. Sandra asked for a second glass of wine. She explained, "I'm not a big girl, and I hadn't had anything to eat"—which was her way of preparing me for the confession, "so actually I got a little drunk."

While soul-building, God-affirming pleasure pleases our Father and brings him pleasure, our tendency to use pleasure to dull the pain makes him grieve. He wants us to turn to *him*. The trap of pleasure divorced from God's governing hand will lead to our ruin: "He who loves pleasure will become poor" (Proverbs 21:17).

In 2 Timothy 3:4, Paul warns against "lovers of pleasure rather than lovers of God." This passage challenges those who pursue pleasure as their primary aim rather than the God-ordained path of pursuing God and finding pleasure as a by-product of a life lived in surrender to Christ's purposes and aims. Pleasure divorced from God's governing hand becomes treacherous.

Frank Sinatra became famous for saying, "I'm for anything that gets you through the night, be it prayer, tranquilizers, or a bottle of Jack Daniels," a sentiment echoed by John Lennon when he sang, "Whatever gets you thru the night, 'salright, 'salright ..."[15]

No, it's *not* all right. Some pleasures affirm, rebuild, refresh, and enhance life, honoring God the Creator and pleasing him. Others destroy life, causing us harm and him grief. We become most vulnerable when we are desperate—and this is precisely when we need to take the most care about our choice of pleasures. It's not merely about getting through the night; it's about what helps us *grow* through life, pointing us toward eternity.

Pure Pleasure, 38–39

MIRROR, MIRROR, ON THE WALL

A businessman in a service industry grew weary of being yelled at. He tired of getting sprayed with spittle from dissatisfied customers who expected five-star service at Motel 6 prices. One day, he became oddly detached during yet another customer tirade; he felt as though he were watching a movie. And he couldn't help but think that the angry woman's antics made her look like a monkey.

That observation gave him a brilliant idea. He posted a giant mirror behind the front desk—and the customer tirades all but ceased. When people saw how rude and hateful they looked while yelling and screaming, they stopped yelling and screaming.

What is true physically is also true spiritually. God offers us a mirror for our attitudes. By living in his presence, we see more clearly how we are treating others. This gift of seeing people and situations from heaven's vantage point needs to begin at home. In our Sacred Marriage seminars, I mention that for married believers, God is our spiritual Father-in-law. When I realized I was married to *God's* daughter, everything changed about the way I viewed marriage. It was no longer about just me and one other person; it was very much a relationship with a passionately interested third partner who sees what is going on and cares very much about how my wife is treated and cared for.

Most of us fail to grasp just how fully God loves the person to whom we are married. As the father of three children, I fervently pray that each one will marry a spouse who will love them generously, respect them, and enjoy them. I realize that each of my children has certain quirks or limitations that may test a future spouse's patience, but I pray that each of their spouses will be kind in these areas. I know my kids aren't perfect, but I want them each to have spouses who will love them despite their imperfections.

In the same way, God is fully aware of our spouses' limitations—and he is just as eager for us to be kind and generous with these faults as we are for our kids' future spouses to be kind to them. By looking at our spouses through God's eyes, we invite God into our marriages in a new and richer way.

Holy Available, 63

RENEWED FLESH

Jesus came to this earth in the flesh, and he left it in the flesh. Any spirituality that ignores the body ignores Christ.

Rooted in this world—in some cosmically mysterious way, a part of the world he created—Jesus' birth, resurrection, and ascension *in a body* calls us to live in this world as he did. Becoming alive to Jesus makes us newly alive and acutely sensitive to the world. We can see with new eyes, hear with new ears, and feel with new hearts. It is as though Jesus tunes us into the world's real frequency —the static stops and true understanding begins.

Relatively few of us, however, see the world as Jesus would have us see and experience it. We can quickly become spiritual lepers, deadened by the distractions around us. The apostle Peter promises that through Christ we "may participate in the divine nature and escape the corruption in the world caused by evil desires" (2 Peter 1:4). In the Greek text, the grammar has us escaping the corruption of the world *as a precursor* to participating in the divine nature; that is, "we may participate in the divine nature, having escaped the corruption in the world caused by evil desires." Sin squelches God's work within us. In fact, one commentator's definition of this *corruption* is "the disintegrating power of evil."[16] This is a remarkable image.

Sin does indeed blind our eyes, anesthetize our spiritual senses, and lead us into many destructive illusions. As sin creeps into more parts of our lives, we grow increasingly deadened to God, as well as to the world he created.

As the disintegrating power of evil takes over, our lives become smaller, more self-absorbed and trivial, and less like Christ's. But as we are made alive in Christ and gain release from this corrupting influence, becoming participators in the divine nature through the uniting work of the Holy Spirit, a marvelous transformation takes place. Formerly wasted and even pathetic lives can become compelling.

Holy Available, 46–47

PAPA GOD

One day, when our daughter Kelsey was two years old, she started pointing at every family member's chair around the table. I was gone at the time. "Mommy," she began, "Allison, Graham, Kelsey . . ." She then pointed to my empty seat and said, "God."

"That's not God, Kelsey," Lisa said. "That's Papa."

"Jesus," Kelsey replied with a smile.

Three days later, all of us were together in a hotel room when Kelsey did it again. She started pointing to everybody and announcing his or her name. When she got to me, she said, "Jesus."

"I'm not Jesus, Kelsey," I said. "I'm Papa."

"You're Papa God," Kelsey replied.

I was flabbergasted and earnestly tried to talk it out with her, but you parents know what a two-year-old is like. By the time I had made my point, Kelsey had found something vastly more interesting than theology — her little toe and how it could be made to wiggle in all directions.

To me, this is one of the greatest ironies of parenting. I think about how big I seemed to my kids when I was just in my twenties, and how little I knew. Now, a bit more experienced in my forties, it's almost laughable how much smaller I seem to my children! Graham knows he could take me in a math test (and he has long since overtaken me when it comes to a round of golf), and there's no chance either one of my daughters would mistake me for deity.

But these early episodes of mistaken identity truly opened my eyes as a young parent. The more time I spent with my kids as they became toddlers and then preteens and teens, the more open they seemed to God's presence in their lives. The less time I spent with them, the less they seemed to pray. Somehow in their minds I helped shape their passion and hunger for God.

The best way to cultivate spiritual hunger in your children is to cultivate spiritual hunger in your own heart first. And you know what? Today is a good day to rekindle such a heart.

Sacred Parenting, 11 – 12

FULL-BODIED CHANGE

We simply must realize the full-bodied transformation that the early apostles preached. When the Jewish religious leaders in Rome ultimately rejected Paul's preaching of Christ (Acts 28:24–25), the apostle used the same passage (Isaiah 6:9–10) that Jesus used to scold them:

> "You will be ever hearing but never understanding;
>   you will be ever seeing but never perceiving.
> For this people's heart has become calloused;
>   they hardly hear with their ears,
>   and they have closed their eyes.
> Otherwise they might see with their eyes,
>   hear with their ears,
>   understand with their hearts
> and turn, and I would heal them."
>
> Matthew 13:14–15

This historic but new faith, this old/new truth, must change the way we see, hear, feel, and think. The hallmark of Christianity, now as ever, is the transformation into a new and far more compelling person. The "spiritual act of worship" of Romans 12 is not just singing songs; it is a total offering of who we are.

How do I worship God? By continually surrendering the members of my body to become his servants and his instruments of peace. This worship goes far beyond singing choruses or trying to obey a few moral laws; it speaks of a profound transformation. The surprising message of the incarnation — and later of Christ's ascension — is this: Don't try to escape the world, but rather go deeper into the world. See it with God's eyes. Hear it with God's ears. Feel it with God's heart. Think about it with God's mind.

Are you ready for some fresh splashes of God's glory in your life? Will you let go of what you've been and embrace what Christ is calling you to become? Are you willing to escape the corruption of evil desires so that you can more fully experience God's presence? Then let the transformation begin.

Holy Available, 51–52

A REVEALING MOUTH

God takes words very seriously. When God called Jeremiah, he sanctified his mouth: "Then the LORD reached out his hand and *touched my mouth* and said to me, 'Now, I have put my words in your mouth'" (Jeremiah 1:9, emphasis added). God never told Jeremiah to take up a sword or a backhoe; instead, his prophet-servant would accomplish his divinely appointed tearing down, destroying, overthrowing, building, and planting by faithfully speaking God's words.

When Isaiah saw God, he cried out, "Woe to me!... I am ruined! *For I am a man of unclean lips*" (Isaiah 6:5, emphasis added). And what did God do about Isaiah's unclean lips? "Then one of the seraphs flew to me with a live coal in his hand, which he had taken with tongs from the altar. With it he *touched my mouth* and said, 'See, this has touched your lips; your guilt is taken away and your sin atoned for'" (6:6–7, emphasis added).

When God called Ezekiel, he said, "Son of man, stand up on your feet and I will *speak to you*" (Ezekiel 2:1, emphasis added). He told Ezekiel that his ministry would essentially be a ministry of words. God is adamant with Ezekiel: "You must speak my words to them" (2:7). He then prepares Ezekiel by asking him to open his mouth and "eat what is before you, eat this scroll; then go and speak to the house of Israel" (3:1). So Ezekiel opened his mouth, and the Lord "gave [him] the scroll to eat" (3:2).

Is it a coincidence that God calls the three major prophets—Isaiah, Jeremiah, and Ezekiel—by sanctifying their mouths? From a biblical perspective, words reveal the state of our hearts. *The mouth reveals what the heart conceals.*

If we allow our tongues to become God's servants, there is no end to the good God can do through us. There is no limit to the encouragement he can unleash, the number of people he can turn from their sins, and the communities he can build. View your tongue as an instrument of grace; use it to sing God's praises, to speak words of comfort, occasional warning, and love.

Holy Available, 75–76

LOOKING BEYOND MARRIAGE

Our close friends have a son named Nolan. When he was just four years old, he saw me carrying some large boxes and asked me, in all sincerity, "Gary, are you strongest, or is God strongest?"

His dad laughed a little too hard at that one. And of course, we adults think it's absurd to compare our physical strength with God's. But how many of us adults have turned around and asked, perhaps unconsciously, "Are you going to fulfill me, or will God fulfill me?" For some reason, this question doesn't sound as absurd to us as the one about physical strength. But it should!

We need to remind ourselves of the ridiculous nature of looking for something from other humans—ultimate satisfaction—that only God can provide.

I believe that much of the dissatisfaction we experience in marriage comes from expecting too much from it. For years I worked on an outdated computer. It didn't have enough memory or processing power to run particular programs or combine certain tasks. It wasn't that I had a bad computer; compared to the typewriter I wrote my master's thesis on, the computer was amazing. It's just that I couldn't reasonably expect more from it than it had the power to give. I had to learn how to appreciate what it could do, without focusing on what it couldn't do.

In the same way, some of us ask too much of marriage. We want to get the largest portion of our life's fulfillment from our relationship with our spouse—and that's asking too much. Yes, without a doubt a healthy marriage should bring us moments of happiness, meaning, and a general sense of fulfillment. But my wife can't be God, and I was created with a spirit that craves God. Anything less than God, and I'll feel an ache. If I ask more of my marriage than God designed it to give, I'll start resenting it for what it fails to provide instead of appreciating it for what it offers. Active thanksgiving kills the marital cancer of bitterness.

We need to look and explore beyond marriage to find ultimate meaning and satisfaction. Just as celibates use abstinence and religious hermits use isolation to grow in their pursuit of God, so we can use marriage for the same thing. Why can't we learn to use marriage in the same way celibates use abstinence—to point us toward God? We can when we accept that the lack of total fulfillment in the most important human relationship we'll ever have is divinely designed to point out our need to build intimacy with God, first and foremost.

Sacred Marriage, 25

TURNING WEAKNESS INTO STRENGTH

Moses demonstrates what happens when an ordinary person allows an extraordinary God to change the way he speaks, thinks, sees, and feels.

When God first tells Moses he is sending him to the Egyptians to free the Israelites, Moses protests, "O Lord, I have never been eloquent, neither in the past nor since you have spoken to your servant. I am slow of speech and tongue" (Exodus 4:10). On another occasion, Moses complains, "Why would Pharaoh listen to me, since I speak with faltering lips?" (6:12). Moses later repeats virtually the same objection: "Since I speak with faltering lips, why would Pharaoh listen to me?" (6:30). When something gets repeated *three times* like this, it's significant. Clearly, Moses views himself as a pathetically incompetent speaker.

God responds to Moses with the words, "Who gave man his mouth? Who makes him deaf or mute? Who gives him sight or makes him blind? Is it not I, the LORD? Now go; I will help you speak and will teach you what to say" (4:11–12). God gave Moses such an effective mouth that when the early church remembered Moses, they thought of him as strongest exactly where he had considered himself weakest. Stephen, an early biblical martyr, calls Moses "powerful in speech" (Acts 7:22).

What happened? How does a man who speaks with "faltering lips" go down through the ages as "powerful in speech"? It happens when an ordinary individual becomes an active instrument of an extraordinary God.

Later, when Moses met with God for forty days on the top of Mount Sinai, his face glowed with such radiance that Aaron and the Israelites feared to approach him (Exodus 34:29–31). It is impossible to spend time in the dynamic and powerful presence of God and to emerge the same person you were before.

Your weaknesses mean nothing in the light of God's equipping call. In fact, your weaknesses can all the better bring even more glory to God by making it clear that you are God's instrument, for nothing else will explain your personal transformation. Offer up what you view as your greatest weakness; once surrendered to God, watch with fascination as this weakness may become an identifying strength.

Holy Available, 79–80

THOUGHTLESSLY CRUEL

A couple of years ago, my wife planted a few blueberry bushes beside our house, about seventy feet away from the nearest faucet. We had a cheap hose at the time that kept splitting as I hauled it across the lawn to water the bushes. I had to cut the hose and reset a new nozzle every time it split, so I finally got fed up, went to the hardware store, and got a "heavy-duty, industrial-strength" hose *guaranteed* not to split.

I was so happy with my purchase — finally, a decent hose! It made me smile, just looking at it. I'd pick it up, feel its weight, and say to myself, "No way this baby is *ever* gonna split."

Imagine my chagrin when Lisa barged into the house one evening and exclaimed, "I *hate* that stupid hose!"

My super-industrial strength beauty proved far too heavy for my poor wife. When she tried to lug it across the front yard and the driveway to reach the side of our house, it felt like she was trying to pull a stubborn mule. I bought that hose thinking of *me*; I never even considered whether Lisa could lift it.

Although some may consider this a simple, inconsiderate act, at a deeper level it revealed my prideful self-centeredness. I wasn't being intentionally cruel, but I did act *thoughtlessly* cruel. I simply didn't pay attention to what was best for Lisa. Worse, I didn't even think about Lisa when I made the purchase. I had grown tired of repairing the hose, so I determined to make my own life better — as it turned out, at her expense.

Spiritual humility invites us to become more thoughtful, more aware, and more sensitive to others. The arrogant get so wrapped up in their own world that they can't see anyone else.

Humility is about the little things in life, and marriage is 90 percent small stuff. We don't build humility on giant gestures as much as forge it with consistent, thoughtful actions day after day. What better arena to learn this in than marriage? What relationship seems designed to confront our self-preoccupation more than living with a spouse?

In what areas in your marriage are you being thoughtlessly cruel? Where are you not even considering how your actions (or inactions) are making life difficult for your spouse?

Devotions for a Sacred Marriage, 53–54

MARCH

With spring comes renewal, both physically and spiritually. We are invited to clear away the debris and get ready for a new season of growth that results in a steady transformation. With our hearts, minds, and tongues remade in God's image—sometimes a process filled with godly sorrow—we get ready to be filled with his fullness.

TRAINED TONGUES

While the tongue can't be tamed, it can be trained. God's empowering presence works in cooperation with our minds to produce a godly transformation in the way we speak.

God's Word is explicit about the content and purpose of God-honoring speech. The apostle Paul tells us to "encourage one another and build each other up" (1 Thessalonians 5:11). This passage doesn't tell us to refrain from saying hurtful things; it compels us to proclaim truthful, redemptive words designed to build others up.

Paul, ever the skillful pastor, knows that simply speaking positive truths won't cut it in a church filled with people who stumble in many ways. So he lays out particular uses of the tongue a few verses later (verse 14): "Warn those who are idle, encourage the timid, help the weak, be patient with everyone."

It would be wrong to encourage an idle person; instead, we're told to "warn" them. Believers living in a state of disobedience need to be gently and patiently confronted. We must love them enough to speak a word that may make them angry but also calls them to repentance: "The tongue that brings healing is a tree of life" (Proverbs 15:4). Silence, in such situations, is cowardly and a curse.

On the other hand, it would be wrong to further overpower a timid person. Such people need a word of encouragement: "Reckless words pierce like a sword, but the tongue of the wise brings healing" (Proverbs 12:18).

All of our words must be seasoned with grace-filled patience. How much havoc we unleash when our expectations for our spouses, our children, our coworkers, or our fellow drivers amount to perfection! People will regularly disappoint us. If our hearts aren't ready for this, we'll speak only with angry exasperation, and our negative words will tear down people for their humanness. Instead, God calls us to use our tongues to cultivate redemptive transformation.

Let's learn to speak the right word in the right season to the right person. Ask God to help you do this today.

Holy Available, 81–82

MINDS GLORIOUSLY REMADE

Kit DesLauriers made worldwide headlines when she became the first person to ski from the summits of the highest peaks on all seven continents. Not just *climb* the peaks, mind you, but *ski* down them. The scene of her last descent was Mount Everest in October 2006.

The danger of such a quest is incalculable. Kit recounts her thoughts as she looked down from twenty-nine thousand feet on Mount Everest: "This was the most serious ski descent we had ever attempted ... One mistake, and you would be unrecognizable at the bottom. It was very, very intense."

Her husband, Rob, concurred: "It was one of the few times in my ski career when it was, 'If you fall, you die.'"

How do you face, much less overcome, such a daunting challenge? What do you do with your fear? Kit's thoughts are illuminating: "I don't make any claims to not being scared. It's important, and it's healthy. I've been scared enough that I'm comfortable with it. When you experience fear, the next thing out of people's minds is, 'I can't.' *We are in control of our minds.* As much as our minds try to control us, it is important to not let your mind run too far."[1]

I greatly appreciate Kit's affirmation that we can control our minds. Our minds need not rule us; they can be ruled. When Scripture tells us that God will transform our minds, it's clear that we *can* grow and develop in this area. In fact, the apostle Paul suggests that a Christ-molded mind is the foundation of transformation. Consider this familiar passage: "Do not conform any longer to the pattern of this world, but be transformed *by the renewing of your mind.* Then you will be able to test and approve what God's will is—his good, pleasing and perfect will" (Romans 12:2, emphasis added). This verse confirms that God is the agent of change, but we have a responsibility to surrender ourselves to God's change. This is the reality of what is involved in becoming holy available.

Begin to take charge of your mind; feed it with God's truth; question your assumptions; ask God to help you think more clearly and more biblically. Make your mind your servant instead of your master.

Holy Available, 113–14

REGAINING GOD'S HEART

Following a trip to Philadelphia, I returned to the West Coast to do a Sacred Parenting weekend seminar. Because of the time shift, I didn't sleep well, and after doing a full Friday night and Saturday morning and afternoon seminar, I came back to the church on Saturday evening for the first "Sunday" service.

When I woke up the next morning, I felt tired, but prayer, adrenaline, and a venti cup of chai tea got me through the first two services. Just before the third service (the fourth overall), I sat alone in an office and finally had to admit: I just didn't care about the fourth service.

At first, I felt appalled—how could I go into that pulpit when I really, honestly, just didn't care? So I prayed: "Lord, before I came here, and again this morning, I asked you for your words. Now, please give me your heart. I don't merely want to give a lecture. I want to share your passion for these people and preach out of that power."

Nothing happened.

I picked up my notes and walked back into the church. As I stood up front, a pastor leaned over and asked if I would pray for people as they came forward during worship. "We're a bit short on elders and pastors for this final service," he explained. "It's pretty packed, and we may need some help."

Four people came directly to me for prayer. Three left in tears afterward. As the final one walked back to the pew, I realized that God had restarted my heart. He reminded me that I was preaching to real, hurting people with concrete problems who sometimes desperately needed his wisdom. In a brilliant turn of events, God had given me a renewed heart.

God knows what he's doing! If this was just a "coincidence," it's the one millionth coincidence of my life—all of which occurred after prayer. God can, and does, take hearts that have stopped feeling and imbue them with his passion, purpose, and concern. All we have to do is ask him: "Lord, I've lost my passion for this. I've lost my heart for such and such. Can you help me out?" The prayer to care, the prayer to love, is a prayer that God loves to answer.

Just try it. You'll see.

Holy Available, 139–40

THE HOUSE OF MOURNING

The Bible sees mourning not as something to run from but as something to learn from:

> It is better to go to a house of mourning
>> than to go to a house of feasting,
> for death is the destiny of every man;
>> the living should take this to heart.
> Sorrow is better than laughter,
>> because a sad face is good for the heart.
> The heart of the wise is in the house of mourning,
>> but the heart of fools is in the house of pleasure.
>> Ecclesiastes 7:2–4

Clearly this verse speaks of the reality of death more than the notion of mourning for mourning's sake; at the very least, it points out the many sad realities of this world. To live as though the world were a perfectly happy place with no disappointment and pain is both foolish and absurd. There is a time for celebration and laughter, but laughter loses its depth and sweetness when entirely divorced (in a fallen world) from occasional sorrow. As my friend Jeromy Matkin points out, paintings require both highlights and shadows to create the appearance of depth. So do people.

According to the Bible, being a true believer requires mourning in certain seasons. Yet so often, our culture—and even the church—looks at mourning as something to be shunned and overcome. During Joel's time, religious leaders were told to lead the nation in mourning: "Put on sackcloth, O priests, and mourn; wail, you who minister before the altar. Come, spend the night in sackcloth, you who minister before my God" (Joel 1:13). While God offered forgiveness, the doorway was mourning, not rejoicing. How often do we use that doorway today?

Christians are often marvelous celebrators—for good reason. But to be mature Christians, we must also become expert mourners.

Authentic Faith, 149–50

SPIRITUAL CONDITIONING

Psychologists describe a process called "conditioning." If I do something that brings pleasure or relief from distress, my brain will immediately draw a strong connection between that pleasure and the action. If a man finds that a glass of whiskey and soda at the end of a long day relaxes him, before long his brain starts yearning for that whiskey and soda. Once he gets home, his mind anticipates the liquid relief.

Should the whiskey bottle be empty, however, the man may feel tremendous stress. His body has come to appreciate the routine of the alcohol's effect; now that the routine is broken, his brain has to find a new way to cope.

The danger is obvious—what if the action that brings pleasure is illicit and forbidden by God? In this case, we enter the world of Romans 7, where we do what we don't want to do and don't do what we want to do. Our spiritual will and our biological conditioning go to war with each other.

All of us have witnessed the inability of willpower alone to win such struggles. Enter the discipline of mourning into the equation, however, and a new patterning may develop. If I allow myself to go through a process of regret and repentance; if I consider why my actions hurt others and offend the power of love; if I contemplate how my evil actions shape me into someone I don't want to become; if I make myself admit that I have dishonored and rebelled against the God who loves me and who saved me—then negative conditioning can begin to take place.

If I know that a certain action will lead me through a difficult period of mourning, then the next time I face that action, I will not feel compelled by its pleasure or relief. Instead, I will remember its consequences, decidedly less than sweet. And so I can find the will to do the right thing the next time.

The next time you are convicted of sin, let it hurt for a while. Feel the pain. Taste the ugliness. But know this: Once we let it go into the grace of God, it is gone forever.

Authentic Faith, 159–60

SEEING THE SHAME IN ANOTHER'S FACE

A young seminarian, married just a few years, confessed to me his lapse into pornography. He had developed the habit before marrying, but early on in his marriage he had avoided it. After a couple of years, however, he once again gave in to the temptation.

Then he did something that some counselors discourage, though it proved effective in his case. He shared his lapse with his wife. He saw the horror on her face. He felt her sense of betrayal and hurt, and a healthy, holy shame covered him. In his wife's face, he was invited to mourn, and he accepted the invitation.

"Now, when I think about pornography," he said, "I think about how much I hurt my wife. I don't want to do that again."

He has conditioned his mind to associate pornography with pain instead of pleasure. Most men who talk to me about victory over pornography share one common trait: They've disclosed their actions to their wives. Most men who talk to me about their struggle with this addiction have kept it secret from those who can most help them, namely, the ones they live with. Sometimes they spiritualize this hiding: "Why should I burden her with my struggle? I don't want her to think she isn't enough for me or that I'm not satisfied with her." Such thinking allows the man to continue looking at pictures of naked women while he keeps deceiving himself with the promise that "this will be the last time."

I do not suggest that every male reader with this struggle should immediately, without counsel, make such a disclosure. It may well be that you should share your struggle with a Christian brother instead of with your wife. But if you truly want to leave a besetting sin behind, you may need to see the shame of your sin in another's face. That's what confession is all about; though not absolutely necessary for forgiveness, it makes our rebellion much more real.

James tells us, "Confess your sins to each other and pray for each other so that you may be healed" (James 5:16)." Not just forgiven, but healed. Do you want to get "better?" Then learn to confess.

Authentic Faith, 160–61

INCREASINGLY STUPID

"It's difficult to watch someone throw off their faith and become increasingly stupid. *That* is the most difficult client to turn around."

Dr. Mitchell Whitman, a clinical psychologist, was describing his frustration over some people's tendency in midlife to reject everything they once believed in and destroy their families, their children, and their character. They make themselves and everyone around them miserable. They become increasingly misguided and seem to make ever-worse choices, until they get buried under a cascading avalanche of stupidity.

Those who study human nature understand that foolishness begets foolishness. We can become "increasingly stupid" when we start making unwise choices; the snowball effect of darkened thinking can cause utter ruin. When Paul writes, "Do not conform any longer to the pattern of this world, but be transformed by the renewing of your mind" (Romans 12:2), he is declaring, as C. E. B. Cranfield observes, that "when Christians allow themselves to be conformed to this world, what takes place is not just a disguising of their real nature but an inward corruption."[2]

We are fallen creatures radically dependent on God's *continuing* mercy and grace. When we shut God off, we become vulnerable to any foolish whim; our emotions and passions may rule us and degrade us. Worse, we even lose the spiritual perception that otherwise can warn us about what is happening. Solomon —who started out so wisely—is the poster child for this sad phenomenon, and his life provides a grave warning to all of us who grow careless: No matter how far we may have progressed, we can lose it all if we start sliding downward.

Christianity exalts the role of the mind as a necessary part of right living, but our faith is unique in stressing how our behavior and our minds influence and act on each other. When our thinking goes, our behavior doesn't lag far behind. And when our behavior slips, our minds begin to slip as well. In other words, don't risk compromising with compromise. Who knows where the downward slide will stop?

Holy Available, 107–8

STEPPING-STONES OR STUMBLING BLOCKS?

When we partner with God to become transformed people, we proclaim the Lord's reality. In other words, true experiential faith is not an exercise of self-glorification, but rather the pathway to giving glory to God. Luke put it this way: "When [the Sanhedrin] saw the courage of Peter and John and realized that they were unschooled, ordinary men, they were astonished and they took note that these men had been with Jesus" (Acts 4:13).

When we allow God to mark our manner, alter our attitudes, and burnish our behavior, people will naturally ask, "What is it about him? What is it about her?" They'll take note that we have been with Jesus — and have undergone dramatic change. This gives glory to God as we become walking billboards that proclaim his reality and redeeming power.

The reverse is also true. If people take note that we claim to be with Jesus and *haven't* changed, that we are still driven by fear of others and our own passions, then the gospel gets robbed of its glory.

Our motivation for calling God's people to embrace experiential, realized holiness is based on upholding the glory of God's name. Paul clearly laid out the driving force behind his spiritual effort: "Through [Jesus] and *for his name's sake*, we received grace and apostleship to call people from among all the Gentiles *to the obedience* that comes from faith" (Romans 1:5, emphasis added).

It is for God's sake, first and foremost, that we are obligated to call people to obedience and to preach the practice of holiness. When I allow God to change the way I view people, talk to people, and hear people, I become a conduit of ministry, an encourager of faith, and a walking advertisement for God's transforming grace. When I wear the label "Christian" but live in a way that denies its truth, I become a stumbling block instead of a stepping-stone to the faith of others. Let's make up our minds to honor God by serving as stepping-stones, not stumbling blocks.

You may be willing to risk *your* reputation, but are you willing to risk God's?

Holy Available, 177–78

ON CALL

A young man, a good friend of my son, suffered a sad injustice. I felt heartsick at this turn of events and woke up early the next morning and started to pray. *God, can I do anything about this? Can you move creatively here? Would you inspire me to do something to make right this obvious wrong?*

I had been sharing a hotel room with my son and three of his friends. While they slept, I figured I would pray better outside than inside, so I went for a walk beside a river. Once again, I poured out my heart to God, asking him to use me to intervene in some way. I waited for God's quiet leading, which led to ... nothing.

Absolutely nothing.

I tell this uninspiring story for an important reason. Just because we make ourselves available to God doesn't mean we'll experience an unending string of miraculous encounters and exciting celestial conversations. God moves as he wills, where he wills, when he wills. But it was still an act of worship to present myself before God, saying, "Here I am. If you want to do something through me, I'm ready."

Maybe you're about to go to a family reunion; you can pray, *Lord, make me sensitive. I'm offering my ears, mind, tongue, hands, and eyes. Fill them with your presence so that I'll be your servant.*

Maybe you know a couple going through a difficult time in their marriage, or a rebellious teenager, a hurting church, or a troubled coworker. Will you at least present yourself to God and make yourself available to be used by him? He may or may not take you up on your offer, but offering yourself is an important step, a holy act of worship.

To help rid yourself of mere moralism and to begin embracing the gospel of transformation, ask yourself these foundational questions: Am I available? Is God using my eyes, my mind, my ears, my hands and feet to build his kingdom? Have I ever offered them up as an act of worship?

If not, why not do so now?

Holy Available, 171–72

FALLING OUT OF ... REPENTANCE

I have a theory. Behind virtually every case of marital dissatisfaction lies unrepented sin. Couples don't fall out of love so much as they fall out of repentance. Sin, wrong attitudes, and unaddressed personal failures slowly erode the relationship, assaulting and eventually erasing the once lofty promises made in the throes of an earlier passion.

All of us enter marriage with sinful attitudes. When these attitudes surface, we feel tempted to hide them or even run to another relationship where someone hasn't seen our "stuff." But Christian marriage presumes a certain degree of self-disclosure. When I got married, I committed to allow myself to be known by Lisa—which means she will see me as I am, with all my faults, prejudices, fears, and weaknesses. This is a terrifying reality to even contemplate, and yet, a necessary one.

Dating is largely a dance in which you always try to put the best face forward —hardly a good preparation for the inevitable self-disclosure implied in marriage. In fact, it wouldn't surprise me if many marriages end in divorce largely because one or both partners are running from their own revealed weaknesses as much as they are running from something they can't tolerate in their spouse.

May I suggest an alternative? Use the revelation of your sin as a means to grow in the foundational Christian virtue of humility, leading you to confession and renouncement. Then take the next step and adopt the positive virtue that corresponds to the sin you are renouncing. If you've used women in the past, practice serving your wife. If you've been quick to ridicule your husband, practice giving him encouragement and praise. View marriage as an entryway to sanctification—as a relationship that will reveal your sinful behaviors and attitudes and give you the opportunity to address them before the Lord.

But please don't give in to the temptation to resent your partner as your own weaknesses get revealed. Be thankful that God has given you a mirror. Of course, we must also give our family members the freedom and acceptance they need in order to face their own weaknesses as well. In this way, we can all use family life as a spiritual mirror, serving our sanctification and growth in holiness.

Sacred Marriage, 96–97

A CRUCIBLE FOR CHARACTER

My brother once asked me, "What is marriage like?" I thought for a moment and said, "If you want to be free to serve Jesus, there's no question—stay single. Marriage takes a lot of time. But if you want to become more like Jesus, I can't imagine any better thing to do than to get married. Being married forces you to face some character issues you would never have to face otherwise."

Jesus, of course, was celibate his entire life, so it feels ironic to suggest that marriage is the preferred route to becoming more like him. But Jesus did live in a family, and that's all he had done at the time the Father proclaimed, "This is my Son, whom I love; with him I am well pleased" (Matthew 3:17).

The real transforming work of marriage is the twenty-four-hours-a-day, seven-days-a-week commitment. This is the crucible that grinds and shapes us into the character of Jesus Christ. Instead of getting up at 3:00 a.m. to pray in a monastery, the question becomes, "Who will wake up when the baby's diaper needs changing?"

Marriage calls us to an entirely new and selfless life. This insight came some years ago when Lisa and the kids were traveling while I stayed home to work. For the first time ever, it seemed, I had a free Saturday. For as long as I could remember, I had awakened each weekend and talked over with Lisa what the family would do; I almost didn't know how to ask the question—what do *I* want to do? Yet that was the question I had asked myself as a single man virtually every Saturday.

Any situation that calls me to confront my selfishness has enormous spiritual value, and I slowly began to understand that the real purpose of marriage may not be happiness as much as it is holiness. Not that God has anything against happiness, or that happiness and holiness are by nature mutually exclusive; but looking at marriage through the lens of holiness began to put it into an entirely new perspective.

Here's the wonder of this approach: if we value the holiness-producing aspect of marriage, we will value our marriage all the more, as the work of holiness is never done. What do *you* value most about marriage?

Sacred Marriage, 21–22

THE RULES CHANGED

I knew the rules had changed just a few weeks after the birth of our oldest daughter. We were driving south to Oregon when we stopped at a restaurant to get a bite to eat. At one time in my life, my favorite food on earth was a Dairy Queen Blizzard. I just knew that the creator of this fine confection had to be a Christian, because I thought it would take nothing less than the Holy Spirit's inspiration to come up with anything that tasted as good as an M&M Blizzard.

We ordered our burgers and fries, and I had my Blizzard. We took it outside on a sunny day, and at exactly that moment our daughter had her once-every-three-day diaper blowout. Our firstborn, as a baby, liked to "save it up." She preferred to wait until we were on our way to church, had just sat down for dinner, had just given her a bath, or some other convenient moment before she expunged the previous seventy-two hours' worth of digestive effort.

I remember the helpless feeling. Cold fries don't taste very good, and melted Blizzards lose a lot—yet I knew I had a good ten to fifteen minutes' worth of work ahead of me. Because this baby did it all at once, changing her meant not just a new diaper but a veritable bath and a full change of clothing. And we were on the road.

"Don't just stand there," Lisa said. "*Help* me!"

"But"—I looked at my fries, already wilting with a shelf life of about ten minutes. I stared forlornly at my Blizzard, teasing my tongue with its promise, yet already looking as though it were about to start boiling in the hot sun. I put the food bag on top of the car and went to work.

Life had changed, indeed. It may sound like a small sacrifice—and even now, as I look back over two decades later, it seems insubstantial—but it marked a major turning point for this then-twenty-five-year-old. I was learning to put someone else's needs ahead of my own. Little did I know that I had just begun the spiritually transformative journey called parenting.

Sacred Parenting, 12–13

FILLED WITH HIS FULLNESS

The hymnist Frances Ridley Havergal prayed for many years that God would grant her a more genuine spiritual experience. She had written as far back as 1858 of her strong desire for a deeper, empowering presence of God: "I want Jesus to speak to me, to say 'many things' to me, that I may speak for him to others with real power. It is not knowing doctrine, but being with him, which will give this."[3]

God made Frances wait—as he makes most of his saints wait—but Frances recorded the following on a Sunday in 1873: "I first saw clearly the blessedness of true consecration. I saw it as a flash of electric light, and what you see, you can never *unsee*."[4]

The intimacy with God, the growth in personal holiness, the power for ministry—everything Frances longed for—she received. She was truly transformed and later asked the church, "Why should we pare down the promises of God to the level of what we have hitherto experienced of what God is 'able to do,' or even of what we have thought he might be able to do for us? Why not receive God's promises, nothing doubting, just as they stand?"[5]

Out of this experience, following a joyous time of fruitful ministry, Frances wrote one of the most beloved worship songs of the past two hundred years: "Take My Life and Let It Be."

Are you tired of trying to keep connected with God through mere morality? Are you tired of knowing an awful lot about God but precious little of God? Are you exhausted from trying to make the Christian life work in your own strength? If so, then enter the experiential side of Christianity, where God becomes not just the goal of our lives but the engine that takes us to the goal. Along with the apostle Paul, I pray that "you may be filled to the measure of all the fullness of God" (Ephesians 3:19). This is, after all, what you were made for.

In other words, you don't have to settle. Open up your life to God. Ask for more of him. He may seem to take his time in answering your prayer, but according to Frances, the fulfillment of the promise will be more than worth the wait.

Holy Available, 31

THE ANTI-DR. FIX-IT

She may be the most famous multiple divorcée in history. After racking up five husbands and at least one lover, she appeared to feel comfortable around men. But she had never met a man like *this* (see John 4).

His first request sounded simple: "Please give me some water. I'm thirsty."

Have you ever lived as a true outsider? If you haven't, you can't imagine what it feels like for someone to say, "You belong." That's what Jesus communicated to the Samaritan woman in the mere act of talking to her. The geographical dispute about the proper place for the holy temple had created centuries of acrimony between Jews and Samaritans. The historical DNA of her ancestors had kept her anathema to any respectable Jewish man, and even more to a prophet.

Yet here came a Jewish man, a rabbi and a prophet no less, asking *her*, a Samaritan woman, for a drink.

When the woman points out the absurdity of the moment, Jesus reveals something to her that he had said only indirectly to the "real" Jews. Jesus announces, point-blank, that he is the Messiah. What an extraordinary pronouncement! God's chosen people, presumably the ones who had the temple in the "right" place, had to glean the truth about Jesus' messiahship through parables, indirect allusions, and scriptural applications. But not this woman! She gets the truth in its most naked form.

Ultimately, she needed to hear nothing else. Throughout this famous conversation, not once does Jesus talk to the woman about how to "fix" her relationships with men or find "true pleasure" in human intimacy. This never becomes a "Dr. Fix-It" moment, because Jesus cuts to the core of her deepest need—she needs to stop looking at men to find fulfillment and turn to God. Because of the way she has lived, she will never know the intimacy of a lifelong marriage as God intended. But Jesus speaks of something even deeper and richer than a rewarding marriage—a relationship with God himself. And that pleasure can be hers for the asking.

Like this woman, you may have made some bad choices, but know this: God speaks to broken, disappointed people all the time and points them to a water that truly satisfies. Drink deeply!

Pure Pleasure, 198–99

SINFUL SILENCE

I once watched a man's career implode, in part because his subordinates refused to speak up and challenge his worsening tendencies. Yes, that man bears the responsibility for his own lack of growth; but his staff members admit that their refusal to use words to lovingly challenge him allowed a bad situation to grow worse until ultimately it blew up.

How many children have fallen over the edge because their parents saw the beginning of a problem but out of fear refused to speak up? Perhaps they noticed that their daughter and her boyfriend were getting a little too "touchy," or that their son's moods seemed fueled by the unhealthy consumption of who knows what—but they also knew the scene it would create to say something. So they stayed silent.

How many marriages have crumbled under the weight of sin because a spouse was afraid to rock the boat? How many friends have continued a downward slide because their brothers and sisters in Christ felt more concerned about appearing supportive than in calling their friends to live for the glory of God?

Not cursing comprises only about 5 percent of cultivating a transformed, God-honoring tongue. When and how and whether you speak accounts for the other 95 percent. Surely this is the point behind God's challenge to Ezekiel:

> "When I say to a wicked man, 'You will surely die,' and you do not warn him or speak out to dissuade him from his evil ways in order to save his life, that wicked man will die for his sin, and I will hold you accountable for his blood. But if you do warn the wicked man and he does not turn from his wickedness or from his evil ways, he will die for his sin; but you will have saved yourself."
>
> Ezekiel 3:18–19

God desires to commandeer our tongues for his service: "The tongue has the power of life and death" (Proverbs 18:21). Will you use this power? Will you begin the journey to have a mouth that speaks the very words of God?

Is there a conversation you need to have, perhaps even today, but have been avoiding? Put it off no longer. Cowardly silence can be among the greatest of sins.

Holy Available, 82–83

GOD'S EYES, GOD'S WOMAN

A friend of mine traveled to another city to conduct a business seminar. After the sessions, an attractive young woman knocked on his hotel room door. The woman worked for the company that had hired my friend, and when he opened the door, she pushed through and walked right into the room.

"You can't be in here," he protested.

"Why not?" she asked teasingly. "Are you scared?"

Then she acted as if she were going to remove her shirt. My friend kept the room door open and said, "Listen, you really need to leave."

The woman made it very clear that she was available for any sexual favor of his choosing. When he insisted that she leave, she finally did something over-the-top provocative. Only then did she leave. Immediately afterward, my friend wisely told two business associates what had happened, in great detail.

Two months later, my friend returned to that city, working with the same company as before, when the provocative young woman pulled him aside. "We have to talk," she said. My friend's heart started racing as he feared the worst. Would she make a false accusation? Would she try to spin what had happened, making him sound like the bad guy? Her first words put him at ease.

"I can't thank you enough for being the first man who has ever cared about me more than about my breasts. I'm going back to church. I need to get my life back together. When I finally met a man like you who was more interested in me than in my body, it showed me how messed up I had become."

Because of the way she dressed, acted, and talked, this woman was a sex object in the eyes of most men. But one man dared to look at her through God's eyes — seeing a spiritually injured soul acting out her hurt. By treating her appropriately, he helped open her eyes, brought her out of denial, and put her back on the pathway to God. That is our calling — to bring the presence of God to everyone we meet, in season and out.

Holy Available, 66–67

MINDFUL CHOICES

Ernest Hemingway didn't suffer fools. The great novelist once dismissed what he considered to be a silly interviewer by saying, "The fact that I am interrupting serious work to answer these questions proves that I am so stupid that I should be penalized severely."[6]

Notice the focus: Hemingway had the sense that he was engaged in something significant — in his case, to create great literature — so he resented unworthy interruptions.

Do we have the same passion, the same guardedness, the same zeal, to make ourselves available for what God is creating and doing in this world? If so, cultivating the mind of Christ will become an essential element of obedience. If our minds are overly preoccupied with cultural amusements, we'll become unavailable, rarely even considering what God might be doing in any particular moment or situation he has called us to.

Certainly, we all need downtime. Recreation is a good thing, as my wife reminded me one day: "You can't read twenty hours a day." But has the "good" thing begun to crowd out the "best" thing — a determined focus to study and "present [ourselves] to God as one approved" (2 Timothy 2:15)? Are we redeeming the time, aspiring to receive and develop a mind marked by God?

Will this amazing invitation — to have the mind of Christ — so captivate us that we will give up lesser pursuits to seize it? As J. P. Moreland brilliantly observes, "The spiritually mature person is a wise person." The mind of Christ and God's wisdom are something we are both given (1 Corinthians 2:16) and told to cultivate (Proverbs 4:1 – 13) — the product, as Moreland puts it, "of a life of study and a developed mind."[7]

Do you want a truly transformed life? If so, this transformation requires a transformed mind. A transformed mind usually requires transformed priorities — less television, more reading; less fretting, more praying; less chatter, more heartfelt sharing. Let's make good, "mindful" choices today.

Holy Available, 107, 117

March 18

A FALSE CHOICE

Authentic faith means looking out for the least. Consider God's own words about King Josiah: "He defended the cause of the poor and needy, and so all went well. Is that not what it means to know me?" (Jeremiah 22:16). Righteousness *always* has a social justice element: "Renounce your sins by doing what is right, and your wickedness by being kind to the oppressed" (Daniel 4:27).

Given this biblical witness, I was amazed to hear the story of Gene and Helen Tabor.[8] The Tabors traveled to the Philippines with a Christian evangelistic ministry, helping Filipinos develop small, self-supporting farming and business operations. Gene thought it was important to minister to economic needs as well as spiritual ones, but apparently his mission organization didn't agree, saying that he was "wasting valuable time" that could be spent evangelizing. Tabor was given what seems an absurd ultimatum: Quit helping the poor, or quit the "Christian" organization.

Tabor sided with hundreds of years' worth of authentic faith, quit the organization, and started his own work, now called REACH Ministries. Twenty-five years later, REACH has helped give birth to twenty thousand new Christians in twenty-one locations throughout the Philippines, India, and Hong Kong. Social efforts have accompanied this astonishing record of evangelism. The Tabors have targeted the academic community by offering scholarships in tandem with discipleship programs. They also offer small loans to help the very poor begin home-based businesses.

We don't have to choose between social mercy and evangelism. The two can be, and are, complementary. We must beware of the warped spirituality that separates "the spiritual life" from our life of caring for others. In any self-based Christianity, faith is almost entirely about how we learn to overcome our sins, grow in the spiritual disciplines, and build healthier, happier families. These are all wonderful things, but authentic faith urges us to take our newfound victory over temptation, our strong character forged by practicing the disciplines, and the stability offered by having a strong family, *and then put them to use by reaching out to those who need God's love the most.*

Authentic Faith, 105–6

THE IDEAL

Jesus made a number of harsh, seemingly unrelenting statements about how we should live, and no man or woman alive has failed to break at least some of those commands. We are all failures at some point. According to Matthew 5:28, for example, I (and virtually every other man alive) must be considered an adulterer. And just one angry exclamation — "You fool!" — and I'm in danger of hellfire (see Matthew 5:22).

When you look at the life of Jesus, however, you see tremendous mercy. He does not condemn the adulterous woman; he simply tells her not to continue in her sin (see John 8:11). Jesus once said that if we put our hand to the plow and look back, we are not fit for the kingdom of God (see Luke 9:62), but he lovingly took Peter back after Peter had disowned him three times (see Mark 14:66–72).

You serve no one, least of all God, by becoming fixated on some sin you've committed that you can't undo. That's what forgiveness and grace are for — a fresh start, a new beginning, including for those who have gone through a divorce.

It's possible that you find yourself mired in a difficult marriage. If so, I urge you to hang in there. Without question, there are severe spiritual repercussions every time you break an oath, and one thing that makes divorce especially perilous spiritually is that the marriage vow is an oath broken over time. Rather than being a sin of passion — something you do but immediately regret — divorce is a considered decision, with plenty of opportunities to reconsider and reject it. This makes it, at best, a very dangerous choice spiritually. Happiness in your marriage may well be unattainable, but spiritual maturity isn't — and God values character far above any emotional disposition. So in most instances I encourage couples to hang in there, to push on through the pain, and to try to grow in it and through it. An intact marriage is an ideal worth fighting for.

But this doesn't mean we should treat those whose marriages have crumbled as second-class Christians. Jesus spoke of high ideals and absolutes — but he loved real people with acceptance and grace. The Christian life is about accepting Christ's ideals as the basis for all our decisions, and then accepting Christ's grace as the cover for all our failures.

Sacred Marriage, 114–15

GENTLENESS

I checked the car seat buckle for the third time. Allison, our firstborn, was thirty-six hours old, and I was determined that she'd live for at least eighty years.

I placed the car seat in the exact middle of the back seat, then positioned rolled-up towels around Allison's body, just in case. We lived about three miles from the hospital, but I drove so slowly and cautiously that it took us fifteen minutes to get home. No telling how slippery the road might be on a perfectly dry, sunny day!

This was my first child, and *nothing* was going to harm her.

Some ten years later, I stood in a pool and hurled my children into the water, throwing them as high as I could. After more than a decade of child rearing, you realize that kids aren't quite as fragile as they first appear. But I'll never forget the gentleness with which I treated our firstborn.

This is the same gentleness that Paul commands us to have toward others. He writes that as apostles—as living examples of the character of Christ—"we were gentle among you, like a mother caring for her little children" (1 Thessalonians 2:7).

Gentleness is so crucial to the Christian experience that Jonathan Edwards suggested gentleness "may well be called the Christian spirit. It is the distinguishing disposition in the hearts of Christians to be identified as Christians ... All who are truly godly and are real Disciples of Christ have a gentle spirit in them."[9]

The Bible predicted that Jesus would be gentle (Zechariah 9:9). Jesus affirmed his gentleness (Matthew 11:29). The early church remembered Jesus' gentleness (2 Corinthians 10:1). The Bible is a veritable guidebook on gentleness.

In a harsh world, Christians should be known for their Christlike, gentle spirit, which should stand in stark contrast to the judgmental, unyielding, condemning spirit of this age.

The Glorious Pursuit, 147–50

SANCTIFIED SORROW

"This is the best drink I've ever had!" my son, Graham, proclaimed as he took a gulp of cold water after a long and hot hike. At the time he thought Barq's Root Beer was one of history's all-time greatest inventions. His thirst, however, elevated his enjoyment, so that he treasured pure water over any sugary alternative.

In a similar way, we will never experience full joy if we have not pierced the depths of true sorrow. Do you remember the odd scene from Ezra's day when Jews who were returning from exile began to rebuild the temple?

> Many of the older priests and Levites and family heads, who had seen the former temple, wept aloud when they saw the foundation of this temple being laid, while many others shouted for joy. No one could distinguish the sound of the shouts of joy from the sound of weeping, because the people made so much noise.
>
> Ezra 3:12–13

The apostle Paul spoke of a godly sorrow, distinguishing it from a worldly sorrow. Godly sorrow "brings repentance that leads to salvation and leaves no regret." It can produce a healthy earnestness, indignation, alarm, longing, concern, and "readiness to see justice done" (see 2 Corinthians 7:10–11). Paul therefore says he has no regrets about causing the Corinthian church sorrow. It hurt them, yes; but the hurt lasted only a little while and produced a much greater good, making the short season of sorrow more than worthwhile.

This clearly implies that if we are not genuinely sorrowful in the face of serious corruption and sin—if we blink at scandal rather than risk confrontation, if we act as though sorrow has no place in the Christian life and insist on harmony instead of holiness—we are living a faith utterly foreign to the teaching of Paul.

While I still believe joy is the primary mark of a mature Christian, joy without occasional mourning is naïveté, not wisdom; it's playacting, not true love. As John Calvin writes, "Though joy overcomes sorrow, yet it does not put an end to it, because it does not divest us of humanity."[10]

It's more than OK to grieve. Doing so is biblical.

Authentic Faith, 154

"I'm One of You Now"

Larry Gadbaugh's grandfather had run bootleg during Prohibition, owned a tavern, and spent time as a professional wrestler. He lived the hard life of a logger and had, according to Larry, "three wives that we know of." But before he died, he embraced the Savior.

At his memorial service, Larry stood by the casket, watching mourners file past. His heart almost stopped when his dad finally stepped up to take one last look. Larry's father was still a self-described "pagan" who loved to tell his son's church members, "I'm not one of you."

Larry watched as his dad softly touched his grandfather's hands before moving on. Suddenly, Larry was seized with the picture of himself standing at his dad's coffin, looking down and saying his final good-bye. If his dad continued in his unbelief, there would be no hope of heaven as there was now with his grandfather. The parting would be as bitter as it was final. There, in front of everyone, Larry started to weep for his dad.

Over the years, Larry had stopped praying for his father. Their relationship had become distant and sometimes very painful, but as the tears kept coming, Larry realized he couldn't give up. His mourning gave birth to a new determination to renew his prayers for his dad.

Later, after a hurtful dispute in which his dad vowed never to set foot in Larry's house again, Larry humbled himself, went to his dad's house, asked for forgiveness, and listened as his dad admitted his own wrongs. This gave Larry one more opportunity to explain the reasons for his beliefs. While Larry's dad didn't embrace the faith immediately, he did start attending church. One Sunday, after a talk over lunch with a pastor, Larry's dad finally surrendered his soul to Jesus. The first thing Mr. Gadbaugh said when he saw Larry was, "Well, I'm one of you now."

Tears—often feared and shunned—broke up the hardened ground and renewed Larry's efforts and prayers to see his father come to faith.

Sometimes the most powerful ministry is born from the deepest act of mourning. Let's allow God to break our hearts and help us to use that truth as motivation to keep pursuing, loving, caring, and reaching out.

Authentic Faith, 164–66

THE DISCIPLINE OF FORGIVENESS

The gospel message is that, from a human perspective, the first person served by forgiveness is the one who does the forgiving. From a broader perspective, God's glory is served. In both cases, the discipline of forgiveness marks a truly authentic faith.

The Old Testament offers some startling pictures of forgiveness, perhaps the most poignant of which is Joseph's forgiveness of his brothers for selling him into slavery (see Genesis 45). Joseph, stuck in a hole, had heard his siblings discuss his fate (see Genesis 37:26–27). He knew that they planned to kill him and that purely financial considerations prompted them to spare his life and sell him off as a slave—Why rub out your brother when you can gain a few bucks by selling him? Yet even armed with this knowledge, Joseph chose to look at the larger picture.

"You intended to harm me," he told his brothers, "but God intended it for good to accomplish what is now being done, the saving of many lives. So then, don't be afraid. I will provide for you and your children" (Genesis 50:20–21).

Joseph so easily could have made his brothers pay. Instead, he took the noble path of authentic faith and not only refused to harbor a grudge, but actually provided generously for the very brothers who had treated him so terribly. It's one thing not to strike back; it's something else to respond with blessing.

The Wisdom Literature of the Old Testament talks much about the agony and brutality that result from our taking offense at others and refusing to forgive: "Better a dry crust with peace and quiet than a house full of feasting, with strife" (Proverbs 17:1). Living in contention, Solomon suggests, is the height of stupidity, the domain of fools: "It is to a man's honor to avoid strife, but every fool is quick to quarrel" (Proverbs 20:3). By such a definition, are you acting like a fool? Or do you live as a wise man or woman—that is, as a person quick to forgive?

Authentic Faith, 128–29

TWO UNIONS

Maryland pastor C. J. Mahaney asks a key question: Will we approach marriage from a God-centered view or a man-centered view?[11] In a man-centered view, we will maintain our marriage so long as our earthly comforts, desires, and expectations are met. In a God-centered view, we preserve our marriage because it brings glory to God and points a sinful world to a reconciling Creator.

More than seeing marriage as a mutual comfort, we must begin to see it as a word picture of the most important news human beings have ever received —that a divine relationship exists between God and his people. Paul explicitly makes this analogy in his letter to the Ephesians: "Husbands, love your wives, just as Christ loved the church and gave himself up for her to make her holy, cleansing her by the washing with water through the word, and to present her to himself as a radiant church, without stain or wrinkle or any other blemish, but holy and blameless" (5:25–27).

Both the Old and New Testaments use marriage as a central analogy—the union between God and Israel (Old Testament) and the union between Christ and his church (the New Testament). Understanding the depth of these analogies is crucial, as they will help us determine the foundation on which a Christian marriage is based.

If I believe the primary purpose of marriage is to model God's love for his church, then I will enter this relationship and maintain it with an entirely new motivation, one hinted at by Paul in his second letter to the Corinthians: "So we make it our goal to please him" (5:9). When something is the motive force behind all we do, it becomes the driving force for every decision we make. And Paul is crystal clear: The first question we should ask ourselves when doing anything is, "Will this please Jesus Christ?"

Sacred Marriage, 32–33

A CROSS ON YOUR SHOULDER

Life can call us into places where we feel as though we're being poured out on behalf of others. If we don't build a spirit of surrender and sacrifice, we're liable to grow resentful and bitter during these seasons.

John Calvin urges Christians to find comfort in Jesus' words to the sons of Zebedee: "Can you drink the cup I drink or be baptized with the baptism I am baptized with?" (Mark 10:38). Calvin makes this observation:

> These words contain no ordinary consolation for alleviating the bitterness of the cross, when in the cross Christ associates himself with us. And what could be more desirable than to have everything in common with the Son of God? For thus are those things which at first sight appear to be deadly made to yield to us salvation and life.[12]

The truths that at first glance appear to be heavy burdens, even "deadly," actually are given that we might yield to God's plan for our salvation and life. This is "no ordinary consolation," for it means we are invited to share in Christ himself—but even this consolation doesn't annul the fact of "the bitterness of the cross."

Calvin goes on to write:

> How shall he be reckoned among the disciples of Christ, who desires to be wholly exempted from the cross? For such a person refuses to submit to the baptism of Christ, which is nothing else than to withdraw from the earliest lessons. Now whenever baptism is mentioned, let us recollect that we were baptized on this condition, and for this purpose, that the cross may be attached to our shoulders.[13]

Calvin's words weighed heavily on my mind when my youngest daughter, Kelsey, was baptized. As she came up out of the water, I placed a cross necklace around her neck. Her eyes lit up at the sign of this ornament, but I prayed that she would learn to yield to this profound Christian truth: *We are baptized on this condition and for this purpose, that the cross of Jesus Christ may be attached to our shoulders.* Even my little girl must learn the lessons of surrender and sacrifice.

Authentic Faith, 206–7

LUKE'S CHOICE, PART 1

Tensions rose as Ohio State prepared to meet Minnesota in an NCAA basketball game in January 1972. Back then, you had to win your conference to get invited to the national tournament. Ohio State was ranked third in the nation and Minnesota fourth, but only one could make it out of the Big Ten conference.

The press didn't help things by playing the racial card. Most of Minnesota's players were black; the majority of Ohio State's players were white. The media hype, the stakes for which the teams were playing, and the intensity of the moment created a tinderbox that could explode at the slightest spark.

In the last minute of that contest, the spark ignited.

Before the game, Minnesota's coach had told his players that the key to victory would be to neutralize Luke Witte, Ohio State's center. If they could take Luke out of the game, the coach reasoned, they had a good chance of winning.

With about a minute to go, Ohio State led by six points. Witte yanked down a defensive rebound, and Minnesota stayed downcourt to put pressure on the ball handler. Luke sprinted to the other end of the court and stood all alone under Ohio State's basket as he got the ball. In a furious catch-up chase, Minnesota player Clyde Turner raced up the court and hit Luke with a roundhouse across his face as Luke went up for a left-handed layup. Luke dropped to the floor, dazed, but as he looked up, he saw a hand come down to pick him up. Luke judged it a friendly hand, but he couldn't have been more mistaken.

Corky Taylor helped Witte get halfway up, and then kneed him in the groin. Luke dropped back to the floor, nearly unconscious from the pain. Minnesota player Ron Behagen—who had fouled out earlier and had been sitting on the bench—rushed onto the floor and kicked Luke in the head three times.

Let's stop the story there for a moment. If you're Luke Witte, writhing on the floor in your own blood—what's your next move, spiritually speaking? *(Continued tomorrow.)*

Authentic Faith, 142–43

LUKE'S CHOICE, PART 2

The next thing Luke knew, he was lying in a University of Minnesota hospital room, one of his teammates in the bed next to him. He had no recollection of the assault from the night before. When his brother called to ask how he felt, Luke still wasn't sure what had happened. He remembers stammering, "Well, my head is covered with bandages, I have a patch over one eye, and I feel like I was drug behind a truck, but other than that, I guess I'm OK."

When Wayne Duke, the commissioner of the Big Ten, later visited Luke in Columbus to watch a video of the assault, Luke couldn't watch; he had to turn his head away. All told, Luke had a scratched cornea, twenty-seven stitches across his face, a cauliflower ear that had swelled and discolored in a grotesque fashion, and the less visible but even more painful aftereffects of being kneed in the groin.

Recovery was slow and unsteady. After failing a neurological exam, Luke missed several games, but basketball wasn't the only part of his life affected. Luke went through several "blackout" periods. He once sat through a class without any recollection of what the professor had said. In fact, when the class ended and the students filed out, Luke didn't realize class was over, so he sat through a second class. Not until a friend walked in for yet a third class and asked Luke, "What are you doing here?" did Luke realize what had happened.

At the time, Luke wasn't a devout Christian. "I classify myself then as a one-hour-a-week Christian," he told me, but he felt God's voice urging him to choose forgiveness over retaliation—this, even though many voices immediately started urging him to sue everybody: the school, the players, the coaches, the state, even members of the police force who had exited the building before the end of the game and left the Ohio State players in an extremely vulnerable situation. Not a single person—not even Luke's dad, a pastor—suggested forgiveness.

How do you forgive someone who won't even say they're sorry? *(Continued tomorrow.)*

Authentic Faith, 142–143

LUKE'S CHOICE, PART 3

Although Luke wasn't a devout believer, he still heard God's voice telling him that he needed to drop it and start the process of healing. In fact, Luke's decision to forgive was a "thirty-year process" made up of many small choices. "I can choose to live in anger and hurt," he said, "but I can also choose to live in the freedom of knowing that Christ is in charge."[14]

About ten years after the attack, Luke got a letter from Corky Taylor, one of the players who had attacked him. Corky was raising two boys and felt that he needed to address his past before he could teach his sons about love, morality, and ethics. Since the incident, Corky had become very involved at his church, even teaching Sunday school. Luke tried to respond with a letter, but could never get it quite right. Finally, his wife suggested, "Why don't you just call him?" Luke did, and the reconciliation began.

Eventually Luke flew to Minneapolis to meet not just with Corky but also with Clyde Turner, who had delivered the original blow. Near the end of their visit, Luke asked Clyde if he could use pieces of their conversation when he spoke or wrote. Clyde, who had become a strong believer, responded, "You know what, Luke? I don't care what you use, except I want you to make sure that, when you use it, you tell the full gospel."

Today, one of Luke's ministries as a pastor at the Forest Hill Church in Charlotte, North Carolina, is divorce recovery. "People come in who have been physically and mentally abused. We talk about forgiveness and what it really means," Luke told me. He has learned that forgiveness is separate from the other person's repentance and commitment to reconciliation. In fact, some Minnesota players from the old days haven't wanted to reconcile; despite the videotape, they see the incident very differently. "It's not our responsibility to make the offender repent," Luke says, "but forgiveness is our part that brings the full freedom of Christ into our lives."

Though the attack physically weakened Luke, through forgiveness and grace he is stronger spiritually than he would have been otherwise. When bad things happen, we can choose to become bitter, or we can choose to grow. In most cases, it will be one or the other.

Authentic Faith, 142–43

AT THE BOTTOM OF THE DRY CREEK BED

Rob Takemura is a lifelong friend, the type of guy everybody likes to hang around. He knows a lot about a lot of things, so he can enter just about any conversation, but he keeps his ego under control and doesn't dominate the discussion. You respect him; he's not usually going to do anything stupid or cruel. On the other hand, he's not insufferably pious; you really enjoy your time with him.

I'm sure you can think of someone similar in your own circle of friends. If you're throwing a party or inviting a group to dinner, you ask him first so you can tell everyone, "Oh, by the way, Rob will be there too."

I probably spend more time with Rob than any other adult male—but being around Rob doesn't challenge my patience, simply because he's such a healthy individual. I can learn from Rob by trying to emulate his character—but he doesn't stretch my ability to forgive and he doesn't make me dig down deep to respond to cruelty with love.

On the other hand, I once knew a man who hated women and acted cruelly toward men. Putting up with his constant criticisms, his lust to be recognized as significant and powerful, and his malicious use of what little influence he did have stretched me like I've never been stretched. I discovered spiritual holes in my own soul I never knew existed and had to develop spiritual muscles in places that had long lain dormant.

To become mature people, we need both kinds of relationships. It takes God-forged *agape* love to forgive someone who spites you, who returns your kindness with hatred, who considers gestures of generosity to be threats.

But in the bottom of the dry creek bed lies spiritual life, the fossil of character formation. If we die to human potential, we can be resurrected to spiritual strength. God invites us (although at times it may feel as though he is forcing us) to lean on a foreign strength—to go further, love deeper, and learn to forgive in a way we never knew we could.

That very difficult person to love? He or she may be more important than you realize.

Sacred Parenting, 148–49

REDEEMING PLEASURE

Redemption remains incomplete this side of heaven. The sin nature still works within us (Romans 7:14–25)—so how can we move forward spiritually? I believe redeemed pleasure can become a powerful force for piety and goodness. We can't "pleasure" our way out of temptation, of course, because with a sin-weakened heart, whenever I'm presented with two pleasures—one healthy and one destructive—I am likely to choose the wrong one.

This is why embracing pleasure must always begin with a heart being renewed by God's Holy Spirit.

Once this powerful act of redemption has begun, by God's grace and mercy in Christ we can embrace and even cultivate pleasure in such a way that we become less vulnerable to the allure of sin. Embracing pleasure instead of remaining suspicious of it is no cure-all, but it can become an effective tool, provided our hearts have been (and are being) changed.

Because we all have sin-stained hearts, the ancient lessons about our need for the spiritual disciplines, sacrifice, self-denial, mortification, and detachment still apply. Without these, I am a fool to generously embrace pleasure, because in a matter of time that pleasure will consume me. With these spiritual practices, however—and while enjoying the benefits of a redeemed life, the active counsel of the Holy Spirit, and the support of God's community, the local church—I can begin to truly enjoy life, perhaps for the first time. I can embrace pleasure as a way to celebrate God and the life he has given me. Pleasure can lead me *to* him instead of *away* from him.

In a progressive journey of faith, God gradually re-centers our desires toward *holy* pleasures, spiritually good and healthy things that leave us satisfied and full, so that sin begins to lose much (but never all) of its appeal. So often we assume that *pleasure* means something illicit—so we warn others against the dangers of pleasure.

When we learn to redeem pleasure and allow our hearts to be shaped by the Creator of all that is good, pleasure can become the servant of holiness, not its enemy. In this context and with this understanding, prayerfully ask yourself this question: What if pleasure isn't the problem but is actually part of the solution?

Pure Pleasure, 23

A Ministry of Reconciliation

Marriage reminds us—sometimes daily—that God has given us the ministry of reconciliation, proclaiming to the world the good news that we can be reconciled to God through Jesus Christ. If my driving force is to please Christ, then I will work to construct a marriage that enhances this ministry of reconciliation—a marriage that, in fact, incarnates this truth by putting flesh on it, building a relationship that models forgiveness, selfless love, and sacrifice.

The last picture I want to give the world is that I have decided to stop loving someone and that I refuse to serve this person anymore. Yet this is precisely the message many Christians are proclaiming through their actions. According to pollster George Barna, self-described "born-again" Christians have a higher rate of divorce than nonbelievers, and those who claim the label "fundamentalist Christian" have the highest divorce rate of all.[15]

We can't deliver a message well if we don't live it well first. How can I tell my children that God's promise of reconciliation is secure when they see that my own promise doesn't mean a thing? What most divorces mean is that at least one party, and possibly both, have ceased to put the gospel first in their lives. They no longer live by Paul's guiding principle, "I make it my goal to please him" —and God says, "I hate divorce" (Malachi 2:16). If a couple's ultimate goal is to please God, then they won't seek a nonbiblical divorce.

One reason I am determined to keep my marriage together is not because doing so will make me happier (although I believe it will); not because I want my kids to have a secure home (although I desire that); not because it would tear me up to see my wife have to start over (although it would). The first reason I keep my marriage together is because it is my Christian duty. If my life is based on proclaiming God's message to the world, I don't want to do anything that would challenge that message. And how can I proclaim reconciliation when I seek dissolution?

Sacred Marriage, 34–35

APRIL

A yard that is planted still needs to be tended. A house that is built still needs to be maintained. A car that is washed still needs to be serviced. The same is true of our souls. Through Jesus' work on the cross, God offers us initial forgiveness and salvation but moves on to take us through redemption, reconciliation, and progressive growth in righteousness. April is traditionally a month of "spring cleaning." May it also be a season of sanctification.

THE INTIMATE BETRAYAL

A stonemason in Seattle followed a grieving wife's directions and carved a headstone for her husband with the traditional words: "Rest in Peace." A few months later, the wife discovered that her husband had been unfaithful, so she returned to the stonemason and asked him to add four more words. The stonemason did as he was told, and the gravestone now reads:

Rest in Peace …
Till We Meet Again

There's something about sin in marriage that strikes us at a deeper level than when others sin against us. A sense of betrayal adds to the sin, so that when we're wronged, we may feel so offended that we want to continue the dispute into the grave.

We get married for all sorts of reasons. "Because it gives us an opportunity to learn how to forgive" probably doesn't top the list of most honeymooners, but the spiritual practice of continually moving toward someone provides an excellent context in which we can practice this vital spiritual discipline. Sin in marriage—on the part of both spouses—occurs daily, resulting in an ongoing struggle that threatens to hold us back. You will never find a spouse without sin. The person you decide to marry will eventually hurt you, sometimes even intentionally. That's what makes forgiveness an essential spiritual discipline.

Paul offers wonderfully helpful words when he states that "no one will be declared righteous in [God's] sight by observing the law; rather, through the law we become conscious of sin" (Romans 3:20). After reading this verse we've been well warned: Our spouses will never achieve a "lawful" sinlessness. It just won't happen. We will be sinned against, and we will be hurt.

When this happens, we have a choice to make: We can give in to our hurt, resentment, and bitterness, or we can grow as a Christian and learn another important lesson on how to forgive. Marriage teaches us—indeed, it practically forces us—to learn to live by extending grace and forgiveness to people who have sinned against us.

Sacred Marriage, 167–68

A NAIL IN MY POCKET

Many Christians complain that they find it hard to stay awake and focused during prayer, especially in the early morning. These Christians might find prayer easier if they held small objects in their hands as they prayed. A paper clip could help them focus on a crumbling marriage; a rubber band could help them pray for a pliable heart.

One Lenten season, I carried a nail in my pocket, reminding me to offer prayers of intercession and repentance throughout Lent. The sharp edge reminded me of Christ's sufferings every time I touched it or bent over and felt it pressing into my leg.

Orthodox worship involves frequent kissing—a cross, an altar, a holy instrument. Touch with our lips is a way to recognize something as precious.

One of my most memorable times of prayer occurred spontaneously. As a young college student I wanted to offer everything to God. I offered God myself by touching various parts of my body. First I touched my fingers and feet, praying that God would consecrate them for his service. "Whenever I reach out, I want to reach out in love. Wherever I travel, I want to do so under Christ's name." Next I touched my lips. "Whatever I speak, let it be the truth and something that will bring glory to your kingdom." I touched my eyes. "Help me to protect my eyes, only letting them see what is helpful for the inner man within, so that my inner eye will not be blind to the sight of the real needs around me." On I went, offering up the various parts of my body for God's service.

Later, my wife pointed out that I had gone through motions similar to blood consecration in Leviticus 8:24 where Moses is described as placing blood on the lobes of the right ears, the thumbs of the right hands, and the big toes of the right feet of Aaron's sons.

I didn't plan this prayer beforehand; it just happened. I don't know how many times I've prayed, but most of them have been forgotten; yet this prayer has remained with me.

Break out of your prayer rut today. Find a few creative ways to commune with God.

Sacred Pathways, 69–70

April 3

FIRST THINGS FIRST

Our natural inclination to make life as easy as possible for our children, coupled with our focus on what we want them to achieve, ultimately tells us parents what we value most about life. What we stress with our children reveals the true passion of our hearts.

In a remarkable message titled "Gospel-Centered Parenting," pastor C. J. Mahaney warns that when we spend most of our parenting energy on producing "successful," intelligent, well-behaved children, our good intentions can suffocate even better aims. What is *the* most important thing for our children? Mahaney asks. Is it to make it into Harvard or Yale Law School? Is it to make it to age twenty-one without suffering a single scar or a single broken heart? Is it to raise a child who says, "Yes, sir," and "No, ma'am," and who becomes financially independent?

Though these are worthy goals, ask yourself, Is a child who has never been in the hospital, who is comfortable and familiar with eating at a fancy restaurant, and who is a managing partner at a major law firm—but whose soul is in eternal peril—the kind of son or daughter you really want to produce?

The Bible gives us a strong warning in 1 Samuel. High Priest Eli had two sons who slept with women workers and who gorged themselves on God's offerings. Their father's position allowed them to live in relative luxury, and though Eli despised what they did, he didn't stop them. You might say he chose his sons' happiness over their holiness and, in doing so, elicited God's wrath. "Why do you honor your sons more than me?" God scolded Eli (1 Samuel 2:29). Eli's sons became God's enemies, to the point that the Bible tells us, "It was the LORD's will to put them to death" (1 Samuel 2:25).

How terrifying to think that my kids could feel happy on the way to receiving the full brunt of God's wrath! The "main thing" of parenting is praying, working, and striving for our children's salvation—and not just their salvation, but that they, too, will become servants of the gospel of Jesus Christ.

Sacred Parenting, 29–30

April 4

HE BLEEDS, SHE HEMORRHAGES

A wayward child wounds a parent in two ways. First, the child wounds the mother by despising her, cheating her, robbing her, or even hitting her. But then, almost inexplicably, he tears his mother's heart in two once more when she grieves over her profligate child's misfortune as he inevitably marches toward his own ruin. When he falls, her heart gets bruised! When he bleeds, she hemorrhages!

Is this schizophrenic? From a secular perspective, yes—but nobody ever said that parenting was easy or that love, or even grace, for that matter, makes sense. We remain deeply vulnerable as parents, risking the pain of betrayal and then grieving over our betrayer's demise.

King David experienced this as a parent. His son Absalom plotted to steal David's throne by cunningly winning the favor of the people. He then hatched a well-executed plan to have himself declared king. Worse, he recruited some of David's closest advisers, publicly slept with his father's concubines, and then sought to kill his dad. In every way possible, Absalom humiliated and challenged his father, even hunting him like an animal.

David had to defend himself, but in doing so he gave strict orders to his men: "Protect the young man Absalom *for my sake*" (2 Samuel 18:12, emphasis added). In spite of everything, David essentially told his men, "Don't treat Absalom like the traitor he is; treat him like my son."

Despite David's instructions, the general in charge of directing the king's forces executed Absalom when he got the chance. When David heard, he grieved for the son who sought to kill him as though this child had been the most faithful and loving offspring a parent could ever want. He mourned his loss; his heart broke in two. David displays the grace-filled love of a parent, mirroring the love of the God who loved us and who died for us while we yet remained his enemies: "God demonstrates his own love for us in this: While we were still sinners, Christ died for us" (Romans 5:8).

Parenting may well break your heart, but while doing so, it will help you understand God's heart for you all the better.

Sacred Parenting, 140–41

THEY JUST DON'T UNDERSTAND

Melissa has to leave her home every Tuesday and Friday at 3:00 p.m. to take Christy to a physical therapy session on the other side of Chicago. Because she wants to leave Christy in school for as long as possible, the late-afternoon trips put them in the thick of commuter traffic and they don't return home until 7:00.

Christy hates these therapy sessions, but they are doing wonders for her ability to walk with a normal gait. As Melissa welcomed Christy into the car one Tuesday afternoon, Christy hissed at her: "I'll never forgive you for doing this to me."

Melissa wanted to ask Christy what she wouldn't forgive: the four-hour trips twice a week through heavy traffic, all to help Christy walk better? The vacations she and her husband, Greg, had given up so they could have the roughly $1,200 a month to spend on special services, education, and therapies to help Christy learn how to cope? The many nights Melissa spent on the Internet, trying to find the best services and support materials to help Christy overcome her challenges? Melissa has given just about every ounce of strength she has to help Christy deal with her disabilities—and for *that*, Christy will never forgive her?

To be a parent is to be misunderstood. To be a mom or dad is to have your kids, extended family members, friends, and even strangers second-guess you, question your motives, and pass judgment on your decisions. And to have our good motives questioned is certainly one of the most frustrating human experiences we face.

But would you like to know the secret blessing behind this pain? When God allows us to confront this process, he is preparing us to handle a fact of life with regard to working on behalf of his kingdom: to minister is to be attacked, questioned, and maligned. When God allows others to think less of you, to judge you, to challenge you, to malign you, he is bringing you into rare but intimate country—the sufferings of Christ.

You may think you're merely raising children, but during this process, God is also raising *you* to become a stronger and more capable servant of his kingdom.

Devotions for Sacred Parenting, 49

WHOSE PRESENCE?

Julie De Rossi was just forty-four years old when her life was cut short in a crash with a drunk driver. Through the miracle of modern medicine, at least thirty-five lives have benefited from Julie's body, among them National Football League quarterback Carson Palmer. Palmer suffered a potentially career-ending knee injury in January 2006, but doctors used one of Julie's tendons to reconstruct his left knee. Dorothy Hyde, Julie's mother, said her family feels "a special connection when we watch Carson Palmer. My grandson, Burke, has become a big fan."[1]

Palmer talks about the wonder of having a piece of someone else inside his own body: "It's an amazing thing. It's something that blew my mind to think that you could use a part of somebody else's body to repair a living body. It's just crazy." Palmer appreciates the opportunity to represent Julie's family on the football field and through his life, to be a living reminder of a much-loved mother and daughter.

"It's like my grandson said," Hyde notes. "No one would have heard of Julie if not for Carson."

No one would have heard of Julie if not for Carson.

While it is a stretch to suggest no one would have heard of Jesus if not for us, the fact is, some individuals might not think of Jesus if not for us. As a piece of Julie resides in Carson's body, so through the Holy Spirit, a "piece" of God resides in us. Like Palmer, our goal should be to represent the One who has given himself for us and to us. The ascension reminds me that since Jesus still reigns — in fact, reigns through me — my goal should be to proclaim his current rule. At best, I'm a signpost, a messenger, for what Jesus is doing even now on this earth.

When I adopt the ascension as a key theological truth, I confess that Jesus reigns — which, by definition, means *I* cannot reign. If Jesus is active today, then I must surrender to his influence every minute of my life.

What would such a surrender look like in your life today? How is Jesus reigning in this world through you?

Holy Available, 37–38

MARKED BY OUR MAKER

Paul's first letter to the Corinthians is often used to debate which gifts God still hands out today, which gift any individual might get, how you can identify your gift, and so forth—but any honest reading says that Paul had one overriding concern: to declare that God is active through his people, manifesting himself in many (and, yes, sometimes miraculous) ways.

The apostle's emphasis on spiritual gifts rests not on which gift we have but on the fact that *one* God constantly works through *many* people in a multitude of ways: "There are different kinds of working, but the same God works all of them in all men" (1 Corinthians 12:6).

Paul insists that God discloses himself through his people and that he offers divine evidence of his reality by the way he works through his church. You may not be able to see God, but you can surely see him working as his people actively engage in becoming "holy available."

Every maturing Christian should bear this dynamic, ongoing mark of God. Your mark will look different from my mark, but the world should plainly see both of our marks. As the living, reigning Lord works in and through us, we can't help but be actively transformed—day by day, week by week, year by year.

Jesus both lived and taught this faith. He lived it: "The words I say to you are not just my own. Rather, it is the Father, living in me, who is doing his work" (John 14:10). And he taught it: "I tell you the truth, anyone who has faith in me will do what I have been doing" (14:12). As far as we know, the apostle Paul never met Jesus before the crucifixion; but he certainly adopted this mind-set. He wrote, "By the grace of God I am what I am, and his grace to me was not without effect. No, I worked harder than all of them—yet not I, but the grace of God that was with me" (1 Corinthians 15:10).

The ascended Christ *still reigns*. Do others see that truth in you and me today?

Holy Available, 41–42

April 8

THE GIFT THAT KEEPS ON GIVING

At age four, our son decided he wanted to pick out a Mother's Day gift all by himself—no more scribbling his mark on a present picked out by his dad. No, he intended to get it himself.

Graham settled on the cheesiest piggy bank ever made. Normally my wife would roll her eyes and laugh at such a pink monstrosity; she has zero tolerance for tacky presents. But when she opened this present, she cried tears of joy. She knew this present came from Graham, and she felt so touched by the gesture that the tackiness didn't faze her. She even put it on her nightstand in our bedroom. Graham wore a hundred-watt smile when he saw Lisa's tears. Nothing made him happier than to give a present that delighted his mom so much that it made her cry.

God, as the giver of many gifts, would love to see us cry tears of joy and gratitude when he gives us gifts that bring us pleasure. If you see this world and your life as a gift from a loving Creator, then let's honor this gift by enjoying it. Too many Christians are suspicious of God's gifts, as if these gifts compete with God, rather than joyfully receiving them as kindnesses from God.

God has given us taste buds, nerve endings, the capacity to laugh, the ability to create, eyes to marvel, minds to wonder, noses to smell, and hands to feel. We give back to him in proportion to how much we enjoy these good gifts. When one of his gifts obviously moves us—as Graham's did my wife—then we bring a smile to God the giver's face.

The first recorded words God spoke to humans introduced a gift: "I *give you* every seed-bearing plant on the face of the whole earth and every tree that has fruit with seed in it" (Genesis 1:29, emphasis added).

Do you think he might be waiting for us, perhaps for the first time in our lives, to truly open up the gift of life and savor it? While we busy ourselves trying to serve God, do you think he might wait for us to honor him by relishing the world he has made? Is your fear of pure pleasure robbing God of the joy he receives in giving generous gifts to his children?

Pure Pleasure, 41–42

April 9

HOW MUCH DO YOU LOVE ME?

When I grew up, my family lived by a simple rule: If you take out an ice cube, you refill the tray before you put it back in. These days I'll pull out a tray and find nothing more than an ice *chip*.

It amazed me how such a small detail irritated me. I asked Lisa one day, "How much do you love me?"

"More than all the world," she professed.

"I don't need you to love me that much," I said. "I just want you to love me for seven seconds."

"What on earth are you talking about?" she asked.

"Well, I timed how long it takes to fill an ice cube tray and discovered it's just seven sec—"

"Oh, Gary, are we back to that again?"

It finally dawned on me that if it takes Lisa just seven seconds to fill an ice cube tray, *that's all it takes me as well*. Was I really so selfish that I would let seven seconds' worth of inconvenience become a serious issue in my marriage? Was my capacity to show charity really that limited?

Indeed it was.

Being so close to someone—which marriage necessitates—may be the greatest spiritual challenge in the world. There is no "resting," because I am under virtual twenty-four-hour surveillance. Not that Lisa makes it seem like that! It's just that I'm aware of it. Every movie I rent comes with the understanding that I will watch it with Lisa next to me. Lisa knows about every hour I take off for recreation. Where I eat at lunch (and what), how I'm doing on a particular diet —my appetites and lusts and desires are all in her full view.

Do I have the guts to let Lisa confront me with my sin? Am I willing to ask her, "Where do you see unholiness in my life? I want to know about it. I want to change it." I often lack the courage—and yet the opportunity remains. Will we take it? Instead of resenting the restrictions marriage places on our sin, or the exposure of our sin, can we embrace marriage as a spiritual adventure designed to help us grow in Christlikeness?

Sacred Marriage, 93–94

THE FALSE PROMISE OF SIN

When you feel dry, that's the time to especially beware of the false allure of seemingly pleasurable sin. Though it may not feel like a step in the wrong direction, it always is. In his book *Future Grace*, John Piper wisely points out, "The power of sin is the false promise that it will bring more happiness than holiness will bring. Nobody sins out of duty. Therefore, what breaks the power of sin is faith in the true promise that the pleasures of sin are passing and poisonous, but at God's right hand are pleasures forevermore."[2]

Insist on true, holy pleasure — or *nothing at all*. I plead with married people to see sexual temptation of any form as a call for them to become more intimate with their spouse. Intimate doesn't necessarily mean "sexual." It means that God created hormones, and when we notice that they are particularly alive and active, it is God's way of telling us we need to tend to our marriage on all levels.

This commitment to pay renewed attention to our spouse is the only holy response to sexual temptation: "Oh, I see I'm sexually tempted; how am I doing with my mate?" What Satan intends for harm, God can use for good, for building up our home instead of tearing it down.

You will literally change your life and your marriage if you begin using sexual temptation as a call to evaluate and improve your relationship with your spouse. Turn the temptation into spiritual reflection and personal evaluation, but be aware that the temptation could signal a growing coldness toward God as well, not just toward your spouse.

When we feel particularly vulnerable, we need to strictly evaluate our pleasures and run them through a fine filter, making sure they are free of pollutants before we breathe them in. Immediately turning to sin to deal with disappointment, deprivation, or hurt is like smoking cigarettes to lose weight. In the short term, it may seem to help; in the long term, it creates an even bigger problem. God *always* offers us the better deal.

Pure Pleasure, 202–3

April 11

NO EASY CONFLICT

What a night it must have been in Gethsemane as Jesus struggled with the reality about to take place. The road before him was so severe, so terrible, so devastating, that he asked his Father, in essence, "If there's an acceptable way out of this, let me know. But if not, I'll move forward."

John Calvin saw Jesus' prayer—"Not my will, but yours be done"—as a revelation of the conflict in Jesus' soul, a conflict that all of us experience as we seek to align our will with God's. Sacrifice, though an essential element of true faith, is never easy. Calvin explains:

> The prayers of believers do not always flow on with uninterrupted progress to the end ... but, on the contrary, are involved and confused, and either oppose each other, or stop in the middle of the course, like a vessel tossed by tempests, which, though it advances towards the harbor, cannot always keep a straight and uniform course, as in a calm sea.[3]

Have you ever experienced this? Perhaps your prayers have had the same chaotic confusion. You begin to pray one way, then stop yourself: "Am I really willing to do that? Do I really mean what I'm praying?"

Calvin is quick to point out that Jesus didn't have "confused emotions" as he prayed about his upcoming sacrifice, but "he was struck with fear and seized with anguish, so that, amidst the violent shocks of temptation, he vacillated—as it were—from one wish to another."[4]

Few of us vacillate in our prayers when we pray for affluence or blessing. It's easy to agree with God that he should step in and help us! But if we dare to enter the true arena of Christianity, if we accept the cross of sacrifice, then prayer becomes a tempest as we seek to die to our own wills so that God's will and purpose might reign supreme and uncontested.

In your prayers today, will you step back from your own requests and pray the perfect prayer of Jesus? "Your will, Father, not mine, be done."

Authentic Faith, 198–99

SACRED SACRIFICE

Those who want to identify with their Lord must understand that sacrifice is at the heart of Christianity. Sacrifice keeps our idealized and often romanticized expressions of divine adoration rooted in reality.

The notion of sacrifice also lies at the heart of why many Christians celebrate Lent. Unfortunately, in our culture we love to celebrate Mardi Gras but rarely get around to Lent! "Liberated" Christians may well ask, "Why observe Lent?" God doesn't need us to give up anything; certainly, he doesn't need my meat; but sometimes I need to learn to deny myself something in order to truly appreciate what really matters.

One year, I decided to give up ice cream for Lent. Since I was raised as a Baptist, I had never considered observing this season, but our family decided to give it a try. During this period, I was traveling and stopped at a grocery store to get something to eat.

Unfortunately, its produce looked as though it had been trucked in from Brazil — three weeks ago. It had no real bread to speak of, and nothing that looked appetizing enough to take back to my hotel room.

Finally, I gave in to the "dark side." "I'll just get a small carton of ice cream," I thought. But as soon as my hand hit that cold container I remembered my commitment — and put the ice cream back.

Suddenly, I got a vivid reminder of the Easter season. What Christ had done on our behalf broke into my consciousness, deepening my Easter "mourning and celebrating." All in all, I'd say it was a fabulously good trade, forgoing the ice cream to live with a deeper sense of the Easter season. That's what fasting is all about, isn't it? It doesn't earn us any extra merit with God, but he can use it to chasten our demanding hearts.

While we can't give anything to God — *everything* is his, including the strength by which we sacrifice — the act of sacrifice reminds us that we are God's servants and that God is not our servant. How might God use sacrifice to form your soul this Easter season?

Sacred Pathways, 98–99

JESUS WEPT

Mourning is a curious thing, revealing the true state of our hearts. A spiritually deadened person mourns over things that should bring celebration, yet often celebrates things that should be mourned.

Shakespeare had fun with the concept of mourning in *Twelfth Night*. Olivia feels tremendous grief over the death of her brother; but even more, she resents the fact that the world goes on. Consequently, for seven years, she walks with a veil and daily sheds tears for her departed brother. She wants the world to stop, or at least slow down, and feels bitter because it doesn't. Shakespeare sends the fool Feste to prod Olivia.

FESTE: Good madonna, why mourn'st thou?

OLIVIA: Good fool, for my brother's death.

FESTE: I think his soul is in hell, madonna.

OLIVIA: I know his soul is in heaven, fool.

FESTE: The more fool, madonna, to mourn for your brother's soul, being in heaven.[5]

It is not easy to mourn well, and even more difficult to mourn for the right reasons in the right way.

As Jesus entered Jerusalem prior to his arrest, the crowds gave him an ovation that surpassed those given to the Beatles on *The Ed Sullivan Show*. "Blessed is the king who comes in the name of the Lord!" they shouted (Luke 19:38). Yet as Jesus drew closer to Jerusalem, he did a curious thing. He wept over the devastating future hidden from Jerusalem's inhabitants, "because you did not recognize the time of God's coming to you" (Luke 19:44).

As I read this, one thought kept running through my head: Jesus wept while the crowds cheered. I wonder how often this happens today—God's church, lost in spiritual ecstasy, worshiping enthusiastically as God weeps about another lost city and longs for us to join him in his sorrow.

Jesus promised that those who mourn will be comforted (see Matthew 5:4), but mourning is a precondition of comfort. We should not long for one without the other, for then we would reveal our desire to be half human.

What are you mourning today?

Authentic Faith, 151–53

GROWING OUT OF OURSELVES

An author answered the phone one day and heard a nervous voice on the line —someone from her publishing house. Some individual had made a mistake, and it was about to make my friend's life a little more difficult. She listened to the news, dealt with its implications, and moved on. The publisher's representative sighed and said, "You know, that's why we like working with you so much. A lot of writers wouldn't be nearly as gracious."

Can I bore you with the obvious? We're talking about a *Christian* publisher who presumably publishes *Christian* authors. If Christian authors are just as self-centered and resentful when someone makes a mistake as anyone else, then what marks them as Christians?

Admittedly, when James wrote, "We all stumble in many ways" (James 3:2), he was talking about teachers; but I think we need to expect a higher standard for those whom God calls to testify publicly to his truth. I think that many teachers (and parents) stop persevering in their Christian growth. They stop making progress, and when they do, their character usually atrophies. Brother Giles, a companion of Saint Francis, warns of this danger:

> Many men who did not know how to swim have gone into the water to help those who were drowning, and they have drowned with those who were drowning. First, there was one misfortune, and then there were two. If you work well for the salvation of your soul, you will be working well for the salvation of all your friends ... I believe that a good preacher speaks more to himself than to others.[6]

At the foot of the cross, we are all toddlers. But on behalf of the cross, we must press on, persevere, and mature in the faith. We may never in this world grow past being spiritual teenagers, but is it asking too much for teachers to move beyond the toddler stage? We must grow out of ourselves, move past our natural self-absorption, and grow in the grace and sweet mercy of our gentle Savior.

Are you seeing growth in your daily life? Are you serving those whom God has placed under your sphere of influence by earnestly pursuing a growing Christlikeness?

Holy Available, 192–93

A PRISON OF FORGETFULNESS

My daughter wouldn't let go of my hand. I sensed her insecurity and asked, "What's up?"

"I'm so fancy," she said, touching her dress, embarrassed. I looked around. People wearing leather coats, colored T-shirts, shiny jackets with professional sports logos on them, and blue jeans surrounded us—the standard crowd in a jail waiting room.

Allison and I had just come to visit an inmate.

"That's all right," I told her. "It's Good Friday. They'll just figure you've been to church."

After an unusually long wait, we made our way to the cellblocks. I had prepared Allison for what she would see—the man we were visiting would be in a glass-enclosed room, and we'd have to talk through a phone.

"It took a long time," I said.

"I was in the gym," he answered.

"Are they going to be doing anything inside for Easter?" I asked later.

"Is it Easter this weekend?" he asked. "I thought that was last weekend. *Jesus of Nazareth* was on television, so I thought it must have been Easter."

I have to confess that my heart sank. The thought of a believer playing basketball on Good Friday without knowing that Easter was around the corner saddened me. His real prison wasn't constructed of barbwire and high walls; he was living in a prison of forgetfulness, which is all the more sad because this person has a hard time submitting his life to Christ. He has the desire, but pressures arise and sometimes he falters. A good four-day celebration like Easter could do wonders.

Religious observances have their place. They can be lifeless rituals or life-altering encounters, depending on how we approach them. If we're willing to step back from the world for a few days, we may find that God can fill our celebrations with a power we never knew existed. Will you give God the opportunity to pour new meaning into this year's Easter celebration?

Sacred Pathways, 84–86

THE FORGOTTEN FATHER OF CALVARY

Every Good Friday, we celebrate Jesus' heroic sacrifice—and well we should. But what about the "forgotten Father" of Calvary? Imagine watching *your* son being humiliated before your eyes, stripped and pierced and beaten and ridiculed and then crucified. Now imagine your son looking into your eyes as he suffers and then speaks the agonized words, "My father, my dear father, why have you forsaken me?"

No father has loved his son as our heavenly Father loved Jesus, yet his love made room for his Son's suffering. In a way that is hard for us to understand, Jesus the Son, the perfect God-man, needed to suffer for his own sake, and for our sake. The writer of Hebrews explains that Jesus "learned obedience from what he suffered and, once made perfect, he became the source of eternal salvation for all who obey him" (Hebrews 5:8–9). If the Father had not allowed the Son to suffer, Jesus would still bear glory as the deity he is; but he would not wear the glorious victory that he won on the cross.

Here's the sobering truth: If God allowed his own Son to suffer—and he is our model as a parent—we can expect times when we will have to watch our children suffer for a greater good. When this happens, we will know how Mary felt when Simeon warned her that "a sword will pierce your own soul too" (Luke 2:35).

But please remember, *suffering isn't the end of the story!* The same Son who said, "My God, my God, why have you forsaken me?" left this world with the words "Father, into your hands I commit my spirit" (Luke 23:46)—a ringing statement of absolute trust, relinquishment, and love. What a tender comment for any son to say to his father!

So, parents, take courage. Occasional frustration and even rage last only for a moment; they pass away. Do not forsake eternal truths for temporal gain. Mimic your heavenly Father, who courageously allowed his Son to suffer, knowing their relationship would survive.

Sacred Parenting, 31–32

LOSING THE "I" IN PIETY

"Hurry up!" I called out to my family. "Get into the car! If we don't get moving, there won't be any good seats left!" Our church has a wonderful and exasperating problem: If you don't get to Sunday services early, then you may have to sit in the overflow area. This was an Easter Sunday, and I expected the services to be even more crowded than usual. My number one goal that morning was to get us to church in time to get decent seats.

I gathered my car keys, only semi-patiently waiting for my wife to finish drying her hair and my daughter to find her shoes. "I put them right by the door," Kelsey insisted. "Somebody must have stolen them!"

"Right, Kelsey," I answered. "Someone broke in last night, forgot about the TV, the VCR, and the computer, ignored my wallet sitting in the kitchen, and grabbed a used pair of little girl's size 7 shoes."

"Well, it's possible!" she hollered.

I walked out to the car for a moment's pause when God's voice broke into my hurried, frenzied spirit. I realized that many of the people I wanted to "beat out" for a good seat would probably be visitors. Our church uses Easter to its fullest evangelistic effect, and God gently spoke to me about my selfish desire to enjoy good worship at the expense of a nonbeliever having the best chance to respond to the gospel. There's nothing wrong with trying to get to church on time, of course, but my competitive nature spit into the face of what our church was trying to do. I needed to lose the "I" in piety.

Self-centeredness can creep up on us in so many ways—including wanting to get good seats on Easter Sunday. Our fallen nature and the values of our culture collide with the force of an avalanche to push us ever further down the hill of self-centeredness, but authentic faith calls us back to the summit—and joy—of selflessness.

Authentic Faith, 19–20

ACTS OF LOVE

Because of the cross — because our divine King defeated Satan and death while pouring out his wrath on Jesus instead of on us — every thought God has toward his redeemed children flows out of his tender mercy. Can you think of any more comforting words for the redeemed than these: "If God is for us, who can be against us?" (Romans 8:31)? The Lord is *for* us. "Therefore, there is now *no condemnation* for those who are in Christ Jesus (8:1, emphasis added).

Even when we sin to escape the pain of life and the ache of our disappointments, God still looks tenderly at us. He looks at our spiritual panic and sees us as travelers lost in the woods who, instead of thinking clearly, in a frenzy push deeper into the woods and get themselves even more lost. He feels sad at our predicament and grieves that we continue to make things worse.

Yet even then, God doesn't condemn us. Yes, he will gently discipline us (Hebrews 12:5–11). At times he will ask us to deny ourselves what could be legitimate pleasures because he knows we can't handle them. You take away belts from those on suicide watch, not because there is anything wrong with a belt, but because the mentally distraught could use those helpful belts to hang themselves.

Every divine prohibition is always *an act of love and concern*. It is never malicious teasing. It is never based on a desire to deny his children any good gift simply to taunt them. God does the denying only with passionate feelings of overwhelming care and compassion.

Some of us dishonor God by the way we think he withholds, forbids, and plays with us. *He is our Father.* He loves us. He delights in watching us enjoy what he has made, which is why we can openly embrace the pleasures he makes possible for us through the work of the cross. Even when he asks us to deny something because we have misused it, he acts out of a parental commitment of love and concern.

Always.

Pure Pleasure, 40–41

UNFINISHED BUSINESS

While I am glad to see an increasing interest in Christian spirituality today, including the prayer life, at the same time, I have to say that any growth in prayer without a corresponding concern and demonstrated compassion for the down-and-out is a sham, according to the teachings of Jesus.

Jesus rejects any notion that "religious obligation" can be used as an excuse to ignore the poor or needy—including church building programs. He chastised the Pharisees for telling people to give money to the temple instead of to their needy parents (see Mark 7:9–13). He said that teachers of the law who specialize in long, showy prayers but who "devour widows' houses ... will be punished most severely" (Luke 20:46–47).

Perhaps the most poignant moment of Jesus' teaching on social concern came as he hung on the cross. The Romans had beaten Jesus virtually beyond recognition. The pain he felt, both physical and emotional, was eclipsed only by the spiritual anguish of having the sins of the world placed on his perfect soul. No one had a more important mission to perform than Jesus. No one was busier in that sense. And no one has ever had a better excuse to think about other things.

But even in the midst of his agony, Jesus focused his compassion on his widowed mother, who was watching her oldest son die. Jesus had one piece of unfinished business, which he nobly dispatched as he looked down from that cross, dripping with blood. He summoned up his last vestiges of strength to say, "Dear woman, here is your son," and to John, "Here is your mother" (John 19:26–27).

Jesus spoke several of his last words on this earth to make sure a widow would be cared for after he was gone. Once he had accomplished that—and only afterward—he could finally say, "It is finished."

Jesus truly cares. He is passionately committed to the welfare of his people.

Authentic Faith, 110–11

JOY IN RAISING SINFUL KIDS

I have participated in more small groups than I can count. During the initial "life story" testimony time, each participant, without exception, describes moments of tragedy, weakness, sin, and brokenness, met finally by the strong, redeeming grace of Christ. At the end of these exercises, I am in awe at the pain everyone has felt and oftentimes caused.

And yet parents still manage to seem genuinely surprised when sin and "common weaknesses" manifest themselves in their children. Spouses seem shocked when partners stumble in any number of ways. Though a world population rapidly approaching seven billion people proves that not one of us has ever reached moral perfection — that, in fact, few could even claim to have reached moral *excellence* — we resent each other for falling short of perfection and even begin to define each other by our sin.

This lack of graciousness demeans the sacrifice of the cross and stops celebration cold. The only chance we have for joy as fallen people living in a fallen world is the gospel of the cross and its corresponding truths of forgiveness and grace. Sadly, however, many Christian homes become places of judgment, accusation, and pronounced disappointment.

Here's the stark reality: If you can't love, celebrate, and enjoy raising a sinful kid, then you can't love, celebrate, and enjoy *any* child. If you can't love and play with a sinful spouse, then you'll never be able to take pleasure in any spouse, for the simple reason that you can't find any sinless kids or spouses.

Let's not allow sin and our universal brokenness to stop our play, cease our celebration, or impair our ability to take pleasure in the company of each other. Parenting books stress the need to raise responsible kids, to teach them discipline, respect, self-denial, faith, and self-control — good things all. But if we sing *only* that song, we'll create tone-deaf, monotone families. Families begin to break down when they stop enjoying each other. If you wisely put pleasure into play, you can restore broken relationships and maintain healthy, intimate ones.

Pure Pleasure, 181–82

THE GOOD BEHIND THE GUILT

Guilt is a fierce reality, an eternal judgment of damnation—but God has provided a cure in the death and resurrection of Jesus Christ. What once was deadly can now play a positive role in our lives and hearts and souls. Just as former Olympic runner Marty Liquori talks about the "gifts that cancer can give,"[7] so we Christian parents can talk about the positive role that guilt can play in our lives.

First, guilt can point us to God. We're going to miss some cues. We're going to feel tired. We're going to occasionally get distracted by our own temptations and failings. Sometimes our parental vision will be impaired by our own health needs, vocational concerns, or even ministry obligations. Since we are finite human beings with limited understanding who require a certain amount of sleep, we can't be God to our kids.

God has different expectations for different parents. Jesus makes it very clear (in Luke 12:48) that, while all of us are guilty, God considers our background when deciding the *degree* of guilt: "From everyone who has been given much, much will be demanded; and from the one who has been entrusted with much, much more will be asked."

The positive side of our limitations is this: weakness on our part can become a strength when we use it to transfer our kids' allegiance from us to God. We need a Savior, just as they do. We can love them—but God alone has loved, is loving, and will love them with a perfect love.

Our children need to know that even if Mom and Dad let them down, there is one who will always be there for them. How freeing it is to admit to my children, "Do you see, kids, why Daddy needs a Savior, just as you do? All of us are helpless apart from God's grace."

I can't be God to my kids, but I can model my need for God. The same principle is true for other relationships. We can't be God to those we love, but we can point them to God. This truth not only frees us from perfectionistic expectations; it also helps to keep us focused on what really matters. Our energy should be directed toward helping people connect with God rather than worrying about whether they appreciate or respect us.

Sacred Parenting, 45–46

April 22

A New Kind of Thinking

"They're blocking Highway 99? In front of the airport? During rush hour?" My pointed questions betrayed my disbelief and frustration.

"It's a funeral procession, sir. A police officer died here last week."

I had been gone for a week. Forty-five minutes crawled by while I waited for a parking shuttle to take me to my car. My desperation grew by the second, as the forty-five minutes became an hour.

Once the shuttle finally took me to my car, God had a few words for me. Yes, my trip home had been delayed by more than an hour. Yes, it was a frustrating inconvenience at the end of two plane trips that equaled six hours of flying. Yeah, I had awakened on the East Coast fourteen hours earlier and only now was in Seattle, still two hours from home.

But the deceased police officer would never come home again. He wasn't just late; he was gone, removed for all of earth's time from ever greeting his wife or children at the end of a long day. And I was frustrated because *I* had been inconvenienced.

I believe my self-absorbed attitude offended God every bit as much as if I had picked up a *Playboy* magazine at the airport, cussed out the attendant who kept telling me that "the shuttle will be here soon," or took the paycheck I had earned on the trip and stopped at a casino to put all my family's money on red.

True transformation takes us beyond the limitations of traditional under-standings about morality and expands it to include deep issues of the heart. Christ grieved for the fallen officer, expressed empathy for the bereaved family, and mourned with a city that lost a servant in the line of duty. When God made this clear to me, I started praying for the city, the officer, and the family he left behind. I have a long way to go to fully experience the blessed mind of Christ.

When you face frustration today, ask God to expand your mind to help you see the entire picture. Does the traffic backup caused by an accident give you a chance to pray for the victims? Does a coworker's temper outburst provide a re-minder to pray for her? Let's stop living on the surface of self-absorbed thinking and instead press deeper to think about this world with the very mind of Christ.

Holy Available, 105–7

April 23

BORED WITH BLESSINGS, PART 1

Jim's story is as sad as it is familiar. He and his wife, Emma, had been married for almost twenty years. Jim grew bored with his wife, his family, and the predictable routines. He began an affair with a much younger woman just when Emma's mom was diagnosed with cancer. When Emma found out that Jim had used her visits to the hospital as open windows to visit his mistress, and that the mistress in question was still in her twenties, Emma declared the marriage over.

At first, Jim felt relieved by the turn of events. "I felt deeper in love with Jessie after six months than I ever felt with Emma," he said; but of course, that all changed within the next eighteen months.

It almost always does.

When Jim started to see Jessie's faults, he dealt with them the same way he had dealt with problems in his first marriage—he sought solace outside the relationship. This time, however, he tried having an "affair" with his ex-wife! He gave her an expensive gift for her birthday, started telling her how she was the one who had always been there for him, and he even tried to talk about the struggles in his second marriage. Emma, to her credit, would have none of this. "You're starting to do to Jessie what you did to me," she told him flatly, "and I won't be a part of it."

Just as painful to Jim were his children's reactions. They were angry at him for breaking up their family. They took their mother's side, and they resented the expectation that they were to spend time with the woman who was at least partially responsible for wrecking their home.

All of this self-inflicted pain wounded Jim deeply in his soul. We'll pick up the rest of Jim's story tomorrow, but for today, consider this: sin often initially tastes sweet, only to turn bitter over time. Are you flirting with any act of disobedience, unable to see the destruction, pain, and even agony up ahead? If so, please reconsider. Let Jim's regret save you from your own. *(Continued tomorrow.)*

Devotions for Sacred Parenting, 151

BORED WITH BLESSINGS, PART 2

As his life became increasingly miserable, one afternoon Jim became honest. "I can hardly bear this," he confessed. "Jessie is so young she makes me feel really old. She's starting to talk about wanting a family, but I'm forty-five! I don't think I can go through the baby stage again. And there's this younger guy at work that she runs with at lunchtime, and it's just horrible. How can I compete with his hair and his energy and his knowledge of all the current music groups? I put in a Bee Gees CD, and Jessie just laughs at me. Besides all that, I see Emma and realize she really is the woman I've always loved. Yeah, she has her faults—plenty of them—but we had so much together, and I was such a jerk."

Not much to argue with there. But he went on.

"And I can't tell you what it's like to try to have a relationship with a daughter who looks at you with hate in her eyes. She despises me. Every time Jessie so much as touches me, Amanda [the daughter] flinches. Do you have any idea what I would give to get back what I lost? All I want is what I used to have—to wake up next to Emma, those crow's-feet around her eyes but a face I've loved for two decades, and to walk downstairs to the kitchen and see Amanda eating a bowl of cereal and hearing her say, 'Hi, Dad,' without any accusation or rebellion in her voice. That's it! Nothing special—just the plain-old boring Saturday morning that used to drive me crazy. I would give everything I have now—I'd even give my right arm—to get all that back."

One of Satan's oldest tricks is to make us bored with God's blessings. Only when we lose these blessings do we realize how precious they are. More than anything in this world, Jim wants back what he once had and yet had despised.

Today, let's thank God for the familiar routines, the peace of a settled but perhaps slightly boring home. Your marriage may seem a bit stale. Your parents may seem old. Your siblings may get tiresome. But remember this: there is often a hidden glory behind the overly familiar that we will notice only after it is gone.

Devotions for Sacred Parenting, 152

WHY PARENT?

Once you have children, what motivation drives your parenting? Some parents bring a child into the world but refuse to make the sacrifices necessary to truly parent that child. Deciding to conceive children is one thing; daily parenting them requires an entirely different set of decisions. What moves you to get up early in the morning to help your child with his homework, or to stay up late at night talking to your daughter about her day? Why do you go without certain things so that your children can have other things? Why do you give up doing some of the things you like to do so that you can stay at home with your kids?

If you're a single mom, why do you keep doing it all, even when exhaustion makes you feel as though you're wearing a fifty-pound coat? If you're a stepparent, why do you bother with all the hassles, negotiate the volatile relationships, and try to do what some have said is virtually impossible—successfully blend two different and often wounded families? If you're an adoptive parent, what makes you willing to take on such an unbelievably high commitment for a person who used to be someone else's child?

We spend so much time talking about the "how-to" of parenting that we neglect the equally important "why" of parenting. God not only commands us to have children (Genesis 1:28), but he tells us that his desire is that we will raise *godly* offspring (Malachi 2:15). Sacred parenting thus becomes an act of worship toward God, faithfully fulfilling his call and claim on our lives. If we parent only because we want to experience parent-child intimacy, what will keep us parenting when our kids are in rebellion? If we parent out of selfishness or pride, what will keep us parenting when we go through seasons of sacrifice and moments of embarrassment?

The "why" behind parenting is crucial, because our motivation for parenting is what will keep us actively parenting, even when parenting disappoints us.

Sacred Parenting, 18–19

April 26

UNGLAMOROUS LIVES

A profound spiritual truth lies behind the unglamorous lives we adopt as parents. In heaven, Jesus was exalted and worshiped as God. To come to earth, he clothed himself in a body, and a very unglamorous body at that. Scripture seems to portray Jesus as less than average in physical appearance (see Isaiah 53:2). People didn't fall down on their faces saying, "I'm a dead man, for I've seen the face of a holy God!" Yet Jesus, encased in that plain human flesh, was no less God. Jesus left the glamour of heaven to get dirty, and even occasionally smelly, on our behalf. He chose a relationship with us over a spotless appearance and heavenly comfort.

Parenting calls us to the same place. Iris Krasnow writes about trading in her bikini for a gray bathrobe that she wore virtually nonstop for the first six weeks of her baby's life. Later, when she returned to writing magazine articles, she got an assignment to write a profile on Ethel Kennedy.

After weeks of trying to reach Ethel, Iris finally got the esteemed mother on the phone; and at just that moment, Iris's little boy started shrieking into the receiver. Iris felt horrified, but Ethel Kennedy, no stranger to the process of parenting, consoled Iris with the words, "We can do this later. You go do what's really important."[8]

The Bible couldn't be clearer. Looks can deceive: "God chose the foolish things of the world to shame the wise; God chose the weak things of the world to shame the strong. He chose the lowly things of this world and the despised things—and the things that are not—to nullify the things that are, so that no one may boast before him" (1 Corinthians 1:27–29).

This sobering message means that if we lived in the first century and felt motivated by glamour alone, we would have missed Jesus Christ. And if glitz motivates us today, we will miss the wisdom and genius of the gospel. Let's choose obedience today, even if this obedience takes us to the "lowly" things, the despised things, the things the world looks down on. Let's be guided by faithful obedience rather than by the superficial allure of glamour.

Sacred Parenting, 131–32

NOTICING THE IGNORED

One day I picked up a few groceries. When the young man behind the cash register handed me my change, I said, "Thanks, Kurt. Have a great holiday weekend." Kurt's head jerked back as though I had yanked it with a steel chain. Though Kurt wears a name tag, few people ever read it, and even fewer use it to treat him like a person. What a rarity that a customer would use his actual name! Now we always share a few words whenever I go through his line.

Having been in lowly situations and having done less than glamorous work ourselves (changing diapers, mopping up vomit, and so on), we parents are set free to notice those whom others ignore. We have awakened to the fact that glamour misleads and that worldly significance isn't all it's cracked up to be.

In this sense, kids can teach us what truly matters. Indeed, children help us grow up, put away our own childish things, and see in the mirror more clearly who God wants us to be (see 1 Corinthians 13:11–12). We act out of reverence for God instead of pursuing what *Vogue* or *GQ* identifies as the latest hot trend.

If you're a new stay-at-home mom, don't look down on yourself because you've traded spaghetti-strap dresses for sweats, extra-large shirts, and towels draped over your shoulder to catch your baby's spit-up! In time, you'll be able to go back to those dresses (though you may have to upgrade the sizes). If you're a dad who traded in his BMW for a minivan with a bumper sticker that reads "Baby On Board," good for you (although it wouldn't hurt to lose the sticker). Hold your head high as you add parenting to your résumé. Though the superficial around you may look down on you, the process to which you've given yourself closely mirrors the most profound movement of all. Consider Jesus — the one who, "being in very nature God, did not consider equality with God something to be grasped, but made himself nothing, taking the very nature of a servant" (Philippians 2:6–7).

Young people and nonparents take note. Most of the world lusts after getting ahead, becoming important, being noticed. The Bible couldn't be clearer that a Christian must live with a different motivation — namely, becoming the servant of all.

Sacred Parenting, 132–33

April 28

FALL FORWARD

Many years ago, a few close friends and I celebrated our high school graduation by hiking Mount Rainier. Before I attempted to jump a fast-moving creek, one of my friends advised me, "Just make sure you fall forward." He meant that even if I didn't complete the jump, my forward momentum would keep me from getting swept into the stream.

His advice has stayed with me through the years, as I believe that Christian marriage is also about learning to fall forward. Obstacles arise, anger flares up, and weariness dulls our feelings and our senses. When this happens, the spiritually immature respond by pulling back, becoming more distant from their spouse, or even seeking to start over with somebody "more exciting." Yet we reach maturity by continuing to move forward, past the pain and apathy.

Falls are inevitable. We cannot control this, but we can control the direction in which we fall—toward or away from our spouse.

In Hollywood, romance is a passive activity. Couples usually say they have "fallen" in love. Or they may talk about being "swept off their feet." Adulterous couples sometimes even say, "We couldn't help ourselves; it just happened." Such passivity is as foreign to Christian love as the moon is to the earth. Christian love is an aggressive movement and an *active* commitment. We choose where to place our affections.

Donald Harvey writes, "Intimate *relationships*, as opposed to intimate experiences, are the result of planning. They are built. The sense of union that comes with genuine spiritual closeness will not just happen. If it is present, it is because of definite intent and follow-through on your part. You choose to invest, and do. It's not left to mere chance."[9]

It took years for me to understand I have a Christian obligation to continually move toward my wife. I thought that as long as I didn't attack my wife or say cruel things to her, I was a "nice" husband. But the opposite of biblical love isn't hate; it's apathy. To stop moving toward our spouse is to stop loving him or her. It's holding back from the very purpose of marriage.

Sacred Marriage, 154–55

GAINING EYES THAT WORSHIP

The first human sin sprang, in part, from the allure of sight: "When the woman *saw* that the fruit of the tree was good for food and *pleasing to the eye*, ... she took some and ate it" (Genesis 3:6, emphasis added).

In fact, God's sight is the only sight that matters. He warned the Israelites to "listen carefully to the voice of the LORD your God and do what is right *in his eyes*" (Exodus 15:26, emphasis added). So what can we do to receive transformed sight?

1. *Ask God to give you light.* God-sight is a God-gift. Begin praying with the psalmist, "Look on me and answer, O LORD my God. Give light to my eyes, or I will sleep in death" (Psalm 13:3). As part of your daily worship, plead with God to give light to your eyes.

2. *Make a covenant with your eyes.* Job declared, "I made a covenant with my eyes not to look lustfully at a girl" (Job 31:1). If we want to see with God's eyes, then we need to accept that God will turn away from some things—and so should we. In an attitude of humble reliance, pray the prayer of Saint Francis: *Lord, all those things that I have loved after the flesh, make me now despise, and from those things that I formerly loathed, let me drink great sweetness and immeasurable delight.*

3. *Train your eyes.* Scripture can help us train our eyes: "The commands of the LORD are radiant, giving light to the eyes" (Psalm 19:8). Through increased familiarity with all of Scripture, we can train our minds to think more like Christ.

4. *Worship with your eyes.* Ultimately, only one object is worthy of our clearest vision, namely, the glory of God: "My eyes are fixed on you, O Sovereign LORD" (Psalm 141:8). We must worship not only with our tongues but also with our eyes as we consciously fix our sight on the majesty and glory of God—and, over time, we will mirror the spirit and life and character of Christ more deeply.

It all begins with the eyes.

Holy Available, 68–70

THE HEART OF THE MATTER

Have you noticed that when Jesus went on the attack, he typically addressed the heart first and foremost? Not behavior or pedigree or habits, but the heart.

"It was because your hearts were hard that Moses wrote you this law" (Mark 10:5).

"Isaiah was right when he prophesied about you hypocrites; as it is written: 'These people honor me with their lips, but their hearts are far from me'" (Mark 7:6).

"For from within, out of men's hearts, come evil thoughts, sexual immorality, theft, murder, adultery, greed, malice, deceit, lewdness, envy, slander, arrogance and folly. All these evils come from inside and make a man 'unclean'" (Mark 7:21–23).

"This people's heart has become calloused" (Matthew 13:15).

Thankfully for us, Christ's death, resurrection, and ascension fulfill a prophecy given long ago: "The LORD your God will circumcise your hearts and the hearts of your descendants, so that you may love him with all your heart and with all your soul, and live" (Deuteronomy 30:6).

Through what Christ has done, our guilty, shame-ridden hearts can be spiritually defibrillated, jump-started to once again beat with Christ passion and heavenly adoration. The Bible states:

Therefore, brothers, since we have confidence to enter the Most Holy Place by the blood of Jesus, by a new and living way opened for us through the curtain, that is, his body, and since we have a great priest over the house of God, let us draw near to God with a sincere heart in full assurance of faith, having our hearts sprinkled to cleanse us from a guilty conscience. (Hebrews 10:19–22)

Once sprinkled, however, our hearts still need to be maintained. If we don't keep our hearts, carefully grooming their affection—if we allow the running of a business or the raising of a family or the maintenance of a church to keep us so busy that we don't take time to cultivate intimacy with God—then we shouldn't be surprised if our souls collapse into the false allure of scandalous sin.

Holy Available, 142

MAY

Life has a way of getting messy, but the ascended Christ has a far greater way of giving us the resources we need to grow and even spiritually prosper in the midst of tough circumstances. Blogger Steve White puts it succinctly: "Do people still talk about the Four Spiritual Laws? I'm thinking Spiritual Law #1 could be reworded. Instead of 'God loves you and has a wonderful plan for your life,' I would say, 'God loves you and has an astonishing ability to give contentment in distressful circumstances.'"

A SOUL-SATISFYING LIFE

For years the church has tried to scare us out of our sin. For example, you could fortify yourself against an affair by meditating on all the evil that could result: the consequences of bringing home a sexually transmitted disease, the shame of getting caught and exposed, the pain of seeing your spouse's hurt, the horror of watching your kids lose their respect for you, or the threat of a revenge-minded mate.

I suppose there's a place for this approach. If you lived *not* to sin, you might even be able to make a case that such an exercise would bring spiritual benefit. *Or* ...

You could focus on building a marriage in which thoughts of straying get pushed out by a real and satisfying intimacy in which no room exists for another lover. You could spend your time actively raising your children, becoming engaged in their lives in such a way that your heart overflows with love for your family, making any thought of tearing apart your family repugnant. You could faithfully pursue the work to which God has called you so that you have neither the time nor the inclination for something as sordid as an affair.

See the difference? We can build lives of true, lasting pleasure and so fortify ourselves against evil because evil has lost much of its allure — or we can try, with an iron will, to "scare" ourselves away from evil while still, deep in our hearts, truly longing for it.

Which life do you want? Which life do you believe will ultimately succeed?

Thomas Chalmers, a nineteenth-century Scottish preacher, called the former method (meditating on the "vanity" of sin) "altogether incompetent and ineffectual." He believed that the "constitution of our nature" demands that we instead focus on the "rescue and recovery" of our heart from wrong affections by embracing the "expulsive power of a new affection."[1]

We need, in G. K. Chesterton's words, "vivid pictures of purity and spiritual triumph."[2] Let's focus on the glory of a truly soul-satisfying life instead of obsessing over the dangers of a life lived foolishly.

Pure Pleasure, 14 – 15

HOLY HAPPINESS

Buried in the book of Deuteronomy is an interesting and neglected verse: "If a man has recently married, he must not be sent to war or have any other duty laid on him. For one year he is to be free to stay at home and bring happiness to the wife he has married" (Deuteronomy 24:5).

In all my seminary training, the thought never occurred to me that God would want me to devote myself to making my wife happy. My wife was there to join me as I evangelized, studied Scripture, taught younger believers, did "the work of the ministry." The thought that God wants me to serve him by concentrating on making my wife happy was extraordinary. Can it mean, then, that if my wife is unhappy, I'm failing God?

Every spouse ought to spend some time thinking about how to make their mate happy — and celebrating the profound reality that making their spouse happy pleases God. On a practical level, a husband who plots how to make his wife laugh every now and then is serving God. A wife who plans an unforgettable sexual experience for her husband is serving God. A husband who makes sacrifices so his wife can get the recreational time she needs is loving God.

Legions of books get published every year that teach us how to care for ourselves. As our society becomes increasingly fractured, we seem to have a virtual obsession with looking out for ourselves, standing up for ourselves, and bettering ourselves. This emphasis on meeting our own needs can become ridiculous. You need only consider the book I once saw advertised with the title, *Sex for One: The Joy of Selfloving*.

While our society has become expert in self-care, we seem to have lost the art of caring for others. *Sacrifice* has taken on such negative connotations that people fear being a "codependent" more than they fear being perceived as selfish. And yet Scripture says, in effect, "Make your wife happy. Sacrifice yourself daily. You'll find your life only when you first lose it."

Instead of obsessing over your own perceived level of happiness, why not pray today about what you can do to make your spouse happy — whether or not you think they deserve it?

Sacred Marriage, 42–43

GOD-COLORED PLEASURES

One of the United States' founding mothers, Abigail Adams, endured years of separation from her husband, John, while he represented the colonies overseas and then the young United States. Someone once asked Abigail if she would have allowed John to leave had she known beforehand how long he would stay away. She responded, "I feel a pleasure in being able to sacrifice my selfish passions to the general good."[3]

If our decision to embrace pleasure focuses on giving pleasure to God, then what gives us pleasure will ultimately reveal our spiritual maturity and the depth of our relationship with him. To the unformed soul, immediate feelings of pleasure represent the quickest and surest path to pleasure; to the child of God, pleasure becomes the destination we reach when we walk the path of obedience. Pleasure is the end result of a process, which is why we can take as much pleasure in sacrifice as we do in having fun.

Walking this journey for any significant period gradually shapes our hearts to look for the deeper side of pleasure rather than the appearance-oriented pleasures that used to captivate us. Which of the following statements, for example, strike you as most honoring to God?

"I have a nice car" *or* "I enjoy driving."

"Look at my book collection" *or* "Let me tell you how a book has recently challenged me."

"Guess which college my kid got into?" *or* "I love spending time with my kids."

"Look how attractive, important, capable [fill in the blank] my spouse is" *or* "I know my wife intimately and enjoy her company."

A vital relationship with God colors our pleasures with a holy passion and leads us to value relationship over possession, intimacy over ambition, and service over selfishness. God sets us free to revel in what he has designed for our enjoyment; eventually, as we mature, we begin to detest what goes against his nature and will.

We do not need to fear pleasure; we need to fear the alienation from God that corrupts our sense of pleasure and that makes the pleasure drive potentially dangerous.

Pure Pleasure, 42–43

An Ascended Monarch

Question of the day: Does Jesus, as we speak, still have elbows? Knees? Fingernails?

These aren't silly questions; they run to the very heart and foundation of biblical Christianity. They also point to a key theological doctrine called "the ascension."

It is difficult for us to ascertain the exact state of Jesus' glorified body, but we know that after the resurrection, Jesus went to great pains to demonstrate that his body was both real and physical: "Put your finger here; see my hands. Reach out your hand and put it into my side" (John 20:27). Even after the ascension, Stephen saw Jesus "standing" (Acts 7:56). Scripture tells us that Jesus "sat down" (Hebrews 1:3), and the last book of the Bible describes Jesus as "walking" among golden lampstands (Revelation 2:1).

Other biblical language describes Jesus as sitting on a throne and paints pictures of heavenly feasts, both of which require some type of body. Paul uses the idea of Jesus' body to describe our future bodies, telling us that Jesus "will transform our lowly bodies so that they will be like his glorious body" (Philippians 3:21).

The Westminster Confession (8.4, emphasis added) affirms, "On the third day [Jesus] arose from the dead, *with the same body* in which he suffered, with which also he *ascended* into heaven, and there *sits* at the right hand of his Father, making intercession, and shall return to judge men and angels, at the end of the world."

Christmas and Easter are ingrained in American culture and stand out on the calendar of the contemporary church. But we lose something when the ascension becomes a forgotten appendage to the incarnation, crucifixion, and resurrection. What do we lose? Here's the answer of Presbyterian pastor Gerrit Scott Dawson: "The ascended Jesus is the reigning Jesus. Of all the meanings of the ascension, this one is preeminent: Jesus has gone up to the right hand of God the Father, exalted above every name and power. He reigns."[4]

Life changes when we live with an *active* awareness that in spite of all appearances, Jesus still reigns, and even wants to reign through us.

Holy Available, 34–35

THE REIGNING KING

Have you ever asked yourself, "What is Jesus doing *right now?*"

Celebrating Christmas gives us faith; it affirms that our beliefs have roots in the historical fact of the incarnation. Celebrating Easter gives us assurance; it affirms that Christ wiped away our sins by his great sacrifice and triumphed over death. Celebrating the ascension gives us hope and points us toward transformation; it affirms that we can become more like Jesus is *right now.*

Without the ascension, we forget that Christ is the ruling Lord of this fallen, broken world. It reminds us that, just as we can get discouraged in our sin and momentarily forget the pardon Jesus won for us, so we can get discouraged by our lack of effectiveness and forget about Christ's present reign — not just that he *will* reign when he comes again or that he *did* reign over death, but that he is reigning *right now.*

Pastor Gerrit Scott Dawson writes, "While the boots of the soldiers of the most powerful army in the world resounded in the streets of occupied Jerusalem, an uneducated fisherman from the north of Palestine declared, 'God has made this Jesus, whom you crucified, both Lord and Christ' (Acts 2:36)."[5] The church must recapture this sacred truth so that all of us can have the hope and courage to embrace the presently reigning Jesus, who manifests himself through believers by the Holy Spirit.

We serve the ascended *and reigning* Christ. The world may mock our King. We may disdain his rule by our own sinful rebellion — but the fact is, *he reigns.* And we can participate in the spread of his kingdom not simply by imitating how he lived while on earth, but by making ourselves "holy available" to his dynamic, life-transforming presence within us, by letting him change the way we see, think, feel, hear, speak, and serve. It is the life of Christ in us, continuing his work, exercising his reign, manifesting his presence. Remembering the ascension helps keep us from smothering the supernatural and the mysterious elements of our faith, recapturing the dynamic reality of Christ manifesting himself through us.

Holy Available, 36–37

MANIFESTED IN ME

When Jesus ascended to heaven and sat down at his Father's right hand, did his work stop? Not according to Gerrit Dawson: "The Son may be 'seated' at the Father's right hand, but he is far from sedentary. Rather, he is actively engaged in strengthening his people and subduing the enemy. Though Jesus parts from our sight in the ascension, he does not withdraw from the exercise of his authority or his continuing labor for our renewal."[6]

How does this affect everyday Christian living? In my life, it means that before I preach, I meditate on Jesus or imagine him speaking to this audience. I not only want Christ's words; I want his tone, his joy, his love of life, his fondness for stories, his favor toward children — but most of all, his passion for giving glory to God. I usually pray, "May the risen and ascended Christ manifest himself in me as I submit myself to be his servant today."

When I meet with someone, I strive to pray, "Father, help me to love this person with the love of Christ." When I pray for my children, I try to fall into line with the intercession of the Holy Spirit (see Romans 8:26), letting him plead his case through me. When I counsel others, I pray that I will model God's attitude and speak the ascended Christ's words. When I'm in a small group Bible study and someone is talking, I try to listen with Christ's ears: "Father, what is this person really saying, and what do you want to say in response?"

A counselor once asked me to meet a local pastor. She didn't tell me why, just that she was praying for God to use this encounter to make some necessary points. During the meeting, I felt almost as though I were watching myself. I truly felt as though Jesus had used *my* ears and *my* tongue to make *his* points. Although I would never ask people to accept my words as God's words, I am striving more and more to let the living, reigning Christ work through me to truly touch others.

Today, make the ordinary extraordinary by actively inviting the risen and ascended Christ to work through you — not merely by trying to copy him but by letting his living presence use your mind, your tongue, your ears, and your heart to spread his reign.

Holy Available, 39–40

GLORIFIED THROUGH GREATNESS

Sometimes speaking a single thought — "You're so focused on becoming a mother; have you ever wondered if God wants you to focus first on being his *daughter*?" — can open many doors of insight, as long as that phrase is born in heaven and delivered to earth by the Spirit.

I treasure nothing more than to experience the ascended Christ manifesting himself through me. Nothing is even half as rewarding as that. It doesn't always happen when I want it to, but when it does, everyone involved gets a refreshing splash of glory. And this same experience is given to God's church through the ascended Christ.

This submissive and dependent view of Christian life and ministry doesn't diminish our role or the importance of our work. On the contrary, it exalts us. "Humble yourselves, therefore, under God's mighty hand, *that he may lift you up in due time*" (1 Peter 5:6, emphasis added). God isn't glorified through weak, indecisive, and defeated subjects; he is glorified through weak but victorious subjects. Gerrit Dawson (whose book *Jesus Ascended* I highly recommend) writes the following:

> The greatness of a king has always been known through the generosity of the gifts he bestows on his people. One of the first acts of the enthroned Jesus was to open the treasure trove of his love and bring forth a gem of inestimable value. In his bountiful rule, the King of kings showers a priceless gift from his infinite largesse upon his subjects. He receives the Holy Spirit from the Father and pours him out upon the disciples (Acts 2:33). The Spirit ... becomes the bond between the still-incarnate Son in heaven and his people still sojourning on earth. By this boon, the physically absent King establishes a living tie between himself and his subjects. The head pours his life-giving energies and constant direction throughout his body (i.e., into his people) through his Spirit.[7]

God's glory gets recognized not just through *forgiven* people but through *transformed* and *compelling* people. This is one way he makes himself visible to many who would never pick up a Bible. This means the Christian life isn't about accomplishment; it is about surrender to the "life giving energies and constant direction" of the Holy Spirit.

Holy Available, 40–41

OUR HIGHEST HOPE

Living a life of incarnational spirituality is not easy; the process of becoming "holy available" is filled with what appears to be constant failure. If we hoped only in what we actually saw, our hope would soon tire out. Every time someone has experienced a "splash of glory" through me, they've had to wade through ten sessions of my inflated sense of importance, arrogant opinions, and glaring blind spots.

But do you know what keeps me in the race? Do you know what challenges me to keep going? The answer is embedded within Christ's ascension. Listen to John Calvin's words of encouragement as he thunders home this timeless truth:

> Thus, since [Jesus] has gone up there, and is in heaven for us, let us note that we need not fear to be in this world. It is true that we are subject to so much misery that our condition is pitiable, but at that we need neither be astonished nor confine our attention to ourselves. Thus, we look to our Head, who is already in heaven, and say, "Although I am weak, there is Jesus Christ, who is powerful enough to make me stand upright. Although I am feeble, there is Jesus Christ, who is my strength. Although I am full of miseries, Jesus Christ is in immortal glory and what he has will some time be given to me and I shall partake of all his benefits." ... This is how we must look at his ascension, applying the benefit to ourselves.[8]

Because Jesus reigns now, we have hope. Even though my eyes are weak and greedy and judgmental and lustful, there stands Christ, with eyes filled with burning purity, holy passion, and selfless love. Even though I sometimes speak with a hurtful tongue or blurt out unkind comments, there is Christ, with his healing tongue in perfect control. And here is where it gets really good: Jesus is not simply watching me, asking me to imitate him; on the contrary, he has released, is releasing, and will release his Holy Spirit to help me see and talk just as he does. *He will live through me.*

Don't beat yourself up today with your weaknesses and sinful failings; instead, find hope in the promised presence of Christ living through us. He is all we need. He provides all we lack. We live for his glory, not our own.

Holy Available, 42–43

THE EMBODIMENT OF ALL WE CAN BE

Jesus Christ reigns in heaven—and this is what makes our transformation possible. Gerrit Dawson sums this up well:

> Out of the most profound hope, the Christian church looks upon the worst setbacks and sufferings and declares, in the very teeth of death and loss, "What of it? Christ reigns in heaven, and so, at the deepest level, all is well. What of my circumstance? I am in Christ, and he has triumphed. In him, by the Holy Spirit, I am kept in heaven." The ascension provides the very ground for our peace in every circumstance.[9]

In this world, we will not experience the full measure of Christ's glorified state. Nor will we see unending victory. But when we look at our weaknesses and our defeats through the lens of Christ's ascension, our trials and sins take on a much different hue.

And since the Bible teaches us that Jesus ascended in a body and will return in a body (see Acts 1:9–11) and that Jesus now reigns in a body, it is fair to infer that real children are sitting in a real lap (providing hope for those who have lost young loved ones). Shamed and hurting men receive an affirming, masculine hug. Women formerly abused, neglected, or forsaken have their cheeks touched with a selfless, nurturing, 100 percent pure hand.

What is happening there—and it *is* happening there, even as you read these words—can also, in a less perfect way, happen here through us as Christ's representatives. With such a possibility before us, how dare we simply play at church?

This is real human experience, exalted by divine impact; it is our birthright through the ascension—a sacred truth we need to hold dear. We simply cannot limit our Christian experience to the incarnation and Jesus' death and resurrection. To be sure, these are precious truths that make our salvation possible. But let us press on to embrace the power, hope, and glory of the ascension, the reality of a living, in-the-flesh Jesus. He is the embodiment of all that we can be when we surrender to his reign.

Holy Available, 43

May 10

LOOK AWAY, LOOK AWAY

The institution of marriage is divinely designed to force us to become reconcilers. That's the only way we'll survive spiritually. Ironically, in this aspect marriage points us *away* from our spouse and toward God. Listen to the wisdom of James, one of the pillars of the New Testament church: "What causes fights and quarrels among you? Don't they come from your desires that battle within you? You want something but don't get it ... You quarrel and fight. You do not have, because you do not ask God" (James 4:1–2).

Many marital disputes result precisely from this: "You want something but don't get it." James says we don't get it because we're looking *in the wrong place.* Instead of placing demands on your spouse, look to God to get your needs met. That way you can approach your spouse in a spirit of servanthood.

Those of us who have been married for a while tend to forget the "single ruse." By that, I mean the tendency on the part of some single young people to think that what they really need is to find "the one." Once they find their life mate, they assume that everything else will fall into place. Their loneliness, their insecurity, their worries about their own significance—all this and more will somehow mystically melt away in the fire of marital passion.

And for a very short season, this may appear to be true. Infatuation can be an intoxicating drug that temporarily covers up any number of inner weaknesses.

But the spotlight of marriage shows us the misguided notion of searching for another human being to complete us. When disillusionment breaks through, we have one of two choices: dump our spouse and become infatuated with somebody new, or seek to understand the message behind the disillusionment—that we should seek our significance, meaning, and purpose in our Creator rather than in another human being. Approached in the right way, marriage can cause us to reevaluate our dependency on other humans for our spiritual nourishment, and direct us to nurture our relationship with God instead.

Sacred Marriage, 82–83

A TOURNIQUET FOR RESENTMENT

A Claude Lanzmann documentary on the Holocaust titled *Shoah* records the gripping moment when a leader of the Warsaw ghetto uprising talks about the bitterness that remains in his heart: "If you could lick my heart," he says, "it would poison you."

Many marriages are like that. The infighting and personal attacks have become so bitter that the participants have developed poisonous hearts. The tragedy is that a poisonous heart doesn't just pollute the person who licks it; it is itself an infected organ that pours toxic bile into a person's own life.

Forgiveness is a tourniquet that stops the fatal bleeding of resentment. Henri Nouwen once defined forgiveness as "love practiced among people who love poorly." I love poorly; you love poorly; all of us love poorly—if we take Jesus as the model of someone who loves well.

In the midst of this mess, marriage forces us to embrace that most difficult of Christian clichés: "Hate the sin and love the sinner." This is a staggering thing to do, as every self-righteous fiber within us pushes us to transform repulsion toward sin into repulsion toward the sinner—and therefore repulsion toward our spouse.

Perhaps we can move in the direction of loving the sinner by thinking what it must have been like for Jesus. Because Jesus was morally perfect, imagine what platform Jesus had to be disgusted! And yet no one loved sinners with the depth that Jesus did.

C. S. Lewis confessed that he struggled with how to truly love the sinner while hating the sin. One day it suddenly became clear: "It occurred to me that there was one man to whom I had been doing this all my life—namely myself. However much I might dislike my own cowardice or conceit or greed, I went on loving myself. There had never been the slightest difficulty about it."[10] We extend this charity to ourselves, so the question begs to be asked: Why do we not extend this same charity to our spouse?

Sacred Marriage, 170–71

WHY HAUGHTY RHYMES WITH NAUGHTY

Mourning played a key role in the faith of the ancients. In his classic *The Ladder of Divine Ascent* (ca. AD 640), John Climacus calls mourning a "golden spur within the soul."[11] When we truly mourn, Climacus says, we become "inordinately compassionate" and nonjudgmental.

I've found that in my own zeal to grow in righteousness, without a balanced emphasis on mourning, I tend to become critical instead of compassionate, angry instead of gentle, and condemning instead of welcoming.

During lunch a pastor asked me, "I don't know you very well, Gary, but you seem really tired. Is everything OK?" The pastor felt genuinely concerned, but I couldn't come up with an explanation. Later that day, as I carried out various tasks, I felt a strong anger rising within me. I couldn't figure it out.

At the same time, I was completing an article for *Discipleship Journal*. "This is hot!" I said to Lisa as I e-mailed the final draft to the editor. "I didn't hold anything back. I really let the readers have it." A week later, I received a very gracious and tactful — but equally forceful — reply. In essence, the editor considered the article terrible; to her ears, it sounded judgmental, cynical, and critical. She said it didn't sound at all like my typical submissions, and she explained in detail exactly why she had drawn that conclusion.

She was clearly right. *What is going on with me?* I wondered.

I needed to learn that *haughty* rhymes with *naughty* for good reason! Although outwardly my Christian life appeared victorious, my "success" gave a foothold to pride. It had been way too long since I had genuinely mourned, and compassion and empathy had abandoned my soul. Unknowingly, I had been skating on the edge of Pharisaism.

Mourning is the handmaiden of repentance, and repentance is the doorway to humility. When my attitudes and actions become prideful, it's usually been far too long since I've repented and experienced the essential discipline of mourning.

Don't let moral success corrupt your heart with pride. Mourning our sins helps us maintain soft hearts by leading us through repentance and into humility.

Authentic Faith, 154–55

CALLED TO CARE

Regardless of where we live—whether in the suburbs of the Midwest, the elite societies of the East, or the rural South—or whatever we do, as a laborer or business owner, all of us are called to care. If your life lacks any evidence of social mercy—if there isn't a single poor person, prisoner, man or woman with a disability, or refugee who cannot stand up and testify that you have lived out your faith with compassionate care—then know this: Scripture, the Christian classics, and contemporary faith all stand in one accord to challenge the sub-Christian religion you have adopted.

Does this seem like a harsh statement? If so, then consider this: you cannot read Scripture with any honesty or read very deeply in Christian history or live with open eyes in contemporary Christianity without being confronted by how central a compassionate outreach to the poor and needy is to the gospel message. The late Klaus Bockmuehl declared, "Living for yourself is too notoriously small an aim for any human soul." If your faith begins and ends with you—your victories over sin and temptation, your ability to pay the bills, your family's health—you are missing the truly profound experience of working with God to make a difference in a needy person's life.

In your financial plan, besides retirement, are you investing in those who are less well-off than you are? Brady Bobbink, one of my early mentors, earns a relatively low salary as a campus pastor, but he made a pledge over fifteen years ago that each year he and his wife would add one more World Vision or Compassion child to their budget. On a limited income, they plan eventually to sponsor two dozen children.

In an interview with *Beyond* magazine, Gary Haugen said, "It's not a side issue, that God's people address suffering and injustice. It's not one of those extra credit options, that if you do everything else, then maybe you can do something on behalf of those who are victimized by the abuse of power. It's the thing that breaks God's heart. And then we have to ask, why is something that is so passionately important to God only mildly interesting to us?"

If you truly want to experience an authentic faith, go where people are hurting the most and get involved in their lives. You'll not only see God at work; you'll also gain his heart and become transformed in the process.

Authentic Faith, 120–21

THERE'S ALWAYS TOMORROW

It's hard to focus on a task for eight hours, much less *eighteen years*. The length of parenting means there will be highs and lows, good days and bad days. Yes, we're going to miss some things. All of us could do better. All of us could do more.

As parents, we need to cultivate the attitude that seventy-five-year-old John has toward golf. I met John while playing on a public golf course. John plays golf seven days a week, weather permitting. As one player missed a putt, someone else offered consolations, and John said, "When you play every day, you don't worry too much about all that because you know there's always tomorrow."

That's not a bad motto for parenting: There's always tomorrow. Of course, there's never a guarantee of tomorrow, but even so, for most of us, parenting lasts decades, not days. We'll have good days and bad days. When we see parenting as a long journey, we don't drown ourselves in guilt on days that rate less than an A+. We won't always be at our best, but we'll usually have another go at it the next day.

Don't look at your failings apart from God's grace and God's provision. Guilt becomes deadweight when you become consumed by your failings, past or present. But guilt can become positive motivation when you hear our Lord say, "Neither do I condemn you ... Go now and leave your life of sin" (John 8:11).

Recognizing that I become deadweight after 9:00 p.m., guilt can motivate me to get more involved before my brain turns to mush. It means I spend more time with my kids on personal lunch dates. Whatever your own scenario, let your guilt lead you to become more involved when you can instead of causing you to pull back in frustration.

Because of the breadth of God's mercy, we get another day, another chance. Joy unspeakable — we cannot exhaust his grace! We can look forward with confidence, use our failings as teachable moments, and wake up with cleansed souls and fresh hearts, knowing we have learned some valuable lessons for the next day.

Sacred Parenting, 47–48

A MESSY BUSINESS

My son, Graham, and the son of our pastor played on the same Little League baseball team. After the final game, we headed to a buffet-style restaurant to celebrate. It was about 8:00 p.m. and Graham's friend bypassed the salads, took a little of the pizza, and went heavy on the ice cream and pudding. I commented to his dad, "Don't you remember the days when we could eat that much dessert and not pay for it?"

My son spent that night at our pastor's house. Graham woke up early the next morning when he heard some commotion and saw our minister, in his underwear, scrubbing vomit out of the carpet. Apparently Graham's friend didn't get away with eating all that ice cream after all. Graham was used to seeing his pastor dressed nicely in front of the whole congregation, so he understandably giggled.

Graham's little adventure provided a good lesson: No matter how exalted our position, if we have kids, the day will come when we'll wind up in some of the most undignified positions imaginable—including cleaning up vomit in our underwear at 2:00 a.m. The positive spiritual benefit is that it slowly transforms us from valuing the superficial allure of appearances and helps us focus instead on the influential aspect of meaningful relationships.

Real relationships aren't sanitary. Things get messy. We see the sordid side of life, and we're asked to forgive and to love unconditionally. Real relationships take us into everything that casual social relationships allow us to avoid. If we embrace real relationships over superficial ones, our taste for intimacy will get trained in a positive spiritual direction. We'll begin to care less about image and more about substance. We'll understand that true intimacy exacts a price, calling us to a far deeper commitment than making an impression or putting on a false front does.

Parenting wakes us up from our self-indulgence and invites us to get involved in something bigger than adventure and even greater than glamour—the shaping of a human life and the destiny of an eternal soul. It's a messy business, but a highly important one.

Sacred Parenting, 123–24

PLEASURE PRESCRIPTIONS

To remain faith-filled and to retain our joy in unpleasant situations, we should strive to find pleasure where we can. I talk to women all the time whose husbands have abandoned them. They want to know what they should do while they work and pray for reconciliation.

They frequently express shock when I stress the importance of learning how to enjoy life as a single mom. "Find new pleasures," I tell them. "Rediscover laughter. Work on appropriate same-sex relationships. The best way to attract a man isn't by nagging him to return or trying to use your children to make him feel guilty; it's by building a life that he wants to rejoin."

If your children are rebelling, if you're losing your job, if your church is crumbling, if your health is failing—whatever the situation—find *some* pleasure to cultivate. Work hard to draw from an appropriate well. Some waters will be closed to you, but God never fails to open up others. You may find that worship practices once considered routine will take on a new dimension, an increased richness, as you savor your walk with God. You may even begin to discover the pleasure found "in weaknesses, in insults, in hardships, in persecutions, in difficulties" for Christ's sake (2 Corinthians 12:10).

A *USA Today* article highlighted the struggles of people suffering from chronic illness or other long-term stresses. One woman who recently suffered two family deaths and has a son stationed in a combat zone listens to Celtic and old country music, laughs at *America's Funniest Home Videos*, and invites a cat or two to share her recliner. She says, "Stroking their fur and listening to them purr always lifts my spirits."[12]

As you walk your own difficult road, keep in mind that even heroes need to eat. Even heroes need to laugh. Even heroes eventually need to rest. If God has called you to heroic faith, do what you must to build yourself up so that God can keep pouring you out. There's nothing wrong with asking him to bring a little God-honoring pleasure your way.

Pure Pleasure, 207–8

CREATION CALLS US TO GOD

Christians often have attested to the scriptural truth that God is revealed and encountered outdoors. Article 2 of the Reformed tradition's *Belgic Confession* says that God is made known to us "by the creation, preservation, and government of the universe; which is before our eyes as a most elegant book, wherein all creatures great and small, are as so many characters leading us to see clearly the invisible things of God."

The famous preacher Charles Haddon Spurgeon put it this way:

Surely, everything that comes from the hand of such a Master-artist as God has something in it of himself! There are lovely spots on this fair globe which ought to make even a blasphemer devout. I have said, among the mountains, "He who sees no God here is mad." There are things that God has made which overwhelm with a sense of his omnipotence: how can men see them, and doubt the existence of the Deity?

One of the great hymns of the faith, "How Great Thou Art," celebrates the way creation calls us to God:

> *When through the woods, and forest glades I wander,*
> *I hear the birds sing sweetly in the trees;*
> *When I look down from lofty mountain grandeur*
> *And hear the brook and feel the gentle breeze;*
> *Then sings my soul, my Savior God, to thee,*
> *How great thou art! How great thou art!*

The existence, wonder, and worthiness of God are broadcast daily for all to see if we will simply step outside and open our hearts to the truth. More than just the beauty of God is revealed outside, however. His awful and fearful terror is revealed as well. It's no surprise, then, that the same rain that nourishes the ground can disintegrate a coastline. The same wind that keeps us cool in the summer can send our houses sailing during a spring tornado.

As the temperature warms up, let's get outside and allow creation to remind us of God's beauty, power, and judgment.

Sacred Pathways, 48–49

A WARM BLANKET FOR COLD HEARTS

On one occasion I faced burnout through a schedule that included a six-week stretch of five out-of-town trips, two of them cross-country. Recognizing my precarious condition, I left my office, walking through Two Chimneys Park in Falls Church, Virginia, then out through an established neighborhood with mature trees, and finally circling Cherry Hill Park. The chill of the cold day helped me wake up. Leaves crunched under my feet, and the trees cast their steadiness into my soul. The distant sun smiled some perspective into my troubled mind.

I poured out my heart to God. "I just can't do this," I said. "It's too much to try to balance work, my family, my writing, my speaking schedule, and everything else. I'm ready to quit." Yet after praying and being outside, I could face a few more hours in the office. And within days, God providentially canceled two upcoming engagements, mercifully overcoming my lack of discretion.

We don't always need a change. Sometimes we just need a rest, and there is no better place to rest our bodies and our souls than outside.

In Psalm 23, David credits God with restoring his soul, but clearly, the pastoral setting plays a role. The outdoors cannot replace fellowship with God, but God can use it in powerful ways. Susan Power Bratton, a Christian writer and naturalist, writes:

> Experiencing the beauty and peace of God in nature is not a substitute for direct interaction with the regenerative powers of the Creator, but ... the mending and binding so necessary to heal our stress-filled lives may flow through creation. For the spiritually oppressed or the socially injured, a pleasing or quiet natural environment can help provide spiritual release. Resting by a clear, free-running river or sitting on a sunny slope in blooming desert grassland can bring peace and joy into very clouded souls.[13]

Creation can be the warm blanket that God uses to wrap our cold hearts. If you feel exhausted, take some time today to get outside and get renewed.

Sacred Pathways, 49–50

NO EXPLANATION REQUIRED

One of the first books I helped write (*Out of the Silence*) told the story of Duane Miller, whom God miraculously healed of a throat ailment.[14] *Focus on the Family* featured Duane's story; the tape that recounts his healing makes the hair rise on the back of your neck. It truly is a miraculous tale.

Yet Duane is the first to admit his astonishment that a young father, present in the same church on the same morning on which Duane got healed, died just a couple weeks later of a brain tumor. Duane's kids were adults; this young man's children were still very young and presumably needed him even more than Duane's kids needed him. Duane's ailment debilitated him but didn't threaten his life; this man battled a terminal disease.

Why did God miraculously heal Duane and allow a man in the very same room, just three rows away, to die from his sickness? Duane would never suggest that his own healing resulted from faith or obedience. Rather, it happened by God's providential choice, offered without explanation or apology.

Here is where the Lord seems to beckon us to what the ancients called the spiritual discipline of surrender. Paganism seeks to manipulate divine forces to serve the human will: Do the right thing, and you obligate God to respond in a certain way. Authentic Christianity looks at this quite differently. In sending his Son, God has already done the right thing, and now we are obligated to respond in a certain way.

At various points we will feel disappointed or frustrated with God, even angry with him—but what matters is that we make Joshua's famous declaration our own: "As for me and my household, we will serve the LORD" (Joshua 24:15).

- We may face unemployment, but we will serve the Lord.
- We may go to three funerals in one year, but we will serve the Lord.
- We may have two of our three children rebel, but we will serve the Lord.

In other words, it is not appropriate to demand an explanation from God; we are rather to be focused on receiving our direction from God. In the midst of this disappointment, this tragedy, this trial—what is God asking of you today?

Sacred Parenting, 111–12

THAT HUNTED AND HATED MAN

Imagine someone who ridicules everything you hold dear, who you know will one day kill you, who exists only to challenge everything you live for. This man is utterly loathsome, the kind of person who sets your teeth on edge.

Now imagine you were accused of being this person.

Jesus came to earth to win back lost men and women from the clutches of Satan — the one who laid claim to this world with a vengeance. Jesus willingly bled and died in order to overthrow his demonic foe. Imagine, then, how hideous, how utterly shocking, it must have been when Jesus heard the Pharisees say, "It is by the prince of demons that he drives out demons" (Matthew 9:34). There is no worse accusation to make against our Lord than to suggest that he was in league with his mortal enemy.

When you love someone to the point of adoration, when your heart feels an almost physical ache at the mere mention of his name, when you love to sing worship songs to him and tears come to your eyes when you consider how much he means to you, then it can be difficult to imagine him as hunted and hated — but that's exactly what Jesus was throughout his life, beginning with his birth and extending to the time of his death.

Jesus accepted this hatred as inevitable, given his message: "The world ... hates me because I testify that what it does is evil" (John 7:7). In fact, Jesus had to face opposition even from the place where it hurt the most: his own family. Just as his public ministry got under way, some of his brothers accused him of being "out of his mind" (Mark 3:21). Members of the synagogue thought so little of Jesus' sermonizing that they attempted to throw him off the top of a cliff (see Luke 4:29 – 30).

Jesus accepted all of this with a surrendered heart.

When your motives are questioned; when someone attacks your integrity; when people speak false words against you, take comfort in the fact that you are walking in fellowship with the holy Son of God, indeed, the very personification of love, who nevertheless became a hunted and hated man.

Authentic Faith, 82–83

SPLASHES OF GLORY OR SHOWERS OF SIN?

Walking through Narita Airport in Tokyo, Japan, my daughter spoke one of her classic "Allison" phrases: "I feel like such an outsider," she said.

I laughed and replied, "That's because you are."

Our trip eventually took us to Singapore, an impressive, cosmopolitan country. As we strolled past the Clarke Quay, I began praying for the people, including those who would hear me speak in a few days.

My mind wandered to an article I had read about sexual tourism in Thailand in which young women and men are often lured into the country with promises of false jobs and then virtually imprisoned and forced to sell themselves into sexual service for tourists. As an outsider in Singapore, I thought of what I was bringing to the country: truth, I hoped; encouragement; a manifestation of the risen Christ; a passion for God. All of these things would be good gifts, precious splashes of glory that I prayed God would spread through me.

But a war also rages within me. Like the "sexual tourists" in Thailand, I could bring something much different: my lust, pride, selfishness. The thought brought me up short. I really *can* bring lust into a country with me, as well as greed, arrogance, prejudice, and condescension.

Or I can bring Christ.

Every time you enter a room, you bring something with you. If you allow your thoughts to roam into impure places, you are both creating and bringing corruption into your environment. When you walk down a sidewalk or stroll through the marketplace, are you bringing with you impurity, or the Spirit of Christ? When you walk into your house following a long day at work, do you bring selfishness, negativity, harshness, condemnation — or the meekness and gentleness of Christ? When you go to church on Sunday, what marks your manner? Christ, or some spiritual failing? Do you bring encouragement or criticism, judgment or grace?

It was a stunning thought to realize that wherever I go, I can choose to spread splashes of glory or showers of sin. What do I want to leave behind?

Holy Available, 121–22

May 22

THE SPIRITUAL GYM

Ever notice how God uses the most ordinary moments of life to bring his word to life?

After reading Ephesians 4:2 ("Be completely humble and gentle, be patient, bearing with one another in love") one day, I jumped into my car.

There's something about getting behind a steering wheel that brings out the worst in me—especially when I'm tired. Eager to return home after a long trip, I was driving in the left lane. A car pulled in front of me and dropped its speed to about five miles *below* the speed limit. I clicked off the cruise control.

A few minutes later, the car signaled its intention to slip back into the middle lane. I waited until it started to change lanes and then resumed my cruise control. My car jumped forward—but the lead vehicle took about forty-five seconds to move over. I came up on the car's rear end and had to click off my cruise control again to avoid a collision.

A policeman observed this encounter and pulled me over. I wasn't speeding, but he thought I'd been riding this guy for a long time to force him over. So I got a ticket—my first in almost two decades. It served me right. I was thinking only of myself and my desire to get home, which made me far from being "completely humble." And even if the guy was taking a ridiculous amount of time to get in a new lane, I wasn't driving "gently."

Five days later, I got another ticket for driving almost forty in a twenty-five-miles-per-hour zone (I thought it was thirty-five). Now I had two tickets in less than a week. Three weeks later, I cut someone off in a parking lot. The driver waved at me—not a frustrated wave, but a polite and friendly one. And then I saw his face.

It was my pastor.

These three events helped shake me out of my complacency. If God urges us to be "completely humble and gentle," there's no room for aggressive driving —or aggressive board meeting tactics or harsh treatment of the kid who's refereeing your child's soccer game. "Completely," I've learned, means "completely." This isn't a truth best carved out while sitting in a church sanctuary; it has to be dug out of the ordinary moments of life, while watching an athletic event, driving through a parking lot, or standing in line at the post office. These common grounds can become our spiritual gymnasium.

Holy Available, 190–92

FROM MIND TO HEART

A young man, eager to be a writer, asked if we could meet. I prayed before our appointment, sensing that God was moving in this man's life. I asked God to help me to be his conduit.

We talked for almost two hours. As I walked away and looked at my watch, my selfish natural heart said, "I can't spend two hours in the middle of the day like this. I've got tons of work to do!" But immediately, God challenged me with his heart: "This young man has a future. You're investing in my kingdom, and that is a wise use of your time. I put you in this place so that you could provide some inspiration and a listening ear."

Perhaps because I'm so selfish, I don't even try to pretend that my own heart cares about people as much as I should. But God has a way, when I allow him, to give me a new passion, a real empathy, a genuine concern.

We gain God's heart by gaining God's mind. Marriage is a great exercise for building on this foundation. If someone married one of my daughters but did nothing except complain about her, my father's heart would shout, "Everything you say may be true, but have you noticed *this* about her? And *that*? And how she excels in this area as well as that area?"

If you feel disillusioned in your marriage, go to your heavenly Father-in-law and let him fill your mind with what you aren't seeing. You may have lost your heart for your spouse, but God hasn't lost his heart for his child. You may have lost your heart for your congregation or your business partner or a sibling or a city, but God, the great Father of all, remains passionate about their welfare.

The quickest way for me to gain God's heart is to gain God's thoughts. God's perspective breeds God's passion. I suggest that you spend time in Bible study and listening prayer, allowing God to transform you so that he can conform your heart to his. As you put down this book, listen to God. Let him speak to you and fill your mind with his thoughts and his perspective.

Holy Available, 152–53

THE DISCIPLINE OF OBEDIENCE

I had a close friend in college who drove at the (at that time) speed limit of fifty-five miles per hour all the way from Bellingham to south of Seattle, a two- to three-hour drive. When we were jogging together once through the middle of town, I suddenly noticed that I was alone. When I looked back, he was waiting for the traffic light to turn. There was no car in sight, but if the sign said, "Wait," my friend was going to wait.

I've since lost track of my friend, so I have no idea if he has experienced the thrill of hurtling down a freeway at sixty-two miles per hour. Certainly, strict obedience can become legalistic; but on the other hand, I wonder if some of us haven't gone too far the other way. We have forgotten the discipline of obedience.

Obedience is an important part of godly living because it assaults our human pride and invites us to live in humility. While laypeople are not likely to enter into the strict obedience of a master/disciple relationship lived out in monastic times, we can still learn the blessing of obedience by obeying government authorities and employers; children can learn by obeying their parents.

I've been in a position of management in past years, and I've talked with other managers about the casualness with which people cross accepted lines of authority. One manager told me that a temp worker who hoped to secure full-time, permanent employment blew his chances when he told the manager he didn't like the way a decision was handled and expected the manager to justify his decision.

"I almost laughed," the manager said, "and managed to stifle the words I wanted to say: 'Who do you think cares about your opinion here? You're a temp!'"

This may sound harsh, but there's a truth underneath it. It can be hard to submit and accept someone else's leadership. But Peter urges young men to "be submissive to those who are older" (1 Peter 5:5), and all of us to "clothe ourselves with humility."

The spirit of rebellion is a dangerous thing. Let's point our hearts toward proper respect.

Sacred Pathways, 118–19

A NOBLE EPITAPH

The book of Esther pictures Mordecai as a man who cared deeply about others. We find our first picture of him in Esther 2:7, where we learn that he raised Esther as his adopted daughter after her parents died. After royal servants took Esther into the palace, Mordecai remained intimately involved in her welfare (2:11). A less-concerned man might simply have washed his hands of her, but not Mordecai.

Mordecai also looked after the king. When he overheard two royal servants plotting against the king, he reported what he heard, thus saving the king from harm. Later he incurred the wrath of a powerful nobleman, Haman, when he refused to bow down in Haman's presence. When Haman retaliated by obtaining permission to wipe out the Jews, Mordecai "tore his clothes, put on sackcloth and ashes, and went out into the city, wailing loudly and bitterly" (4:1). By undergoing such humiliation, Mordecai communicated the urgency of Israel's danger to Esther. When Esther balked at the only route of escape, Mordecai stood firm. "Do not think that because you are in the king's house you alone of all the Jews will escape ... And who knows but that you have come to royal position for such a time as this?" (4:13 – 14).

It has always amazed me how true caregivers — shepherds — can become lions when necessary. Through Mordecai's insistence, God's providence provided a way for Israel to defend itself. After the Jewish victory, Mordecai established a yearly festival to celebrate God's protection and intervention, decreeing that the Israelites celebrate by giving gifts to the poor.

At all points, Mordecai looked after others: first an orphan, then a king, then a nation, then the poor. His epitaph is fitting: "Mordecai the Jew was second in rank to King Xerxes, preeminent among the Jews, and held in high esteem by his many fellow Jews, because he worked for the good of his people and spoke up for the welfare of all the Jews" (10:3). Who could hope for a more notable epitaph?

What would yours say if you were to die today?

Sacred Pathways, 147 – 49

CHOOSE UNITY

Unresolved disputes in marriage can greatly affect one's prayer life. While Jesus didn't specifically address marriage in the following statement, clearly, his counsel applies to marriage. "If you are offering your gift at the altar and there remember that your brother has something against you," he said, "leave your gift there in front of the altar. First go and be reconciled to your brother; then come and offer your gift" (Matthew 5:23–24).

Imagine someone approaching God in prayer. As she kneels, she remembers that things aren't right between her and somebody else. Before she continues praying, she should direct her energies on reconciling with that other person. Sometimes, that other person is a spouse.

God hates dissension (see Proverbs 6:19) and treasures unity (see Psalm 133:1). Marriage can force us to become stronger people, because if we want to maintain a strong prayer life, we must learn how to forgive and become expert reconcilers. Friction inevitably develops. Anger surely heats up. So we must learn to deal with conflict as mature Christians—or risk blowing off our prayer life.

Marriage virtually forces us into the intense act of reconciliation. It's easy to get along with people if you never get close to them. I could undoubtedly allow a certain immaturity to remain in my life as a single man, choosing not to deal with my selfishness and judgmental spirit; I have, in fact, done that on a number of occasions. While I'm not proud of this, I can think of one or two people with whom it has been very difficult for me to get along. I've chosen to handle this by not going deeper in a relationship with them. I'm not obligated to be in a relationship with everybody, so there's nothing inherently wrong with simply "sidestepping" people who really raise your blood pressure.

That option is obliterated in marriage. My wife and I are going to disagree about some things, and I am unquestionably obligated to maintain my intimacy with her. If you want an unimpeded prayer life, then Jesus makes it clear that you must choose unity. Dissension is a major prayer killer.

Sacred Marriage, 81–82

GENERATIONAL SINS

Psychologists and counselors today are discovering that sins tend to get handed down generationally. One account by Patrick Carnes, a counselor who specializes in sexual addiction, shocked me. One of Dr. Carnes's patients felt deeply ashamed of his exhibitionist compulsion and entered therapy. With great embarrassment and shame, he assumed that only he struggled with this problem —until a little detective work disclosed that his father, two uncles, and two cousins were also exhibitionists.

Dr. Carnes has found that, among his patients, "within the family, addictions would be like overlays whose reinforcing shadows simply deepened the patterns of family pathology."[15]

A woman and man fighting their own personal temptations do not fight merely for themselves; they man the front lines in a generational war against evil. When we fall into sin, we open a gap that spiritually exposes our children and grandchildren. While God's provision in Jesus Christ means we can never use "generational influence" to excuse our sin, at the same time it makes no sense to deny our family tendencies. As Dr. Carnes explains, "For the addict, part of therapy is to discover the role of the previous generation in the addiction."[16]

What does this mean to me as a parent? Sinning as a father is worse than sinning as a son, in that when I sin as a father, I risk perpetuating an evil for generations. It may take twenty or thirty years for our spiritual failures to show up in the lives of our descendants—but we can surely leave an easier or harder road for them to follow. If this doesn't motivate us to take our own spiritual formation more seriously, I don't know what will.

If you struggle with a tendency toward sin that you know has run in your family for generations, why not seek help now? Why not determine before God that you will break this chain? Remember that God assures us his "divine power has given us everything we need for life and godliness through our knowledge of him who called us by his own glory and goodness" (2 Peter 1:3).

And singles, take special note: the longer you accept compromise, the more difficult it will be to leave a life of compromise. Deal with your sin *now*, before you become parents; in doing so, you are fighting for a generation yet to be born.

Sacred Parenting, 174–75

THE VICE OF THE VIRTUOUS

We hear much today about the *message* of Christianity—a crucial discussion, to be sure. We also hear a great deal about the *methods* of our faith—how to witness, how to pray, how to handle finances, and so forth. But an emphasis on the *manner* of our faith often gets lost—how believing in God changes the way we act and molds our dispositions.

Henry Drummond, author of the nineteenth-century classic *The Greatest Thing in the World*, warns against a bad disposition, writing that "ill temper" is "the vice of the virtuous."[17] Sadly, an ill manner often isn't considered a serious failing. On the contrary, we're quick to excuse ourselves in a way we would never excuse other sins. We say, "I was overly tired and stressed, that's all." And yet, would we excuse getting drunk in front of our children simply because we were under a lot of stress?

So how do we deal with our ill temper? The best antidote is *humility*.

When we remember how much God has forgiven us, remaining sensitive to how mercifully he has treated us and giving thanks for his grace, we feel compelled to forgive and be merciful and gracious to others. Drummond counsels that "souls are made sweet not by taking the acid fluids out, but by putting something in—a great Love, a new Spirit, the Spirit of Christ. Christ, the Spirit of Christ, interpenetrating ours, sweetens, purifies, transforms all."[18] In other words, we become yielded worshipers, regularly putting ourselves before the presence of God, allowing his Spirit to penetrate our hearts and transform our manner from the inside out.

Linger in your heavenly Father's presence, asking him to fill you with the sweet attitudes of Christ. You've taught your kids the gospel message—good for you! You've showed them how to pray and urged them to give generously out of their allowance—excellent! Now model the *manner* of their faith. Demonstrate the loveliness of God's disposition toward us so they'll fall in love, not just with what God has said and done, but with *who he is*.

Devotions for Sacred Parenting, 74–76

THE OBLIGATION OF RESPECT

Why is it that comparatively few Christians seem to think of giving respect as a command or a spiritual discipline? We obsess over being respected, but rarely consider our own obligation to respect others.

All of us have a visceral desire to be respected. When this desire goes unmet, we tend to lapse into self-defeating responses—that is, we tear down our spouse in a desperate attempt to convince ourselves that his or her lack of respect is meaningless. Spiritually, this becomes a vicious and debilitating cycle, extremely difficult to break.

God has a solution that, if adopted, will revolutionize our relationships.

While many people fight to receive respect, Christian marriage calls us to focus on giving respect. God calls us to honor someone, even when we know only too well his or her deepest flaws. We are called to stretch ourselves, to find out how we can learn to respect this person with whom we've become so familiar. In this exploration, the Lord urges to "have contempt for contempt."

A failure to show respect is a sign of spiritual immaturity more than it is an inevitable pathway of marriage. Consider Paul and the members of the Corinthian church. Even though he addressed a congregation full of quarrelers (1 Corinthians 1:11), unlearned and simple people (1:26), "worldly" infants (3:1–3), arrogant egocentrics (4:18), a man sleeping with his stepmother (5:1), greedy men suing fellow believers (6:1), and childish thinkers (14:20), still he honored them by saying, "I always thank God for you ..." (1:4).

He knew their faults, yet he continued to thank God for them. Why? The key is found in the second half of verse 4: "I always thank God for you *because of his grace given you in Christ Jesus*" (emphasis added). We can be thankful for our fellow sinners when we spend more time looking for evidences of grace than we do in finding fault. Giving appropriate respect is an obligation, not a favor; it is an act of maturity, birthed in a profound understanding of God's good grace.

Sacred Marriage, 54–55

ACTIVE HONOR

My family once went through the National Gallery of Art, looking at some original Rembrandts. One of our children reached out to touch a painting. My wife let loose with a harsh whisper and grabbed our child's hand. "This is a *Rembrandt!*" she hissed under the guard's glare. "You can't touch these!"

Rembrandts certainly are valuable—but God himself created my wife! How dare I dishonor her? In fact, shouldn't it even give me pause before I reach out to touch her? She is the Creator's daughter, after all.

The fact that my wife is made in the image of God calls me to a far more noble response than simply refraining from exhibiting a condescending attitude toward her. While it is wildly inappropriate for me to look down on Lisa because she's a woman, her creation in the image of God really calls me to actively and enthusiastically honor her.

Honoring our spouse calls us to adopt attitudes and actions that go far beyond merely saying that we won't dishonor him or her. As Betsy and Gary Ricucci point out, "Honor isn't passive, it's active. We honor our wives by demonstrating our esteem and respect: complimenting them in public; affirming their gifts, abilities, and accomplishments; and declaring our appreciation for all they do. Honor not expressed is not honor."[19]

I've found that the more I honor my wife in particular, the more I honor other women in general. The reverse is also true. The glib statement "Oh, that's just women for you" betrays a serious spiritual disease. "*Just* women" are made in the image of God. Such a comment comes dangerously close to maligning the Creator who made women just the way they are. A good marriage, carried by appropriate honor and respect, increases a man's respect for women in general. Belittling your wife or withholding honor from her is the doorway to becoming a misogynist.

Giving respect to others brings light and life into our lives. It leads us in the end to respect the God who created all of us and shapes us as he sees fit. It is an essential discipline, and marriage provides daily opportunities for us to grow in this area.

Sacred Marriage, 62–63

GAIN A NEW UNDERSTANDING

My wife and I entered a new journey in our marriage when I became self-employed. To save on overhead, we decided that I would work out of our home. The only problem was that, at the time, we lived in a town house. With three children.

In other words, I'd really be working out of our *bedroom*.

When other married couples found out what we were doing, they frequently expressed amazement. "And you still *like* each other?" they would ask.

In fact, working at home did wonders for our marriage. For the first time, I could see for myself what it was like to spend an entire day being Lisa. What makes her life difficult isn't an occasional forty-eight-hour stretch—it's the cumulative, never-ending, day in, day out responsibility of raising and teaching kids, while also cleaning the house, planning meals, and preparing for her own Bible study. And then, when your husband comes home, you're supposed to have enough energy left over to act like a wife.

On the other hand, my wife saw what it was like for me to sit in front of a computer all day long. Some days I got tired. Other days I was sick. Sometimes the beautiful weather outside called to me, but always I stayed in my chair and worked. She saw my determination and discipline. And she had a front-row seat from which to witness the pressure of meeting deadlines or accepting tough assignments.

Both of us now understand in a much clearer way the challenges facing each of us. We're not married in a carefree garden of Eden. This new understanding has ushered in a stronger empathy for each other.

You don't have to work out of your own home to experience such empathy. As a spiritual exercise, discover what your spouse's day is really like. Draw them out—what is the most difficult part of your day? When do you feel like just giving up? Are parts of your day monotonous? Is there something you constantly fear? Take time to do an inventory of your spouse's difficulties rather than shortcomings.

Sacred Marriage, 65–66

JUNE

The coming of summer often brings opportunities to slow down, take stock, reconnect with family, and refocus on God. Let's allow his warmth to seep into our souls, refresh our spirits, and renew our passion.

THE HEALING EFFECTS OF A GOOD BARBECUE

For some Christians, reserving even five hours a week for something they truly enjoy—be it painting, gardening, or watching a movie—seems selfish, weak, and shameful. If they do finally give in, they may battle with regret and shame instead of finding rest and relaxation in the activity. Instead of feeling renewed, these poor Christians just feel guilty.

If pleasure becomes painful, if it gets so surrounded by guilt and regret that you can't enjoy it, then you may be under Satan's guns. It's time to take some concerted action. Pleasure enjoyed and cherished is worth fighting for.

If you aren't reserving five hours a week for restorative pleasure, then you are likely running on deprivation and are susceptible to any number of spiritual ills. Five hours is an arbitrary number—I'm no therapist—but it seems a reasonable weekly portion. If anything, five hours a week is probably understating our need. One of the ways we can fight sin is to build lives of holy pleasure.

In a difficult life episode, author Shauna Niequist discovered the "healing effects of a barbecue."[1] She got lifted out of discouragement by getting together with close friends and eating great food.

For you, it may be the healing effects of a solitary round of golf, a long afternoon spent reading a novel straight through, or a morning in the garden. Don't despise these practical helps.

Remember the biblical story of Naaman, commander of the army of the king of Aram? He sought out Elisha, hoping to be cured of his leprosy, and felt deeply offended when Elisha told him to dip into the Jordan River seven times. Fortunately, Naaman had a wise servant, who said, "My father, if the prophet had told you to do some great thing, would you not have done it? How much more, then, when he tells you, 'Wash and be cleansed'!" (2 Kings 5:13).

You may want a mystical cure for your ailing soul when what you really need is a good barbecue.

Pure Pleasure, 91–92

THE REAL SIN OF SODOM

Repeatedly the Bible challenges us to love God by caring for others. Jesus emphasized compassion in so many of his teachings that it's no surprise his followers also urge us to love God this way.

John tells us that "we know that we have passed from death to life, because we love our brothers" (1 John 3:14). In fact, lack of love for others calls into question whether we love God at all: "If anyone has material possessions and sees his brother in need but has no pity on him, how can the love of God be in him?" (1 John 3:17).

The writer of Hebrews equates loving others with loving God: "God is not unjust; he will not forget your work and the love you have shown him as you helped his people and continue to help them" (6:10). The breadth of this teaching and the fact that so many writers of the New Testament repeat it leave us with no doubt as to the importance of loving God by loving those he has made. Though some people excel in this avenue of loving God, it should be a part of every Christian's life.

One verse in particular has greatly challenged me. The city of Sodom is often alluded to as *the* wicked city, but listen to Ezekiel declare the city's guilt: "Now this was the sin of your sister Sodom: She and her daughters were arrogant, overfed and unconcerned; they did not help the poor and needy" (16:49).

I definitely have plenty of pride in my life. On a worldwide scale, I am certainly overfed. I also have to own up to an attitude of unconcern. The only thing keeping me from the sin of Sodom — the biblical picture of wickedness at its basest form — is whether I "help the poor and needy."

We like to define holiness by avoiding transgression, but in God's book, the sin of omission (not doing what we should do) ranks right up there with the sin of commission (doing something we shouldn't do). And love says, "Take action!"

Sacred Pathways, 152–53

June 3

GOD'S SON, GOD'S DAUGHTER

One day in prayer, I sensed God exhorting me that Lisa wasn't just my wife; she's also his daughter — and I was to treat her accordingly.

The force of this insight grew once I had kids of my own. If you want to get on my good side, just be good to one of my kids. Conversely, if you really want to make me angry, pick on my kids. You'll fire up my righteous anger faster than anything you could possibly do to me.

So when I realized I am married to *God's daughter* — and that you, women, are married to *God's son* — everything about how I view marriage changed overnight. It was no longer about just me and one other person; it was very much a relationship with a passionately interested third partner. We rightly contemplate the Fatherhood of God, a wonderful and true doctrine. But if you want to change your marriage, spend time thinking about God as Father-*in-Law*. Because he is!

When I fail to respect my wife or mistreat her in any way, I am courting trouble with the heavenly Father, who feels passionately about my spouse's welfare. Most of us fail to grasp just how fully God loves the person we married.

As the father of three children, I fervently pray that each one of my children will marry a spouse who will love them generously, respect them, and enjoy them. I realize that each of my children have certain quirks or limitations that might test a future spouse, but I pray that their spouses will be kind in these areas rather than use them to belittle my children or make them feel smaller. I hope with all my heart that they'll find a partner who will encourage them with a gracious spirit. In the same way, God is fully aware of our spouse's limitations — and he is just as eager for us to be kind and generous with these faults as we are for our kids' future spouses to be kind to them.

Think about how you treated your husband or wife this past week. Is that how you want your son or daughter to be treated by their spouse? Never forget: you didn't just marry a man or a woman; you married God's son or God's daughter.

Treat him, treat her, accordingly.

Devotions for a Sacred Marriage, 21–22

EMPTY ACCOMPLISHMENTS

Bill McCartney became famous in Christian circles during the early 1990s. He was a highly successful college football coach who was also running the hottest ministry of the decade, Promise Keepers. Yet during this time, his wife was lonely and hurting. She described herself in "an emotional deep freeze," her depression becoming so great that she lost eighty pounds.[2] McCartney was too preoccupied to take notice. As McCartney's star rose, his wife Lyndi said something truly gripping: "I just felt like I was getting smaller and smaller and smaller."

In his book *Sold Out*, McCartney reflects, "It may sound unbelievable, but while Promise Keepers was spiritually inspiring to my core, my hard-charging approach to the ministry was distracting me from being, in the truest sense, a promise keeper to my own family." To McCartney's credit, once he realized what was happening, he took the drastic step of retiring as a football coach—an incredible sacrifice that his wife took to heart—and the McCartneys were able to put their marriage back together.

Making someone else feel smaller so that we can feel larger completely rejects the Christian virtues of humility, sacrifice, and service. Jesus often left the crowd to minister to the individual, while we rationalize leaving the individual—particularly our spouse—to curry favor with the crowd. Today, the evangelical world tends to value accomplishers, people who get things done. The danger is that spouses often pay the biggest price for some of these accomplishments, and true spirituality can easily suffer.

Faithful participation in God's kingdom invites and encourages others as we serve; it doesn't diminish them. Biblical truth finds its basis in community and in serving the community. If a man or woman is willing to ignore or to sacrifice a spouse in pursuit of their agenda, he or she almost inevitably will be unrelentingly ambitious toward others as well. And this does not bode well for mutual kingdom service.

God doesn't need to kill a marriage in order to give birth to a ministry. In a healthy situation, any ministry God calls you to will build your marriage rather than threaten it. Beware of arrogant religious ambition!

Sacred Marriage, 76–77

THE HEART OF UNFORGIVENESS

At the heart of unforgiveness lies obstinacy—a stubbornness that refuses to let up, that marches relentlessly toward mutual destruction: "An offended brother is more unyielding than a fortified city, and disputes are like the barred gates of a citadel" (Proverbs 18:19).

By contrast, the picture of wisdom and refinement, biblically speaking, is learning to overcome the baser part of our nature that gets so easily offended and that demands immediate revenge: "A man's wisdom gives him patience; it is to his glory to overlook an offense" (Proverbs 19:11).

This is a crucial quality in the workplace. Inevitably people let us down, sin against us, and maybe even deliberately malign us. If we spend our energy trying to get back at and ruin the other person, we debase ourselves; even worse, we become like the very person we despise. It is a glorious thing to respond to sin with forgiveness, grace, and mercy. Any simpleton can respond with hatred; only one who possesses a truly authentic faith will habitually respond with gentleness, understanding, and forgiveness. When you can respond that way, you know that Jesus is operating within you.

Being unwilling to forgive means that we hold everyone around us to a standard of perfection—something that we ourselves will never achieve. In wisdom, we learn to forgive because we know that we, too, have sinned—often in the same way that others have sinned against us: "Do not pay attention to every word people say, or you may hear your servant cursing you—for you know in your heart that many times you yourself have cursed others" (Ecclesiastes 7:21–22).

I hate it when others gossip about me; it hurts when I hear that someone has ridiculed me or put what I said in a bad light. But if I'm honest, I know I've done the same thing to others. By God's grace, we can respond to such revelations by trying to become more sensitive to our own tendency toward this sin rather than continuing to gossip about the one who maligned us. We do not need to participate in mutual spiritual destruction.

Authentic Faith, 129–30

A PROUD MOMENT

I revel in watching my kids laugh and enjoy themselves, but I feel even prouder when I see them act selflessly and with great courage.

This feeling of pride came on my wife and me recently when we went out to dinner with our younger daughter, Kelsey. Kelsey had just turned sixteen. She's an extrovert with a capital *C* and provides an enormous amount of fun. For years, another family begged us to let Kelsey go on vacation with them because, in their words, "she supplies all the entertainment."

As our little girl started becoming a young woman, she began attracting attention from a number of teenage boys. As a cross-country runner, she's in great shape; even more, she has a marvelously captivating personality and loves God — so it's no surprise that boys would find her company appealing.

I "prayed up" for the dinner, asking God to give me wisdom and the right tone to communicate with Kelsey about this new season in her life; but I felt led by God to begin the dinner by asking Kelsey to speak first. Our daughter opened up a notebook where she had written out her philosophy for relating to the opposite sex. She declared her belief that marriage is primarily about giving glory to God, not about one's personal pleasure. She intends to conduct her relationships accordingly.

I glanced at my wife and saw tears filling her eyes. Then I told our daughter, "This is the most impressive conversation I've ever had with a sixteen-year-old."

The pleasure my wife and I felt in the face of Kelsey's maturity and character far outweighed the pleasure we take in seeing her laugh and have fun. I suspect the same is true of our heavenly Father. He certainly delights in our laughter and play, but he also takes great pleasure in our obedience.

Mirroring God's heart, John wrote, "I have no greater joy than to hear that my children are walking in the truth" (3 John 4). What decisions can we make today to give God this joy?

Pure Pleasure, 44–45

MEETING GOD OUTDOORS

The sun cast crystal rays off the water on a summer day in Birch Bay, just below the Canadian border and about one hundred miles north of Seattle, Washington. The water that day, calm and gentle, lapped at the sides of my kayak. A small baby couldn't have felt more comfortable at her mother's breast.

Steve, a college friend and now a pastor, pulled his kayak close to mine. We stopped paddling and let ourselves be rocked by the small, graceful waves. Then we talked of how life had changed over the past dozen years. We talked of what God was doing in our lives, how we felt challenged and encouraged. We talked about mutual friends. We laughed, and we thanked God. We appreciated each other's company and the world God had given us in which to enjoy it.

As we paddled toward the shore, I marveled at what I had missed growing up. I grew up farther south of the Bay, under the shadow of Mount Rainier. The Pacific Northwest's evergreen forests provide one of the strongest memories of my childhood.

Although I was in the forests a lot, most of the time I was running. My heart hadn't grown to the point where I could enter a forest and think of it as a sacred place of prayer. In our modern age, where we're born in the antiseptic environment of a hospital, taken home to a nursery that consists of sheetrock coated with paint, and driven through the countryside in a metal contraption called a car, our ability to appreciate and meet God in creation is stunted, to say the least.

We need to be spiritually reawakened to fully appreciate the outdoors. Elizabeth Barrett Browning understood this when she wrote the now famous words:

> Earth's crammed with heaven and every common bush afire with God.
> But only he who sees takes off his shoes
> The rest sit round it and pick blackberries.

If you're able to enjoy a summer picnic, or even simply take a walk out to your mailbox, pause for just a moment, open up your heart to God's presence, and see if Browning's words don't prove true.

Sacred Pathways, 51

SACRED SORROW

When you want to keep a vicious dog at bay, do you pelt him with bread? Probably not. So the seventh-century believer John Climacus said, "The man who mourns at one time and then goes in for high living ... on another occasion is like someone who pelts the dog of sensuality with bread."[3] If we fail morally, say a glib, "Oh, I'm sorry," and immediately return to our former pattern of living, we're feeding the sin rather than being redeemed from it—and we're using forgiveness as an aid to continue in our sin rather than as a tool to be delivered from it. When we fail God, a certain season of mourning is entirely appropriate as we look honestly at our actions.

I've followed this practice in my own life and encourage others to do so as well. Too often, we want to rush into experiencing God's joy and forgiveness, yet fail to truly mourn our sins—and mourning can be an effective deterrent to habitual sins.

John Climacus recognizes that we cannot manufacture tears: "Regarding our tears, as in everything else about us, the good and just Judge will certainly make allowances for our natural attributes."[4] Whether you are a "wailer" or tears come out one by one (or not at all) isn't nearly as important as the disposition of our wills—which includes, but is not limited to, our heart and emotions. When John Calvin was asked, "Is weeping requisite in true repentance?" he replied, "Believers often with dry eyes groan before the Lord without hypocrisy, and confess their fault to obtain pardon." He adds, however, that "in more aggravated offences" we must be particularly "stupid and hardened" if our sorrow does not lead to tears.[5]

At times I have sat and cried over how I have failed God, forcing myself to face my despicable actions and my hypocritical behavior. This is not some "spiritually correct" parroting of Paul's "I am the chief of sinners" but the stark realization that I really *am* the chief of sinners. I don't rush for consolation, because mourning has a critical role to play in my life. It does in yours too. When is the last time you truly mourned over your sins?

Authentic Faith, 155–56

WHY HAVE CHILDREN?

If I want to get people smiling during my Sacred Marriage seminars, all I have to do is to ask people why they got married. A lot of us got married for superficial and selfish reasons. Few of us understood the deep commitment and call to service that biblical marriage asks of us.

Sadly, most of us end up having kids for equally superficial reasons. Some single young women tell crisis pregnancy center counselors that they wanted to get pregnant to create someone who would love them. Some men think it's important to "carry on the family name." Other couples have children because little babies "seem so cute." Still others get lost on a narcissist's binge to create another human being who looks just like the two of them combined. A few may even think having a baby will save a lonely marriage.

I have to confess that I felt eager to have kids, in part because I longed to experience a close father-son relationship as well as an intimate father-daughter relationship. I wanted to be a hero to my kids, as my dad was a hero to me. I had a sense that these children would validate me as a man. Yet these motivations, as noble as they may sound, are still narcissistic at root, based on an idealized notion of children and a romanticized view of family life.

Before long I discovered what every parent has discovered: babies come to us as sinners in need of God's grace and as dependent human beings demanding around-the-clock care. We need something more concrete, something more eternal, to see us through the challenges of parenting.

The best reason to have kids is so simple that it may not seem profound: God commands us to have children (Genesis 1:28). Elsewhere in Scripture we learn that he wants us to raise spiritually sensitive children who will serve God and work for the glory of his kingdom. In other words, having kids isn't about *us* —it's about *him*. We are called to bear and raise children for the glory of God.

Sacred Parenting, 15–16

A PROMINENT PLACE IN THE STORY

It is amazing to realize how often the men who surrounded Jesus simply didn't get it, while the women did.

One time a woman poured costly perfume over Jesus' head (Mark 14:3–9). Some disciples said to themselves, "What a waste!" while Jesus thought, "Finally someone really gets who I am."

Jesus also elevated women in his teaching. In Mark 10:11, Jesus astonishes his disciples when he tells them, "Anyone who divorces his wife and marries another woman commits adultery against her." According to rabbinic law, a man could commit adultery against another married *man* by sleeping with that man's wife, and a wife could commit adultery against *her husband* by sleeping with another man; but no provision stipulated how a husband could commit adultery against his wife. Jesus was telling those first-century men, "Your wife has equal value in God's sight. It is possible for you to sin against her every bit as much as it is possible for her to sin against you."

And consider Jesus' death. While one male disciple betrayed our Lord and ten others cowered behind locked doors, several courageous women (and just one male disciple) dared to watch Jesus' final minutes on this earth (Mark 15:40–41). Modern readers may read right over this narrative fact, but in the early history of the church, this was a startling truth and a challenge to any false view of male superiority.

But perhaps the boldest statement came after Jesus' resurrection. According to ancient Pharisaic law, a woman's testimony was inadmissible in a tribunal. Only men could give witness. So when Jesus rose from the dead—the most important event that has ever occurred or ever will occur—who was present to give witness and testimony? Women! Jesus pointedly uses women, whose testimony could not be heard in contemporary courts of law, to proclaim his glorious resurrection.

This elevation of women at all points should astonish us, given the male-oriented culture in which the Bible took shape. Thousands of years before *feminism* had become a word, God repeatedly stood up for women, giving them a prominent place in the story of all stories.

Don't think I am promoting a radical feminist agenda. I believe it is important to affirm differences in gender roles. Men and women aren't the same, but they are equal in God's eyes, and there is a unique glory in both genders.

Christian women owe it to the God who created them—and to themselves, to the husbands who married them, and to any kids they've birthed—to become the women he designed them to be, in all their glory, power, strength, and wisdom.

Sacred Influence, 24–25

DELIVERED FROM SELFISH PREOCCUPATION

Several years ago, I walked unbothered through the halls of my old elementary school. Had I been alone, a police escort may well have ushered me out. Hand in hand with my six-year-old daughter Allison, however, explaining that she wanted to see my old school, I had free rein to roam.

Why? At that moment I was a "nurturing" man — and nurturing men pose no threat.

A man or woman bent toward care and nurture no longer lives for himself or herself; they live for others. This is the spirit of Jesus, who even while being led away to the cross consoled those who mourned on his behalf: "Daughters of Jerusalem, do not weep for me; weep for yourselves and for your children" (Luke 23:28). Even in his darkest moment, Jesus looked after others. His body was bloody, dirty, disfigured, and bruised. Even then, he was busy loving us, sacrificing for us, taking care of us. In his glorious state, the Son was beauty beyond compare; in his incarnation, he was despised, broken, and bruised.

Not once do we read of Jesus asking his disciples for a comb; there isn't a single instance of assistants hovering over him with makeup. Jesus served in a fantastically unpreoccupied and humble way.

The world becomes a far different place when we learn to care about others more than we care about our appearance or making an impression. Being glamorous is all about selfish preoccupation; giving care is all about focusing on others. It is the distinction between narcissism and love.

Parenting leads us to turn a vital bend in the road toward adulthood, toward caring and love and away from narcissism. It helps us explore new truths and gain new respect — men for their wives in particular and for women in general, and women for their own astonishing capabilities and spiritual insight, as well as to alter the things they value most about men. This is why I believe that when a baby suckles at her mother's breasts, more than one is being nursed. The small one receives milk, but both husband and wife receive spiritual insights and life-altering awareness. Indeed, spiritually aware parents nurse their own souls. They will never look at their own body or others' bodies in the same way.

Sacred Parenting, 129–30

June 12

FOLLOW ME

Do our lifestyles leave something our children must overcome, or are we blazing a godly path for them to follow? If children catch some of our strengths and some of our weaknesses, then the process of raising them calls us to get more serious about our own character growth. If we start to veer off course even fifteen degrees, and our kids maintain that direction, and their kids follow them, soon the entire family line will be radically off track.

My esteem for the apostle Paul only grows over time. The deeper I get into his writings, the more the depth of his faith humbles and challenges me, particularly in this issue of leaving an example. Paul has the temerity to tell the Corinthians, "Therefore I urge you to imitate me" (1 Corinthians 4:16). In case they didn't get it, he later repeats himself: "Follow my example, as I follow the example of Christ" (1 Corinthians 11:1). To the Thessalonians, Paul gives essentially the same advice:

> For you yourselves know how you ought to follow our example. We were not idle when we were with you, nor did we eat anyone's food without paying for it. On the contrary, we worked night and day, laboring and toiling so that we would not be a burden to any of you. We did this, not because we do not have the right to such help, *but in order to make ourselves a model for you to follow.* (2 Thessalonians 3:7–9, emphasis added)

And to the Galatians, the great apostle says, "I plead with you, brothers, become like me ..." (Galatians 4:12).

Paul set a plumb line for others to follow. He had to make sure he stayed headed in the right direction, because he told others to model themselves after him.

This is the call of a parent times ten! Even without requesting that our children follow us, they will do so, at least to some degree. What kind of example are we giving them?

Sacred Parenting, 176–77

A CENTRAL PART OF OUR MISSION

While many people assume that "religion" and caring for others go hand in hand, it is only because of Jesus that this is so. He is most responsible among religious leaders for associating love for God with love for others—particularly the downtrodden. Islam was founded in warfare; the morality of Buddhism is based on refraining from evil; and Hindus are concerned with avoiding bad karma and thereby escaping from the wheel of life, death, and rebirth.

Entwining love for God with love for others and adopting a positive morality rather than a negative one were radical messages in Jesus' day—an expansion of Old Testament calls for social mercy. The spread of Christ's message is the main reason that people today assume religion and caring should be interwoven.

One picture in particular reveals the caregiving heart of Jesus. When he saw a crowd of needy people, despite his own weariness, "he had compassion on them and healed their sick." The crowds eventually grew hungry—providing a great excuse, the disciples thought, to get rid of them. But Jesus, full of the caregiver's heart, looked at them and said, "They do not need to go away. You give them something to eat."

I can imagine the disciples' calculations: "If we have to feed this lot, we're talking days before we can eat in peace!" So they pull out the trump card. "We have only five loaves of bread and two fish." And then, in spite of his exhaustion, Jesus exerted himself once more and performed yet another miracle to feed the people—again sacrificing his own needs before sending them away. Jesus had a more important mission to accomplish than anyone in history, and yet he found time to care for the basic needs of a sick, hungry, and unruly crowd.

His example continues to challenge me today. It is easy to ignore the needs of others around us because we have "more important things" to do, but Jesus defines these very needs as a central part of our mission. Following Jesus isn't merely about avoiding sin or being faithful in the spiritual disciplines; it's about learning to truly care.

Sacred Pathways, 149–52

NOT AN OPTION

Wise persons learn to forgive because the Old Testament insists that vengeance belongs to God alone: "Do not say, 'I'll pay you back for this wrong!' Wait for the LORD, and he will deliver you" (Proverbs 20:22; see also Leviticus 19:18; Proverbs 24:29).

The New Testament declares that offering forgiveness to others is a Christian obligation. Paul tells believers in Christ to forgive each other, "just as in Christ God forgave you" (Ephesians 4:32). In fact, mature believers are told to forgive beyond count (see Matthew 18:21–22). Christians must have nothing to do with revenge; on the contrary, they are to care for their enemies rather than seek their harm (see Romans 12:17–21).

The shocking truth about Christianity is Scripture's insistence that forgiveness is not an option but an obligation. Refusing to forgive has serious repercussions. Jesus warned that God will treat us unmercifully if we refuse to forgive those who sin against us (see Matthew 18:35). He even suggests that divine forgiveness is tied to our willingness to forgive others: "And when you stand praying, if you hold anything against anyone, forgive him, so that your Father in heaven may forgive you your sins" (Mark 11:25). Jesus speaks even more forcefully in Matthew 6:14–15: "For if you forgive men when they sin against you, your heavenly Father will also forgive you. But if you do not forgive men their sins, your Father will not forgive your sins."

All of this sounds so unlike the gospel that some theologians spout torrents of words trying to convince us that it doesn't mean what it clearly sounds like it means—namely, if we refuse to forgive, we will not be forgiven. Augustine had no such reticence. About this verse he wrote, "The man whom the thunder of this warning does not awaken is not asleep, but dead; and yet so powerful is that voice, that it can awaken even the dead."[6] Better to awaken from the dead now when there is still time to repent.

Authentic Faith, 130–31

PLUMBING THE WRETCHEDNESS

Howard Hendricks told about a time he had just delivered a sermon and an eager young man came up to him and called him a "great man." On the drive home, Hendricks turned to his wife and said, "*A great man.* How many great men do you know?"

"One fewer than you think," she answered.

When someone receives constant adulation, it is invaluable to have another person come alongside who will see through to the real you. François Fénelon, an eighteenth-century Christian mystic, wrote, "We have not sufficiently plumbed the wretchedness of man in general, nor our own in particular, when we are still surprised at the weakness and corruption of man."[7]

Being married forces me to realize where I fall short; it encourages me to plumb both the wretchedness of man in general and myself in particular. As a spiritual exercise, few things are more profitable than this kind of examination.

The great Anglican writer William Law wrote that humility "is so essential to the right state of our souls that there is no pretending to a reasonable or pious life without it. We may as well think to see without eyes or live without breath as to live in the spirit of religion without the spirit of humility."[8]

And what is humility? Fénelon tells us that it is "a certain honesty, and child-like willingness to acknowledge our faults, to recover from them, and to submit to the advice of experienced people; these will be solid useful virtues, adapted to your sanctification."[9]

We must embrace having our flaws exposed to our partner, and thereby having them exposed to us as well. Sin never seems quite as shocking when only we know it; when we see how it looks or sounds to another, it gets magnified ten times over. The celibate can hide frustration by removing herself from the situation, but the married man or woman has no true refuge. It is hard to hide when you share the same bed!

What is marriage—or relationships in general—teaching you about the depths of your own sin?

Sacred Marriage, 95–96

June 16

FAMILIAR FOOTSTEPS

I was driving home from speaking at a church one Sunday evening, after promising our seven-year-old Kelsey that I'd be home in time to tuck her in bed. As the clock crept past 8:30, I started to get anxious and called Lisa to tell her to keep Kelsey awake.

"She's spending the night at Laura's house," Lisa said.

"But I promised I would tuck her in!" I thought for a second and added, "I have an even better idea. Call Jennie and Tim [Laura's parents] and tell them I'll be there about 9:00. Ask them not to tell Kelsey, though. I want it to be a surprise."

Thirty minutes later, Tim welcomed me into his house and silently pointed toward Laura's bedroom. I walked down the hallway, opened the door, and saw Kelsey's face peeking out of Laura's bed.

"Hi there, Pop-tart!"

Kelsey giggled but didn't look the least bit surprised.

"Did you know I was coming?" I asked.

"No, but I heard your footsteps coming down the hall, so I figured you came here to tuck me in."

How did Kelsey know it was me when she had no reason to expect my arrival? Apparently she had become so familiar with the cadence and rhythm of my steps that she knew them anytime, anywhere, even when they were unexpected.

May we become so familiar with God's footsteps, and may our hearts be so accustomed to the cadence of his approach and the gentle footfall of his shoes, that when he breaks into our lives, we will know it is him, regardless of the environment or where we're sleeping. If we have this kind of relationship with God —if we're this captivated by his love—we won't be caught off guard if we find his footsteps guiding us through difficulty and suffering; we won't feel abandoned if his footsteps take us through persecution. Listening for God's footsteps in even the most difficult circumstances will lead to a fire-tested life and a truly authentic faith. Although some may call it a hard life, I believe it is the richest and most meaningful life possible.

Authentic Faith, 243–44

June 17

IF IT'S NOT SIN ...

After Wendy and Don married, their personal differences started becoming irritants. "I was always in a hurry," Wendy says, "and Don was methodical. I flew by the seat of my pants, and he was so organized. I let things slide, but he has to know every little detail."

Inevitably, these personality differences created moments of tension—little frustrations that crept up at the grocery store, while sitting around at home, or during the basic rituals surrounding dinnertime. In the aftermath of one such moment, Wendy found herself praying, "God, what do you want me to do here? Show me what my response is supposed to be."

The tension had been building and now seemed about to boil over. Wendy felt "really frustrated and angry," but she had learned enough to ask God for his perspective. His insight sent Wendy to her knees. She felt suddenly overcome by peace, and God, in his quiet voice, whispered, "Wendy, if it's not sin, you can't demand that it change."

Wendy realized that she could ask her husband to change, but she couldn't demand that he change or nag the change out of him. If the irritating action or character quality wasn't sin, she'd have to learn to put up with it unless Don decided to change it voluntarily.

Her quiet conversation with God radically changed Wendy's attitude. "Because Don is organized and meticulous and takes his time when I want him to hurry up, that's not sin. Yeah, it can be frustrating shopping with him, but I can't demand that he become like me. Accepting this freed up our relationship, and I stopped being such a nag. After all, it was really *my* problem, not Don's. Once I accepted this, our marriage started to come together and everything became easier. We have our struggles and our moments, but when I hear others talk about their marriages, I think Don and I have an unusually good one."

God's words to Wendy can revolutionize any marriage. We need to realize that the man or woman we're married to is their own person. Some things about him or her might not be to our liking, but if the things that bug us aren't sin, we have no right to demand that they change.

If you've been working on an issue for a long time and it's a matter of annoyance rather than morality, here's my advice: *let it go*. Instead of trying to resolve the differences, find harmony in learning to live with them. Such a response calls us to humility, in which we no longer assume that our way is the only way or even the best way.

"Accept one another, then, just as Christ accepted you, in order to bring praise to God" (Romans 15:7).

Devotions for a Sacred Marriage, 66–67

POWER IN OUR VEINS

Many years ago, our oldest daughter became enthralled with Olympic figure skaters. One night she asked me, "Papa, if you enter the Olympics, you get a gold, silver, or bras, right?"

I was in the middle of a book and eager to return to it, so I decided to overlook her "bronze" faux pas.

"That's right, Allison," I mumbled.

"But little girls can't wear bras, can they?" she asked in a worried voice.

Only then did I understand the problem. My precious daughter feared that she would enter the Olympics, take third place, and receive an award for which she had no use.

"That's right, honey," I said. "Little girls don't need to wear bras." Immediately Allison hiked up her shirt just over her stomach, looked down, and said, "But I'm on my way, right?"

Allison understood that physical development is a natural part of life. Her spiritual development, however, won't happen nearly as naturally or easily. She'll have to *choose* to grow.

And so do we.

Jesus' followers testified to a dynamic inner reality that resulted in outward growth: "Inwardly we are being renewed day by day" (2 Corinthians 4:16). But a conundrum soon presents itself. Read the following verse slowly, as Paul suggests something that at first glance seems quite strange: "To this end I labor, struggling with all *his* energy, which so powerfully works in me" (Colossians 1:29, emphasis added). Paul is laboring, but he is struggling with *God's* energy, not merely his own. Elsewhere he writes, "Continue to work out your salvation with fear and trembling, for it is God who works in you to will and to act according to his good purpose" (Philippians 2:12–13). So which is it? God or us?

These truths complement rather than contradict one another. We must choose to cooperate, giving over our minuscule powers of will and muscle instead of canceling out the working of God's grace in us. The Christian virtues mark the force of God's empowering and transforming work.

Are you actively cooperating with God's work in your life today in such a way that you are reminded of your need for his empowering grace?

The Glorious Pursuit, 38–39

AN INCREDIBLE OFFER

Imagine that one night God wakes you from a dream and offers you the basketball ability of LeBron James. That would be something, wouldn't it? Or imagine being bestowed with the computer or entrepreneurial capabilities of Bill Gates. "You can create the next Microsoft," God says. "Interested?"

Or maybe you're more the cultural type, and your heart would beat faster if God enabled you to sing like Andrea Bocelli, to write like Jane Austen, or to paint like Rembrandt.

We could get lost all day in fantasies such as these, but, in fact, reality for the Christian is much more stunning. Suppose God says, "You can have *my* eternal life in you." The truth of Christianity is that God offers us something infinitely more valuable than all human abilities put together. According to the apostle Paul, we can have "the mind of Christ" (1 Corinthians 2:16).

Think about it for a moment. Somehow, spiritually, as Christians, we have the mind—that is, the knowledge of God and the attitudes of heart—of Jesus, the one who is the Word become flesh. This is an incredible offer! We are talking about a possibility that should take away our breath. We are being told that we can become like the greatest human being who ever lived.

God is telling us that we can forsake the eternally inconsequential pursuits that consume our time, energy, and passion and can adopt a new pursuit, namely, spiritual growth in the character of Christ. It's bold. It's daring. It sounds unachievable—but the Bible promises that it is within our grasp. We *can* become like Christ!

But how?

The apostle Peter tells us that God's "divine power has given us everything we need for life and godliness" (2 Peter 1:3). God, said Peter, gives us everything we need to live—not merely to exist in body, but to *live*! He also has given us everything we need for godliness—in other words, everything we require to experience and become trained in the character of Christ.

This is a pursuit for the ages. Offered this opportunity, how could we ever settle for less?

The Glorious Pursuit, 35–36

PENITENCE

The Christian's spiritual life doesn't begin with hope. It doesn't begin with chastity. It doesn't even begin with obedience. It begins, according to the gospel of Matthew, with penitence.

The first public words of ministry that came out of the mouths of both John the Baptist and Jesus were, "Repent, for the kingdom of heaven is near" (Matthew 3:2; 4:17).

Penitence is being willing to exchange our old view of the things that we thought would give us satisfaction for the things from God that really will give life and health. It involves sorrow for going the wrong way and a willingness to turn toward the right way. It is a change of heart accompanied by a change of mind, perfected by a change of direction — all three changes bending toward the will of God.

Since penitence rights us after our failure to obey God, it is the virtue that keeps us connected to the life-giving fellowship of God. Penitence returns us to humble reliance as it releases in us a spirit of surrender. The people who lack penitence receive the death sentence — sobering, but true — while the people who mourn get saved.

In fact, the first two beatitudes are related to penitence: "Blessed are the poor in spirit, for theirs is the kingdom of heaven. Blessed are those who mourn, for they will be comforted" (Matthew 5:3–4). Not only was penitence God's first word to his people; it provided the entry point for Jesus' first major address in the New Testament.

Penitence keeps us soft toward God and wary toward sin. Since our sin nature is crippled but never fully dies this side of heaven, penitence needs to be a frequent practice. If our prayers are focused solely on petition — begging God to do what we want him to do — we are missing out on a vital, life-giving spiritual practice. Spend time regularly in penitence, asking God to reclaim your heart, to turn you from your sinful inclinations, and to help you exchange your natural foolishness for his excellent wisdom.

The Glorious Pursuit, 172–75

NO TRAITOR FOR A PARENT

Kids desire parents they can be proud of—even in the most extreme situations. While in a Communist prison because of his Christian beliefs, a father named Florescu was tortured with red-hot iron pokers and knives. When the torture didn't break Florescu's spirit, the Communists put starving rats into his cell through a long pipe, which meant that Florescu could never get any sleep. As soon as he started to nod off, he would literally get eaten, so he had to stay awake to defend himself. This went on for fourteen days, but still Florescu refused to reveal the names of other Christians in his fellowship.

Then the Communists brought in Florescu's fourteen-year-old son and whipped the boy in front of his father. As the young boy cried out, the Communists taunted Florescu, telling him they would continue to beat his son until he told them what they wanted to know.

Finally Florescu had had enough. "Alexander," he cried out, "I must say what they want. I can't bear your beating anymore!"

Astonishingly, young Alexander answered with an even more impassioned plea: "Father, don't do me the injustice of having a traitor as a parent. Withstand! If they kill me, I will die with the words, 'Jesus and my fatherland.'"[10]

Florescu never forgot his son's words: "Father, don't do me the injustice of having a traitor as a parent." For Florescu's son, having a father he could feel proud of was even more important than his own life. Maybe that's why Joshua's famous line, "As for me and my household, we will serve the LORD" (Joshua 24:15), begins with *me*. Before my household serves God, I commit myself to serve God. "As for *me* and my household ..."

I don't want a traitor for a son, but, even more, my son doesn't want a traitor for a father. What are we doing that will make our children proud? Do they ever see us acting with courage, conviction, and sacrifice?

Let's love our kids by making them proud to be our children.

Devotions for Sacred Parenting, 44–45

AN OLD PATH TO A NEW LIFE

Our ancient Christian forebears understood how to grow spiritually by nurturing the Christian virtues. John Climacus, who wrote a fifth-century classic of the Christian faith titled *The Ladder of Divine Ascent*, assures us that "a [Christian] is shaped by virtues in the way that others are shaped by pleasures."[11]

If you approach the virtues as nothing more than obligations, then you are going to labor without being able to rest. And unless you're carried along by God's power working within you, you'll be crushed by the seeming impossibility of spiritual growth. But as we progress, we come to understand how seemingly contradictory truths are really complementary. In Christ we are already perfect, even as we are being made perfect; we labor with God's strength, but sometimes this requires a lot of conscious effort.

Consider an analogy. My oldest brother came to visit our house when we lived in Virginia. As we sat in the backyard one day, he looked at our flowerbeds and said, "I think I'm going to do some weeding." I thought he was crazy. Here he was, on vacation, wanting to work in our flowerbeds? But to him it wasn't work; it just looked like work *to me*. To my brother, this was a restful thing to do, and he really enjoyed it.

When God re-creates us, what looks like "work" to the outside world becomes a delightful "rest" to us. We love it, even as we sweat. Why? A dynamic change has occurred within us. We cherish the spiritual freedom created by each virtue as it begins to blossom; we experience the power of a transformed life, and we are drawn to want more of godliness in the same way we used to be drawn to sink deeper into sin.

Throw any pleasure in front of a hedonist, and he can't resist. He is captivated by its imprisoning force. Dangle a virtue in front of a healthy Christian, and her heart is liberated to walk in that light. She is enchanted by it, can't wait to revel in it, and runs after it.

What are you running after today?

The Glorious Pursuit, 40

SPIRITUAL BEAUTY

I once boarded a small commuter airplane and was assigned a seat directly across the aisle from a very attractive woman. I was the last person off the plane, so on my way to the baggage claim, I surveyed the reactions of the men in the airport as this woman walked down the hall.

Sometimes a man's casual glance would be followed by a quick jerk back and then a long, piercing stare. Other men would not be quite as bold. They kept turning their heads—a quick look at the woman, followed by quick nervous glances back at their wives. Three skycaps rammed their carts against each other in an attempt to ask the woman if she needed help.

You know what? This woman may be a bear to live with—demanding, selfish, and cruel. Or perhaps she is amazingly kind and thoughtful. Nobody watching her had a clue, but it didn't matter because beauty, in and of itself, arrests us.

The beauty of God is even more powerful than humankind's reflection of beauty, because God is not just beautiful; he is beauty itself. And just as men will do silly things to attract a beautiful woman, so we will do radical things to live in obedience to a beautiful God—if our eyes are opened to his beauty. Grasping the beauty of God is thus a key to holiness and discernment.

Jonathan Edwards states that spiritual understanding begins with this sense of spiritual beauty: "For whoever does not see the beauty of holiness cannot appreciate the graces of God's Spirit. Without this there is ignorance of the whole spiritual world."[12]

God's beauty is the basic component of spiritual understanding and insight. If we miss this, we miss the spiritual contours that really matter, and we get used to (or even become enamored with) a fallen world with its skewed angles. Spiritual beauty creates the context for our obedience and serves to refine our spiritual taste. We then value what God values, and seeing things his way becomes our passion and joy rather than a legalistic obligation.

Ask God to open up your heart and mind to his beauty. Spend time in his Word meditating on his glory, and let the beauty of God draw you from the ugliness of sin.

The Glorious Pursuit, 129–30

A DIFFICULT ROAD

When Mary approached Joseph with her incredible news, she must have been full of wonder. God had chosen *her* for the incredible task of raising the Son of God.

Did Mary's wonder and excitement slip into confusion and fear when she saw the doubt in Joseph's eyes and heard the disbelief in his words? We're not given any details about their encounter, but we can conclude that Mary knew two things after she left that meeting. First, Joseph didn't believe her, and second, her life was in danger. From John 8 we know that the Pharisees were not slow to carry out the punishment for adultery (death by stoning). Who would stop the Pharisees once Mary's pregnancy began showing?

I can imagine her questions.

"How can you do this to me, God? I said yes to you, and this is the thanks I get? I held nothing back, only to be called a liar and have my life threatened by my own people!"

God could have made it easy on Mary. He could have directed the angel to visit Joseph *before* Mary told him about the child. Then Joseph could have immediately comforted her and said, "It's OK, Mary; I believe you. God visited me last night and told me all about it." Why didn't God make it easy on Mary? Maybe God wanted to do a work *in* Mary before he did a miraculous work *through* Mary. Perhaps. But one thing is clear: God asked Mary to travel a difficult road.

He continues to call his saints to great challenges.

Perhaps more than today, Christians in earlier centuries widely recognized that the spiritual life is very difficult. The classics speak with one voice, best typified by Johannes Tauler: "Beloved, no one can escape suffering. Wherever a person may be, he must suffer."[13] God's wonderful plan has a painful beginning and many difficult hills to climb before we reach our final resting ground. Ignatius, imagining Jesus speaking, stated it this way: "Whoever, therefore, desires to come with me must labor with me, in order that following me in pain, he may likewise follow me in glory."[14]

Thirsting for God, 179–80

A RAUCOUS CHEER

Just before my family moved from one state to another, Gordon Dunn, a dear missionary in his eighties, invited Lisa and me over for a good-bye dinner. As the night wore on, Gordon pulled me aside and opened his well-worn Bible to Acts 26:19, where Paul tells Agrippa, "I was not disobedient to the vision from heaven."

"Gary," Gordon said as he looked me in the eye, "at the end of your life, will you be able to say, as Paul did, that you were not disobedient to the vision given you from heaven?"

I've never forgotten that conversation. I particularly try to remember it—as well as Jesus' words on the cross, "It is finished" (John 19:30)—every time I participate in the Lord's Supper. Every time we take Communion, we should do so with the awareness that, just as Jesus' work on earth had a beginning and an end (as he ministered in a human body), so the mission he has given us has a beginning and an end.

One of my editors told me of a writer, not well-known in the United States, who died at a relatively young age. He had worked tirelessly to get Christians more actively involved in the arts. His life was a testimony to God's grace and creativity. By all accounts, this man had been a faithful husband, a good father, and an earnest servant of the gospel.

Many tears were shed at the funeral for a man most thought should have had several more decades to live. Yet as his casket was picked up by the pall bearers and carried down the church aisle, something curious happened: Mourners turned into celebrators. The crowd erupted into a spontaneous standing ovation. This was a life well lived—a life in which death revealed a victory, not a defeat; a life marked by faithfulness and service. It deserved a raucous cheer.

May we all live in such a way that our passing evokes a standing ovation, not only by believers on earth, but also by the saints and inhabitants of heaven.

Thirsting for God, 177–78

CHRISTIAN, KNOW YOUR GOD

Humility embraces two truths — the lowliness of humanity and the greatness of God. According to the classic devotional writers, the way to build humility isn't to obsess on how lowly we are but to spend time reflecting on the surpassing glory of God. Consider these words from *The Cloud of Unknowing:* "[We] should choose rather to be humbled under the wonderful height and worthiness of God who is perfect than under [our] own wretchedness, which is imperfect. That is to say, take care that your particular attention is directed more to the worthiness of God than to your own sinfulness."[15]

Jonathan Edwards writes, "The greater the view and sense that one has of the infinite excellence and glory of God in Christ, and of how boundless is the length and breadth, depth and height of the love of Christ to sinners, the greater will be the astonishment one feels as he realizes how little he knows of such love to such a God, and to such a glorious Redeemer."[16]

Without a direct experience of God, humility is impossible because our frame of reference is distorted. Have you ever been invited to a home just after the family had done some remodeling? Let's say they fixed up their kitchen by increasing the floor space, adding new cupboards, doubling their counter space, and maybe even putting an island in the middle of the kitchen. When you go home, you walk into your own kitchen — and sigh.

In the same way, we can easily get proud of our holiness or character — until we catch a glimpse of God's holiness. Once we see his, humility comes as a natural response.

While we can use any human measurement to reveal our humble state, Fénelon noted that such reasoning "only skims the heart. It does not sink in." Therefore, only a direct encounter with God shakes the depths of our being. A work of humility requires a supernatural touch and even a mystic's pursuit. Merely reading about God won't cut it; we must actually *encounter* God to have our hearts transformed in this way.

Thirsting for God, 143–44

OPEN MARRIAGE

The call to become one requires an open marriage of honesty and truth. I talked with a couple once in which the wife suspected the husband of viewing pornography. He denied it but admitted to keeping a post office box he had kept a secret. "I can't think of a single good reason to have a secret post office box," I confessed, "but I can think of several bad ones."

The post office box amounted to a giant sinkhole sucking the intimacy out of his marriage. Not surprisingly, he and his wife got divorced several months later. When you start to build a separate life, you pave the way to the ultimate separation—divorce.

Lisa and I laughed one time as we listened to a talk radio host scold a woman who felt terrible because her husband caught her going through his wallet. "What's so bad about that?" Lisa asked. She considers my wallet her personal ATM machine. She likes it because it doesn't require a PIN. Maybe Lisa and I are just weird, but she can go through my wallet anytime she wants. She knows my e-mail passwords, and I know hers. She has a key for our business post office box. Neither of us has a single relationship that the other doesn't know about.

It all comes down to this: Are we going to be married, or not? Are we going to be 60 percent married or 90 percent married, or are we committed to living life together 100 percent?

The irony is that most of us desire to be fully known. This desire creates a sense of belonging and intimacy and fulfillment. But then we create static in our marriage by lying or carrying out secret activities. In doing this, we sabotage the very fulfillment that we seek. We may lie out of shame, embarrassment, or selfishness, but whenever we do, we strangle the intimacy that comes from knowing and being fully known.

Make the courageous choice to be fully married. When you lie to your spouse, you reject the very spiritual benefits that marriage provides: the chance to repent, the motivation to change, the opportunity to be spiritually transformed, the journey of loving and being loved. As soon as you lose the spiritual benefits of marriage, the structure of marriage will start to feel like a restriction instead of an intimate relationship. Before long, you'll want out. In relationships, deception is the threshold that leads to destruction.

How about deciding this week to create a new start—a new honesty and openness, a commitment to truly walk in the light? God didn't design a relationship as intense as marriage to be fulfilling when it's done halfway. Be fully married, completely open with each other.

Devotions for a Sacred Marriage, 131–32

IN OUR IMAGE

As a single, I looked at righteousness self-centeredly—how my choices would displease God, how moral decisions might affect my future, how bad choices could damage my reputation. But as a parent, I must consider my children. Andrew Murray said, "If the parent is to be God's fellow-worker,... the parent himself must be in harmony with God. He must hate sin with a perfect hatred and seek above everything to remove and keep it out of his home."[17]

Every time a man talks to his son about women, he creates a moral example. Will he be in harmony with God, or will he pass on a predatory mind-set? Every time a woman speaks of her husband in front of her children, she creates a moral example. Will it be a good one, or a negative one? Whenever she talks on the phone, not realizing that a child can overhear her, will her children hear words of encouragement and blessing, or gossip and slander?

Every time a man sits in front of a computer and logs onto the Internet, he creates a moral trail. Will he hate sin "with a perfect hatred and seek above everything to remove and keep it out of his home," or will he allow it to infiltrate his children's home?

When our kids see us dealing with failure, disappointment, frustration, and our own limitations, they are learning. Are we building a secure refuge, or a shoddy cardboard house that won't make it through a single storm? Do they witness a faith that will last through cancer, unemployment, frustration, and stress, or are they looking at a belief that wilts under the slightest spiritual assault?

Just as God created man and woman in his own image, so we parents end up creating boys and girls very much in *our* image. As Jesus said, "Everyone who is fully trained will be like his teacher" (Luke 6:40). Do these words encourage us, or do they convict us?

Devotions for Sacred Parenting, 16

DRAGON SLAYER

One of the chief aims of Christian spirituality, second only to knowing God, is to enter other people's lives—to become others-centered. Consider the contrast between the Pharisees, who sought to make themselves holy, and Jesus, who sought to help others be delivered from the unholy things that held them captive.

Evangelism is a holy, necessary, and primary calling. We would do well, however, to also prioritize surgery of the soul—the ability to work with God to bring back to health those suffering from spiritual problems.

Every spiritual problem has an individual genesis and therefore requires an individual exodus. Generalized preaching is crucial to the Christian community, but individual needs call for individual attention. Most believers have had their fill of simplistic answers and general platitudes that leave people impressed but still broken. Instead, they want and need someone to be with them, to encourage them to continue on in the journey and find the help they desperately require.

Such needs call us toward maturity so that we might become surgeons of the soul.

We do not need to be mature to reach heaven. In just moments, God can transform us from enthusiastic pagans into children of the heavenly King. Without maturity, however, we will have neither the motivation nor the ability to get involved in the lives of others.

God must do a work *in* us before he can work *through* us. This is why a lack of growth is so dangerous. We live in a world of wasted human lives. Part of the problem has to do with sin, and much of it has to do with complacency, as lives slowly waste away in front of television sets, in gossip sessions, and through other means of escape.

True fulfillment comes as we receive God's love and respond to it by loving others. This is the essence of Christian spirituality. Let God do his work in you today. Seek to grow, so that you can help others grow. The one thing more rewarding than seeing God slay a dragon in your own life is seeing him use you to slay a dragon in someone else's life.

Thirsting for God, 15–16

JOYFUL SURRENDER

On the night of November 23, 1654, Blaise Pascal had an ecstatic experience that affected him for the rest of his life. He wrote down the insights he gained that night and sewed them into his jacket, transferring them from garment to garment as each one wore out.

About two years later, Pascal began making notes for what he hoped would become a full-scale apology for the Christian faith. Pascal's notes now fill up several hundred pages in the book we call *Pensées*. The scope of what Pascal intended must have been enormous, because he stated that it would take ten years of good health to bring the book to completion — this from a man who had accomplished more in his first thirty-five years than most people accomplish in a lifetime.

He made the notes in 1657 and 1658, but in 1659 Pascal entered a period of serious illness from which he never fully recovered. In the midst of his illness he wrote a prayer titled "Prayer Asking God for the Right Use of Illnesses," in which he tried to find a Christian meaning for his suffering so he could discern God's will and submit to it wholeheartedly. Pascal asked God to dispose of his health and his sickness, his life and his death, first for the glory of God and then for his salvation and the good of the church.

Pascal could have grown bitter. He could have argued that God had treated him unfairly. He could have prayed, *God, I gave up everything to serve you, and now I'm too sick to complete it. How could you allow this to happen?* Rather than complain, however, Pascal devoted his final years to ministering to the poor. While he could no longer summon the strength for a serious intellectual enterprise, he could hand out blankets and pour soup. Instead of retreating back to the world, he found a new way to serve God. Pascal placed *everything* on the altar and expressed no bitterness when God decided to keep it. Pascal just kept serving him.

This is a mark of a truly classic spirituality. Will we live similarly surrendered lives today?

Thirsting for God, 89–90

JULY

According to the U.S. Department of Agriculture, the average American eats 156 pounds of sugar a year. It's hard to believe, but a little bit every day adds up. The same is true in a positive sense when it comes to things like prayer. Many Christians feel understandable (and perhaps appropriate guilt) over how little they actually pray, but consider this: if you pray just ten minutes a day, over the course of a year, you will have spent about sixty hours talking with God. As we enter this month, let's consider how even small steps of daily communion can pay big dividends.

NO FAITH WITHOUT PRAYER

To be strong Christians, we must be strong pray-ers. There is no other way. The words of Jesus and his disciples, in addition to two thousand years of Christian tradition, bear witness to the fact that prayer is essential to the Christian life.

Paul urges us to pray *continually* (1 Thessalonians 5:17). This puts prayer on a far higher plane than mere intercession. It marks prayer as the heart of our devotion, the constant awareness of God's presence, our consistent submission to his will, and our frequent expressions of adoration and praise.

John Henry Newman, a nineteenth-century English scholar and churchman, wrote, "Prayer is to the spiritual life what the beating of the pulse and the drawing of the breath are to the life of the body."[1] Martin Luther insisted, "As it is the business of tailors to make clothes and of cobblers to mend shoes, so it is the business of Christians to pray." J. C. Ryle observed, "Prayer is the very life-breath of true Christianity." A modern writer, Terry Glaspey, sums it up well: "Prayer is a work to which we must commit ourselves if we are to make sense of our lives in the light of eternity."

I like this last phrase — prayer is how we *make sense of our lives in the light of eternity*. Prayer helps us to regain the proper priorities, discern biblical wisdom, and make right judgments. Without prayer, Glaspey might say, we live as temporal people with temporal values.

Prayer pushes eternity back into our lives, making God ever more relevant to the way we live our lives. The Christian who fails to pray will fail to grow as she should and will be trapped in a perpetual spiritual adolescence. Listen to J. C. Ryle again:

> What is the reason that some believers are so much brighter and holier than others? I believe the difference, in nineteen cases out of twenty, arises from different habits about private prayer. I believe that those who are not eminently holy pray *little*, and those who are eminently holy pray *much*.

In light of this ancient wisdom, are you willing to make a bigger investment and put in more effort to build what is rightly called the fundamental spiritual discipline of prayer?

Sacred Marriage, 74–75

THE MYSTERY OF PRAYER

Is there anything more mysterious than prayer? Prayer moves us to call on a Being we cannot see and ask him to alter that which we can see. Formulas do not work; rituals cannot guarantee success. Neither the length nor the form of the prayer makes the prayer potent. This is why we need to create pockets of prayer in our lives, learning to trust God to come through in unexpected ways.

There is an element of mystery, however, against which we sometimes rebel — the mystery of unanswered prayer, or, perhaps more appropriately stated, prayers that receive the answer "no."

Because God sometimes answers our prayers with a yes, it can become intoxicating, and this intoxication can become so addicting that we begin to demand that God answer every prayer with a yes. When a prayer doesn't get answered in the way we want it to be, we may mistakenly assume there must be hidden sin, lack of faith, or some other buried obstruction, which then sends us into hours of fruitless introspection.

But to demand that God answer all our prayers with a yes is to ask for his omnipotence (power) without having the benefit of his omniscience (knowledge).

Looking back, I'm thankful that God said no to some of my prayers. The mystery of faith calls us to love and serve a God whom we can't always understand. We love this when the result satisfies us and God answers in ways that make our knees weak. It is much less exciting, however, when the mystery leads us to believe that God is silent, indifferent, or even cruel.

Mystery is mystery. It has its exhilarating elements as well as frustrating ones, and we can't expect one without the other.

The pursuit of maturity will lead virtually every one of us through this canyon of unanswered prayer, where expectancy runs dry and the only mystery seems to be where God is hiding. Understand that this is a necessary avenue on the destination to holiness and that it usually has an end — in God's timing, however.

Sacred Pathways, 174–75

GOD MADE REAL *THIS*?

I've always loved movies, but movies are not always a safe recreation. So in this activity, Lisa acts as a sort of conscience for me. For some reason that I'm not proud of, I suspect that my standards would be even lower if I knew that Lisa wouldn't be in the room watching the movie with me. Even after almost two decades of marriage, watching a movie with Lisa feels a little like watching it with God. I can imagine her thinking, "You rented *this*?"

Dietrich Bonhoeffer shocked the theological world when, as a Lutheran theologian in the early part of the twentieth century, he began advocating that Protestants reinstitute the practice of confession. He did so not because he felt confession to a fellow human was necessary in order to gain forgiveness from God, but because human confession has a practical purpose: it makes our sin seem more real to us.

If you question this, ask yourself: Why is it much easier to confess sins to God than to your pastor? Why is there more shame when another sinful human being observes my weakness than when I pronounce them before an all-holy God?

Could it be because God's presence is so weak in our lives? If we truly understood and cherished the beauty and holiness of God, we would shake a bit more when approaching him. But his invisibility often creates a buffer, thereby softening the impact of his presence.

In and through our spouse, God becomes real to us in human form. There is a flesh-and-blood person sitting next to me who flinches when she sees what should make me flinch, but doesn't—and I see my hard heart exposed by her soft one.

We can help each other become aware of God's presence by gently encouraging each other toward growth in holiness. Yet we need to be sure to undertake this with extreme caution. We want to bring God's presence into the other's life, not our own judgment. Pointing each other to God's presence is a fundamental spiritual discipline for spouses.

Sacred Marriage, 239–40

THE PLACE

When Graham was quite young, we talked one day about heaven.

"There's no better place, Graham," I told him as he snuggled close. "No crying, no sickness, no bullies; the girls there don't have cooties; there aren't any under-the-bed monsters—plus, we'll all be together."

Graham nodded. "I can't wait to sit on God's lap," he said, "and your lap too."

There may be no safer place in the world, spiritually, than a parent's lap. Take the most frightened child; take a little girl who skinned her knee or a boy who was picked on by a bully. Let their hearts race at a hundred beats a minute, tears cascading from their eyes—then place this child in the all-encompassing lap of a parent. Suddenly, the heartbeat drops in half and the tears slow to a trickle. The child is safe. A parent's lap is the most secure refuge ever invented by God.

Even as adults, we secretly harbor the desire to lose ourselves in a lap—the spiritual lap of God. In fact, one Hebrew name for God is "the Place." Mystics throughout the ages have sought to reach this destination, a quiet, spiritual refuge in a rushed world. The task of raising children points us the way there. True spiritual listening is about climbing into God's lap, restful and secure, and hearing his soft words of love, affirmation, correction, and challenge.

The biggest change in my prayer life probably occurred as the result of reading about Teresa of Avila. Teresa didn't define prayer by time or frequency but by *intimacy*. It revolutionized my prayer life. Teresa's book *The Interior Castle* charts the soul's progress, beginning with the prayer of meditation, moving on to the prayer of recollection, the prayer of the quiet, the prayer of union, and, ultimately, the "interior castle," which she describes as the "fullness of spiritual marriage." I benefited greatly from this insightful woman who taught me how to approach God a little more softly and who pointed out that much of prayer is about climbing into God's lap and resting.

Spend some time today thinking about finding refuge and peace in the lap of God.

Sacred Parenting, 61–62

AN ACHINGLY DIFFICULT PROCESS

The Israeli housewife hated cockroaches, and this one wouldn't die. So the woman stepped on it, threw it in a toilet, and then sprayed a full can of insecticide on it until finally the cockroach stopped moving.

Her husband returned home from work later that day. While sitting on the toilet, he threw a cigarette butt into the bowl. The insecticide fumes ignited, and the husband received serious burns in a sensitive area of his anatomy.

The wife immediately called the paramedics. They arrived within minutes, examined the man, and decided that the burns warranted hospital attention, so they put him on a stretcher and carried him downstairs. After they found out how the husband had been injured, the paramedics found it difficult to contain their laughter. They ended up laughing so hard that they dropped the husband on the stairs, breaking his pelvis and ribs.[2]

I imagine that this man's ability to forgive was sorely tried! But even in the best of circumstances, forgiveness isn't easy. Our natural minds work against it.

One time, I spoke at a staff retreat at a Roman Catholic retreat center. Shortly after I arrived, I poked around the small but distinguished chapel. I saw a confessional in the back, so I opened the door and found, of all things, a file cabinet.

Sometimes that's what marriage is like. Our spouse has confessed sins and weaknesses to us, which we've kept in a mental file cabinet, ready to be used in our defense. But true forgiveness is a process, not an event. Rarely are we able to forgive "one time," forever settling the matter. Far more often, we must relinquish our bitterness a dozen times or more, continually choosing to release the offender from our condemnation. Philip Yancey writes, "Forgiveness ... is no sweet platonic ideal to be dispensed into the world like air freshener sprayed from a can. Forgiveness is achingly difficult, and long after you've forgiven, the wound ... lives on in memory. Forgiveness is an unnatural act."[3]

Here's the hope: Any life situation that exercises our ability to extend forgiveness is a life situation that can mold us further into the character of Jesus Christ.

Sacred Marriage, 169–70

July 6

FOSTERING EXPECTANCY

As a young collegian, I met with a number of students for prayer every Friday afternoon on the top floor of a dorm. We called these meetings "the Upper Room." They were powerful times of preparation for our Friday night campus meetings.

One of the things that charged these lengthy prayer times was expectancy. We expected that God wanted to do something, and he often met that expectancy—and then some. Our prayers often coincided with the theme of the Friday night meetings, even when we had no idea what had been planned for those meetings. This happened so frequently that my future wife (then girlfriend) frequently asked me as we walked into the meeting, "So what are we going to hear about tonight?"

Expectancy can energize our faith. Try it! Ask God to bring someone in your path to whom you can minister. This sense of watching, whether it presents an evangelistic opportunity or a chance to encourage a downhearted believer, energizes our faith because we see God moving in visible ways.

The needs of the "real world" are great and known to God. By cooperating with him, we can move even in supernatural ways. I once walked through the mall heartbroken, helping a friend pick out a tiny bear to place in the coffin of his stillborn son. We tried to carry on a normal conversation with various store clerks, while emotionally we felt ripped up inside.

Virtually every time we step inside a mall, a church, or any public place, the odds are that *somebody* feels just like my friend and I did that day. Maybe they just found out they have cancer, a relationship has ended, or a job has been lost. But in our busyness, our lack of expectancy, we miss opportunities to minister to people in supernatural ways.

Be willing to stretch yourself. Create room in your life for God to move.

Sacred Pathways, 173–74

THE PREYER

Previous generations of Christians may have paid too much attention to the devil, but our age tends to pay him too little heed. The severe truth is that Satan hates your marriage and makes its destruction a daily aim.

While Francis of Assisi once prayed for his Order, "by divine revelation he saw the whole Place surrounded and besieged by devils, as by a great army." Much to Francis's satisfaction, the demons couldn't find a place to enter, until one of the friars was stirred to anger and began to plot revenge on a brother. "As a result, the gate of virtue being abandoned and the door of wickedness being open, he gave the devil a way to come in."[4]

Francis called for the offending brother and confronted him. The brother confessed that he had indeed been making vengeful plans; he repented, and the gate to hell slammed shut.

While many today snicker at such a primitive worldview, our modern naïveté concerning spiritual realities is at least as pathetic. When we quarrel with each other, hold resentment, allow bitterness to simmer, play petty games of control, manipulation, and revenge, we do, in fact, open the door to spiritual beings who seek to destroy the holy family God has called us to create.

Jesus taught constant vigilance when he told his disciples how to pray. The Lord's Prayer includes these words: "And lead us not into temptation, but deliver us from the evil one" (Matthew 6:13). Notice, Jesus didn't pray, "Deliver us from *evil*," but, "Deliver us from the evil *one*." Jesus told his followers to regularly petition God so that they might not fall prey to the evil one's schemes.

A married couple's relationship is the inner fortress in a cosmic spiritual battle. This fortress is not limited to just a man and woman; it also protects the children and grandchildren who result from that union.

With so much at stake, can we afford to be lackadaisical? Dare we forget that a powerful, pernicious being aims to wreck what God is trying to build? Even worse, are we cooperating with his agenda? By our actions, whether physical (flirting with an office mate, viewing pornography, getting so busy you have little time to work on your marriage) or spiritual (refusing to forgive, holding a grudge, neglecting to build spiritual intimacy), are we foolishly putting our marriage at risk?

One little thing, left untended, can be nursed to become a major issue. Guard what God has given you; give Satan no place to enter.

Devotions for a Sacred Marriage, 40–41

PRAYER OF THE HEART

When Westerners think of *prayer*, they usually think of talking to God. But other Christians have found that a prayer of the heart, without replacing a prayer of the mind, is an essential ingredient for a full life of prayer.

God created us with more than intellectual or cerebral faculties, yet we do little to develop the emotional element of our being. One writer describes it this way:

> Never would we come to true peace and fulfillment if only our cerebral faculties were involved in conversing with God. And yet it is a fact that, in comparison with the overwhelming rational and cognitive training, we receive very little education in our emotional growth. Often the affective dimension of adults is either infantile or of a crudity which is neighbor to a barbarian attitude.[5]

Prayer of the heart does not call us to abandon our mind. But it does call us to use the mind to focus on our heart. What are we feeling as we enter God's presence? Is our adoration centered on God or on something else? Are we content to enjoy the presence of God, or are we too restless to quiet the mind for just a few minutes?

That our faith must not be ruled by our feelings does not mean that feelings are irrelevant or unimportant. God created our emotions for a purpose. It is true that we cannot entirely trust them, but it is also true that we shut off part of our true selves if we entirely ignore them.

Prayer of the heart is more "being" than "doing." It aims not to get an answer from God, make a request known to God, receive an insight from God, or even express our commitment to God. Rather, the prayer of the heart focuses on emotional attachment to, or adoration of, God. It develops and matures the affective faculty of our souls that is so frequently crippled in our society. Its aim is to love God, to have our hearts enlarged so that God owns more and more of us.

Will you give God more of your heart today?

Sacred Pathways, 199–200

BUILDING A HABIT OF PRAYER

Invocation

In the name of the Father and the Son and the Holy Spirit. Amen.

O God, be merciful to me, a sinner.

Prayer of Cleansing

Lord, cleanse me of my sins and have mercy on me.

Prayer to the Holy Spirit

Glory to You, O Lord. Glory to You.

O Heavenly King, O Comforter, the Spirit of truth, Treasury of good things and Giver of life, come and abide in us. Cleanse us from every stain and save our souls, O Good One.

The Trisagion Prayers

Holy God, Holy Mighty, Holy Immortal, have mercy on us.

Glory to the Father and to the Son and to the Holy Spirit, now and forever. Amen.

O Most Holy Trinity, have mercy on us. O Lord, cleanse us from our sins. O Master, pardon our iniquities. O Holy One, visit and heal our infirmities for Your Name's sake.

Lord, have mercy.

Our Father in heaven, hallowed be your name, your kingdom come, your will be done on earth as it is in heaven. Give us today our daily bread. Forgive us our debts, as we also have forgiven our debtors. And lead us not into temptation, but deliver us from the evil one, for yours is the kingdom and the power and the glory forever. Amen.

Call to Worship

Come, let us worship and fall down before God our King.

Come, let us worship and fall down before Christ, our King and our God.

Song

"Come Let Us Worship and Bow Down"

Read or Sing a Psalm

Read Scripture

Choose a Hymn or Song for the Day

Intercessions

Closing Prayer

Glory to the Father and to the Son and to the Holy Spirit, now and forever. Amen.

O Lord, thank you for hearing my prayers. Give me the strength to serve you this day. Have mercy on me and save me, for you are good and love humankind. Amen.

Sacred Pathways, 89–91

FAITHFUL FRANCIS

Shortly after Francis of Assisi embraced a life of faith, he sensed God telling him, "Francis, all those things that you have loved in the flesh you must now despise, and from those things that you formerly loathed you will drink great sweetness and immeasurable delight."

Almost immediately, he applied the divine admonition in a horrifically beautiful way.

As the young Christian rode his horse out of town, he saw what he once most despised: a leper. It is difficult for us to understand the terror of that once untreatable disease—an insidious malady in which bacteria seek refuge in the nerves and proceed to destroy them, one by one. Even apart from the macabre appearance of a leprosy victim, no one wants to end up alienated from the world, which made leprosy one of the most feared diseases of its time. "During my life of sin," Francis wrote, "nothing disgusted me like seeing victims of leprosy."[6]

Exuberant in his newfound faith and remembering that he was now to love and even treasure those things that he formerly loathed, Francis chose not to run from the leper, as he would have earlier in his life. Instead, he leapt down from his horse, knelt in front of the leper, and kissed the diseased hand.

He *kissed* it.

Francis then further astonished the leper by giving him money. But even that wasn't enough! No, Francis was determined to "drink great sweetness" from what he formerly loathed, so he jumped on his horse and rode to a neighboring leper colony. Francis "begged their pardon for having so often despised them." He gave them money and refused to leave until he had kissed each one, joyfully receiving the touch of their pale, encrusted lips. Only then did Francis go on his way.

In that indelible moment, Francis's faith became incarnate. His belief didn't just inspire him; it transformed him.

Francis's initial conversion was invisible, exhibited only in the changed expression on his face. This is as far as many of us ever go—a superficial change of mind in response to a compelling argument for faith. *This* act was astonishingly explicit—a grotesquely gorgeous parable of a radically changed man. The very instant that Francis's lips touched the leper, what might have been merely a religion crumbled under the weight of a new way of life. The horse no longer carried a man; it transported a saint, whose example continues to challenge us today.

Holy Available, 13–15

ACTIVE PEOPLE, LIVELY PRAYERS

If ever there was a group I would want to see plugged into prayer, it would be Christian activists. Fortunately, many of the activists I know regularly participate in various forms of prayer.

Many activists find "walking prayer" particularly helpful. The evangelist may intercede for a city block by walking around it as he prays silently; the intercessor may walk around a government building while she prays for justice. Some Christians will spread a map in front of them and pray for unreached people groups.

"Jesus marches," in which large numbers of Christians gather to march in celebration of Jesus, made a surprising comeback in the early 1990s. I say *comeback* because the practice can be found as far back as the Baroque period (roughly 1550–1750). The marches of the 1990s were a bit different, as they focused on praise and celebration, whereas the earlier community marches tended to seek some spiritual favor and frequently were solemn affairs.

Karl Barth urged Christians to pray with the Bible in one hand and a newspaper in the other. I remember rising early once a week in college to attend missions prayer meetings. We didn't bring a newspaper with us, but we did carry materials prepared from various missions groups. Such meetings still take place in many churches.

Prayer should be an important part of the life of every Christian, and especially for those called to active ministry. Work as prayer is important and valid, but coming away to pray is crucial. Activists need to stay focused and unpolluted so they don't let hatred for sin become hatred for people when they become tired and spiritually depleted. Do yourself and the church a favor: cultivate an active prayer life. If you truly want to make a God-sized difference in your neighborhood and community, partnering with God through prayer has to remain a priority.

Sacred Pathways, 139–40

Marriage: A Tool to Refine Prayer

Few verses are more astounding than 1 Peter 3:7: "Husbands, in the same way be considerate as you live with your wives, and treat them with respect as the weaker partner and as heirs with you of the gracious gift of life, so that nothing will hinder your prayers." Much Christian teaching on prayer has gotten it exactly backward. We're told that if we want a stronger marriage, we should improve our prayer lives. But Peter tells us that we should improve our marriages so that we can improve our prayer lives. Instead of prayer being the tool that will refine my marriage, Peter tells me that marriage is the tool that will refine my prayers.

If prayer is the essence of spirituality, and if a wrong attitude in marriage destroys prayer, then it behooves men to pay careful attention here. Never again will I be able to approach prayer "as if" I were a single man!

When Peter says that men must treat their wives with respect so that nothing will hinder their prayers, he is directly connecting our attitude toward our wives with the fundamental Christian discipline. God sees me, in one sense, through my wife. So if I want to grow as a married pray-er, I can't pretend that I'm a celibate monk. I can't simply parrot the practices of medieval scholars who addressed single men and women in their pursuit of God.

Why do many of us find it more difficult to pray as married men? The truth is, the rules change when we get married. A condition is placed on our prayer life—and this condition is tied directly to how we view and treat our wives.

A man may be able to preach a sterling sermon, write inspiring books, and quote the Bible front to back. But if he hasn't learned how to serve his wife, to respect her, and to be considerate of her, then his spirituality is still infantile. And his prayer life—the lifeblood of his soul—will be a sham.

Sacred Marriage, 75–76

A SLAVE TO EVERYONE

Many years ago, *The New Yorker* ran a cartoon in which a smiling woman jabbered nonstop to a glum-faced companion. The smiling woman finally said, "Well, that's enough about me. Now let's talk about you. What do you think about me?"

Instead of being preoccupied by what others thought of him, the apostle Paul learned the theme song of an authentic faith oriented around the needs of others: "We who are strong ought to bear with the failings of the weak and not to please ourselves. Each of us should please his neighbor for his good, to build him up. For even Christ did not please himself" (Romans 15:1–3).

In fact, Paul took this line of thinking to a radical and even shocking conclusion: "Though I am free and belong to no man, I make myself a slave to everyone, to win as many as possible" (1 Corinthians 9:19).

Where did Paul get this selflessness? How could a man become so humble, so others-oriented, so willing to play the role of a servant? I believe it comes down to this: Paul took literally the words of Jesus—"It is more blessed to give than to receive" (Acts 20:35)—and he found them true!

I confess to being in awe of Paul, particularly when I think about how many communities he stayed in touch with and how many churches he genuinely cared about. Paul's letters reveal an ongoing, passionate, and loving relationship with churches across the Mediterranean. It amazes me to see not just the depth but the breadth of Paul's active love. One may be tempted to think he didn't have much else going on in his life, for if he had, he would have lacked the emotional energy to remain actively compassionate, loving, and involved with so many people.

Yet Paul derived genuine enjoyment from serving others and sacrificing for them. These are not the words of a man who serves grudgingly but the words of a man who found a life of service to be the most meaningful one imaginable. A mature Christian is never focused on himself or herself; he or she is devoted to the welfare of others.

Authentic Faith, 20–21

"I Knew You'd Come"

During World War I, two American soldiers bonded as they talked about their families, what they wanted to do when the war ended, and even how they dealt with the fear of living so close to death.

One night the order came to leave the trench and attack the enemy. In the fierce and desperate fighting, the two friends got separated. After a long and arduous battle, the call went out to retreat. When the one soldier returned, he began asking about his buddy. Eventually he discovered that his friend was still out there, wounded and bleeding. Without considering the danger, he announced he was going back to get his friend.

"Absolutely not," the commanding officer replied. "It's suicidal to go back out there, and it's not worth the risk. I've already lost more men than I can afford to lose."

The soldier waited until the officer turned his head, then jumped out of the relative safety of the trench and crawled toward his wounded buddy. Immediately, he paid the price — mind-splitting reverberations from the shelling, thick smoke choking him, and bullets zipping overhead, which kept his face smashed into the blood- and gore-infested ground.

Still, he crawled on. Finally he reached his friend, shared a few words, and then began pulling him back toward the trench. Sometime before the pair made it back to safety, the wounded friend died. With great sorrow, the man pulled a precious corpse into the trench.

"So, was it worth it?" the angry officer barked.

"Absolutely," the friend replied. "My buddy's final words made it all worthwhile."

"What could he possibly have said that made it worth risking your life to hear?" the officer demanded.

"When I reached him, he saw my face and said, 'I knew you'd come.'"

In a culture that celebrates the self, that calls us to be true to ourselves, a prophetic power gets released when people act with selflessness and learn to put others first — and even to sacrifice themselves on another's behalf.

Authentic Faith, 34–35

SACRED INTERRUPTIONS

During the Second World War, C. S. Lewis took in numerous children fleeing London and other British cities vulnerable to German bombing. Bringing children into his home, the Kilns, entailed a lot of extra work—in addition to coping with the excess noise.

Be careful not to look at Lewis's sacrifice too lightly. As a writer, I work out of my home, so I can imagine what it would be like to try to prepare college courses and keep writing books and articles and respond to correspondence while unruly kids run around the house (kids who miss their parents). Certainly, Lewis must have realized that his work would take a severe hit. Yet this act of sacrifice helped produce Lewis's most famous writings.

You see, one afternoon one of these children grew interested in an old wardrobe and asked Lewis if there was anything behind it. Thus was planted the seed for perhaps the most beloved of all of Lewis's books, *The Lion, the Witch, and the Wardrobe*.

In another book, *Mere Christianity*, Lewis writes,

> Give up your self, and you will find your real self. Lose your life and you will save it. Submit to death, death of your ambitions and favorite wishes every day and death of your whole body in the end: submit with every fiber of your being, and you will find eternal life. Keep back nothing. Nothing that you have not given away will ever be really yours. Nothing in you that has not died will ever be raised from the dead. Look for yourself, and you will find in the long run only hatred, loneliness, despair, rage, ruin, and decay. But look for Christ and you will find Him, and with Him everything else thrown in.[7]

If you think selfless living is costly, then you haven't honestly considered the steep price we pay for living selfishly. Those interruptions of our "important" work may be the threshold of a deeper ministry than we ever could have imagined.

Authentic Faith, 26–27

A LAVISH DEDICATION

A Christian magazine asked me to write an article on selflessness. These people get it right far more often than not, so I'm not intending to disrespect them. But after I submitted the article, I received an e-mail from the editor praising much of the article but then making this request: "What we need now is for you to beef up the section on the rewards of selflessness."

I understand that the article's tone could seem too negative, but there is a somewhat comic irony that our culture says, in a sense, "I'm willing to be less selfish, but *what's in it for me*? Where's my reward?" Even in our selflessness, we tend to adopt a selfish attitude!

My editor's request was not entirely inappropriate, for many ancient believers do testify to the many rewards of selflessness. But when we revisit Paul's astonishing statement in Romans 9:3—where he says he would choose damnation for the sake of others—we realize that "reward" as a motivation to become less selfish can take us only so far; it will never usher us into the joyful self-abandonment experienced by Jesus, Paul, Augustine, C. S. Lewis, and other well-known believers throughout history.

Keep in mind, this selflessness isn't reserved solely for mature Christians. Paul urges all of us to adopt it: "Do nothing out of selfish ambition or vain conceit, but in humility consider others better than yourselves. *Each of you* should look not only to your own interests, but also to the interests of others" (Philippians 2:3–4, emphasis added).

My mentor J. I. Packer put it this way: "The happy state which we know only rarely, is the unselfconscious state in which all our attention is being given to the people around us, to the situation outside us, and we're forgetting ourselves in the service of others. You see that to perfection in the life of Jesus."[8]

Spiritual health is marked by a vibrant, others-centered compassion and concern. Far from simply absorbing blessings, we are called to lavish God's love on others. If you're frustrated in your faith, do a spiritual inventory: Are you focused primarily on your own blessings and spiritual health, or are you dedicating yourself to serving others?

Authentic Faith, 29–30

July 17

A REAL SAINT'S DAY

One night during the early years of our marriage, I woke up astonished at my wife's endurance—and immensely grateful for it. We had two children at the time. It was a stressful season for me, and my wife had gone out of her way to schedule a romantic evening to ease my mind. Later that night, however, our children became ill. One of them was still nursing, and the other insisted that Lisa care for her.

An exhausted Lisa had been up late with me, and now she suffered a hungry baby's desperate sucks for breast milk that wasn't there. When Lisa put the baby down, she had to hold a feverishly hot toddler in her lap, stroking her hair and placing a damp cloth on her forehead.

I saw my wife give virtually every inch of her body in selfless service—and the thought hit me, *She is a saint!* As a younger man I had often idealized the religious devotion of those who chose the life of a celibate monk or nun, thinking that marriage required much less devotion, much less commitment. But that night, the life of a celibate nun surely would have sounded like a dream vacation to Lisa compared to the service she was being asked to give. I gave thanks for her amazing heart of self-sacrifice.

Which is the preferred pathway to holiness—celibacy or marriage? Christians have walked both paths successfully. The important thing is to view the challenges of your particular life situation as a platform for spiritual growth. An athlete who truly wants to improve his performance doesn't look for the easiest workout; he looks for the most challenging one. Marriage and parenting certainly have their challenges, but when we face them head-on, they can nurture our devotional life and shape our hearts in enriching ways.

Sacred Marriage, 91–92

WHAT MATTERS MOST

My friend Matt came home one afternoon and paused on his way into the house. His eyes caught sight of a long white scratch down the side of his one-week-old minivan.

"What happened?" he bellowed.

His daughter confessed that she had ridden her bike into the garage and scraped the brand-new vehicle with her handlebars. Matt responded with some heat, because his daughter had broken an ironclad rule and cost him a lot of money and hassle.

Laura, Matt's wife, came out when she heard the "conversation" and immediately took their daughter away, saying just three words: "It's a *car*."

Those three short syllables were enough to chasten my friend. "My daughter had scratched metal," Matt admitted, "but I crushed a person."

Matt's insight — comparing scratched metal to a crushed person — helps me keep perspective. What matters more? It's impossible for any kid to live in a house without occasionally making a mess, breaking something, or leaving behind a permanent mark. Yet it's easy to make them feel guilty for inconveniencing us. It's also easy to forget what matters most.

During his induction ceremony into the Baseball Hall of Fame, Harmon Killebrew spoke fondly of his parents. He recounted how one day he and his brother were playing in the yard, upsetting their mother. "You're tearing up the grass!" she complained. To which Harmon's dad replied, "We're not raising grass; we're raising boys."

Harmon's dad was on to something. In the end, what matters more? Life today demands — even ensures — that some *good* aims will have to get temporarily shelved in order for us to fulfill the *ultimate* aim. In the twilight of these choices, we determine what matters most. Set yourself — and your family — free. Few of us with kids around will ever qualify for a *Better Homes and Gardens* spread. Visitors or passersby may not gawk at our lawns. But we're not raising grass; we're raising kids. Let's remember Matt's insight: Scratched metal doesn't justify crushing persons.

Devotions for Sacred Parenting, 30

SACRED GRIEF

Ralph Venning, a seventeenth-century Puritan, urged believers to grieve over other persons' failings as well as their own. "All sin is against God," he wrote, "and for that reason he who truly grieves for his own sin will grieve for other men's too." Venning adds, "Oh, that there were more crying persons, when there are so many crying sins!"[9]

John Wesley writes in his journal, "My soul has been pained day by day, even in walking the streets of Newcastle, at the senseless, shameless wickedness, the ignorant profaneness, of the poor men to whom our lives are entrusted. The continual cursing and swearing, the wanton blasphemy of the soldiers in general, must needs be a torture to the sober ear ... Can any that either fear God, or love their neighbor, hear this without concern?"[10]

While I studied at a public park one sunny afternoon, the sound of children playing in a creek provided background noise. Their words suddenly jumped out at me. Two girls — maybe ten years old — were singing, "I'm a bitch; I'm a sinner ... " Apparently it was a well-known song, though I had never heard it and haven't heard it since.

My heart deflated. What has gone so wrong that ten-year-old girls should happily sing such lyrics? In the face of such loss of innocence, am I supposed to "claim the joy of the Lord" and move on in happy and silly forgetfulness? Or am I, like John Wesley, Paul, and Jesus, to be personally grieved over this offense and implore God to use his church — and me! — to shine light into this dark world?

I know what Ezra would have done. When he heard about how the Israelites had disobeyed God by intermarrying with the neighboring peoples, he tore his clothes, yanked hair from his head and beard, and "sat there appalled until the evening sacrifice" (Ezra 9:4). He then undertook a complete fast (10:6). To be a Christian is to grieve when we encounter such sadness. Not to be moved by such things is the hallmark of hardened hearts and deadened consciences.

What are you grieving over today?

Authentic Faith, 157–58

SHARING THE PAIN OF OTHERS

Almost two decades ago, a close friend of ours miscarried her first child. In a misguided attempt to console her, a number of friends and family members said some hurtful things: "Don't worry. You're young. You can have lots of other children." "It was probably for the best. After all, the baby might have been deformed."

She had just lost a baby! *It was right for her to mourn.* It would have been unhealthy *not* to mourn. The spiritually immature try to minimize others' pain, while authentic faith calls us to share others' pain with a sympathetic, compassionate, and loving spirit (see 1 Peter 3:8).

It is uncomfortable to mourn or to be around people who mourn, so sometimes we try to short-circuit the process. Authentic faith and the call to love require us to respect the role that mourning plays and to let people mourn — including ourselves. There is no rush to "get over" something. Trying to "talk away" a legitimate grief is naive at best and cruelly superficial at worst.

Our call is not to approach grief as something to talk people out of so much as it is to share their hurt. We will never "get over" some losses but will in fact carry them to our graves.

We must gain a new respect for the discipline of mourning and allow ourselves to mourn our sins, our losses, the rebellious state of the world — surely not to the extent that we forget joy and grace and renewal, but enough so that we recognize the discipline of mourning as a legitimate tool, a true blessing that God provides for us as fallen people in a fallen world. Let mourning fulfill its function. Don't fear it, but embrace it, use it, and baptize it for God's glory.

Authentic Faith, 163–64

LIVING FOR GOD'S CHURCH

This may sound shocking, but biblically, living for God means living for his church. When God calls us to himself, he calls us to his church, to a purpose bigger than ourselves. There is a glory in the presence of Jesus Christ, seen when believers come together, that will necessarily go missing in a strictly individual pursuit of God. When the gospel gets turned from a community-centered faith to an individual-centered faith ("Jesus would have died for me if I had been the only one!"), we eclipse much of its power and meaning.

But because we live in a me-first culture, we often try to individualize corporate promises. We tend to have more concern about what the Bible says to us *individually* than about how it calls us to live in *community*. Too easily we forget that we are called to be part of Christ's body, the church.

Peter tells us that, corporately, we are "a chosen people, a royal priesthood, a holy nation, a people belonging to God." Why? Not for any individual purpose, but for a corporate one that honors God: "that you may declare the praises of him who called you out of darkness into his wonderful light. Once you were not a people, but now you are the people of God; once you had not received mercy, but now you have received mercy" (1 Peter 2:9–10).

All of us need to lay a new groundwork if we want an authentic faith based on a God-centered life. Rather than the believer being the sun around whom God, the church, and the world revolve, God becomes the sun around which the believer revolves. This means the believer becomes willing to suffer—even to be persecuted—and to lay down his or her life to build God's kingdom and to serve God's church.

What are you doing in your life right now to serve God's church, to build God's church, to participate in God's church? We should be passionately devoted to the bride of Christ.

Authentic Faith, 10–11

RUNNING FROM YOURSELF

One time, after tossing and turning all night long, I glanced in the hotel mirror and was shocked at what I saw — the tired eyes, the messed-up hair, the pale color. I said to myself, "Gary, at this very moment you may well be the ugliest person on the face of this planet."

In the same way, looking at our reflection through the mirror of our marriage can be hard to take. We are horrified by how we've acted, astonished at our own selfishness, pettiness, laziness, or even cruelty. Satan can use this to tempt us to run. In truth, we don't just want to run from our spouse; we also want to run from ourselves, the person we are in that marriage. We want to be with someone new who hasn't seen our bad side. Some may even try to deceive themselves into thinking that the other person is at fault for bringing out the flaw in them. We think we can just start over without having the bad side follow.

This is, of course, the great myth. We have enough energy either to run from who we are or to cooperate with God's Holy Spirit to change who we are — but never enough to do both.

If we accept the fact that God designed marriage to help us grow in holiness, we know that we are a work in progress. Instead of running from hurtful revelations, we can welcome them, realizing that our marriage is showing us what we need to know and pointing out where we need to grow.

Rather than run from ourselves, we can focus on *changing* ourselves! Let's be honest — some things about you and me are ugly. Our spouse will see that ugliness, whether it is an attitude, habit, or disposition. After marriage does its work and our weakness gets exposed, we'll have a decision to make: Will we run from this revelation into the arms of another person who doesn't yet know our weakness, or will we embrace the call to grow in holiness, accepting Scripture's admonition to "think of ourselves with sober judgment" (Romans 12:3)?

Don't run from yourself. Be humble, stay where you are, and focus on changing your attitudes instead of your spouse.

Devotions for a Sacred Marriage, 89–90

SACRED LIVES

What drew so many people to the Christian faith in the first century? Primarily it was the way of life of its adherents — the reality of God's presence in them. People saw how these Christ-followers treated others differently, and their changed lives provided compelling evidence for the supremacy of Jesus. Church historian Aaron Milavec states:

> Potential members assessed the movement not so much on the basis of claims made on behalf of Jesus who was absent, but on the basis of their experience of the way of life of members who were very much present to them. It is no surprise, therefore, that the entire system of the *Didache* [an early first-century document explaining the Christian life to new believers] displays little taste for negotiating, defining, and defending the exalted titles and functions of Jesus. Rather, the *Didache* is taken up with the business of passing on the Way of Life revealed to its authors by the Father through his servant Jesus. Converts came forward ready to assimilate that Way of Life as it was formulated and lived out by the tried and tested members of the movement.[11]

This emphasis continued into the third century, particularly during a terrible epidemic around AD 260 that wiped out vast swaths of the population. People saw Christians acting differently. Dionysius, the bishop of Alexandria at that time, explains:

> Most of our brother Christians showed unbounded love and loyalty, never sparing themselves and thinking only of one another. Heedless of danger, they took charge of the sick, attending to their every need and ministering to them in Christ, and with them departed this life serenely happy; for they were infected by others with the disease, drawing on themselves the sickness of their neighbors and cheerfully accepting their pains. Many, in nursing and curing others, transferred their death to themselves and died in their stead ... The best of our brothers lost their lives in this manner.

When Christianity combines its intellectual basis with a commitment to practice its compelling truth, it can't help but radically influence a culture.

Holy Available, 29–30

POWER AND AUTHORITY

One morning I began reading Scripture and stopped cold after just thirteen words: "When Jesus had called the Twelve together, he gave them power and authority" (Luke 9:1). "That's what your church needs, Lord," I prayed. "It's what *I* need. Your power and your authority."

I wondered what it must have been like to receive such amazing gifts. Imagine the gravitas, the weight, of God's imprimatur. Twenty-four hours later, I read what happened after the disciples received such remarkable gifts. As the disciples went out, they conquered both sickness and ignorance (see Luke 9:6). But as the days turned into weeks, these "authoritative" and "powerful" prophets proved almost pathetic. Three of the best of them witnessed the transfiguration and all but lost their minds trying to comprehend it. Peter makes a ridiculous suggestion, which Luke dismisses with, "He did not know what he was saying" (9:33).

Some authority!

Next, Luke tells us the disciples failed miserably at healing a demonized boy (9:40).

Some power!

The very next snapshot showed the disciples arguing about who would be the greatest (9:46). This sad picture transitioned into yet another sorry example when a Samaritan village insulted Jesus. The "powerful, authoritative" disciples knew exactly what to do: "Lord, do you want us to call fire down from heaven to destroy them?" (9:54). Jesus promptly rebuked them. After these glaring failures, you might think Jesus would pull the disciples away for another year of training. Instead, he sent out seventy-two others (Luke 10:1).

Even with God's power and his authority, we can be pathetic and dim-witted. Yet in the midst of our failures and limitations, God still sends us out and allows his power to break through and accomplish something through us that we could never do on our own.

Even the most mature among us will display moments of sheer stupidity. But Jesus entrusts his ministry to a body of believers, knowing that *together* we can exercise the weight of God's power and properly proclaim God's authority.

Holy Available, 214–16

WE NEED EACH OTHER

I once met with a fellow church member over a serious theological disagreement. We were virtual strangers, but out of our discussion, a friendship grew. Though we continue to disagree on the issue, we both sense Christ in each other. My friend said to me, "After we met, I was shaking for three hours." His spiritual journey and love for Christ, his passion for Scripture and truth and God's power, inspire me. Being with me seems to do the same for him. In middle age, discovering a friendship like this is one of life's truest gifts. God made us and designed us for community.

I swim in a stream of inspiring witness, infectious faith, and shared power. I am humbled by ordinary women and men who have devoted themselves to God and whose lives bear the mark of his reflected glory. Having seen what is possible in them, I will never be content to settle for less in me.

The best gift you can give to God's church is to become your best and by your best to inspire others to fully embrace the experiential, realized life of the glorified Christ living through you. Elton Trueblood writes, "The renewal of the church will be in progress when it is seen as a fellowship of consciously inadequate persons who gather because they are weak, and scatter to serve because their unity with one another and with Christ has made them bold."[12]

Your life is part of God's overall tapestry. Don't settle for anything less. A single thread is just a thread, but remove that single thread from a beautiful tapestry and the first thing you notice is the missing thread. As you weave it back into that tapestry, both the greater work and the single thread complement each other's glory.

The red thread needs the yellow thread. The "contemporary" church needs the "traditional" church, and vice versa. We can and should challenge each other, occasionally rebuke each other, and even try to persuade each other—but we can never stop loving each other.

Holy Available, 219–20

NOURISHED BY THE NEW

That didn't take long, I said to myself as I stood up from the old wooden pew and made my way to the side door of the church, up near the altar. "These Episco- palians sure know how to hold a short service."

The priest turned and saw me walk up the aisle. A distinctly puzzled look covered his face. I glanced sideways and realized to my horror that people were sitting down, not leaving. The service wasn't over at all; it was just beginning.

With a face redder than the wine served for Communion, I slunk down into the closest available pew. "Passing the peace," I learned, wasn't a benediction; it was like the Baptist, "Take a moment and shake everybody's hand."

The experience was all the more embarrassing because I was not a new Chris- tian; I had attended thousands of church services. But this was my first liturgical service, and I felt as ill at ease as when my college missions group attended a Sikh wedding to get a cross-cultural experience.

If you weren't raised in a liturgical setting, it takes a while to get used to it, but the benefits can be tremendous, even for someone raised a Baptist. The written prayers of confession in that liturgical service, for instance, gripped my soul in a powerful way.

Presbyterian writer Kathleen Norris stopped going to church after high school. What eventually drew her back? The Benedictines. She remembered, "They would sing or recite psalms, have a Bible reading, and some prayers four times a day. Being able to say and hear poems out loud was a whole new approach for me, even though it's about 1,700 years old. It really nourished me."[13]

Many Christians want to remain in their tradition but have found some ele- ments of worship in other Christian traditions that greatly increase their faith. If your devotions seem stale, if worship feels old and tired, reach out and experi- ence how other Christians have learned to worship and adore God.

Sacred Pathways, 79–80

SOUND-ENERGIZED SOULS

What kind of facility best prepares God's people for worship? For those who believe that the quieter a building is, the more holy the environment, using sound to worship God might seem paradoxical. Certainly we need times of silence, but there is also a great tradition of sound being used to serve God—a tradition celebrated in the Bible.

Psalms 147, 149, and 150 urge believers to worship God through making music on instruments. And Psalm 81 states, "Begin the music, strike the tambourine, play the melodious harp and lyre. Sound the ram's horn at the New Moon, and when the moon is full, on the day of our Feast" (verses 2–3). The psalmist then reminds his audience that this is more than a mere recommendation: "This is a decree for Israel, an ordinance of the God of Jacob" (verse 4).

As our Creator, God knows that language and music together stimulate the brain more than just language on its own; in a real sense, the congregation may be more "alive" during special music than during the sermon.

Beautiful music has been a part of church life since its beginning. The great composer Handel recognized what he called the "transcendental keys." Any key signature with five, six, seven, or eight sharps he associated with heaven. He used particular chords to bring forth various feelings—G minor, to evoke urgency or jealousy; E minor, to create a sorrowful, lamenting mood; G major, to create moods reminiscent of bright sunlight and green pastures; F minor, to provoke gloom and despondency.[14]

It is interesting to note that Martin Luther argued that God meant Scripture to be heard more than read. Our hearts are most transformed and challenged, he thought, when we hear the Word of God. Science has proven the validity of Luther's insight. When we hear Scripture read, our brains are more active than when we are just reading with our eyes.

Today, consider some ways you can use the God-created reality of sound to energize your soul.

Sacred Pathways, 66–67

THINKING GENERATIONALLY

Is there a little girl somewhere who *hasn't* dreamed about being a princess, at least once in her life? Maybe, but I've never met one.

When we think of a princess today, we think of luxury, servants, a palace, respect, power, and lots of money. When Sarah (her name means "princess"), Abraham's wife, hears that she will become a princess, the promise didn't include an opulent setting, a throne, or ruling power over a city. What made her a princess in God's eyes was that she would have countless descendants: "I will bless her so that she will be the mother of nations; kings of peoples will come from her" (Genesis 17:16).

Just as immature Christians think of their faith only individually (how God is blessing them, using them, building them up), apart from their role in the corporate church, so immature fathers and mothers think of themselves only individually, apart from their descendants (both spiritual and physical). When God makes a promise to Abraham, he extends it well beyond his own lifetime to that of his offspring: "All the land that you see I will give to you and your offspring forever" (Genesis 13:15).

As a mature couple, Abraham and Sarah thought generationally, just as a mature Christian must learn to think corporately (of the church). It is our calling and our glory to look beyond ourselves to the good of God's church and toward the future of our children.

This is God's own perspective. We're told that God chose Abraham, not just for the sake of Abraham, but for the generations to come: "For I have chosen him, so that he will direct his children and his household after him to keep the way of the LORD" (Genesis 18:19). Paul tells us that God loves to answer our prayers in surprising and even thrilling ways: "Now to him who is able to do immeasurably more than all we ask or imagine, according to his power that is at work within us, to him be glory *in the church* and in Christ Jesus throughout all generations, for ever and ever! Amen" (Ephesians 3:20–21, emphasis added).

Are you living in such a way that you are dedicated to the spiritual vitality of generations yet to come?

Sacred Parenting, 161–62

COSTLY OBEDIENCE

My wife startled me with what seemed like a bizarre suggestion. "I think we should let the Smiths borrow our van for the weekend," she said.

"Where are they going?" I asked.

"Eastern Washington."

"You mean, over-the-mountains-and-across-the-state eastern Washington?"

"Yeah."

Just weeks earlier, we had purchased our first brand-new vehicle in almost fifteen years. I was determined to make the car last—and keep the mileage down—for as long as possible. The thought of someone else dropping a thousand miles on it in three days (when the vehicle had just seven hundred miles on it to begin with) didn't thrill me.

But I knew God had set me up. My devotions that morning came from the book of Acts: "All the believers were together and had everything in common. Selling their possessions and goods, they gave to anyone as he had need" (Acts 2:44–45). Sometimes it's safer to schedule your Bible reading in the evening, after you've made all your important decisions!

When I saw how serious Lisa was, I winced. Obviously God had provided for us and we could help another Christian couple. Even so, I felt reluctant. I argued against the idea. But after all our years of marriage, Lisa knows how to read my face. I wasn't acting nobly, but I certainly was feeling guilty, and guilt usually wins out in me. "Should I call them?" she asked.

"I don't want you to," I confessed, "but I think God wants us to." Sigh. Deep breath. Second sigh. "Yeah. Go ahead."

Later as I was out for a jog, God seemed to say to me, "So, you're willing to act like a Christian only if it doesn't cost you anything?" Those words hit me so hard that I almost fell off the road, which is tough to do when you plod along at my speed. But they were true.

Is there anything God may be asking of you today, but you're resisting because you're willing to act like a Christian *only if it doesn't cost you anything?*

Authentic Faith, 192–93

REAL LOVE MEANS REAL MOURNING

The woman described the difficulties and heartbreaks she had endured. You'd have to be stone-cold not to feel for her; but then she said something that stopped me dead in my tracks. She concluded her saga by saying that God had visited her and told her she was done mourning. She would have nothing but joy and celebration for the rest of her life. The studio audience clapped, shouted "amen," and celebrated vigorously as I shook my head in dismay.

How is it possible to be "done mourning" and still be part of a church? While I suppose it's possible a person might have nothing personally to mourn over (in very rare circumstances), if a Christian truly wants to be done mourning, she had better not read the newspaper. She had better plug her ears when prayer requests are offered. She had better not read Romans 12:15. And she had better learn how to achieve a state of moral perfection.

Otherwise, how will she protect herself from stories of couples who love the Lord but get slammed in the face every month with the painful reality of their infertility? How can she love fellow believers who for decades have prayed for their relatives to become Christians, but who watch with anguish as those loved ones pass into eternity without submitting to Christ? How can she escape sadness when others with whom she is called to fellowship face the struggles, burdens, and pain of a fallen world? And how will she repent when she does something that grieves our Lord?

To be "delivered" from mourning is to be delivered into a lonely existence, cut off from real life and, even worse, cut off from real love. There is no real love without real mourning. The time *will* come when all of us will be done mourning—but that time is not now. We need to mourn. Mourning invites us to a deeper life and takes us beyond the surface to give us a glimpse of the world as God sees it.

Authentic Faith, 148–49

THE SAMUEL SYNDROME

During the rule of the prophet Samuel, Israel transformed itself from a tribe ruled by a judge to a people ruled by a king. Samuel was a seminal figure in Israel's history and, by all accounts, a faithful servant of God (1 Samuel 2:35; 12:1 – 5). Yet both his kids rebelled against God. They "turned aside after dishonest gain and accepted bribes and perverted justice" (1 Samuel 8:1 – 3).

Some Christian books put the blame on Samuel. The authors assume that Samuel failed as a father; but nowhere does Scripture even hint at this. It just says that Samuel's sons went bad. Eli—whom Samuel succeeded—is specifically charged with not restraining his sons (1 Samuel 3:13), so the Bible's silence about Samuel's alleged failure leads me to conclude that Samuel should not be faulted for his kids' choices to lead ungodly lives.

We live in an era of linear thinking. Do good, we're told, and God will bless you, and all your children will become godly believers. Mess up, and God will curse you financially, relationally, and vocationally, and your kids will destroy their lives.

But we are not raising robots; *we are shepherding image bearers of the Creator God* who live with freedom of choice, their own wills, and a personal responsibility of their own. The Bible records instances of faithful servants of God who raise ungodly children (Samuel), and servants who abandon God but who yet have faithful, God-fearing offspring (Asa). It even records egregiously wicked kings (Ahaz) with heroic, God-following sons (Hezekiah).

This teaches us that none of us can be such good parents that God becomes obligated to save our children's souls. On the other hand, none of us can mess up so badly that our children somehow extend beyond the reach of God's mercy.

I am not saying that children can't be damaged by deficiencies in our parenting, but that the failure of kids does not necessarily mean we have failed as parents. We find our only refuge in God's grace and mercy.

Sacred Parenting, 42 – 43

AUGUST

The residents of Houston, Texas, where I now live, say that "August is the price you pay for living in such a great city." The humidity and heat index can be brutal. Yet in the winter months, as so many Northerners scrape ice off windshields and brace themselves for blasts of the cold wind, Texans often enjoy some of the most pleasant weather in the country.

In the same way, Christians experience many benefits and blessings—more than we count—but we also have our "Augusts"—seasons when God calls us to hard work, service, and even sacrifice for the benefit of his people and the advancement of his kingdom. A full Christian life involves accepting every "month" God calls us to—the particularly pleasant seasons of tranquility and blessing as well as the difficult months of trials and testing.

LIGHT IN THE DARKNESS

John of the Cross grew up under difficult circumstances. His father died when he was three, and John's family fell into hunger and poverty. John eventually received a proper education but chose to enter a religious order. Because of his connection with Teresa of Avila, he was arrested, classified as a rebel, and given the usual penalties—imprisonment, flogging, and fasting on bread and water. John languished in a small room, six feet wide by ten feet long, with one two-inch window for his only source of light. For nine months he lived in darkness with little food and hardly a change of clothing.

Yet a divine light pierced the darkness, and John's teaching on the dark night of the soul has inspired many Christians to persevere through the spiritual desert. John wrote about difficulty, "The darknesses and trials, spiritual and temporal, that fortunate [*fortunate*, he says!] souls ordinarily undergo on their way to the high state of perfection are so numerous and profound that human science cannot understand them adequately." He added later, "Both the sense and the spirit, as though under an immense and dark load, undergo such agony and pain that the soul would consider death a relief."[1]

John had no easy life, but he didn't mention the physical pain, the cold, the hunger, or the loneliness. Instead, he focused on the difficult war within, the battle for his soul. This struggle captivated his attention.

In John's mind, internal pain became the doorkeeper to further spiritual growth. He wrote that souls often do not advance because they refuse to face the dark night that would lead them to a closer walk with God. He also warned of unwise counselors who do not understand the necessity of difficulty.

When many Christians today face difficulty, their counselors and pastors and friends feel compelled to fix it—to help suffering believers out of their trials. John believed precisely the opposite. We must allow God to take believers through some soul-crushing experiences in order for them to mature. John taught that we do not "fix" these things; we endure them and learn from them.

Thirsting for God, 188–90

LET IT PASS

A few years ago, a man who may well be the most influential pastor in the United States invited me to address his staff and then afterward shocked me to my core by offering me a position in his church.

As a writer, I couldn't have had a better platform to promote my books. But my family had settled in Bellingham. On the very day this pastor talked to me, we had just closed on a house, and my kids — who had moved with us from the East Coast four years prior — felt settled into their relationships with friends, schools, and youth groups. I felt like a fool for letting the offer pass. There seemed little question about the choice I should make vocationally. But my dreams do not and cannot begin or end with me.

One year later, a seminary sent me a job description as a "writer in residence" that felt so inviting it made my wife laugh. She said it seemed as though they had read my mind. "They couldn't have come up with something more inviting if they had tried," she exclaimed.

Yet that job offer felt like a dagger through my heart because I eventually realized, kicking and screaming, that I would have to let this opportunity pass too. When we moved our kids to Washington, I promised them, "This is it until you're out of the house. I won't disrupt your lives like this again." Yes, the offer represented a lifelong dream, a job description that couldn't suit me better — but I'm not just a man, I'm a father. And in this case, I believed my fatherly responsibilities had to count more than my personal ambition.

Part of carrying out our parental responsibilities requires adopting the attitude of Jesus Christ. Jesus made himself poor so that his spiritual children could become rich. Jesus allowed himself to be humiliated so that we could be glorified. He died so that we could live. Everything we have spiritually comes on the back of Jesus' sacrifice. Sacred parenting invites us to adopt this same attitude.

Sacred Parenting, 183–84

THE ONE THING THAT MATTERS

My son's middle name comes from a courageous, passionate, and sometimes embarrassing Old Testament king. Astute readers may immediately guess that I'm talking about David. Who else?

The young shepherd grew into a powerful leader who could be totally right and utterly wrong (sometimes almost simultaneously). But what marks him most is when Scripture calls him a man after God's own heart: "I have found David son of Jesse a man after my own heart; he will do everything I want him to do" (Acts 13:22).

Did you catch that last line? "He will do everything I want him to do."

I pray that my son, my daughters, myself, and you will do everything God wants us to do. Henry Drummond waxes eloquent when reflecting on this charge:

> One man will tell you the end of life is to be true. Another will tell you it is to deny self. Another will say it is to keep the Ten Commandments. A fourth will point you to the Beatitudes. One will tell you it is to *do* good, another that it is to *get* good, another that it is to *be* good. But the end of life is in none of these things. It is more than all, and it includes them all. The end of life is not to deny self, nor to be true, nor to keep the Ten Commandments—it is simply to do God's will. It is not to get good nor be good, nor even to do good —it is just what God wills, whether that be working or waiting, or winning or losing, or suffering or recovering, or living or dying.[2]

This makes it much easier, doesn't it? If I am to offer my hands and feet back to God, then all of life becomes a matter of discovering and fulfilling God's purpose for these hands and these feet. So what is your purpose? And are you fulfilling it? Are you driven first and foremost by God's will for your life at this very moment?

Holy Available, 125–26

KICKING AGAINST THE GOADS

What if God should will for me to be poor, or wealthy, or famous, or anony-mous, or influential, or ignored? In that case, my call is to be faithful in the midst of God's will, whatever that will may be. The question then becomes, "How can I be faithful in the midst of this situation?" Henry Drummond writes:

> That is the object of your life and mine — to do God's will. It is not to be happy or to be successful, or famous, or to do the best we can, and get on honestly in the world. It is something far higher than this — to do God's will ... A man may think he is doing God's work when he is not even doing God's will. And a man may be doing God's work and God's will quite as much by hewing stones or sweeping streets as by preaching or praying. So the question just means this — Are we working out our common everyday life on the great lines of God's will?[3]

As believers in Christ, we will search in vain to find happiness outside of his will. I don't pretend that God's will is always easy to discern. I also doubt that God's will is always the narrow road we sometimes make it out to be. If a man loves working with wood, who is to say that his working with wood doesn't fulfill God's will?

But one thing I do know. Almost without question, the happiest, most joy-filled people I meet are those who believe they are exactly where God wants them to be. And the most frustrated people on this planet tend to be those who are fighting God rather than surrendering to him. Remember what Jesus said to Saul (later the apostle Paul) on the road to Damascus? "Saul, Saul, why do you persecute me? It is hard for you to kick against the goads."

If you're "kicking against the goads," stop! It will get you nowhere. Surrender to God's will and experience his best for you — whatever that may be.

Holy Available, 126

WORKING WITH GOD'S STRENGTH

One day while I was feeling overwhelmed and anxious about all I had to do in the coming months, I found solace in something I had written in my journal many months before:

> God hasn't lost courage. God isn't wavering on endurance. God doesn't fear another day or another test, and God is standing behind me. He is making available for me all that he is. By grace through faith, I have nothing to fear, no reason to feel defeated.

The words struck me as though someone else had written them. Their truth felt like a late-afternoon explosion of sunlight into an otherwise dreary day. It was a refreshing liberation to remember that ministry in its purest form is radically God-dependent and God-empowered. As David declared, "I do not trust in my bow, my sword does not bring me victory; but you give us victory over our enemies, you put our adversaries to shame. In God we make our boast all day long" (Psalm 44:6–8).

Paul had this same mind-set: "But by the grace of God I am what I am, and his grace to me was not without effect. No, I worked harder than all of them —yet not I, but the grace of God that was with me" (1 Corinthians 15:10). We see this marvelous image of Paul paddling furiously while he is carried down the river by God's great current. Peter shared the same sentiment: "If anyone serves, he should do it with the strength God provides, so that in all things God may be praised through Jesus Christ" (1 Peter 4:11).

David, Paul, and Peter—three key biblical characters—all testified to learning the secret of working with God's strength, of leaning into the wind of God's Spirit and letting his empowering presence enable them to do what they could never do on their own.

Don't be discouraged today by comparing your call or duties to your own limitations. God will make available all that he is, to cover all that you're not.

Authentic Faith, 31–32

RADICALLY ALIVE

From childhood, I've wrestled with how to rely on Christ's strength, as Paul speaks of it: "To this end I labor, struggling with all [Christ's] energy, which so powerfully works in me" (Colossians 1:29).

This is not an imitation of Christ; it is an ongoing reliance on Christ, almost (dare I say it?) a mystical dependence (there, I did say it). I once checked two commentaries on Colossians 1:29, both written by well-known and well-respected evangelicals, and was astonished by how little they had to say about it. They not only failed to consider what "struggling with all his energy" actually means; they barely even mentioned it, as if it has nothing to say to us today.

We evangelicals experience a huge gap between the mystical force of God promised in the New Testament and our actual experience of it. Our focus on imitating Christ may have blinded us to how we are to *appropriate* Christ, receiving his ongoing power. Other traditions can help us gain insight. An Eastern Orthodox monk looks at Christ's presence and power this way:

> Not only Paul but the author of the book of Revelation, the Alexandrine exegetes, martyrs like Ignatius of Antioch, Felicitas, and Perpetua, and many others have witnessed—(the "cloud of witnesses")—to the Spiritual Christ, to the actual charismatic presence of the Lord, as the great fact behind the whole Christian movement. Do *we* believe as intensely in the reality of the Spiritual Christ?... We, in our day, should endeavor to take the possibility of direct communications from the Risen Lord most seriously, to become more vividly aware of the absolute reality of his presence, to open our eyes and ears more readily to the deeds and words of the Spiritual Christ. The Christ of the Spirit is no figure of speech, no mere symbol of a surviving influence; he is forever alive and present.[4]

Christ is radically alive, available to all who will align themselves with God's purposes. Living in awareness of this truth will bring a spiritual depth to our lives and efforts that otherwise would be missing.

Holy Available, 127–28

EMBRACING THE EMPOWERING PRESENCE

I can't tell you how many times I have stood in front of a group, feeling tired or sick or defeated, and then watched in awe as God's Spirit carried me through the day or evening. Self-empowered ministry is so limiting. We are rarely at our best—fully rested, totally prepared, highly energetic, feeling strong. Something niggles at us that holds back our ministry: sinus headache, insomnia, family concerns, an overly busy schedule, nervous anxiety, financial problems—you name it. But when ministry flows out of God-reliance, when our service issues from supernatural dependence, then a full night of sleep, a clear head, or even a clear conscience matters far less than allowing God to do what he does best, namely, glorify his name through us.

How do we open ourselves up to this kind of ministry?

First, *we believe in Christ's empowering presence.* Although the Bible certainly teaches it, too many believers don't even consider it; they rely on natural means for a supernatural ministry.

Second, *we humbly ask God to fulfill his Word in us.* I like to pray these words: "Lord, you've created this moment. You've created these people, and you've created me. Not only have you created me, but you've shaped me and prepared me for such a time as this. You've brought us all together, and now I ask you to release your life-giving power to accomplish your aims and your purpose. May the ascended Christ manifest himself through me today."

Third, *we cultivate our relationship with Christ by living daily in the reality of his indwelling power.* We don't turn this relationship on and off. I can't ignore God for days on end and then get in front of a group and expect to rest in and rely on his empowering presence. But when my life becomes a prayer, when my service becomes an act of worship, when God-granted humility becomes my companion, then relying on God becomes the only thing I know how to do.

Holy Available, 128–29

AN INWARD CURE

"Gary, I need some help."

I winced. I knew what was coming, but I didn't want to hear it. Gordy moved his wheelchair a little closer and whispered, "I had a little accident."

"Sure, no problem, Gord," I answered. "Let's go take care of it."

Gordy and I had attended the same university, but he was in the advanced stages of muscular dystrophy and was just two years away from dying of pneumonia. As Gordy's condition worsened, his need for extra help increased.

I had seen another Christian taking care of him just a week before during a different bout of diarrhea and remembered saying to myself, "I couldn't do that." I was about to find out differently.

Gordy was more familiar with the situation than I, and we were able to enjoy ourselves through the whole experience. Since I had been duly "initiated," I also became someone Gordy could, and did, frequently call on when his paid person wasn't available.

Once I took off his shirt and was folding it when I heard this patient but very urgent, "Gary!" I turned and caught Gordy before he fell all the way back. Gordy laughed, and I laughed, and the next time I remembered to prop him up with my knees while I pulled his shirt over his head.

I remember his feet the most. They showed all the signs of never being used. Gordy had been unable to walk for ten years by the time I met him, and he wore slippers instead of shoes. As I was putting his socks on him one day, I realized Gordy was the holy one in all our efforts. He was serving *me* and in practical ways sacrificing the privacy of his body to do it. I was disabled inside, afraid to let people see my faults and struggles. Gordy's outward disability became, in a very real sense, my inward cure. His willingness to let another see his weakness revealed an inspiring inner strength.

A humble spirit is far more beautiful than the most gorgeous or glamorous body.

Sacred Pathways, 145–46

CREATURES OF THE CREATOR

I once officiated at a funeral service for a young man who died of AIDS—one of the more difficult things I've ever done. He never married and didn't father any children. Because he had built a list of legal offenses and arrests long enough to fill a computer screen, he ultimately died in prison. The last few years of his life were a torturous affair. He just couldn't learn to live without heroin (which is how the HIV virus was introduced into his body). This young man had great promise, but he died with most of that promise unfulfilled.

Christians rightly believe that life is a gift from God, something we shouldn't waste. We celebrate God by using the life he has given us to create other things. Whether it's building a business, writing a poem, painting a picture, or planting a garden, creating something can be a profoundly holy experience. Far more than hobbies, these activities can be powerful expressions of worship. One of the most powerful antidotes to addiction is participating in different activities that lift addicts out of themselves and into positive, constructive acts of creation.

Healthy Christians create. It is the nature of our God to create. He is introduced in Genesis 1 as the Creator of everything. One of the last images given to us in the book of Revelation is that of God creating the new heaven and the new earth. The Bible is literally framed around the act of God creating.

With the Spirit of God living in us we also have a need to create. A business, a poem, a song, a piece of art—all of us should find some outlet that is an act of creation. It is what we were made to do.

Without lapsing into perfectionism, do your best to make something shine for the glory of God. God gave you your mind, your hands, your strength, and your skill. Create something, anything, to give that mind, strength, and skill back to God.

Sacred Pathways, 179–80

CHOIR ROBES AND WORK BOOTS

On a weekly basis, most of us sing songs of amazing commitment, making seemingly heartfelt promises—but how many of them will we keep? Yes, music helps us rest in God's presence, but too often we walk out of church and go our own selfish ways, forgetting all that we sang and promised just moments before.

You will find no verse in the New Testament in which Jesus commands his disciples to sing for at least a half hour once a week. But you can hardly go two pages without encountering Jesus' call to commitment, a call he applied and fulfilled in glorious fashion. Jesus prayed to his heavenly Father, "I have brought you glory on earth *by completing the work you gave me to do*" (John 17:4, emphasis added).

It's not helpful to pit musical worship against service; the two should go hand in hand. But if we lack Jesus' sense of giving God glory by completing the *work* he gave us to do, our worship will suffer accordingly. Consider how often Paul calls believers "fellow *workers*" (see 1 Corinthians 3:9; 2 Corinthians 6:1, emphasis added), not "fellow *singers*."

One of the great misunderstandings of our day is that *worship* and *singing* are considered synonyms. If only *working* received the same top billing!

Music is a wonderful gift from God that can constitute a true act of worship, but once the worship service is over, if we do not exchange our choir robes for a good pair of work boots, our empty promises will count for nothing, no matter how beautifully they were sung.

What work—that is to say, what *worship*—is God calling you to be involved in today?

Holy Available, 124–25

SOUL SALSA

My wife has a penchant for all things organic. She buys products touting low salt, no trans fats, no poisonous preservatives — and, many times, *no taste!*

My savior when downing these insipid delicacies? *Extra hot salsa.*

Service is salsa to the soul. People often talk about the blessings of believing, usually referring to financial provision, physical healing, reunited families, and the like. While God does indeed offer such gifts, we should remind ourselves that service is among the most cherished of God's blessings. Remember what the Lord told the Israelites: "I am giving you the service of the priesthood as a gift" (Numbers 18:7).

Without this sense of mission, our lives become intolerable. In the words of Elton Trueblood, "Man can bear great physical or spiritual hardship, but what he cannot bear is the sense of meaninglessness."[5] Even war, Trueblood said, brings out this truth: "Evil and horrible as war is, there is no doubt that it brings tremendous zest and even mental health to multitudes whose lives normally have no element of victory in them ... War gives significance to little lives."[6]

Our greatest foe is what we often seek — unencumbered lives and unbroken leisure, free of any care or concern. Trueblood believed this would destroy us: "The ultimate enemy is not pain or disease or physical hardship, evil as these may be, but triviality."[7]

After he won the U.S. Open, one of the most prestigious tournaments in professional golf, Johnny Miller found himself saying, "Is this it? Is this really all there is?" Perhaps he heard the whispers of Trueblood's insight: "If a man begins each day as just another unit of time in which he wonders what to do with himself, he is already as good as dead. The man who really lives always has vastly more to do than he can accomplish."[8]

Holy Available, 130–31

THE DOORWAY TO SATISFACTION

Do you ever feel frustrated with God? Maybe you are irked with the Lord at this very moment. If so, chances are that you've turned your faith on its head. You are likely frustrated because God isn't ordering your life in the way you would choose; he's not answering your prayers like you want him to. Could it be you want blessing but no responsibility?

It is interesting how Jesus often calls us "to work in his vineyard" (Matthew 20:1) in contrast to "doing nothing" (verse 3). Elsewhere Jesus says, "Ask the Lord of the harvest ... to send out workers into his harvest field," for "the harvest is plentiful" (Matthew 9:37 – 38). Christianity involves a call to work. Being a Christian is an honor and joy and comes to us as undeserved grace, but it also entails a responsibility and a task to fulfill.

In the parable of the tenants, Jesus points to exactly what his work will include: betrayal, mocking, flogging, and crucifixion (Mark 12:1 – 12). This was Jesus' *work*. It's easy to think of Christianity for all its benefits while forgetting the work aspect. And the thing about work is that you don't always get to choose your job. Our employer has the right to tell us what we're going to do; he assigns the jobs. Kingdom work is kingdom *work*.

In fact, this work is the doorway to our greatest satisfaction. Elton Trueblood reminds us, "The greatest unhappiness ... comes from focusing attention on ourselves."[9] If your comfort, fame, and success indicate the level of your happiness, then you will feel perpetually frustrated, for who among us can be comfortable enough? Famous enough? Rich enough?

You must ask yourself, "Do I really want a fulfilling life?" Remember, you never find satisfaction in cajoling God to adopt your agenda, but in surrendering to God's agenda. Instead of accusing God for what he's not doing, spend some time asking him what you're supposed to be doing. Listen carefully — and then get busy, as his Spirit empowers you.

Holy Available, 131 – 32

BEHIND THE SCENES

Elijah's confrontations with the rulers of Israel rival Moses' confrontations with Pharaoh. Elijah displayed great courage in his confrontation with Ahab and the prophets of Baal, but his demeanor also reveals pride. Elijah thought he was the only true prophet left, and the only one who demonstrated true zeal (1 Kings 18:22; 19:10). However, God assured Elijah that seven thousand others were still true to the faith (1 Kings 19:18).

Elijah reveals some classic activist symptoms (the negative kind) in feelings of exhaustion and isolation (1 Kings 19:4; 18:22). Activism can spiritually feed many Christians, but it can also exhaust them.

Elisha, Elijah's replacement, was also an activist, and he showed great maturity in his confrontation with Hazael, who would eventually become king of Israel. Elisha saw the harm that Hazael would do and wept over it, but he didn't become consumed with it (2 Kings 8:11 – 13). Most Christians have to learn that whenever God calls us to action, we must leave the results to him or we will be consumed and driven by immediate results rather than by the Holy Spirit. I've seen a number of activists who just can't accept defeat. When their political or social campaigns fail, their faith is rocked. Elisha would be a good role model for such people to emulate, in part to keep them from responding like Habakkuk did.

Habakkuk cried out, "How long, O LORD, must I call for help, but you do not listen? Or cry out to you, 'Violence!' but you do not save? ... The wicked hem in the righteous, so that justice is perverted" (Habakkuk 1:2, 4). God responds that he is working behind the scenes. Justice is coming, even though Habakkuk can't see it.

Activists need to learn the message of the book of Habakkuk: live by faith. Life circumstances can tempt us to question God's sovereignty and goodness, but we see with a finite eye. God is not blind to injustice, nor is he indifferent. When we think our concern for righteousness exceeds God's, we have slipped into the delusion of being self-appointed messiahs. "[The proud] is puffed up; his desires are not upright — but the righteous will live by his faith" (Habakkuk 2:4).

Sacred Pathways, 129 – 31

INTIMATE ALLIES

Many years ago, Francis Schaeffer wrote this in *The Mark of the Christian*:

> There is only one kind of person who can fight the Lord's battles in anywhere near a proper way, and that is the person who by nature is unbelligerent. A belligerent person tends to do it because he or she is belligerent; at least it looks that way. The world must observe that, when we must differ with each other as true Christians, we do it not because we love the smell of blood, the smell of the arena, the smell of the bullfight, but because we must for God's sake.[10]

When activists live to see justice and righteousness worked out so that it becomes visibly evident in the church and in society—doing it as a way of loving God—then the confrontation will bring fulfillment, not exhaustion; thanksgiving, not anger; and often a deeper sense of intimacy with God rather than self-righteousness.

I found this to be especially true in my open-air preaching days. Temptations abound on a college campus. Tight accountability groups can help, but nothing was more effective to banning the lure of temptation than knowing I would be preaching the next morning.

The fear involved in confrontation creates a dependence on God not normally there. You don't just love him; you need him—*desperately*. You fear that he may leave you to face the challenge on your own. Facing this fear and stepping out in faith, finding God to be faithful as he steps in to carry you, can do wonders for your intimacy with God. You appreciate him more.

The fear of confrontation keeps many of us from acting when we should. But walking through a confrontation with God is one of the more pleasantly intense experiences Christians will ever know.

If God is calling you into an arena of conflict, don't run, and don't fight with your own passion. Enter it as an act of worship. Learn to depend on him, and you may well experience an intimacy you have never known before.

Sacred Pathways, 133–34

CALLED TO GET INVOLVED

The Christian church has often led the way in societal reform. John Wesley wrote that there is "no holiness but social holiness ... and to turn Christianity into a solitary religion is to destroy it."[11] Charles Finney refused to baptize Christians who still believed in slavery, while William Wilberforce fought slavery in his own country, England. Today many believers fight such evils as sexual trafficking and child pornography.

I worked a number of years for a pro-life organization, and one of the most difficult challenges I faced was how to encourage other Christians to adopt this sense of social responsibility. Too often we think that as long as we attend church regularly, give faithfully from our income, and keep from willingly living in sin, we've done our Christian duty. Yet the Bible is filled with calls for God's people to reach out to the less fortunate (Matthew 25:35 – 36; James 1:27; and others).

There is a tension in this, however. Good Christian minds disagree on many issues — the government's use of welfare and capital punishment, to give just two examples. While we may find Christian brothers and sisters advocating an opposing position, as Christians and as citizens we have a responsibility to be fully informed, prayerfully decisive, and actively involved.

Writers, preachers, politicians, academics, artists, and homemakers can all be activists, faithful in their own sphere to stand up for the truth. And, of course, the content of Christian activism can move beyond protest to provide positive alternatives. Instead of just writing letters to Congress, Christians can run for Congress. Instead of merely protesting immorality in entertainment, Christians can become part of the entertainment industry.

The key question is: To what form of activism has God called *you*?

Sacred Pathways, 137–38

THE PARABLE OF THE GARDEN

Suppose two women are each planting a vegetable garden. On the same day, they prepare the earth and plant their seeds. One then neglects her garden while the other woman works in her garden regularly. She puts cages around the young tomato plants, drives in stakes beside the plants that would grow high, and puts netting around plants that are particularly attractive to rabbits.

Several months later, the two women go out for the harvest. One finds tomatoes rotting on the ground, beans whose vines had spread among the other plants, weeds that have choked out most of the carrot plants—all of which have been raided by birds and squirrels. She pulls up a handful of food and figures that planting a garden wasn't worth it—the food isn't as good, the harvest is small, and, well, grocery stores are so much more convenient.

Her neighbor, however, harvests a basketful of good vegetables every other day, which all tastes much better than grocery store vegetables. She figures that, when everything is added up, she probably saved a good 15 to 20 percent on her grocery bill during the summer months. Both women planted, but only one tended.

I've known Christians who have committed their lives to following Jesus at about the same time; but the influence this commitment had on their lives soon became markedly different. One lived a life of self-absorption. Christianity made sense, but it became almost a convenience—no need to take it too seriously or to reorder one's life around it. The other person took a different approach. She made Bible study a regular part of her life. She kept her prayer life fresh and varied. New character traits came to the forefront, and before she knew it, people were asking her for advice and counseling.

Both planted a spiritual garden, but only one tended.

Some of us live with the mistaken impression that our faith needs only to be planted, not tended. Becoming a mature Christian, some think, is like becoming six feet tall—either it happens or it doesn't. They couldn't be more wrong. The difference is tending.

Sacred Pathways, 231–32

THE "WORTHY"

For years I worked with a ministry that reached out to women facing crisis pregnancies. One of the challenges—in some people's minds, at least—was that these women were merely reaping what they had sown, so why should we help them?

To be sure, many people are in desperate straits because of sinful choices and actions. But John examines it from another angle: "If anyone has material possessions and sees his brother in need but has no pity on him, how can the love of God be in him?" (1 John 3:17).

For John, there's no mention of a *sinless* brother or sister in need. His teaching is far more blunt—their need defines our obligation. It's a matter of God's love, not human evaluation or judgment.

I reach out to people because God has loved me and asked me to love others in return, not because the people I love are "worthy" of love or because they'll thank me for it in the end. It's not for me to make judgments about their worthiness. I am to love God by loving others.

God is always worthy of being obeyed and served, so when I act out of obedience to him, the person who receives my service doesn't have to be deserving. They are benefiting from what I owe God.

This truth applies abundantly in marriage, where demands and expectations are plentiful. But it's hard. I try to remind myself that God is always worthy of being obeyed, and God calls us to serve our spouse—so regardless of how our spouse may treat us at any particular moment, he calls us to respond as a servant.

Jesus' example has challenged me greatly in this regard. None of the disciples deserved to have their feet washed at the Last Supper—all of them abandoned him within a few hours—yet Jesus did it anyway (see John 13:1–17). Jesus even washed the feet of Judas, who already had arranged to betray him.

The worthiness of God is more than sufficient motivation for us to love "unworthy" people.

Sacred Marriage, 188–89

THE SPIRIT OF SERVICE

In almost two decades of marriage, Lisa and I have settled into certain habits like an old pair of jeans. When we come back from a trip, Lisa invariably checks the phone messages while I unload the car. Lisa hates filling up the car's gas tank, so before I leave on a trip, I try to make sure it's full. If Lisa knows I'm coming home, she'll nurse that tank until she's riding on nothing more than fumes.

I don't resent this, and Lisa doesn't resent the fact that she's usually folding laundry when she watches a movie while I just sit there like an all-star couch potato.

We're not just after the imitation of Christ's *actions* in our home; we also want to model Christ's *spirit* and *attitude*. There are times to serve, and times to receive service.

The beauty of this commitment is that it makes both Lisa and me God-dependent rather than spouse-dependent. If Lisa is faithfully serving me when I'm in a surly mood, she still receives an inner affirmation and sense of fulfillment from God. She has the joy of that inner witness declaring that her Creator is pleased with her.

To become a servant is to become radically strong spiritually. It means you are free from the petty demands and grievances that ruin so many lives and turn so many hearts into bitter cauldrons of disappointment and self-pity. There is true joy when true service is offered up with a true heart.

I've learned to guard not just my servant's actions but my servant's *spirit*. If I serve Lisa with little puffs of exasperation, grunting every time I lift a finger on her behalf, I'm exhibiting a proud, false-martyr's spirit, not the attitude of Jesus Christ. The attitude of Jesus is the attitude of service: "The Son of man did not come to be served, but to serve" (Matthew 20:28).

Every Christian home should be marked by the spirit as well as the act of service.

Sacred Marriage, 190–91

HUMBLE PIE

Our house has three levels. When the phone rings, any phone *always* seems at least two levels away—even if I'm on the middle floor. This may sound impossible, but I always guess wrong. I run downstairs, thinking that's where the phones are, only to discover they're all on the top floor. If I guess upstairs, the phones will almost certainly be downstairs, tucked under the couch cushions or kicked under the computer desk.

Oh, and all this running has to be completed within four rings.

I got so frustrated over this seemingly immutable law that I bought five phones (three cordless and two stationary) to cover our three levels. I figured if I bought enough phones, eventually one of them would have to remain on each level.

But no! We regularly miss calls because all the cordless phones somehow find themselves in the same corner, buried under a pile of laundry or a kid's gym bag. One afternoon, after missing yet another call following a mad dash up the stairs, my frustration reached a breaking point. "Look," I complained to my wife and kids, "we have at least one phone for each floor. How difficult is it to leave the phone on the floor where you found it? This is the *black* phone. It stays on *this* floor!"

"Gary," Lisa said, "*you* were the last one to use that phone. Remember? You had a call about a half hour ago, and you took it upstairs where it was quieter. *You're* the one who left it upstairs."

Boy, the kids had a good laugh about that one—and I could say nothing in my defense. Lisa had caught me red-handed. How difficult is *that*?

Parents find it so easy to act as though we never make mistakes, as though we have arrived and only our children need to shape up. Yeah, I had a good slice of humble pie that day. But spiritually speaking, it was one of the best meals I've had in years.

Devotions for Sacred Parenting, 64–65

MAKE EVERY EFFORT

Because we feel secure in our trust in the finished work of Jesus Christ, we sometimes take for granted our continued growth in holiness. "I know getting into heaven isn't a matter of my morality," we may think, "and of course I'll repent of any major sin I fall into — so what's the big deal if I tolerate a few bad habits?"

Well, the Bible makes spiritual growth a *very* big deal. In fact, Peter tells us that we should "make every effort" to add to our faith "goodness; and to goodness, knowledge; and to knowledge, self-control; and to self-control, perseverance; and to perseverance, godliness; and to godliness, brotherly kindness; and to brotherly kindness, love" (2 Peter 1:5–7).

"Every effort" looks nothing like the casual trot of Barry Bonds as he ambles toward first base while "running out" a fly ball he knows will be caught. "Every effort," rather, recalls Ichiro Suzuki as he barrels toward first base trying to beat out a soft grounder in the infield. That's the kind of exertion to which Peter calls us spiritually. According to him, laziness about increasing in these virtues is to be "nearsighted and blind" and to forget that we have been cleansed from our past sins (2 Peter 1:9).

If heaven doesn't give us the motivation to make every effort, perhaps having kids will. If we don't seek to add to our faith in this aggressive manner, Peter warns that we will be "ineffective and unproductive" in our "knowledge of our Lord Jesus Christ" (2 Peter 1:8). We may indeed be saved, but we won't bring others along with us.

Peter challenges us to look at our own hearts to see if we are truly making every effort to add to our faith the virtues Scripture calls us to practice. Christ's cross-won forgiveness doesn't mean God excuses us from growing in righteousness; it means he frees us from being self-centered as we do so! Growing in godliness is not about trying to achieve heaven but rather about leaving an authentic example for others to follow — beginning with our children.

None of us live perfect lives, but especially if you're a parent, ask yourself this: Am I building an increasingly holy life?

Sacred Parenting, 172–73

THE HEAT OF ANGER

After preaching a sermon on anger, a pastor invited church members who needed special prayer for their struggles with this emotion to come forward. Nineteen individuals responded.

Every one of them was the mother of small children.

Raising children often leads to certain spiritual hazards. On occasion, my children have caused me to laugh as hard as I've ever laughed; at other times, I've become so angry at them that it frightened me, to the point where I almost didn't recognize myself.

Parenting brings real emotions to the surface — emotions too strong to ignore or deny. The process of parenting forces us to become more mature in handling some of the trickier emotions, particularly anger.

Motivation is everything when it comes to anger. The difference between righteous anger and unrighteous anger ultimately comes down to why we feel angry, what we feel angry about, and what we do with our anger. Nehemiah provides a healthy example. When he heard that some of his own people were taking advantage of the poor, he didn't shrug his shoulders, deliver an arrogant opinion on human nature, or ignore the situation. Instead, he became righteously white-hot: "When I heard their outcry and these charges, I was very angry. I pondered them in my mind and then accused the nobles and officials" (Nehemiah 5:6–7).

Nehemiah became angry, but he then paused to ponder his reasons for feeling angry. After thinking through the reasons and determining that he had good reason to be upset, he went into action, confronting the nobles and officials and demanding they make a change. He didn't deny, ignore, or repress his passion; instead, he used it as motivation, subjected it to wisdom and rational thinking, and then took action.

Let's consciously and prayerfully evaluate how we process and then act on our anger, making sure that we are providing a godly example for our children when walking in the land of a sometimes treacherous emotion.

Sacred Parenting, 103–4

RETHINK THAT AMBITION

Deacon John Adams, a common farmer and shoemaker in the eighteenth century, lived by a simple axiom: *The only truly sound investment is land, and once purchased, land should never be sold.* Historians believe that Deacon John made just one exception to this rule. He sold ten acres to send his oldest son, John, to college. Deacon John willingly made that sacrifice in order to give his son the best chance at success.

John didn't waste his father's sacrifice. He went on to become the first vice president and second president of the United States.

The act of raising children invites us to sacrifice our own welfare on behalf of another human being—which, of course, provides marvelous spiritual training.

A man once told me that he would never incur debt to send one of his children to college, nor would he reduce his retirement contribution by a single dollar just so they could get a diploma. Perhaps my wife and I have been irresponsible by taking a different approach, but it has been our joy to lay aside some of our own dreams for the sake of our children in the hope that they can accomplish even more for God's kingdom than we can.

Wasn't this Jesus' own modus operandi? Didn't he willingly give up his life at the remarkably young age of thirty-three? Imagine how much more he could have done with another three or four decades on this earth. Yet Jesus told his disciples, "I tell you the truth, anyone who has faith in me will do what I have been doing. He will do even greater things than these" (John 14:12).

How will we do greater things than Jesus? On the back of his sacrifice, that's how. How could John Adams get an education and climb out of his lower-middle-class background to become one of the most influential men of his day? On the back of his dad's sacrifice, that's how. How do kids get nurtured with the active love, wise counsel, and prayerful presence they so desperately need? On the backs of their parents' sacrifices, that's how.

Sacred Parenting, 181–82

A BLANKET OF SACRIFICE

In the first flush of adolescence, an eighth grader felt increasingly embarrassed about the clothes her mom typically wore. Finally, the mom couldn't take it anymore. "Look, honey," she said, "I realize the clothes I wear are out of style, but you need to know something. I dress like this so you can dress like that. We can't afford for both of us to buy the latest fashions."

I think of the homeschool moms I've met who sacrifice huge chunks of time to educate their children. Or the working moms whose schedules are packed so tightly and who yet find a way to engage in long conversations with a child even when a report is due the next morning. Or the dads who endure frustrating jobs rather than "pursue their dreams" because their family needs the paycheck more than the dad needs his fulfillment.

God calls parents to lay down a blanket of sacrifice on behalf of the next generation. This is the way of Jesus. In many ways, sacrifice defines love. It was one thing for Jesus to *tell* the world, "I love you." It was another thing entirely when he demonstrated his love by dying on our behalf. Paul states, "For you know the grace of our Lord Jesus Christ, that though he was rich, yet for your sakes he became poor, so that you through his poverty might become rich" (2 Corinthians 8:9). Jesus allowed himself to be humiliated so that we could be glorified. He died so that we could live.

Without sacrifice, love becomes mere words and empty sentiment.

A few years ago a cultural icon told the press how much he "loved" his children, even while admitting that he hardly ever saw them. Court records revealed that from 1995 to 1997, this celebrity spent almost twice as much feeding and housing his animals (including over a thousand pigeons and plenty of cats) as he did on child support.[12]

Words and feelings are the cheap currency of sentimentality; sacrifice is the backbone of true biblical love: "Greater love has no one than this, that he lay down his life for his friends" (John 15:13).

Sacred Parenting, 184–85

LAYING DOWN LEGITIMATE NEEDS

Journalist Iris Krasnow once prepared for a "delicious" afternoon and evening out, a needed break from parenting four young boys. First, she planned to get her hair done. Then she intended to teach a class on writing at American University. Then she hoped to meet a close friend at a restaurant to have some "grown-up conversation." It all sounded too good to be true.

Unfortunately it was.

As Iris pulled on her black wool pantsuit with satin lapels, dreaming about what she would eat and drink, one of her sons came into her bedroom and informed her that he had just thrown up and that his head was "on fire." Iris took his temperature: 103.

Iris didn't just *want* this break from her kids; she felt she *needed* it. But her son needed her as well. Whose rights would prevail? Krasnow writes, "As I held him in my lap, his sticky face burrowed into my black blazer. I picked up the telephone and called the pediatrician, then canceled the hair appointment ..., the writing class, and the Cactus Cantina date."[13]

The way Iris responded reminds me of Jesus just after he heard the news of John the Baptist's execution. Jesus knew that John's death provided a tame precursor of what would soon happen to him. Understandably, he felt drawn to seek out a much-needed time of solitude with his Father (Matthew 14:13).

But when the crowds heard that Jesus was nearby, they followed in large numbers. Jesus could have legitimately sent them away and no one could have faulted him. But instead Jesus "had compassion on them and healed their sick" (Matthew 14:14). This went on *all day long*. And at the end of the day, Jesus fed the five thousand.

How many parents have felt at wits' end, eager for time alone, only to have to sacrifice it on behalf of their children? When God calls us into this arena, remember that Jesus has been there. He knows exactly how we're feeling and invites us to turn this difficult moment of sacrifice into a profound place of intimacy and understanding with him.

Sacred Parenting, 186–87

If Only We Had the Time

One of the first great sacrifices we make for our kids involves giving up time. Family needs and desires redefine our weekends and evenings, independent of our individual wishes. For parents who stay at home, the sacrifice grows even larger; just about every minute gets spoken for.

Rachel Cusk describes a scene I'm sure most mothers have experienced — the thrill of seeing an infant falling asleep, perhaps offering a few quiet moments for oneself:

> Her eyelids begin to droop. The sight of them reminds me of the possibility that she might go to sleep and stay that way for two or three hours ... The prospect is exciting, for it is when the baby sleeps that I liaise, as if it were a lover, with my former life. These liaisons, though always thrilling, are often frantic. I dash about the house unable to decide what to do: to read, to work, to telephone my friends ... Watching her eyelids droop, my excitement at the prospect of freedom buzzes about my veins. I begin manically to list and consider things I might do ...[14]

All children require loads of time. Since parents don't get any more hours in a day than childless couples, they have to crucify some activities in order to make way for the new demands. Nothing can substitute for time spent with kids, and this time frequently must come from something else we would prefer to do.

But isn't all ministry this way? Wouldn't all of us like to volunteer for Habitat for Humanity, volunteer for a crisis pregnancy center, or do some other works of service *if only we had the time*? Those who do these things have no more time in their day than those who don't — just as fathers who talk to their children don't have twenty-eight hours as opposed to silent dads who have just twenty-four. Time is no respecter of persons. It's all about where we choose to spend our hours and what we will willingly sacrifice in order to free up some of those hours.

Sacred Parenting, 188–89

August 26

EVERYONE HAS A ROLE

God is building an entire church, and *each* member is crucial. The eye, the hand, the foot, the mouth—all have a role to play (see 1 Corinthians 12:14–31). We are just one cog in the machine, and, quite frankly, God could replace any one of us without hesitation.

When I was in college, I was deeply saddened by the tragic death of Keith Green, a Christian musician who had an amazingly effective ministry in reaching teens. "How could God let such a strong leader die?" I wondered. But neither Dietrich Bonhoeffer, the great German writer and teacher, nor Blaise Pascal, a brilliant thinker and Christian apologist, lived to the age of forty. Jesus himself didn't even make it to his thirty-fifth birthday.

This truth teaches me plainly that my faithfulness is important, but my service isn't essential. The Christian church can carry on very well if I never write another book, preach another sermon, or speak at another retreat. But God is gracious, and I continue to live.

Therefore we need to learn to live with *passion* and *humility*. As Christians, to marginalize ourselves is to marginalize the God who empowers us and who has used imperfect vessels throughout history. We need to let his power flow while we are still alive!

On the other hand, while serving, we need to remember our humble estate. If God rendered the service of so many brilliant and seemingly capable saints unessential to the well-being of the church, allowing them to pass on at such a young age, who are we to assume that we are irreplaceable?

Our focus should be on God, the Commander who works through his church, and not on the individual (and even expendable) soldiers who can be replaced.

Sacred Marriage, 261–62

August 27

A TWO-STEP PROCESS

I asked a friend about her impression of a Christian conference she had attended. This friend is by no means a critical woman, but I could hear her heart's sadness as she replied, "Virtually all the emphasis was on how to become more fulfilled, more successful, healthier, you name it. It seemed like a very self-centered approach to me."

It's a fine line to walk, because, in general, we will prosper when we listen to God's wisdom for handling money. Our relationships and families will grow stronger when we adopt the attitudes of Jesus Christ. We will have more joy as we walk in obedience, and God does bless us in many ways—but if any of these blessings become the focus, or even worse, the purpose, of our faith, we have substituted a gross distortion for an authentic faith.

In fact, God blesses us in order that we may bless others. Proverbs 11:25 reads, "A generous man will prosper; he who refreshes others will himself be refreshed." A little later in the same book, the writer states, "A generous man will himself be blessed, for he shares his food with the poor" (Proverbs 22:9). The apostle Paul applied this concept to the believers at Corinth when he urged them to share their bounty with the less fortunate: "At the present time your plenty will supply what they need, so that in turn their plenty will supply what you need" (2 Corinthians 8:14). Does this sharing sometimes pinch us? Of course. But receiving a blessing from God is just the first step in a two-step process. The second step is asking, "How can I turn this personal blessing into a way to bless someone else?"

Paul urges us to offer ourselves as living sacrifices (Romans 12:1). Both Scripture and the ancients present a faith motivated not just by how much we are blessed and how far we get catapulted into affluence, but by our willingness to sacrifice those blessings, to literally give up everything for the pearl of great value (Matthew 13:45–46).

Authentic Faith, 194–95

August 28

WE DON'T GET TO CHOOSE

My former seminary professor, Klaus Bockmuehl, once described to his students the pain of living so far apart from his grown children. "Elizabeth [his wife] and I always prayed that our children would serve God," he said to us, "and all of them are doing so — in separate countries."

His sacrifice was living apart from his children. Others who have mentally or physically challenged children sacrifice by living with their children for decades beyond the "normal" duration.

What makes sacrifice so difficult is that we don't get to choose our crosses. Only one man could die for our sins — Jesus Christ, the perfect one — so his destiny was written in stone from the day he was born. In the same way, God has placed us in settings where certain sacrifices become necessary. The only thing that can make these sacrifices precious is recognizing where the sacrifice is pointing.

Francis de Sales once wrote, "The more a cross is from God, the more we should love it." We're not masochists; we don't enjoy pain for its own sake. But we value obedience to God and the intimacy it builds over any pleasure that takes us further away from enjoying his presence. In this light, God's invitations to sacrifice are not April Fool's pranks; they are February's Valentines, if we receive them in this spirit. They become precious because of the One who sent them to us. They mark us as his, and thus we wouldn't trade them for anything in the world.

The human-centered faith often embraced today leads to great disillusionment when life doesn't turn out perfect. The truth is, no life turns out perfect. All of us will be called to give up something. When Christians are told up front that the Christian life is a life of sacrifice, they will be better equipped to live out an authentic faith.

By its nature, sacrifice makes our faith more precious. It is human nature to value most that which has cost us something. If you don't highly value your faith, then perhaps you've never sacrificed for it.

Authentic Faith, 200–201

GIVING PAST THE POINT OF PAIN

King David once declared that he would not sacrifice to the Lord anything that cost him nothing (1 Chronicles 21:24). In contrast, my attitude is often exactly the opposite: "I'm willing to act like a Christian as long as it doesn't cost me anything. I'll give—but not when it hurts. I'll volunteer—as long as it's enjoyable and doesn't disrupt my schedule. I'll give up something—as long as I don't really want it."

Jesus commended the destitute widow for giving up all she had, even though she gave a relatively small gift (Luke 21:1–4). God looks not at the size of the gift, but at the size of the sacrifice.

As Christians, we no longer sacrifice animals as burnt offerings, but we can offer financial gifts, food for the hungry, and good deeds toward others. The writer of Hebrews implores us, "Do not forget to do good and to share with others, for with such sacrifices God is pleased" (Hebrews 13:16). We will never think about this aspect of faith, however, if we continue to define our faith in terms of God being obligated to bless us.

Where are you today?

Are you willing to be a member of your church—as long as they don't ask you to start serving (or work with the young people)? Are you willing to give a few dollars to God's work—as long as you won't really miss them? Are your daily decisions based on what brings you the least amount of discomfort and the greatest amount of affluence?

If you feel dissatisfied or frustrated with God, try this: Instead of accusing him, ask yourself what you've been holding back. Instead of waiting for God's blessing, ask him where you can begin serving. Rather than becoming disillusioned by what God seems to be withholding, remember that we are called to present our bodies as living sacrifices to accomplish God's work on earth. Are we willing to keep giving past the point of pain?

Authentic Faith, 195–97

THE NOBLE ROAD

In the mid-1990s, doctors diagnosed Lance Armstrong, a professional cyclist who demonstrated great promise but had little to show for it, with testicular cancer. They told him he had a 40 percent chance of survival, but that was optimistic. In reality, the physicians didn't want to tell him he probably wouldn't reach the age of thirty.

After chemotherapy and the cancer's remission, Lance returned to his bike. He placed a respectable fourteenth in the Ruta del Sol, but in the middle of the Paris-Nice race he pulled to the side of the road and told his teammates he was through with racing.

Back home in Austin, he became a self-described bum. He played golf every day, water-skied, drank beer, lay on the sofa, and channel-surfed. He ate at his favorite Tex-Mex restaurant and violated every rule of his training diet. "I intended never to deprive myself again," he said.[15]

After several weeks of this, his future wife told him that he needed to decide if he was going to be a golf-playing, beer-drinking, Mexican-food-eating slob for the rest of his life. She'd love him anyway, she said, but if he was, she was going to go out and get a job.[16]

One week later, Lance was back on his bike, training hard. About a year later, he won the most grueling sporting event in the world, the Tour de France, eventually repeating the performance for a record total of seven victories. Today he credits his cancer with helping him to win the Tour: "Without cancer, I never would have won a single Tour de France."[17]

We pay a price when we become leisure-oriented, self-serving, pleasure-seeking people. Something within us dies. We lose a certain nobility and self-respect, for we know we are becoming less than we could be. Sacrifice sharpens our character and refines our faith.

If you feel disillusioned about your life and faith, it's not because Christianity isn't fulfilling; it's because you've stopped thinking and acting like a Christian —someone who has sold everything for the pearl of great value, someone who considers everything a loss compared to the greatness of knowing Jesus Christ.

Authentic Faith, 201–2

THE TWO ESSENTIAL QUESTIONS

A journey toward complete surrender to God leads us to grapple with two fundamental questions: "Is God good?" and "Is God the Lord?" Only if we truly believe in God's goodness can we entrust ourselves completely to his care, and only if we trust that God actually rules over the affairs of this world can we have confidence that he can make a difference for our good.

Both the goodness and providence of God are well established in Scripture, but both are questioned today. Many ask, "If God is so good, then why does he allow evil things to happen?" and "If God is in control, then why is the world such a mess?" Until we resolve these two questions for ourselves, we will remain at odds with God, and surrendering to him—along with the intimacy that such surrender brings—simply will not be possible.

Thomas à Kempis wrote about the goodness of God: "Do with me whatever it shall please thee. For it cannot be anything but good, whatever thou shalt do with me. If it be thy will I should be in darkness, be thou blessed; and if it be thy will I should be in light, be thou again blessed."[18] William Law wrote of God's providence: "Every man is to consider himself as a particular object of God's providence, under the same care and protection of God as if the world had been made for him alone. It is not by chance that any man is born at such a time, of such parents, and in such place and condition."[19]

Many of us carry wounds that require healing before we can embrace these two truths, so we need to do whatever soul work may be necessary for us to embrace God's goodness and providence. Others of us may have some intellectual mountains to climb before we can wave our white flags of surrender. We must do whatever we need to in order to resolve these two fundamental questions.

Until we do, we'll never find rest in God.

Thirsting for God, 95–97

SEPTEMBER

With summer vacations over, it's time to get back to school. God wants to teach us, to open up his Word to us, and to train us to listen for his voice. He wants to prepare our minds to discern his wisdom and to lead us through the school of godly character.

September 1

SACRED STUDENTS

Every month, without fail, I eagerly read *Runner's World* magazine. Because I love running, I want to read about the latest training techniques and running gear. I revel in the inspiring personal stories. I check my calendar against upcoming races. I want to know about the latest shoes. I even pore over the ads.

The Bible could well be called *God's World*. If we truly love God's world, Bible study will be a joy. We will eagerly embrace the filling of our minds with his inspired words and want to read the insights of others as they interact with God's Word, which is why being a diligent student also usually means reading other books.

Is it possible to be a faithful disciple and not be a diligent student? No. Contemplative prayer, social activism, fellowship, and enthusiastic worship all have their place, but it is impossible to be serious disciples of Jesus if we do not also become serious students of his truth.

Do not allow laziness or lack of fondness for reading, discipline, and study to imprison you in spiritual immaturity. Someone may prefer not to exercise, but if they are fifty pounds overweight and trying to ward off diabetes, high blood pressure, and clogged arteries, then they had better get over it. They will never get healthy until they find a way to exercise.

In the same way, if someone is ignorant of God's Word, then they will reflect this ignorance in their beliefs, their speech, their purpose in life, their motivations, and in all sorts of spiritual illnesses. They need to get over their distaste of disciplined study.

Christianity is not like some Eastern religions that try to circumvent the mind with meditations designed to put the mind in a state of paralysis. Christianity gives a reasonable explanation of the universe and our relationship with the God who created us. Ignorance isn't just sin; it leads to ever-increasing sin. And it has no place in a maturing believer's life.

Holy Available, 115–17

TAKE CHARGE OF YOUR MIND

The Bible makes it clear that we need to take charge of our minds. On their own, minds can be instruments of anxiety, doubt, worry, fear, and romantic fallacies. Paul urges us to exert ourselves more strongly in the arena of our minds than in any other area of the spiritual life: "Finally, brothers, whatever is true, whatever is noble, whatever is right, whatever is pure, whatever is lovely, whatever is admirable — if anything is excellent or praiseworthy — think about such things" (Philippians 4:8). He gets even more forceful when writing to the Corinthians: "Stop thinking like children. In regard to evil be infants, but in your thinking be adults" (1 Corinthians 14:20).

We need to mature to the point where we take charge of our minds, Paul insists, because God holds us accountable to do so. Jesus challenged some teachers of the law for their faulty reasoning when he said, "Why are you thinking these things?" (Mark 2:8).

Some Christians act as if they are helpless victims of their own thinking, as if they can't stop certain fantasies, infatuations, negative thinking, rumination on fears, or hateful prejudices. This simply doesn't square with a biblical worldview that tells us to pivot toward pure thought. We are taught to stop thinking about evil and to start thinking about what is pure and admirable and excellent.

For understandable reasons, we give our brains a little more power than they deserve, but ultimately, the Bible tells us we must not allow any organ to rule over us — not our stomachs, not our genitalia, and not our brains. We must take dominion over each aspect of our humanity, surrender it to God, and allow it to be transformed by God. For this reason Paul wrote, "We demolish arguments and every pretension that sets itself up against the knowledge of God, and *we take captive every thought* to make it obedient to Christ" (2 Corinthians 10:5, emphasis added). To "take captive" implies wartime conditions, and so it is. We must capture rogue thoughts and substitute godly ideas that glorify Christ.

Holy Available, 118

NEW MEANING TO AN OLD PRACTICE

Meditating on Scripture is an important source of nourishment for any Christian. The Old Testament first recommended this repetitive practice: "Do not let this Book of the Law depart from your mouth; meditate on it day and night, so that you may be careful to do everything written in it" (Joshua 1:8). Certain scriptural rituals can add new meaning to an old practice. Consider trying the following:

Read Scripture aloud. I did this in a hotel room the first time. Tired from being on the road, I tried to silently read the Bible. The words seemed to meld into one another, and I was getting nowhere. I knew I needed to be replenished, however, so I got up, paced around the room, and began reading the Scriptures aloud. The words came alive. Hearing them spoken seemed to ram them into my soul.

Use the Psalms. The early church father Chrysostom urged every Christian to read through Psalm 62 in the morning and Psalm 140 in the evening. According to Caesarious of Arles, all Christians knew Psalms 50, 90, and 103.[1] There can be great benefit in reading the same passages of Scripture over and over until you know them by heart. Imagine the power of reading a psalm at age eighty that you read daily in your thirties. Rituals can tie our years together with the common thread of faith.

Begin your day with the Bible. In my early teens, I started the practice of reading a chapter of the Bible first thing in the morning and last thing in the evening—my first and last conscious activity would be God's Word. I've heard of another Christian who places his Bible on his shoes at night. Before he can get dressed the next morning, he will have to read the Scriptures.

Whatever helps you to get into the Bible, and the Bible into you, is well worth the time and effort it may require. All of us need continual renewal, and God's Word is one of heaven's best tools in bringing it to us.

Sacred Pathways, 87–88

CULTIVATING THE QUIET

"God," I prayed as a ten-year-old, "I'm staying in here until I see you. You showed yourself to Moses; you can show yourself to me."

Silence. The linoleum floor pushed back against my knees. I started to get hungry.

"OK," I said out loud. "I'm going to close my eyes. When I open them again, I want you to show yourself to me. *Please.*"

I closed my eyes and bristled with anticipation. When I opened my eyes, I saw a sink and a bathtub, but no God incarnate. But then I heard a loud knock on the door. My heart leapt.

"Gary," my mother's familiar voice rang out, bringing my heart back to normal, "are you OK? You've been in there a long time."

God never did show up in bodily form.

At the time, I thought giving God thirty minutes to appear seemed quite generous, but years later, while reading through the book of Exodus, I changed my mind. When Moses went up on a mountain to meet God, he waited for six days before God spoke to him (chapter 24). *Six days!* When I sit down to pray and wait for six *minutes*, I am proud of myself. And what about the people of Israel? Sadly, the Israelites got swept into idolatry by mere boredom. They simply got tired of waiting (32:1).

The same is true for many of us. Ask us to give money, and we'll write a check. Ask us to show up for a demonstration, and we're there. But ask us to face boredom, and we turn on the TV, tune in the radio, or plug in our iPods. Please don't ask us to be bored!

In the midst of the noise, God calls us into the quiet (Isaiah 30:15). If we would live and love the way Christians throughout history have, we must learn to value silence. Listen to Lorenzo Scupoli: "Silence, beloved, is a safe stronghold in the spiritual battle, and a sure pledge of victory. Silence is the friend of him who distrusts self and trusts in God; it is the guardian of the spirit of prayer and a wonderful help in the attainment of virtues."[2]

In a loud and busy world, will we allow silence to lead us forward?

Thirsting for God, 113–14, 117–18

TAKE AND READ!

"Tolle, lege!"

A young child's singsong voice calling out, *"Tolle, lege!"* ("Take and read!") first pierced the ears and then shook the heart of a man who would become one of Christianity's most famous teachers. Something told the young and proud Augustine that these words sprang from a divinely ordained source. He knew of no child's game that used the words "take and read," so he accepted them at face value, opened the New Testament, and soon surrendered to the power of God's truth. Thus began a long journey of faith that would leave an indelible mark on what was then a relatively new faith.

Perhaps it is not surprising, given the genesis of his faith, that throughout his life Augustine remained sensitive to the God who speaks. In *The Confessions*, Augustine writes:

> You [God] are Truth, and you are everywhere present where all seek counsel of you. You reply to all at once ... The answer you give is clear, but not all hear clearly. All ask you whatever they wish to ask, but the answer they receive is not always what they want to hear. The man who serves you best is the one who is less intent on hearing from you what he wills to hear than on shaping his will according to what he hears from you.[3]

The young man who once had an insatiable desire for renown and a woman's touch evolved into a strong bishop who sought God's divine guidance: "Whisper words of truth in my heart, for you alone speak truth."[4]

Though the practice of listening to God remains controversial to some, earnest believers have understood that the blessings of this biblical practice far outweigh the occasional problems that result. Frank Buchman, whose ministry touched private individuals and influential world leaders during the early part of the twentieth century, argued, "Divine guidance must become the normal experience ... Definite, accurate, adequate information can come from the mind of God to the minds of men. This is normal prayer."[5]

Do you pray only with your tongue? Are you willing to pray with your ears as well?

Holy Available, 87 – 88

DOES GOD STILL SPEAK?

Some people today teach that God speaks only indirectly through preaching and applying the Bible's timeless principles. To be sure, Scripture is the only infallible record we have of God's revelation. Yet this same Bible bursts with stories of God communicating to individuals.

Every Old Testament patriarch, as well as the psalmists, not only heard from God, but begged him to keep speaking. The book of Acts overflows with accounts of God speaking to individuals—to Peter, Stephen, Philip, Ananias, Paul, Cornelius, and many others. Jesus himself set the example of humble listening: "He who sent me is reliable, and what I have heard from him I tell the world ... I do nothing on my own but speak just what the Father has taught me" (John 8:26, 28). I love how my spiritual mentor, Dr. Klaus Bockmuehl, summarizes Jesus' stance:

> The common denominator in these passages is a God-inspired, fundamental, and comprehensive suspension of judgment: I will not judge, decide, speak, or do anything on my own, but I will first listen to God. This reservation represents the end of human autonomy or self-governance and establishes, in practice, the primacy and reality of God's kingship in the earthly life of Jesus.[6]

Some earnest believers have taken "listening to God" to an unhealthy extreme, making mundane tasks (which road to take on the way home, whether to order chicken or beef) take on cosmic importance. On the other hand, I've known some staunch believers who insist that we're simply supposed to use our own reasoning to apply the general principles given in Scripture. This borders on practical atheism and undercuts the Holy Spirit's role as our Counselor.

In addition to study, we need to *experience* God. How real is your God? Does your faith have a pulse? Do you enjoy a dynamic relationship, or are you limiting yourself to simply trying to follow "timeless biblical principles"? Whether you believe that God speaks today will have a major impact on your spiritual life.

Holy Available, 88–89

DEAF TO GOD'S GUIDANCE

When God speaks, how well do we listen? Can we improve in this practice? See if anything catches you off guard as you take a fresh look at one of Jesus' famous illustrations:

> No one lights a lamp and hides it in a jar or puts it under a bed. Instead, he puts it on a stand, so that those who come in can see the light. For there is nothing hidden that will not be disclosed, and nothing concealed that will not be known or brought out into the open. Therefore consider carefully *how you listen*. Whoever has will be given more; whoever does not have, even what he thinks he has will be taken from him.
>
> Luke 8:16–18, emphasis added

I remember reading this passage and being struck by the seemingly out-of-place "consider carefully *how you listen*." For whatever reason, I didn't expect the instruction. Jesus is talking about what we *see*—what is hidden, what is disclosed—but then makes his main point about what we *hear*. If our *hearing* goes bad, he seems to be saying, even what we think we know will be taken away. But if we learn to listen—to truly hear—we will receive spiritual wealth and understanding beyond imagination.

The Greek imperative translated "consider carefully" is *blepete*; it means "to watch" or "to take care," "to give the matter due attention." "How you listen" translates *pos akouete*, which addresses the way in which we hear. Put together, these words mean that we should hear with great thought, not haphazardly. We should make a concerted effort to tune in to spiritual truth, an effort that addresses not just whether we hear from God's Word but how, in what manner, in what state, and in what frame of mind.

If we fail to listen or listen in the wrong way, we become spiritually deaf. Eventually, we'll lose even what we have. But if we take heed, we will be blessed with new insight and understanding. The transformative process will take hold in our lives, and God will increase our understanding.

Holy Available, 91–92

ACTIVE, AVAILABLE EARS

How well do we listen to the Word of God? While the parable of the soils seems to address how we receive the truth of the salvation message, it is significant that in Luke 8:16–18, Jesus is talking to his disciples, who already have heard the gospel. It's to them that he says, "Consider carefully how you listen." Hearing, then, is an ongoing process.

This is almost completely backward from how we view biblical teaching and communication. As people walk out of church, they are often evaluating the preacher. "How was the sermon?" someone will ask.

"Well, a little long, kind of boring, but overall a noble effort."

But the Bible never addresses giving a good sermon; it only addresses how we *receive* that sermon—which means that the conversation after church, from a biblical perspective, should go like this:

"How was your hearing today?"

"Pretty good. I was attentive, and I've taken the truth to heart. I want to hold on to it, so I've taken some notes, and I'm going to be praying about it this weekend. I don't want to lose what God has given me."

The sad truth is, most of us worry more about losing our wallets in church than we do about losing the truth that God laid out for us. And doesn't this put us in the dangerous category Jesus warned about when he spoke of "those who hear, but as they go on their way they are choked by life's ... riches ... and they do not mature"?

What does this mean in practice? Every time the Word of God is proclaimed, my priorities get tested. My future spiritual health will be governed in no small part by my hearing. Careless hearing will stop up my spiritual understanding; over time, it can even take away what little I already have. Have your ears become active, available servants of God?

Holy Available, 92–93

LISTENING FOR OTHERS

I'll always remember when my good friends Rob and Jill Takemura got engaged. Rob organized such an elaborate proposal that it made the evening news.

When you truly love someone, you'll go out of your way to show it. That's why I can empathize with a paralyzed man's friends who cut through a roof to get their friend in front of the wonder-working Rabbi. When the attending teachers of the law heard Jesus say to the paralytic, "Son, your sins are forgiven," they started grumbling in their hearts: "Why does this fellow talk like that? He's blaspheming! Who can forgive sins but God alone?" (Mark 2:5–7).

And Jesus *heard* them. I emphasize *heard* because they weren't actually speaking: "Immediately Jesus knew in his spirit that this was what they were thinking in their hearts" (verse 8), and he rebuked them.

In a similar way, Peter "heard" what was unspoken about Ananias and Sapphira, the deceitful couple who pretended to give all their earnings to God while keeping back a share for themselves (see Acts 5:1–11). This type of hearing has served me personally. In college, when I was dating a young woman, a woman who listened to God "saw" me in prayer one morning and then asked, "Tell me, is your relationship with _____ absolutely above reproach?" This act of great courage and love kept an unhealthy situation from growing even worse. God arrested my slide before it was too late. *I* had stopped hearing—but this woman had not! And I thank God for her faithfulness.

If we listen carefully, God may give us an encouraging word to sustain the weary. We can listen for others who have stopped listening but who still need God's perspective. This must be done humbly, without prophetic arrogance— and usually without tipping our hand that we think it may be a divine nudge. We're simply speaking with an instructed tongue in the hope that God's insight may be embraced.

Will you humbly be open to listening for others? God may occasionally choose to speak to us in order to reach another believer with stopped-up ears.

Holy Available, 94–95

A MOST PRECIOUS GIFT

I'll never forget my first appearance on *Focus on the Family*. I rarely get nervous about public speaking, but the reality that I was about to tape a program heard by millions seemed daunting. Complicating matters was that when I speak, I have notes. I know where I'm headed, and I'm working with familiar material. That morning the thought hit me, "What if I get asked an unexpected question and I freeze?"

Since I'm not used to dealing with a bad case of nerves, I'm not particularly experienced at making them go away. So I took refuge in the restroom just outside the studio wing and started pacing in front of the sinks. Finally, God's voice broke through so clearly, so convincingly, so therapeutically: "This is *so* not about you."

As I listened to God's still, small voice — not audible, but unmistakable nevertheless — I realized that my nerves came from my pride. I wanted to make a good impression. I wanted to be entertaining, thought-provoking, the type of guest my hosts would want to ask back. But God wasn't as concerned about me that day as he was about reaching families with the message contained in *Sacred Marriage*.

I heard a clear call to focus on those struggling in their homes because of a faulty understanding of Christian marriage; and once I began focusing on the ones God really wanted to reach, the nervousness dissipated like my daughter's beloved soap bubbles. It just vanished.

And God's words, "This is so not about you," remain to this day one of the most precious gifts my heavenly Father has ever given me. Whenever I stumble toward nervousness, I now know that the reason is pride. I'm trying to make an impression instead of focusing on being a servant.

Holy Available, 96

THE TURNED CHRISTIAN

I get a lot of requests to write endorsements for books. During one month I received two books, one on prayer and one written by David Benner called *Desiring God's Will*. Benner's book has the wonderful subtitle *Aligning Our Hearts with the Heart of God*. I could have endorsed the book just for its focus, but it proved to be a rich spiritual read as well.

I'm at a place where I desire to hear God's voice ten times more than I desire to lay out any particular request. Of course, asking is important, but I tend to think, "If I don't have it, how badly do I really need it?" And I need to hear God's perspective far more than I need to tell him mine.

This is why I especially appreciated David Benner's book. For every one book on listening to God, there are a thousand on talking to God. We need to become completely enamored with hearing God's voice: "Speak, LORD, for your servant is listening" (1 Samuel 3:9).

Brother Lawrence, Frank Laubach, and many other practitioners of divine listening attest to the development of "turned" Christians. "Turning" to hear God usually begins as an act of the will, involving hundreds of tiny but significant conscious decisions. Over time, this turning becomes our normal bent and we become what the ancients called "turned Christians."

Once we reach this point, what once was discipline becomes delight — and it has come to delight my own heart. I don't take credit for this practice; it's simply one of the many delights I enjoy as God's adopted son. You and I *can* work toward a "turned" relationship, a propensity to listen to God; and when we do, we can be amazed at how easily God's voice can break through.

You can start this process today. As you go about your daily tasks, consciously choose to remain sensitive to God's voice, God's direction, God's guidance. He will take it from there.

Holy Available, 97–98

TESTING, 1, 2 . . .

Through his church, God has left us with many concrete, traditionally understood tests for accurately discerning God's voice.

The First Test: Scripture. God will never contradict himself. Anything we think we hear from God that does not align itself with scriptural revelation should automatically be disregarded. The only certain revelation is God's written Word. But if we listen as we read, God can help us apply those words in practical and specific ways. Our first step to hearing God is to become biblically informed. The Bible shapes our thinking and provides the framework for all of God's communication to humankind. If someone truly wants to know God's will, he or she should begin by developing a biblically informed mind — the kind of mind that trains us to understand wisdom and God's perspective.

The Second Test: The Church's Witness. I am suspicious of anyone who has a novel interpretation of the Word of God. Creativity has its place, but when it comes to understanding truth, faithfulness is a much higher priority. Frank Buchman observed, "No one can be wholly God-controlled who works alone. It is to a group of willing men and women that God speaks most clearly."[7]

We need to heed the warnings of the Reformers. They said that when *anyone* can claim divine inspiration, the end of the church is in sight. We listen to God humbly, as daughters and sons of God's church. None of us should delight in swimming against the current; we must do so only when we are convinced that Scripture insists on it.

On the other hand, Calvin may have inadvertently helped create the personality-centered church that has existed for too long, a one-man show that can undercut the priesthood of all believers by limiting God's speaking almost exclusively to trained preachers. In this case, we must seek a middle ground in which we base our understanding on God's Word, while also receiving personal instruction, comfort, and advice that must be tested. Even then, we always hold these things secondarily as *possible* applications of God's written Word. *(Continued tomorrow.)*

Holy Available, 100–101

TESTING, 3, 4

If we truly want to hear from God, then we must listen to the church's witness about how it has effectively been done.

The Third Test: A Holy Life. Sin may not block our salvation, but it does tend to stop up our ears. It leads us down a path of deception and hinders further understanding and direct hearing. If we are serious about listening to God, we must take seriously the words of God in Leviticus: "Be holy, because I am holy" (11:45). If you haven't dealt with your pride, then your own voice and ambition eventually will begin to sound suspiciously like God's. And if you haven't gained some mastery over your fear, you'll mistake your worry for the Holy Spirit's "warning."

Transformation is a process; growth in one area helps us grow in other areas as well. Augustine honestly faced the consequences of sin. He clearly believed that "true understanding depends on moral uprightness, for an evil will does not comprehend the truth."[8] The listening life must therefore be a devout life. Hypocrisy stops up our ears and tends to lead to self-justification and empty rationalization rather than humble hearing. Obedience becomes an essential component of maintaining ears that hear.

The Fourth Test: Growing Familiarity with God's Voice. If you speak with those who are practiced in listening to God, they testify that, over time, God's voice becomes familiar in a way that nothing else can match. We begin to experience Jesus' promise in John 10:4–5: "His sheep follow him because they know his voice. But they will never follow a stranger; in fact, they will run away from him because they do not recognize a stranger's voice."

God's voice has a certain style and tone that mark it as genuine. Just as those who catch counterfeiters train by becoming obsessively familiar with the real thing, so we build walls between ourselves and deception by patiently, perseveringly, and faithfully practicing the presence of God.

You *can* hear from God. The question is: Are you ready to listen?

Holy Available, 100–101

FINGER-POINTING

Religion professor Jerry Sittser captures one of family life's most fundamental spiritual problems: finger-pointing.

> Most homes are like mine, single parent or not. They seem to follow a similar pattern. Family members use the misbehavior of each other to excuse their own. A wife whines, "My husband is never home on time." Her husband responds, "She's such a crab when I'm home that it makes me want to stay away." A brother accuses a sister, "She comes into my room all the time without asking." She counters, "He's always taking my CDs. I can get them if I want to. They're mine."[9]

What can break us out of this spiritual morass? If everybody always blames someone else, how can the home life ever change? Instead of offering a three-step resolution process, Jesus prescribes the spiritual virtue of *humility*. Humility is the only antidote strong enough to take a household filled with blame and backbiting and turn it into a place of growth and encouragement.

But here's the tricky part. The person most in need of this lesson is the *parent*. We need to take the lead and set the example. We set an entirely new tone in our household when our kids occasionally hear us say, "I was wrong; I'm sorry. Please forgive me." Suddenly, the kids won't feel like they're the only ones always being challenged. They'll understand that God is at work in all of us, and they'll be far more likely to admit their own shortcomings.

Learning to question ourselves is among the most difficult experiences in life. It is graduate school spirituality. If humility does not get purposefully taught and consistently modeled, our kids will never get it. Only when we admit our own sin and take responsibility for it can we live in peace and harmony.

Because sin is as tenacious as it is terrible, it has to be continuously crucified, which means we must model humility again and again. If you've worn yourself out with all the "methods," why not give Jesus' words a try and begin modeling humility and self-examination?

Devotions for Sacred Parenting, 105

September 15

A Soul Filled with God

Personal worship is an absolute necessity for a strong marriage. It comes down to this: If I stop *receiving* from God, I start *demanding* from others. Instead of appreciating and loving and serving others, I become disappointed in them. Instead of cherishing my wife, I become aware of her shortcomings. I take out my frustrations with a less-than-perfect life and somehow blame her for my lack of fulfillment.

But when my heart gets filled by God's love and acceptance, I am set free to love instead of worrying about being loved. I'm motivated to serve instead of becoming obsessed about whether I'm being served. I'm moved to cherish instead of feeling unappreciated.

A wife complains about a lack of spiritual intimacy in her relationship with her husband. "He's never been what you might call a spiritual leader," she says, and this has become almost an obsession for her — as if her own spiritual health depends on her husband suddenly becoming mature.

Spiritual intimacy is a legitimate desire, but whenever we place our happiness in the hands of another human being, we guarantee ourselves some degree of disappointment. This is why worship sets us free. It meets our most basic need — to rest in the fact we are known and loved, that we have a purpose, and that our eternal destiny and delight is secure — so that lesser needs (including spiritual companionship) serve the role of an occasional dessert rather than our main meal.

It's simply not fair to ask our spouse to fulfill us. No one can. If we expect our spouse to be God for us, our spouse will fail every day and on every account. Not only that, should our disappointment lead us to divorce, our second, third, and even fourth spouse will fail us too!

There is no one else who can love us like God, with a steady and giving love. When the one thing we seek is to dwell in God's house, gaze on his beauty, and seek him in his temple (Psalm 27:4), our soul's sense of desperate need is met in our heavenly Father's arms. Then we leave that temple and find tremendous joy in giving, loving, and serving rather than in keeping close accounts as to whether we are being loved or being served.

Devotions for a Sacred Marriage, 31–32

THE ROAD TO RUIN

When Jesus fed the five thousand, even those closest to him didn't fully understand the true nature of the miracle. So when Jesus conquered the waves and the storm — no greater feat than feeding so many with such a small amount — "they were completely amazed, for they had not understood about the loaves; their hearts were hardened" (Mark 6:51 – 52).

When they later missed Jesus' point about the "yeast of the Pharisees," Jesus seemed almost exasperated: "Do you still not see or understand? Are your hearts hardened? Do you have eyes but fail to see, and ears but fail to hear?" (Mark 8:17 – 18). Confusion — lack of perception — breeds further uncertainty. So for his men's sake, Jesus becomes literal:

"When I broke the five loaves for the five thousand, how many basketfuls of pieces did you pick up?"

"Twelve," they replied.

"And when I broke the seven loaves for the four thousand, how many basketfuls of pieces did you pick up?"

They answered, "Seven."

He said to them, "Do you still not understand?"

Mark 8:19–21

You can see Jesus' point: they *saw* what happened, so how could they not *see* his point? While they used their physical eyes, their hearts were hardened to the spiritual implications — and so their minds remained dim.

In short, we can either develop or lose our ability to discriminate. I've seen churchgoing adults suddenly act as though feelings are all that matter and thus destroy their families in order to follow their infatuation. Then, five years later, they are surprised at how costly their choice has been for their children and their checkbook.

Don't be among the surprised. Sharpen your mind, stay close to God, and keep confusion at bay. When we lose the ability to discriminate, ruin is never far away.

Holy Available, 108–9

THE TRUE TEST

Most people think of religion as a bunch of dos and don'ts, but I believe a relationship with God is distinguished first of all by listening. During the transfiguration, God the Father admonished Peter, James, and John, "This is my Son, whom I love. *Listen to him!*" (Mark 9:7, emphasis added).

Like Father, like Son. Listening is a constant refrain in the teaching of Jesus:

"Listen and understand" (Matthew 15:10).

"Again Jesus called the crowd to him and said, 'Listen to me, everyone, and understand this'" (Mark 7:14).

"Consider carefully how you listen" (Luke 8:18).

"Listen carefully to what I am about to tell you" (Luke 9:44).

What distinguishes a Christian from those who don't believe or from those who make no room for God in their lives? A Christian *listens* to God while the world ignores him. Frankly, being flat-out ignored offends as much as anything. Does anything feel more irritating than talking to kids who tune us out?

God remains active in our world—and he speaks to us if we will only listen:

"Call to me and I will answer you and tell you great and unsearchable things you do not know" (Jeremiah 33:3).

"The LORD confides in those who fear him" (Psalm 25:14).

"Everyone who listens to the Father and learns from him comes to me" (John 6:45).

Many of us don't actively rebel against God. We don't shake our fist at him or malign his name, but we do ignore him. We are a prideful people by nature, and pride keeps telling us we don't need God to handle the situation at hand. Humble people listen; prideful people never seem to have the time to wait on God. Listening to God provides the true test of our humility.

Sacred Parenting, 56–57

THE IMPORTANCE OF "AND"

Several years ago, one of our kids was having incessant, angry outbursts. Confronting this challenge revealed some of my own weaknesses. Lisa and I went to an insightful counselor to get a better grip on how to handle the situation.

"Gary," the counselor said, "I'm thinking you have a difficult time dealing honestly with your anger about all of this. What are you going to do? As soon as this child makes your life miserable for two hours, are you going to slip off into your study and write about gentleness and peace?"

That's when Lisa laughed. "Well, as a matter of fact," Lisa said, "gentleness *is* one of his talks people like most."

While it is true that gentleness is a key component of who God is — and therefore an indicator of what we should become — it is also true that God wears his gentleness with his strength. Consider these words: "See, the Sovereign LORD comes with power, and his arm rules for him ... He tends his flock like a shepherd: He gathers the lambs in his arms and carries them close to his heart; he gently leads those that have young" (Isaiah 40:10 – 11). God can come "with power" while also "gently" leading his lambs. He is not either strong *or* gentle; he is both, simultaneously.

In many ways, kids become indicators for us, making clear the places where we've gravitated toward extremes. We see our sharp edges, our weaknesses, and the convincing evidence that we are not yet fully rounded people. Children come along and point out where we need more work. They unmask our prejudices and uncover our most glaring weaknesses, the areas where we find it most difficult to love, accept, and forgive.

In the coming days, watch as God uses your children to show you exactly where you're not perfect. I suspect you know about many of these areas. But be open to surprises. Expect the process of parenting to put a spotlight on a hidden weakness — and thank God for providing such help for your spiritual growth.

Devotions for Sacred Parenting, 101 – 2

September 19

LET GOD SET THE AGENDA

I was headed down a wooded trail once, preoccupied with trying to solve a problem at work. As I made my way farther down the trail, I sensed God correcting me. In a matter of yards, my mind was clear and my heart was listening to God, loving him, being with him.

The trail bent and began descending slightly. A freely flowing stream now blocked a creek bed off Bull Run, which I had run across all winter. The same small path of earth I had easily crossed for several months lay under several inches of water. The suddenness of the change overwhelmed me and God's voice broke in: *Opportunities change. If we don't cross when we can, we may not be able to cross at a later date.*

Thoughts, analogies, and ideas flooded through my mind as I hiked around the creek bed to the small wooden footbridge that crossed it. There God planted new directions in my heart, and I lingered at that bridge, enjoying a rich time of worship. Yet I almost missed this blessing because my mind was so full when I entered the woods. God in his mercy broke in, and I left the woods deeply in love with a God who shares his heart and purposes with me.

We cannot receive unless we set aside time for God to speak—and then let him set the agenda for our discussion. He knows what we need to hear. When we're consumed with our temporal problems, we miss the blessing of being outdoors. So when you come to the woods, come to receive. Leave your worries at home.

I've found that most people who ask for my advice don't need my answers as much as they need help asking better questions. In the same way, when I pray, I want to give God room to challenge my assumptions and to help me see my concerns from an entirely different perspective.

Today, don't enter prayer with an agenda. Let God direct the discussion.

Sacred Pathways, 54–55

THE NORMAL EXPERIENCE

I've read a number of books about Frank Buchman (he died in 1961, the year of my birth), who founded a powerful movement known as "Moral Re-Armament." Buchman urged believers to spend time each day listening to God. In a 1935 address to ten thousand people in Denmark, he made this declaration:

> We accept as commonplace a man's voice carried by radio to the uttermost parts of the earth. Why not the voice of the living God as an active, creative force in every home, every business, every parliament? ...
>
> The Holy Spirit is the most intelligent source of information in the world today. He has the answer to every problem. Everywhere when men will let him, he is teaching them how to live ... Divine guidance must become the normal experience of ordinary men and women. Any man can pick up divine messages if he will put his receiving set in order. Definite, accurate, adequate information can come from the Mind of God to the minds of men. This is normal prayer.[10]

This practice of listening to God influenced the highest levels of many national governments and made a major impact on millions of individual lives. Christianity, Buchman insisted, begins with listening.

To a group of twenty-five thousand people in Great Britain, Buchman proclaimed, "The lesson the world most needs is the art of listening to God ... God gave a man two ears and one mouth. Why don't you listen twice as much as you talk? This is a daily possibility for everyone—to listen to God and get his program for the day."[11]

Many of us would enjoy far more effectiveness in our lives if we would *do* less and *listen* more. We stand on dangerous ground if we ever let service to God crowd out our time of listening to God. In his book *On the Way*, Gordon Smith writes bluntly, "It is inconceivable to think that God would give us so much to do that we can no longer spend extended time with Him."[12] Listening doesn't detract from our service; it empowers it.

Sacred Parenting, 63–64

GREAT SPIRITUAL WEALTH

Over the years, solitude has become one of my best friends. There is a quietness and depth to solitude that nourishes me while other spiritual activities—preaching, for instance—deplete me. Even in a crowd or at a party, sometimes I'll try to sneak in a few moments of solitude. In these solitary moments, colors regain their brightness for me, truth regains its clarity, and reality loses its fog. Without some time alone, I feel like I've lost my anchor.

M. Basil Pennington wrote, "If one note is to characterize the true monk, it is this: He is the one who has gone apart, to be in some way alone."[13] Even if we are married or have a busy church ministry, spending some time apart is essential for a deepening walk with God.

For a young mother or father, or a child living at home, getting completely away may not be possible, but we should try to be proactive. A family can create a prayer room; perhaps your local church will allow you to have keys to the sanctuary. Even a walk around the block can suffice. Just the act of getting away can serve as a call to worship.

For years I thrived on arriving hours before anyone else came to the office because I found the quiet and solitude essential for my faith. The early morning was my favorite part of the day. It took some time for me to adjust when another "early bird" joined the staff. I began using the afternoons as a time to get away.

We all need a certain amount of time alone, some of us perhaps every day. You may prefer yours late at night, early in the morning, or at midday. Find the time, even make the time, if need be. Guard it as you would your most treasured possession. Solitude is often the key to great spiritual wealth.

Sacred Pathways, 110–11

BEATING BURNOUT

As an introvert, it's a bit ironic that God has called me to a rather visible, people-oriented job. I frequently speak at conferences, and weekend services at Second Baptist in Houston can have me addressing twenty thousand people. All my insecurities (and not a little sin) come rushing to the forefront.

Yet my job requires me to do this. It is what God has called me to do at this stage of my life, so I need to make allowances for spiritual nourishment within this context. To keep my sanity, I have to schedule time to get outside when I'm on the road, and I almost always reject the idea of sleeping in someone's house. I need — not just want — time alone, without any demands of propriety or politeness. Otherwise I will grow frustrated with my responsibilities and not be able to fulfill my calling.

Some Christians get recharged by getting together and talking about what has happened or just kicking back and enjoying each other's company. I prefer to be alone to think and pray and wind down slowly.

I used to struggle with this need, wondering if I was being selfish. Now I know that if I serve God in a blazing two weeks, or a blazing ten years, and then become burned-out for long periods of time, I will not have been a good steward of my life. I want to faithfully serve God for fifty or sixty or seventy years, which means I need to consider how I can be spiritually replenished.

I've met too many godly men and women who burned out before they entered their most productive years. Sometimes burnout led them to quit the ministry and never look back. Others sought escape through illicit activity and brought scandal on the church of Christ. If God grants it, I want to serve him just as zealously in my sixties, seventies, and eighties as I do now.

Are you taking time to recharge your spiritual batteries? I now believe it's not a selfish thing to do; it's about being a good steward of a lifelong call.

Sacred Pathways, 235–36

A Simple Faith

One time I spoke at a Sacred Marriage seminar on the East Coast. I had covered the material many times, but I like to ask God if he would like me to customize it for a particular audience. That weekend I focused—for the first time—on the idea that the participants' marriages were very precious to God, even if they were no longer precious to them. The word *precious* kept coming up.

Afterward a young wife approached me with tears in her eyes. "What you said," she began, "about our marriage being precious to God ..." She paused, composed herself, and added, "My *name* is Precious. I can't tell you how much that spoke to me."

What are the odds? How many people have *you* met named Precious?

But that's the point. I wasn't playing the odds. I was listening, and God spoke, hitting at least one woman at a deep level.

This kind of thing happened to author Frank Buchman all the time. One evening, while walking down the street, he clearly had the thought to speak to the man strolling in front of him. At first Buchman hesitated, but God seemed insistent. Finally Frank called out, "I felt I ought to speak to you. I thought you might need something."

"Of course I am in need," the man replied. "God must have sent you to me."

The man's mother was dying in the hospital. His brothers and sisters had remained at the bedside, and he had stepped out to clear his head. Frank returned with him to the hospital and had a powerful time of ministry.

An impressed Japanese prime minister once told Frank, "You must feel very proud of all this," to which Frank replied, "I do not feel that way at all. I have had nothing to do with it. God does everything. I only obey and do what He says."[14]

What a wonderfully simple faith: "I only obey and do what He says."

Sacred Parenting, 64–65

A SECURE PLACE

Sometimes listening can feel painful—in a good way. I've found that many times God will gently correct me with a question. On one occasion, the question went something like this: "Are you spending more emotional energy this summer getting to know what's going on in your adolescent daughter's heart or in trying to lower your golf scores?" He didn't say *time*; he didn't say *money* (both of which I could defend). God wanted me to consider the focus of my *emotional energy*—what did I find myself thinking and talking about?

This gentle challenge is a source of great comfort. You gain a calm assurance when you walk in the confidence that God will quietly let you know when you start to stray. You don't feel alone, unprotected, or unwarned. It is a secure place to be, as you rest in God's shepherding care and listen to his voice.

My friend Annie Carlson, who has four children, has an admirable perspective. "We're usually so concerned about finding God's will in major life decisions," she said, "but if we are constantly checking in with God on a daily basis, we get used to listening and then don't panic when big decisions come along."

In other words, we learn to discern God's voice for major life choices by constantly seeking his guidance in our day-to-day decisions and listen to him on a regular basis. Raising kids means we need God's guidance on a daily, if not hourly, basis!

More than anything else, having kids forces me into the posture of listening. In my parental pride, I feel tempted to talk more than to listen, but I've found that talking without listening is a lousy way to build relationships with children. Raising kids has thus reoriented my entire approach to relationships, both with God and other people: *listen, listen, listen*. I've found that the very skills we must possess in order to hear children as they go through their various stages in life are the same skills that sharpen our spiritual sensibilities toward God.

Sacred Parenting, 65–66

THE TRUTH OF TOLERANCE

Our youngest daughter once expressed frustration with one of Lisa's lastborn quirks. "You know what, Kelsey?" I replied, not meaning to sound harsh. "That's never going to change, so you may as well get used to it."

One day Kelsey is going to marry a man, and the day will surely come when she must learn to live with real disappointment. This disappointment will inconvenience her, frustrate her, at times perplex her, and occasionally even anger her.

How providential, then, that God has given her two imperfect parents who can teach her the value and necessity of tolerance! As my kids get older, I'm more and more aware of my responsibility to prepare them for married life. I stress how the skills for family life they develop as brother and sister, son and daughter, will come into great use as husband and wife, father and mother. If they don't learn these skills now, they're going to have to learn them then, and it'll be much easier if they can begin marriage with these skills rather than weigh down a future relationship in its early stages.

Tolerance is a key virtue for communal living. I hesitate to use the word *tolerance*, as it has been co-opted by many in our culture to justify obscene forms of evil—but the word still has meaning, value, and truth. Family life grows miserable without tolerance and patience.

Are you looking for prime opportunities to teach tolerance? How do your kids see you respond to your spouse's limitations or personality quirks? Are they learning that you deal with frustration by belittling your spouse in front of your kids? By gossiping about him or her to your friends? Or do they see you building up your spouse and being gracious when he or she falls short?

A tolerant wife or husband can make the difference between a home where joy and peace reside and a home where pressure and tension become so thick you get a headache by merely walking through the door.

Let's teach tolerance.

Devotions for Sacred Parenting, 149–50

NOT SORRY FOR THE LESSON

Family life will disappoint us, wound us, and frustrate us. Yes, there will be moments of sheer joy and almost transcendent wonder. But make no mistake —family life can cut us open.

If we have only a selfish motivation, we will run from parenting's greatest challenges. Once disappointment seeps in, we'll pull back into the same shells we inhabited as children and run from the pain, not to our bedrooms or backyards, but to our offices, boardrooms, workout clubs, Starbucks, or even churches.

Let's accept that both marriage and parenting provide many good moments while also challenging us to the very root of our being; let's admit that family life tries us as perhaps nothing else does. But let's also accept that, for most of us, this is God's call and part of his plan to perfect us. Once we realize that we are sinners, that the children God has given us are sinners, and that together, as a family, we are to grow toward God, then family life takes on an entirely new purpose and context. It becomes a sacred enterprise when we finally understand that God can baptize dirty diapers, toddlers' tantrums, and teenagers' silence in order to transform us into people who more closely resemble Jesus Christ.

What I've just said, most of us already know in our hearts; we simply haven't put words to it. A pastor-friend of mine confessed to me, "My wife and I would certainly consider our experiences with our son Jeff to be one of the most influential things in our lives, spiritually speaking." A mother who gave birth to a child with a developmental disability said, "I wouldn't change anything. I'm glad I had him, because I wouldn't be the same person. I would have desired for him to be normal, but I'm not sorry I learned what I've learned."

I'm not sorry I learned what I've learned.

That's the message here. Get to the place in this journey of sacred parenting where you can say, "It may have been difficult at times, but I'm not sorry I learned what I've learned."

Sacred Parenting, 17–18

September 27

WATCHFUL LITTLE EYES

Although in a single act of sexual intimacy we can reproduce children who look like us, the real reproduction is spiritual—living in front of children who will imitate us in dramatic ways.

Early one spring when Graham was just four years old, he was "helping" me work on the car when I turned my head and spit.

"Why did you spit?" he asked.

"I don't know. Sometimes guys just need to spit."

"I need to spit too," Graham said, and he let one fly.

Later in the day I was teaching him to play tennis and took off my shirt.

"Why are you taking off your shirt, Dad?" Graham asked.

"I'm just a little hot," I answered.

Instantly I heard his racket drop to the ground. "I'm hot too"—and suddenly his shirt was off as well.

Later, our family decided to go for a walk and Graham couldn't find his shoes. "You look upstairs," I told him, "and I'll look downstairs."

As soon as I reached the landing and looked down, my heart skipped a beat. In the middle of the floor, I had taken off my shoes. About six inches from my shoes lay Graham's little tennis shoes, placed right next to mine, mimicking the same angle at which my shoes had been dropped.

What a sobering weekend! I realized that every move I made was being watched. Every word I chose, every time I did something without even thinking about it, Graham was watching me and coming to the conclusion, "This is what I'm supposed to do because that's what my daddy does."

To be a parent is to teach by example. It gives a whole new meaning to Paul's words to Timothy: "Watch your life and doctrine closely. Persevere in them, because if you do, you will save both yourself and your hearers" (1 Timothy 4:16).

Sacred Parenting, 171–72

September 28

The Joy and Peace of Surrender

Just as complaining leads to bitterness, resentment, and smoldering anger, so surrender leads to tremendous joy and peace. François Fénelon wrote, "O bridegroom of souls, thou lettest the souls which do not resist thee experience in this life an advance taste of felicity."[15]

The glory of the Christian life is found in the fact that God doesn't ask us to surrender only to difficult things. Eventually, if we don't hold back, we'll find that God wants us to surrender to many wonderful things. When we surrender to a good God, we shouldn't be surprised that we must surrender to good things. Sin tastes sweet but turns bitter in our stomachs. Holiness often tastes bitter initially but later turns sweet, like fine wine that seasons over time.

One of the joys of surrender is a deep peace. Rebellion means war, so surrender logically brings peace. This peace gives us new freedom in our relationships, not only with God, but also with others. Thomas à Kempis warned that if we are not surrendered to God, we will also be at war with others: "He that is well in peace, is not suspicious of any man. But he that is discontented and troubled, is tossed with divers suspicions: he is neither at rest himself nor suffereth others to be at rest ... He considereth what others are bound to do, and neglecteth that which is bound to himself."[16]

I suspect that someday we'll have a better understanding of why our lives have gone the way they have. But for now, we must content ourselves in trusting that God knows what he is doing. One thing is for sure: God will not lay down his arms. He has declared war on all who stand in rebellion. The vanquished receive eternal life; the obstinate are condemned by their own foolishness. And there will be no peace for us until we surrender.

Surrender to God is the essence—and the greatest blessing—of the Christian life.

Thirsting for God, 109–10

September 29

THE FREEDOM OF HUMILITY

One day, Brother Masseo, an early follower of Francis of Assisi, asked the saint, "Why does all the world seem to be running after you, and everyone seems to want to see you and hear you and obey you? You are not a handsome man. You do not have great learning or wisdom. You are not a nobleman. So why is all the world running after you?"

Francis sat before God a long time before answering.

> You really want to know why everyone is running after me? I have this from the all-holy eyes of God ... For those blessed and all-holy eyes have not seen among sinners anyone more vile or insufficient than I am. And so in order to do that wonderful work which he intends to do, he did not find on earth a viler creature, and therefore he chose me, for God has chosen the foolish things of the world to put to shame the wise ... so that all excellence in virtue may be from God and not from the creature, in order that no creature should glory before him, but "let him who takes pride, take pride the Lord," that honor and glory may be only God's forever.[17]

Do you understand the freedom in this? We don't have to defend ourselves or even prove ourselves worthy. We can spend 100 percent of our energy and time glorifying God and pointing people to his goodness and sufficiency. And if our weaknesses and limitations spotlight God's glory even more, so much the better.

John the Baptist was the quintessential example of a humble servant of God. He was willing to serve humbly and obscurely in the desert while God readied him for his ministry. He spoke forcefully when God exalted him to become a famous and powerful prophet, but then he willingly handed his ministry over to Jesus the Messiah when the time was right.

May God raise up many more such servants!

Thirsting for God, 163

TINY TEACHERS

The idea that God can use children to teach us, that we have an opportunity to gain spiritual insight from those we are called to raise and teach, comes from our Lord himself, who in this regard was something of a revolutionary.

In the first century, children enjoyed little esteem and virtually no respect. While families appreciated their own children, society merely tolerated them. The language of the day reveals this first-century prejudice. One Greek word for child (*pais* or *paidion*) also can mean "servant" or "slave." Yet another term (*nepios*) carries connotations of inexperience, foolishness, and helplessness. Greek philosophers regularly chided a stupid or foolish man by calling him *nepios*. Even biblical writers admonished Christians to "stop thinking like children [*paidia*]" (1 Corinthians 14:20)—though it is interesting to note that in this same verse Paul writes, "In regard to evil be infants, but in your thinking be adults."

Imagine, then, the people's astonishment when Jesus brings a little child and places him in front of the crowd (Matthew 18:1–9). With his hand on the lad's shoulder, Jesus has the audacity to suggest that this small tyke provides an example to be followed. "Unless you humble yourself like one of these," said Jesus, "you'll never enter the kingdom of God." He means, "Look at them, learn from them, and aspire to become like them."

Jesus seemed to delight in the fact that inexperienced, simple children had an understanding superior to the trained adults. We find the genius of children, spiritually speaking, in their helpless state. The Bible has consistently seen pride as the greatest spiritual failing known to humankind. The message of the gospel scandalizes the proud. It insists that we admit we are fallen, helpless, and in need of someone to pay the price on our behalf. It forces us to let ourselves be imbued with a foreign power so that we can live life the way it was meant to be lived. An infant incarnates this truth perfectly.

How, then, can we become more like a child?

Sacred Parenting, 13–15

OCTOBER

October is my favorite month of the year. The chill of fall, with its shorter days and falling leaves, inspires reflection that brings the noisy days of summer to an end. In many ways, the season's symbol of death (falling leaves, the harvest being gathered, the days getting ever darker) eventually lead to spring's rebirth. Isn't this the metaphor of the Christian life—learning to die so that we might learn to live?

A LONG-RUNNING STORY

In today's busy world, we pride ourselves on how fast we move. One restaurant in Tokyo, Japan, has no prices on the menu. Why not? Because the owners don't charge you by what you eat; they charge you by how long you stay. And at lunchtime, there's a line to get in.

In his book *Faster: The Acceleration of Just About Everything*, James Gleick provides several telling anecdotes about the modern obsession with speed, including "one-minute bedtime stories," condensed so a busy parent can get on with his evening.

In the summer of 2000, an up-and-coming computer publishing executive died at the age of twenty-six. Aaron Bunnell was overwhelmed at the way the world was opening up before him. His fantastic success and wealth thrilled him, but in his desire to keep the ball rolling, he pushed himself a little too far and a little too fast. After Aaron's body was discovered in the Waldorf-Astoria Hotel, his dad publicly admitted that Aaron may well have been ingesting stamina-boosting drugs to "keep going and going ... He pushed it too far."[1]

The irony isn't hard to miss. In a desperate desire to keep things moving faster and faster and to boost his production just a bit more, Aaron brought everything to a crashing halt. All his frantic efforts didn't just get put on hold; they disintegrated in a premature and tragic end.

Despite our obsession with instant results, we serve a God whose calendar moves by millennia, not minutes, and who thinks in terms of generations, not seasons. Unless we understand this about God, we will never understand his ways. Peter is clear: "With the Lord a day is like a thousand years, and a thousand years are like a day" (2 Peter 3:8). While we obsess over where we are today and with what is going to happen in the next year, God's plans for us and this world usually take a long-term view.

When we lose our patience for God's unfolding providence, we lose our perspective. In the end, our lives are but a sentence in the long-running story of God's redeeming work.

Authentic Faith, 36–37

October 2

WAITING: THE BACKBONE OF LOVE

If we are to take seriously Christ's call to love, then we must learn to wait.

I experience this regularly when I spend time with my friend Scott Hope. Scott's life changed irrevocably nearly three decades ago when, shortly before his high school graduation, a drunk driver plowed into his car and injured him severely. He now spends his days in a wheelchair and has difficulty speaking clearly.

Though I enjoy Scott's company, sometimes I have to admit I feel sad whenever I leave his small apartment, where he lives alone. I wish he had a family to share his days with. I wish he could swing the clubs with me instead of just riding around in the cart when we go out on the golf course.

There's no cure to this sadness. The only way I can completely avoid it is to stop spending time with Scott, which isn't an option. Instead, I reinforce myself spiritually with the call to wait. One day, Scott will be healed. One day, he'll stand taller than I stand. One day, he won't need to lean on me for support as we stand together in the presence of God and worship before the throne.

Waiting is the portal of hope, a necessary element of spirituality in facing the troubles of this world. If you work with people suffering from Alzheimer's disease, with people who have disabilities or addictions, with people who are imprisoned or are nearing the end of their lives—eventually love will require you to learn how to wait. You may have to wait weeks while someone you're called to love recovers from a serious illness. You may have to wait months as you patiently help a profligate spender climb out of debt. You may have to wait years for an imprisoned and repentant individual to be released from jail. You may have to wait decades for a disabled person finally to be given a new "spiritual body." But one thing is certain: If you're called to love, you're called to wait. There is no love without patience, no love without waiting, no love without hope.

Authentic Faith, 48–49

October 3

AN EXCRUCIATING EXERCISE

Abraham was a sprightly seventy-five years old when God promised to make him into "a great nation"—a bold promise given to a childless old man (see Genesis 12:1–5). A whole quarter century passed before Isaac was born, and a full century went by before the promise about the land took concrete shape.

Abraham's excruciating exercise of waiting marks the essence of the Christian life. The psalmist recognized that God's blessings do not always come with the speed of a bullet, but rather with the slow, steady approach of a glacier: "I wait for the LORD, my soul waits, and in his word I put my hope. My soul waits for the Lord more than watchmen wait for the morning" (Psalm 130:5–6).

God won't be rushed. Without a willingness to wait, we will regularly get frustrated with God and may become disillusioned with our faith. God never promises that our present circumstances will always make sense. Sometimes we'll have to wait a long time before our current difficulties become even remotely understandable to us.

The book of Psalms, for example, teaches that we cannot understand how "the wicked" seem to get away with everything, unless we are willing to wait. "Be still before the LORD and wait patiently for him," David writes. "Do not fret when men succeed in their ways, when they carry out their wicked schemes" (Psalm 37:7). Neither rewards nor punishments always come immediately. God sees what's going on and he pronounces a judgment, but rarely does he carry it out within what many of us would consider a normal time frame.

This waiting can debilitate us and suck our souls dry—unless we put our hope in God. Waiting, for the believer, is not the futile and desperate act of someone who has no other options, but rather a confident trust that God *will* set things right. "Those who hope in the LORD will renew their strength," Isaiah tells us (Isaiah 40:31). If you want strength, then you need to hope in God; and hope relies on the discipline of waiting.

Authentic Faith, 39–40

Not Yet Christmas

The Christian naturally longs for what is to come, even to the point of groaning. Paul writes, "We groan, longing to be clothed with our heavenly dwelling ... For while we are in this tent, we groan and are burdened ... We live by faith, not by sight. We are confident, I say, and would prefer to be away from the body and at home with the Lord" (2 Corinthians 5:2, 4, 7–8).

A similar passage appears in Romans: "We ourselves, who have the firstfruits of the Spirit, groan inwardly as we wait eagerly for our adoption as sons, the redemption of our bodies ... Who hopes for what he already has? But if we hope for what we do not yet have, we wait for it patiently" (Romans 8:23–25).

This is by no means an easy waiting—as if we don't really want it. On the contrary, we wait passionately: "Our citizenship is in heaven. And we *eagerly* await a Savior from there, the Lord Jesus Christ" (Philippians 3:20, emphasis added).

The spirit of waiting is the spirit of godliness. It is a combination of contentment, gentleness, and humility—three key Christian virtues. The plain truth is that we are not given all we want on this earth. Regardless of how much God blesses us, if we are spiritually in tune with the Holy Spirit, we will live in perpetual waiting and anticipation, in a holy anxiety for the better life that is to come.

For us, it is always just past Christmas Eve but never quite Christmas morning. We can smell the turkey roasting; we can see the presents under the tree; we can anticipate the joy on our children's faces—but the full celebration lies just minutes beyond our reach: "Here we do not have an enduring city, but we are looking for the city that is to come" (Hebrews 13:14). So James advises us, "Be patient, then, brothers, until the Lord's coming ... Be patient and stand firm, because the Lord's coming is near" (James 5:7–8).

Authentic Faith, 40

PRODUCTIVE WAITING

Has God given you a vision that burns in your soul? Perhaps you received the call with excitement and enthusiasm—but it's been several months or even years now, and you feel like that work has never been further away. What attitude will you have as time goes on? Will you take comfort from God while you wait, learning the lessons God wants you to learn, or will you begin accusing God of playing games with you?

Remember this: God is not merely concerned with results but also with character—and few things produce character like learning how to wait. Paul's three cardinal virtues—faith, hope, and love—are all built on the foundation of patient waiting.

Perhaps you are in the middle of a difficult relationship, pleading with God for deliverance and answers and direction, and all you hear is, "Wait." You want God to move mountains on your behalf, and you want those mountains moved *now*. Why can't the marriage be healed today? Why can't your child or friend come back to their senses this weekend?

I can't promise you that the relationship will ever be healed, but I can tell you that many people have written to me or told me how, over time, God has worked a mighty change. Nothing dramatic happened in any one week, but steadily, over the years, God brought a gentle healing. All families go through seasons; sometimes we just have to weather the difficult ones.

In the midst of your waiting, take care to pursue refreshing recreation instead of soul-numbing narcotics (sin in any form). We can choose to dull the ache of waiting with a narcotic and regress, or we can take the path of inspiration and grow.

In the midst of your frustration, find activities and thoughts that inspire you. Gradually weed out those things that are just passing time. Choose to grow —toward God, in character, toward others—and this season of waiting will eventually produce an abundant crop.

Authentic Faith, 50

A PATIENT PURSUIT OF HOLINESS

I have a friend who in his college days had a notoriously brusque manner. As an intelligent and quick thinker, he became the master of the humorous put-down. Then he married an unusually sensitive and amazingly empathetic woman.

Some time ago, my friend and his wife were under a mountain of pressure. If you had rated my friend on the stress scale, he would have rocketed off the charts. One evening, while my wife and I were present, he slipped back into his old style and said something to ridicule his wife.

The next morning, I received an e-mail from a contrite friend. He wanted to express how ashamed he felt, how sorry he was, how much he loved and respected his wife, and how much he wanted me to know that he wasn't the same guy I knew in college.

God has worked deeply in this man's life, refining the quick thinking and good humor, but my friend didn't change overnight and the change still isn't complete. Change is a process. Even so, my friend is in a vastly different place today than he was twenty years ago.

Habitual sins have to be put to sleep. Faithful obedience, over time, weakens temptation's allure. As we begin to find new ways to deal with stress or insecurity or other "sin triggers," we learn to live without the sin that often has served as a crutch.

Sanctification has two elements—a declared holiness and a realized holiness. This explains why waiting plays such a crucial role in our growth in righteousness. In general, our pursuit of holiness should be patient. Instead of a frantic and desperate clutching, we should adopt a hopeful expectation: "Keep yourselves in God's love as you wait for the mercy of our Lord Jesus Christ to bring you to eternal life" (Jude 21).

You'll get there. Just give God time.

Authentic Faith, 41–42

IF AT FIRST YOU DON'T SUCCEED ...

Moses received what sounded like an impossible mission. Take a nation of slaves, with no government, no army—that means no captains, sergeants, privates, or weaponry—and no leverage, and break free from one of the most powerful regimes in history.

After some hesitation, Moses finally agreed and approached Pharaoh. "Let my people go," he said. Of course, things went from bad to worse. Pharaoh increased Israel's workload, and as it turned out, Moses not only had Egypt to contend with, but now the people of Israel hated the very thought of him. Even so, Moses returned to Pharaoh, and once again success eluded him. Pharaoh refused to let Israel go.

That's when the ten plagues began. And we have no evidence—none at all—that God pulled Moses aside and said, "Listen, Moses, there are going to be ten plagues. After the tenth one, you'll be out of here. Hang with me, though. One day, this will play great in Hollywood. You'll be played by Charlton Heston, a famous actor who is going to be a lot better looking than you are. Put up with this, and together we'll make history." Moses knew only that God was sending him back to Pharaoh one more time. Not until the twelfth confrontation did Moses actually succeed in getting his people released.

Scripture presents perseverance as a hallmark of Jesus' disciples. The apostle John wrote as "your brother and companion in the suffering and kingdom and *patient endurance* that are ours in Jesus" (Revelation 1:9, emphasis added). Being called often means being asked to persevere, even in the face of failure. It means maintaining an overarching attitude of patience and hope in the face of resistance.

Perseverance is one of the most difficult lessons we will ever have to learn, but it is essential as we travel this Christian journey.

Authentic Faith, 47–48

MASKED OPPORTUNITIES OF SAINTHOOD

Without perseverance, spiritual maturity will remain forever out of reach. James writes, "Perseverance must finish its work so that you may be mature and complete, not lacking anything" (James 1:4).

R. Somerset Ward makes this observation: "Of all the tests of the saint, I suppose this is the hardest for us. To go on day by day without getting slack, without continual stimulus, is an awful task. Look back on life and you will see how often we have had the opportunities of sainthood, and how often we have lost them because we would not persevere."[2]

Isn't it often true that divorce comes because of a refusal to keep working on the relationship? It's saying, "Things have become too difficult, too frustrating, too hard. I want something easier, more fun, more pleasurable, so I'm going to try to start over with someone else." (Of course, some divorces are forced on well-meaning believers, who fight the dissolution of their marriage but are unable to keep it together.)

Individuals who give up miss out on the experience of God's power doing a soul-scouring work in the midst of difficult relationships—and this goes far beyond marriage to include parenting, office politics, and even church life. But this works only when we realize, as Ward reminds us, that the difficult relationships and situations we find ourselves in are really masked "opportunities of sainthood."

These qualities of a saint come at a premium price. We cannot wake up one day and suddenly see a saint looking back at us in the mirror. The tapestry of Christlikeness is laid down stitch by stitch, as God weaves events, attitudes, relationships, and personal affliction through our daily experience. As we lovingly respond to him, he shapes us by his firm and gracious will—and through Spirit-empowered perseverance, we become what he intends us to be.

Holy Available, 203–4

No Guarantee of Quick Success

"That's exactly what they needed to hear!"

Parent after parent came up to shake my hand after the commencement address. I knew that 99 percent of the kids wouldn't remember a thing I said, so I prayed about leaving them with a word picture that would stick with them. I found it in my rejections box.

My wife and kids helped me staple and tape together more than 150 rejection letters that I had received over the years from publishers and editors. The length of that roll still staggers me, and each note represented a professional telling me my work didn't measure up. When I told the young graduates that God's calling doesn't mean an easy way—without doubts and without rejections—I nodded to a few students who then began to unroll my rejection letters. Murmurs, laughs, and then gasps rumbled through the auditorium as the roll grew longer and longer, ultimately stretching across the entire ballroom.

I had been invited to speak as the author of numerous books and as one who travels nationally and internationally to speak—but I wanted the students to see the insecure seminary graduate who wondered if anyone would ever want to hear what he believed God had given him to say.

Many Christians don't fail; they just quit before they get ripe. I've met too many young Christians who mistakenly think that if they're called, God will "open every door." By that, they mean the road will be easy, obstacles will vanish, and God will "bless" their obedience. They think there will be no waiting, or perhaps only a minimum amount of time between the promise and the fulfillment.

Being called is no guarantee of quick success. The writer of Hebrews tells us, "Let us run *with perseverance* the race marked out for us" (Hebrews 12:1, emphasis added).

Authentic Faith, 46–48

A BUNDLE OF DIFFICULTIES

Have you ever noticed that most trials come in batches and bundles?

In one year, a pastor I know suffered through the loss of his father, an attack of kidney stones (perhaps the most painful ordeal any man can go through), and then a diagnosis of prostate cancer. Later that year, a staff member resigned due to a moral failure. This four-pronged attack just about took my breath away — and I wasn't even the one feeling the pain!

During the same year, a good friend of mine watched his daughter fight off a serious infection, discovered that his mother had Alzheimer's, and then had one of the most difficult business years of any self-employed person I know. His business entirely depends on two items: the phone and his computer. Someone misappropriated his toll-free number; his phone system crashed two times; a computer glitch lost vital information; an allegedly Christian client cheated him out of tens of thousands of dollars — and then accused my friend of cheating *him!* When I spoke to him, his deadened voice told me something very wrong had happened. Life had broken him, but he remained solid in his faith and commitment to God.

Why do these bundles of trials seem so common? Why do I not even feign surprise anymore when earnest believers lay out similar stories as they desperately seek direction?

We have only one way to become mature and complete in God. We must develop the difficult but crucial discipline of perseverance. Jesus said that only through perseverance do we bear fruit: "The seed on good soil stands for those with a noble and good heart, who hear the word, retain it, *and by persevering* produce a crop" (Luke 8:15, emphasis added).

There's only one way to develop perseverance. We have to surrender to God as we feel pushed past the human breaking point. We have to reach the threshold of exhaustion, and then get pushed even further. One trial can help us deal with fear. Two trials can lead to wisdom. But perseverance? That takes a bundle of difficulties.

Sacred Parenting, 144–45

It Hurts

We live on a fallen planet, and thoughtful Christians have long understood the necessity of warning fellow believers about the suffering inherent in such a world. When Christians are taught only that Christianity makes life easier, they become disenchanted when they find themselves or a loved one walking through cancer, unemployment, or other challenges.

I once heard a well-known revivalist/faith healer say on television, "We must become as serious about fighting sickness as we are about fighting sin." He suggested that just as faith overcomes sin, so true faith overcomes all sickness. My then nine-year-old daughter looked up from her puzzle and asked me — skepticism dripping from her lips — "Is that true, Daddy?"

We looked at Galatians 4, in which Paul confesses he had physical challenges. "As you know," he writes, "it was because of an illness that I first preached the gospel to you. Even though my illness was a trial to you, you did not treat me with contempt or scorn. Instead, you welcomed me as if I were an angel of God, as if I were Christ Jesus himself" (Galatians 4:13 – 14).

If sickness and suffering always revealed a lack of faith, then Paul, Augustine, Teresa of Avila, Brother Lawrence, Martin Luther, and at least half of the Puritans have nothing to teach us. Absurd! Because Christians live with an eternal worldview, they know that God can use temporal suffering to create a greater, long-term good.

Larry King interviewed Billy Graham after it was publicly announced that the evangelist suffered from Parkinson's disease. "You pray not to be in pain, don't you?" Larry asked. "Not at all," Graham responded. "I pray for God's will." Graham explained he was more than willing to suffer if God had another lesson for him to learn — even in his eighties and nineties! Billy Graham has led more people to the Lord than perhaps anyone in history. He has lived a long and fruitful life, yet he still wants to learn, even if it requires pain. If Billy Graham has this attitude, then how much more should we?

Authentic Faith, 59 – 60

October 12

DON'T EXPLAIN IT AWAY

Stephen Asonibare serves as a pastor in Nigeria. Three weeks prior to a class I taught at Western Seminary, armed robbers raided his family's village. Stephen's wife and youngest son were severely beaten and a neighbor woman was gang-raped by six men. "What I'd like to do," Stephen told the other pastors in our class, "is hold a thanksgiving service. As bad as it was, it could have been a lot worse. No one was killed. The problem is that I don't want to antagonize the robbers. If they hear about the service, they might come back and do something even worse."

He had a tough choice to make. On the one hand, Stephen wanted to bring spiritual care and nurture to a hurting village. On the other hand, he didn't want to bring further violence.

Answers don't come easy in such situations.

Two friends from college were driving a stretch of highway with a newborn baby in the car when a buck crashed into their vehicle, killing their baby. As you try to respond pastorally to such a horrific event, you are led to think, *God, couldn't you have delayed that buck for half a second? Couldn't you have delayed my friends' departure for five seconds? Why did this have to happen?*

This is a fallen world, and horrific things happen in it, even to believers. It's understandable that we want to have an answer for every dilemma, but reality often fights against this. In fact, we dishonor our suffering sisters and brothers when we try to explain everything away. We are called to suffer with them, not to try to "cure" them of their suffering. Paul tells us to "carry each other's burdens" (Galatians 6:2), not try to explain the deeper wisdom buried under every tragedy.

If you're facing a tough ministry situation today—in your life, or someone else's—be encouraged that we're not expected to provide an answer. All we are obligated to provide is love. If you think you have to provide an answer for everything, you won't last long in ministry. If you excel at providing love, you'll never grow weary.

Authentic Faith, 66–67

FROM AFFLICTION TO GLORY

Thomas Watson, a seventeenth-century Puritan pastor who ministered in London, wrote a book titled *A Divine Cordial*, in which he lists the many ways that affliction works for the good of those who love God.

Watson wrote that affliction works as our "preacher and tutor." He said that sometimes a sickbed can teach us more than a sermon. If we value wisdom more than comfort, we won't casually dismiss the role of suffering. Watson also said that in prosperity, we can be strangers to ourselves, but affliction teaches us to know ourselves, including the corruption of our hearts. It's easy to be pleasant when all is well, when our finances are in order, and when we don't have a headache or back pain — but take away these comforts, and how patient are we then?

The apostle Paul taught that afflictions work for our good in that they make way for glory. Paul describes a time-tested spiritual exercise in Romans 5:3 – 4 that emphasizes this truth: "We also rejoice in our sufferings, because we know that suffering produces perseverance; perseverance, character; and character, hope. And hope does not disappoint us."

Paul doesn't say that he has learned to tolerate suffering or even to wait patiently during suffering. On the contrary, he says he has learned to *rejoice* in his sufferings. In Paul's mind, what suffering produces is so amazingly wonderful that it leads him to rejoice when suffering comes his way.

Don't misunderstand; suffering *hurts*. The Greek word used here carries a sense of considerable oppression and affliction, not some minor inconvenience. Paul is talking about pain. Without pain, there is no need to persevere. A man sitting in his easy chair doesn't need to persevere; a man running a marathon does. It is only through discomfort that we can learn to persevere. And it is only through perseverance that we can develop character. When we learn to persevere through suffering and respond with biblical hope, affliction becomes our divine preacher instead of our persecutor.

Authentic Faith, 63 – 64

NOT A DAY WITHOUT SUFFERING ...

Paul didn't welcome suffering for the sake of suffering; he was no masochist. He welcomed suffering for the sake of hope, a virtue infused with an eternal perspective, the promises offered to us in the gospel. He saw suffering and affliction as but a doorway, not a house to dwell in; and the place they lead is blessed indeed. So he can write in Romans 8:18, "I consider that our present sufferings are not worth comparing with the glory that will be revealed in us."

Ancient Christians followed Paul's example. Basil wrote in the fourth century, "Good men take sickness as athletes take their contest, waiting for the crowns that are to reward their endurance."[3] Basil obviously believed that we can gain spiritual benefit from enduring even a common malady.

Listen to Teresa of Avila: "When the Lord begins to grant greater favors here on earth, greater trials can be expected."[4] In her autobiography, Teresa confesses of herself, "I know a person who cannot truthfully say that from the time the Lord began forty years ago to grant the favor that was mentioned she spent one day without pains and other kinds of suffering."[5] Through her writings, Teresa has taught generations of Christians how to enjoy a more intimate communion with God, yet she testifies that not a single day went by without some form of pain and suffering to accompany it. When Teresa faced her migraines, she didn't have the benefit of Percocet or Vicodin. She didn't even have Tylenol or Bayer aspirin. Her medicines were of a far different kind: hope, endurance, and patience.

Thomas à Kempis reminds us that when we suffer, we don't experience anything different than everybody else also suffers, in one way or other: "There is no person on this earth without some trouble or affliction. Who is it then who is most at ease in the midst of suffering? He who is willing to suffer some affliction for God's sake."[6] When suffering is ordained on our behalf, we must endure it with hope and patience, valuing it for the spiritual benefit it brings.

Authentic Faith, 65–66

October 15

IN THE NICK OF TIME

During the height of his writing years, C. S. Lewis cared for a very sick woman named Janie King Moore. Whenever she called, Lewis had to go to her—and she called him many times a day. George Sayer, Lewis's biographer, explains: "[Lewis] would leave his work, go upstairs and do her bidding, and then return to his writing. There were two maids in the house, but they quarreled with each other and sometimes with Mrs. Moore too. Jack's role was to try to make peace, over and over again."[7] Added to this was the constant irritation of the alcoholism of his brother, Warren, and Lewis's constant fears that he was about to go bankrupt.

As one who writes for a living, I can sympathize with the difficulty of continuing work amid many interruptions; yet it was precisely under these conditions that Sayer says Lewis wrote "the best known and most widely loved of all his books" — *The Lion, the Witch, and the Wardrobe*. Sayer explains, "That the Narnia stories are full of laughter and the fact that they breathe forth joy does not mean that the years of their writing were happy for Jack. What it does mean is that his faith had taught him how to cope with difficulties and to rise above miseries that would have overwhelmed most men."[8]

Sayer goes even a step further, suggesting that the brilliance of the Narnia series came from its creation in a situation of human suffering. "If [Lewis] had lived the cloistered existence of a bachelor don, his writing would have suffered from a loss of warmth, humanity, and the understanding of pain and suffering."[9]

Lewis did not consider a life with no difficulty as ideal precisely because it tempted him to become what he despised: overly comfortable, complacent, and apathetic. In fact, when war broke out in 1939, Lewis wrote to a friend, "I daresay, for me, personally, [the war] has come in the nick of time; I was just beginning to get too well settled in my profession, too successful, and probably self-complacent."[10]

Has one of your recent trials come "in the nick of time"?

Authentic Faith, 72–73

PERSONAL TRANSFORMATION:
A PAINFUL PROCESS

Why do we sin? Usually it is to meet some immediate demand or desire. Merely stopping the sin does nothing to address the yearning that led to the sin, which is why we must pass through the desert to embrace the virtue of detachment. We must separate ourselves from anything that takes the place of God in our lives —which can be a painful process. But while holiness may make our lives more miserable in the short run, it will make them far more joyful in the long run.

The ancients taught that we experience true holiness through the desert. When it comes to emotional satisfaction, there may be a dip before there is a rise, until we learn to live without the narcotic of sinful behavior. It takes time—and sometimes considerable suffering—for us to separate from our sin.

If you insist on avoiding suffering at all costs, then you will never be free of your addictions. If you are serious about spiritual growth or overcoming a long-term bad habit, then you had better be prepared to go to war. A halfhearted effort usually ends with half-baked results.

While an alcoholic can expect many difficult times ahead, he also will find that once the initial cravings have passed, he has far more time and energy than he ever dreamed possible. His initial suffering produces tremendous long-term benefits. But there will be intense, short-term battles on his way to freedom.

A celebrity revealed in an interview that he valued sobriety above anything else. I have never treasured sobriety, in large part because I've never been un-sober. This man can appreciate something in a way I cannot, because he has suffered to get what I take for granted.

Being willing to suffer and experiencing personal transformation go hand in hand. If we refuse to face the discomfort of change, we will endure even more severe consequences as the idol increases its hold on our heart. Worst of all, we will forever remain strangers to experiential holiness. If we don't practice the virtue the ancients called "detachment," we will not live as free people in the grace of Jesus Christ.

Authentic Faith, 69–70

October 17

THE SPIRITUAL DISCIPLINE OF PERSEVERANCE

Some have called this "the generation of quitters." Employees quit their jobs as soon as the going gets tough. Employers quit on their employees as soon as profits dip a quarter of a percentage point. People routinely quit on their church. The Bible even warns that some will quit on their faith (1 Timothy 4:1).

Jesus talks about this temptation in the parable of the soils. In Luke 8, Jesus warns that some will hear God's Word and believe for a while, "but in the time of testing they fall away" (verse 13). Others hear but have their faith choked by "life's worries, riches and pleasures" (verse 14). But those commended by Jesus are those who "hear the word, *retain it, and by persevering* produce a crop" (verse 15, emphasis added).

True Christian spirituality has always emphasized perseverance: "To those *who by persistence* in doing good seek glory, honor and immortality, he will give eternal life." (Romans 2:7, emphasis added). Righteousness—true holiness—is seen over time in our persistence. It is relatively easy to flirt with righteousness —being occasionally courteous to other drivers (if you happen to be in a good mood), helping someone in need (if you have time), throwing a few extra bucks into the offering plate (as long as you won't miss them). But the righteousness God seeks is a *persistent* righteousness, a commitment to continue making the right decision even when you feel pulled in the opposite direction. Holiness is far more than an inclination toward occasional acts of kindness and charity. It is a commitment to persistent surrender before God.

Marriage is a beautiful and effective reminder of this eternal priority. Consider one of the most poetic lines in Scripture, one that I wish every husband and wife would display in a prominent place in their home: "May the Lord direct your hearts into God's love and Christ's perseverance." (2 Thessalonians 3:5). That's what I want my heart filled with: *God's love* and *Christ's perseverance*. It's the Bible's best recipe for holiness and a successful life here on earth!

Sacred Marriage, 107 – 8

How Hard to Submit . . .

C. S. Lewis's life was filled with struggle and hardship. By the summer of 1949, stress had reached such high levels for him that he developed a severe infection. His symptoms included a high temperature, delirium, a splitting headache, a sore throat, and swollen glands. Lewis's doctor said the real problem was exhaustion resulting from his work and difficulties at home. His brother, Warren, arranged for Jack to spend a month in Ireland, to which Lewis said, "It seems too good to be true."

Unfortunately it was. Warren drank his way into an asylum, ultimately requiring Lewis to forgo his own convalescence so that he could look after his alcoholic brother. Lewis wrote, "It would be better that the door of my prison had never been opened than if it now bangs in my face! How hard to submit to God's will."[11]

All this prepared Lewis for his real test — having to watch the suffering of his wife as she fought a losing battle with cancer. Lewis wanted, like Christ, to put himself in Joy's place and take her suffering on himself. He actually prayed for his wife's pain to be transferred to him. Although some may question the theology undergirding his prayer, shortly afterward Joy seemed to get much better, while Lewis suddenly endured such great pain that, according to a man who worked at his house, there was "screamin' and 'ollerin' and no sleep without dope."[12]

Lewis later said, "The intriguing thing was that while I (for no discernible reason) was losing the calcium from my bones, Joy, who needed it much more, was gaining it in hers."[13] During this time Lewis could hardly walk and was fitted with a surgical brace to support his weakened spine. Yet out of this seemingly bitter stew emerged the honey of a proven character, a seasoned soul, and a stalwart defender of the faith. This is Christianity in its truest and finest form, the extension of Christ's own work — the one who suffered and died that we might live.

Authentic Faith, 73–74

October 19

THE UNWELCOME MAT

From the beginning, Jesus told his followers to expect the same kind of ugly treatment that he received: "All men will hate you because of me, but he who stands firm to the end will be saved" (Matthew 10:22). Imagine that promise. There will *always* be someone who hates us; we will never run out of places where we are unappreciated. Until Jesus comes back, someone can always make a living churning out "unwelcome mats."

You don't see *that* in too many "Bible promise" books!

As we serve God, others will call us disgusting names. When we act out of love, we may be accused of hatred. When we proclaim a message of joyful life in Christ, some observers might blast us with the charge of intolerance. When we seek to spread a message of salvation, others will rush to condemn us.

But lest any of us are tempted to pity our plight, let us remember that none of us will ever be more maligned or slandered than was our Lord. Regardless of what you are called or how much your motives are mischaracterized, the injustice done to you will never approach what the Pharisees perpetrated on Christ, whom they accused of being in league with his worst enemy.

I don't know how many lectures I attended at Regent College in Vancouver, British Columbia, but a few I will never forget. Among them was one given by Don Lewis, who surveyed a terrible but glorious time in church history when martyrs fell like branches in a storm. This was clearly no mere academic exercise to my professor. Dr. Lewis barely managed to complete the lecture, finally uttering Tertullian's famous phrase with an emotion-packed quiver, "The blood of the martyrs is the seed of the church."

Expect opposition. Expect to be ridiculed. Expect to have your good motives questioned. Assume that you will be called everything you find repugnant. Remember: Satan is the father of lies. His followers will not hesitate to unleash any charge, however baseless, if in doing so they think they can frustrate a work of God.

Authentic Faith, 83–84, 88

No Wasted Pain

As dawn broke over the Polish countryside on September 1, 1939, a nineteen-year-old acolyte helped his priest celebrate Mass in the heart of Krakow. Near the altar lay a silver casket bearing the remains of Saint Stanislaw, the patron saint of Poland.

Suddenly the wail of air-raid sirens pierced the morning air. Antiaircraft fire shot into the sky and German bombs pummeled the city. Peace took flight and chaos ruled. Hitler's grab for Poland — and after that, the world — had begun.

The people celebrating Mass fled, eager to find secure shelter. But the young acolyte and his priest stood their ground and finished the Mass. It was a tailor-made proving ground for the young man, who was already familiar with suffering. He had lost his mother when he was just six years old. At age twelve, he suffered through the death of an older brother. As an acolyte, he faced German occupation of his homeland. Two years later, his father died. Following the war, the Communists took over.

When the archbishop of Krakow position became vacant, Communist party leaders backed this young priest, assuming that his youth would work in their favor by allowing them to control him — a grievous error, as Karol Wojtyła eventually ascended to the papacy, becoming Pope John Paul II. From there he played a major role in the fall of Communism in Poland.

Soviet boss Leonid Brezhnev later warned Polish leaders not to let Pope John Paul II back into Poland, but the leaders thought they could control what happened. Another grievous error. In a once-in-a-century, nine-day tour in 1979, Wojtyła's courage and charisma all but sounded the death knell for Communism while preserving the future of the Solidarity movement.

It would be difficult to measure the pain and suffering that the future pope experienced prior to assuming leadership of the Roman Catholic Church, and yet out of this crucible of a life that no one addicted to comfort would ever choose arose the character of a man who changed the course of history.

God doesn't waste our pain.

Authentic Faith, 77 – 78

A NECESSARY PART

You think of yourself as reasonably intelligent and thoughtful. During a group discussion, the questions start coming: "Do you really believe that everyone came from Adam and Eve? "You don't honestly think there's a heaven and hell, do you?" "Isn't it true that the Bible is full of contradictions?"

When your heart starts pounding and your palms start sweating, will you choose to stand with your Lord, the apostles, and two thousand years' worth of faithful witnesses, or will you sell your soul in a vain attempt to impress a few cynics and to spare yourself a little mocking laughter?

When a family member or employer gives you an ultimatum — shut up or be cut off — will you rest in eternal glory or grasp at earthly comfort?

Let's say a fellow believer mocks you, lies about you, and seems obsessed with destroying your reputation. When persecution does come — as it surely will — what attitude toward God will you adopt? Will you rejoice that you have been counted worthy to suffer for his name? Or will you resent God and accuse him of not protecting you?

Enduring persecution creates a titanic testimony, a vibrant marker, of an authentic faith. The shots — either verbal, financial, emotional, relational, or literal — will come. Some will bounce off us. Others will wound us. A few might cripple us, and the rare bullet may even kill us. But through it all, Jesus tells us this: "Love your enemies and pray for those who persecute you, that you may be sons of your Father in heaven" (Matthew 5:44 – 45).

Persecution is a necessary part of worshiping and serving a persecuted Savior.

Authentic Faith, 99

October 22

THE FALL AND YOUR MARRIAGE

Our world is profoundly broken. As a result of the fall, I will labor with difficulty and angst (Genesis 3:17–19). Lisa will mother our children and enter relationships with mixed motives and frustrated aims (Genesis 3:16).

Even an unusually good marriage is unable to erase the effects of sin's curse. Dan Allender and Tremper Longman write, "We must never be naive enough to think of marriage as a safe harbor from the fall ... The deepest struggles of life will occur in the most primary relationship affected by the fall: marriage."[14] The problem is that even though we can't go back to the idyllic existence prior to the fall, we know what relationships should be like, but we cannot make them perfectly in tune with that ideal: "Our souls are wired for what we will never enjoy until Eden is restored in the new heaven and earth. We are built with a distant memory of Eden."[15]

This calls me to extend gentleness and tolerance toward my wife. I want her to become all that Jesus calls her to become, but she will never fully get there this side of heaven, so I must love and accept her in the midst of a sin-stained world with all its ill effects.

When I still worked outside the home, I remember occasions when Lisa and I would plan a romantic evening. Flush with morning's zest, we would plan a "hot" night. Romance would fly. For a few brief moments, we would make the earth melt away and enjoy the blessed fruits of conjugal intimacy. Then I'd go to work, throughout the day occasionally thinking about what marital pleasures awaited me. When I came home, however, sometimes I found a wife who wanted nothing more than a solitary bath and an early start on a good night's sleep.

I realized it was nothing personal. Sometimes wives get tired. That's just the way it works in a fallen world—for all of us. Extend to your spouse the empathy they need while living in a broken world. Tiredness, discouragement, illness, exhaustion just happens, even when we don't want it to.

Sacred Marriage, 67–68

October 23

A CALL TO DESTINY

Mary Todd Lincoln was hardly the type of woman with whom one could enjoy a quiet evening. She was a woman of intense impulses and tremendous temper, though this held part of her attraction for the sixteenth president of the United States. Abraham Lincoln called her the "first aggressively brilliant, feminine creature" who had crossed his path.

Lincoln suffered numerous indignities at the hand of his wife, from Mary's publicly throwing coffee in his face to her profligate spending. In those days, presidents were not quite as well off as they are today, but Mary went on bizarre spending binges, during one stretch buying hundreds of pairs of gloves.

When the Lincolns lost Willie—Mary's favorite son—the ensuing grief began to crack Mrs. Lincoln's fragile psyche. It became more and more difficult for her to control her hysteria.

It was in the aftermath of this tremendous grief (the loss of his son) and distraction (watching his wife fall apart) that the president was called on to give the now famous Gettysburg Address—a speech that would mark him for posterity. Lincoln's political life was as precarious at this point as was his home life; even so, his words created a steady foundation on which even a country at war could find stability.

It's important to see that not only did Lincoln's difficult marriage not deter him from achieving greatness; one might argue that it actually helped prepare him for it. Lincoln's character was tested and refined on a daily basis so that when the national test came, he was able to stand strong.

Had Lincoln obsessed over happiness, he wouldn't have mustered the strength to put up with Mary or to hold the nation together. But he sensed a call to destiny, something that in his mind superseded personal comfort—and his obedience to that destiny made world history.

May we never run from the very trials that will make us strong.

Sacred Marriage, 134–37

FORCEFUL MEN

As a cross-country runner, my most satisfying victories took every ounce of strength I possessed. Races that I won easily felt less satisfying. I remember one race against a smaller school. I went out hard, but not too hard, and lost their lead runner within the first mile. I then slowed up and allowed our number-two runner to catch up, and we ambled through the rest of the race together. We even talked as we raced over the familiar trails — a pleasant race, but nothing to feel proud of. What is there to be proud about when you haven't even been tested?

But in another race involving six high schools, I went out at a bruising pace and nearly ran myself into the hospital. It was an unusually hot day, and about a dozen times in that three-mile race I had to make a conscious decision not to quit as yet another runner pushed up to challenge for the lead. When I finally collapsed across the finish line, I was almost too tired to feel elated over the win. I developed a high fever that night and remained sick for three days — but even in the pain of my recovery, I knew I had given it my all. A certain awe came with that knowledge. What the race lacked in fun it made up in meaning

Isn't it true that when we have to fight for our marriage, our children, our jobs, or when we sacrifice for our church, we almost invariably end up appreciating them all the more? Coasting in any arena rarely leads to a sense of fulfillment.

Are you willing to go to war with your apathy to develop a life of prayer? Will you wrestle the obstacles that keep your children from Jesus? Will you break down all the barriers blocking your marital intimacy? Will you engage in spiritual warfare to serve at your local church?

The easy road is usually a boring road, devoid of meaning and joy, and providing little fulfillment. Don't allow a little challenge to hold you back. Ironically, the fulfilled person is the person willing to go to war: "From the days of John the Baptist until now, the kingdom of heaven has been forcefully advancing, and forceful men lay hold of it" (Matthew 11:12).

Sacred Marriage, 129–30

Going on a Bear Hunt

When my kids were small, they loved a book about a family that goes on a bear hunt. The father and his children face all kinds of obstacles—a deep, dark forest; oozing mud; a swirling, whirling snowstorm. At each dilemma they conclude, "We can't go over it; we can't go around it. Oh, no! We have to go through it."

This children's book holds a lesson for adults as well. We can't always run from pain; sometimes we just have to go through it. We may be forced to work with unhealthy people. We may be married to a cruel spouse or be the child of a cruel parent or the parent of a cruel child. A friend of mine was locked into a difficult relationship with her boss: "I've had four bosses, and they've all been like this one. There's no use running. I just have to learn whatever it is that God wants to teach me."

Remember that Jesus purposely chose twelve disciples who would have problems with each other. If I were seeking peace and harmony, I certainly wouldn't put a tax collector with a zealot—two natural enemies. But Jesus knew that real spirituality is proven in our relationships with others, and he was willing to call people into relationships that stretched them beyond their comfort level.

God is well aware of the difficulty of living in a world of sinners. Jesus, on his way to the cross, told some sobbing women, "Daughters of Jerusalem, do not weep for me; weep for yourselves and for your children … For if men do these things when the tree is green, what will happen when it is dry?" (Luke 23:28, 31).

No doubt Jesus appreciated the women's sympathy, but he displayed a remarkable empathy of his own, mentioning his sorrow that they lived in a world where people get treated brutally. God understands that ours is not an easy world to live in.

If you evaluate your circumstances by what makes you most comfortable, this world is going to frustrate you. If you evaluate your circumstances by what fosters your growth in character, you're going to see tremendous potential in every day.

Thirsting for God, 194–95

THE CLIMBER'S APPROACH

Jesus portrayed struggle as the entry point into the Christian life: "If anyone would come after me, he must deny himself and take up his cross *daily* and follow me" (Luke 9:23, emphasis added). To many Western Christians, this verse may sound melodramatic. When I look at my life honestly, I have to admit I have it unusually easy. I am not ridiculed or persecuted for my faith; in fact, as a Christian writer and speaker, my faith has the favorable effect of supporting my family.

We have it so easy that we can begin to get lulled to sleep, thinking that life should be easy or will always be easy. Once it gets a bit difficult, we tend to feel consumed with trying to make our lives comfortable again—but by doing so we miss a great spiritual opportunity.

As mountain climbers plan their assaults on Mount Everest, many step back from a particularly difficult overhang or stretch and discuss how to surmount it. Much of the fun in the sport is encountering the challenges and figuring out ways to get around them. If mountain climbing were easy, it would lose a great deal of its appeal.

We can look at our family relationships in the same way. Instead of immediately thinking about how we can take a helicopter to the top, we might take a climber's approach and think, "This is really tough. This is a challenge, no doubt about it. How do I keep loving this person in the face of this challenge?"

Thomas à Kempis noted that "the more the flesh is wasted by affliction, so much the more is the spirit strengthened by inward grace. And sometimes he is so comforted with desire of tribulation and adversity, for the love of conformity to the cross of Christ, that he would not wish to be without grief or tribulation." Ask yourself, "Would I rather live a life of ease and comfort and remain immature in Christ, or am I willing to be seasoned with suffering if by doing so I am conformed to the image of Christ?"

Sacred Marriage, 130–31

October 27
CONFLICT'S CHOICE

Mature adults realize that every relationship involves conflict, confession, and forgiveness. The absence of conflict demonstrates either that the relationship isn't important enough to fight over or that both individuals are too insecure to risk disagreement.

Conflict provides an avenue for spiritual growth. To resolve conflict, we must become *more* engaged, not less. Just when we want to tell the other person off, we are forced to grow quiet and listen to their complaint. Just when we are most eager to make ourselves understood, we must strive to understand. Just when we want to point out the fallacies and abusive behavior of someone else, we must ruthlessly evaluate our own offensive attitudes and behaviors.

When conflict arises and is overcome, the couple has had to move toward each other. They've "fallen forward," sought resolution, and in the process built an urgent hunger for each other. Glossing over disagreements and sinful attitudes and behaviors isn't fellowship; it's play acting.

Learning to successfully negotiate conflict will have a direct influence on our relationship with God, for the time will come when we feel we have a bone to pick with him too. One of the most famous fights in the Bible involved God and Jacob. The two combatants wrestled all night long, and the encounter so transformed Jacob that his name was changed to Israel ("he struggles with God").

Sometimes we will find ourselves wrestling with God. It is no mark of Christian maturity to pretend that our heavenly Father's silence or rejection of our wishes does not bother us. A healthy spirituality will call us to fall forward with God no less than with our spouse. Like Jacob, wrestling with God may well result in an unforeseen blessing. We may also—as did Jacob—receive a lifelong limp, but any interaction with God will prove beneficial, provided the movement is always toward him.

In all relationships, conflict is guaranteed. To fall *forward* is a choice—the mature choice.

Sacred Marriage, 162–64

335

MARSHMALLOWS AND MARRIAGE

Mature Christians recognize and appreciate the sweet side of suffering. Teresa of Avila wrote, "Lord, how you afflict your lovers! But everything is small in comparison to what you give them afterward." John Climacus experienced the same thing centuries before. He wrote, "If individuals resolutely submit to the carrying of the cross, if they decidedly want to find and endure trial in all things for God, they will discover in all of them great relief and sweetness."

This teaching mirrors Paul's words in 2 Corinthians 4:17: "Our light and momentary troubles are achieving for us an eternal glory that far outweighs them all."

Because we have hope for eternity, we do not become nearsighted, demanding short-term ease that would short-circuit long-term gain. We should periodically ask ourselves, "Am I living for God's kingdom and service, or for my own comfort and reputation?"

A heavyweight boxing champion who dodges all serious contenders to consistently fight marshmallows gets derided and ridiculed—and rightly so. Christians who dodge all serious struggle and consciously seek to put themselves in the easiest situations and relationships do the same thing. They are coasting, and eventually this coasting will define them and, even worse, shape them.

If young engaged couples need to hear one thing, it's that a good marriage is not something you find; it's something you work for. It takes struggle. You must crucify your selfishness. You must at times confront, at other times confess, and always be willing to forgive.

It helps when we view our struggles in light of what they provide spiritually rather than what they take from us emotionally. If I'm in my marriage for emotional stability, I probably won't last long. But if I think it can reap spiritual benefits, I'll have plenty of reason to not just *be* married but *act* married.

Don't run from the struggles of marriage. Embrace them. Grow in them. Draw nearer to God because of them. Through them you will reflect more of the spirit of Jesus Christ. And thank God that he has placed you in a situation where your spirit can be perfected.

Sacred Marriage, 132–33

GOD'S EMPATHY

I am indebted to John Calvin for a helpful reminder. Calvin taught me that after I become God's adopted son, the Lord doesn't treat my sin the way a judge would, but rather as a physician would. God knows that I sin, and he will discipline me accordingly, but he does so with the spirit of a doctor who wants to make me well, not a prosecuting attorney who wants to make me pay.

Works from the Eastern Orthodox branch of Christianity have also helped me. While the Reformed tradition emphasizes that Jesus' death absorbed God's wrath against us (and many biblical passages support this emphasis), the Orthodox branch emphasizes that Jesus died not primarily to absorb God's wrath but to defeat the powers of sin and darkness that war against his people.

Because we are guilty, we cannot paint ourselves primarily as victims. But in another sense, God does see us as victims because he knows that, on our own, we are powerless against the force of sin in our hearts. This may sound like double-speak, but we need to view God's anger through the lens of his empathy toward us.

Growing up in my tradition, I was intensely aware of God's wrath and disappointment. The Eastern branch has helped me to see that God is also empathetic toward my struggles, that he sent his own Son as a statement of just how sorry he is that we must bear the burden of our sin.

Romans 8:31, "If God is for us, who can be against us?" is the hope of every believer. Our sin nature provides a daily struggle, and we are right to assume God's disappointment and even anger when we fail. But we are wrong when we forget his empathy. If we could only see how he is rooting for us, and how he grieves that we must fight this bruising battle!

God hates your sin, but he loves you, more deeply than you can know. You are not alone. God's mercy triumphs over judgment; his empathy exceeds his anger.

Thirsting for God, 196–98

THE BLESSING OF DUTY

Family life teaches us that we do some things simply because they must be done. We may even grow to resent them, but duty calls us to remain faithful. If we lived merely by inclination or happiness, our lives—and our world—would become a ruin. G. K. Chesterton confesses, "In everything on this earth that is worth doing, there is a stage when no one would do it except for necessity or honor."

It helps to know that every family—and I mean *every* family—faces times when weariness leads the parents to ask, "Why bother?" Elton Trueblood has this gentle counsel:

> The desire to escape family responsibilities is practically universal at some time or other and if mere inclination were followed every family would break to pieces ... Countless humble homes have been made scenes of enduring wonder by the fact that an *accepted bond* has held the members together in spite of hard work, poverty and much suffering.[16]

By fulfilling God's call to keep our marriages and families intact, we find the spiritual blessing that results from hanging in there despite the pain. Sacred parenting, which rejects socially approved exits, invites us to experience the benefits behind these trials to an even greater degree simply because the escape isn't so easy.

The crux of the issue is this: Our first and natural inclination in any trial is to pray for God to remove the difficulty. But God's first priority is often to strengthen us in the midst of the difficulty rather than to take us out of the difficulty. That's because he can see the treasure that lies at the end of the trail.

No matter how difficult our children may be, God can and will use them to shape our souls into his Son's image. No matter how many bumps we may hit or bends we may have to negotiate along the road to raising our children, God promises to guide our steps, strengthen our stride, and refresh our souls.

Sacred Parenting, 147, 151

FACE YOUR FEARS

One day I was throwing batting practice to my son. Eventually he hit just about everything that crossed the plate. His confidence soared, and during one break, he said, "Now that I know I can hit a fastball, the only thing I'm worried about facing is a right-handed pitcher who throws side-armed. That really throws me off."

So as soon as we began playing again, do you know what I did? I threw side-armed, as hard as I could, until Graham could start hitting it. He needed to face his fears in order to grow as a hitter, just as we need to face our worst fears in order to grow as children of God.

I can't predict your aversions. I'm not even qualified to diagnose them! But you need to know that they exist. When you react to an unkind (but not necessarily cruel) remark in a manner way out of proportion, when you feel as though your world is falling apart just because of tension in an important relationship, then it's time to pray—and perhaps to discuss your feelings with a wise friend who can help you pinpoint the aversion so that it doesn't rule over you.

Why is this necessary? Because beyond our aversions and addictions, we yearn to belong completely and unreservedly to God. God will often walk us through paths that deliberately confront our attachments, prejudices, fears, and aversions that stand like roadblocks in our relationship to him. If we are averse to pain, hunger, rejection, insecurity, ridicule, or anything else, at that very point we are vulnerable to the worship of idols—whether that idol is comfort, fame, security, wealth, or acceptance. This is why God seems relentlessly bent on walking us through our worst fears.

I threw side-armed to Graham that day because I love him and want to help him grow. He smiled and gave me the benefit of the doubt. Will you do the same for God—give him the benefit of the doubt—if he chooses to take you past your worst fears?

Authentic Faith, 71–72

NOVEMBER

As we look forward to Thanksgiving, we have the opportunity to prepare our hearts by remembering all the good things God gives us. As we meditate on his blessings, our hearts turn to praise and gratitude as we find contentment in his love. Our thankfulness, in turn, reminds us to be generous with others, which multiplies the thanksgiving.

THE SPIRITUAL AIR FRESHENER

A number of years ago I returned from a long trip, dog-tired from being away. But as soon as I got home, my wife met me at the door with a recital of things that had broken during my absence—a closet door out of its track, a leaking toilet, a broken refrigerator shelf...

"Stop!" I wanted to yell. "Just tell me what *isn't* broken so I can leave it alone."

The next morning as I hugged a toilet, I began to grow bitter. I wanted a day off; no, I *deserved* a day off. I could use a walk in the open air. I could be playing with the children. The "I" statements poured out of me as fast as the water poured out of the back of the toilet.

Then I remembered how my wife and I had prayed for God to provide this house—at a time when we weren't sure we could afford one. I remembered how cold it had been outside and how nice it was to come into a warm place. I began thanking God for the benefit of space, protection from the weather, and a living room that my wife could decorate in a way she loves.

In short, I found things to thank God for, and my heart felt drawn to God.

Wait a minute, you might object. *What about the reality of a legitimately frustrating situation? Isn't thankfulness naive?*

Let me pose a different question: Has an attitude of bitterness ever healed a disabled child? Filled a bank account? Repaired a car or a leaky toilet?

No, being thankful doesn't fix broken lives or restore bitter losses. But it does transform our spirit as we face them. And since we all have to live through hardships in this fallen world, we need the power—the very great power—of a spirit filled with peace and joy to carry us through the toughness of life.

The virtue of thankfulness is power to the soul. God offers it to us to drive out the spiritually degenerative illness of bitter, negative thinking. I like to think of thankfulness as "God's spiritual air freshener." It replaces the stale odor of resentment with clean, fresh-smelling air for the soul to breathe.

The Glorious Pursuit, 138–39

AN UNFORGETTABLE BALD HEAD

I'll never forget that bald head. The man probably was still in his thirties, but I was nineteen years old at the time, and thirty-two seemed ancient. The two of us were battling it out for the lead in a six-mile road race. He had more speed; I had more strength. On the flats, he broke away. When we got to the hills, I passed him.

My whole view of training changed that day. On training runs, I wondered why I was doing this to myself. My legs would have that weak, blown-out feeling; my lungs would burn. I thought, "Is the pain really worth it?" But during this race, every time I saw my competitor fall back as we reached another hill, I felt thankful for the times I had endured training on the hills. In this case, because the finish line was at the top of a hill, I won.

The same principle holds true for my spiritual struggles. Perhaps we find it too difficult to thank God for a hard struggle while we are in it, but afterward we can look back and say, *God, you really helped me mature during that last difficult time. Thank you.* Once we begin thanking God for the easy things, it is possible to progress and begin thanking him for the difficult things that happened to us in the past. Eventually we can thank God for what he's doing through current difficult circumstances.

Of course, there's a difference between thanking God *for* the difficult things and thanking God *in* the difficult things. I began to see the difference when I combined "giving thanks in all circumstances" with Romans 8:28–29: "And we know that in all things God works for the good of those who love him, who have been called according to his purpose. For those God foreknew he also predestined to be conformed to the likeness of his Son." If we miss this, we miss everything. *It is God's will that we be conformed to the image of his Son.*

God can use virtually any circumstance — no matter how painful or pleasant — to shape the character of Christ in us. And we can be thankful for this shaping.

The Glorious Pursuit, 142–43

MORE THAN A LOVER

During our engagement, I gave Lisa a poem titled "My Sister, His Bride." I said that while the step we were taking toward marriage was monumental, there already existed an even more significant eternal bond between us that would outlive our status as husband and wife: namely, brother and sister in Christ.

Otto Piper explains it this way:

> The believer who conducts his marriage as in the Lord will seek to make his marriage transcend mere sexuality by emphasizing his fellowship with God. Then the spouse is not only a sexual partner but also and above all a brother or sister in Christ. In this way the instinctive longing inherent in all love becomes real: our earthly lives are transmuted into lives with God.[1]

This means that while physical pleasure is good and acceptable, we mustn't reduce sex to a merely *physical* experience. It is about much more than that. Sex speaks of spiritual realities far more profound than mere pleasure.

When Paul tells us that our bodies are temples of the Holy Spirit (1 Corinthians 6:19), our contemplations on the significance of sex take on an entirely new meaning. What a woman is allowing inside her, what a man is willingly entering—in a Christian marriage, these are *sanctified* bodies, bodies in which God is present through his Holy Spirit, bodies coming together and celebrating in a spirit of reverence and holiness.

Paul tells us that a man is not to join himself to a prostitute because his body is a holy temple, but can't this imagery be used in a positive way? Isn't a Christian husband somehow entering God's temple—knocking on the door of *shekinah* glory—when he joins himself to a fellow believer? And isn't this a tacit encouragement to think about God as your body joins with that of your spouse?

Otto Piper urges us to view the sex act as a physical picture of a deeper spiritual reality, namely, that we are no longer two, but one. In Christian marriage, husband and wife are more than lovers. They are brother and sister in Christ.

Sacred Marriage, 209–10

A QUIET ELATION

It had been an exhausting week, with two or three more hard weeks ahead. I was flying from coast to coast, so I requested an aisle seat. I needed the room to get some work done.

"Sorry, sir," the agent said, "but all that remains are center seats."

I sighed as I got in line to board, knowing that work would be impossible. I dug a novel out of my shoulder bag and found my seat between a large man and an elderly woman. I didn't even have my seat belt on when the woman started talking. She was in her seventies, with a sweet demeanor. But I was tired from speaking at several events, and I looked wistfully at the book in my hands. How could I open the cover without being rude?

"I'm sorry," the woman said, perhaps catching my glance. "I'm sure you probably want to read."

I smiled politely and began to crack open my book.

"I just don't get to talk very much," she said quietly. "Not since my husband died."

Her words felt like a spiritual body-slam. I had allowed myself to fill up with self-pity, selfishly demanding four hours of duty-free living on a cross-country flight. Suddenly it occurred to me. Out of all the seats I could have been assigned, I found myself seated next to this elderly woman who felt lonely and was hoping for someone to talk to. Wasn't it at least *possible* that God had placed me beside her?

We talked for the next four hours—about her children, her life, her church. I listened a lot, even though the novel kept summoning me. *This is God's daughter*, I kept reminding myself.

As the flight ended, a surprising thing happened. The extreme weariness I had been feeling was gone. I actually felt buoyant. That's the energizing reality of obedience. I had surrendered to the situation, believing it was not a random circumstance but one in which God had placed me. I had surrendered my will to his will—and in doing so, I had experienced Jesus, the delight of my soul. A quiet elation filled my soul.

Let's make ourselves available to God today; let's be aware of his providence, and surrender to its sometimes masked joys.

The Glorious Pursuit, 25–26

FASTING AND FEASTING

Christian spirituality is largely about maintaining our thirst and passion for God and his purposes. Admittedly, at times our passions can lead us astray, but Christian marriage teaches us to manage these passions, like the dam keepers in Washington state. Sometimes dam managers opt to let the water flow freely; other times they hold it to a trickle. This is what marriage teaches us to do. Sometimes it is healthy and good to let marital passions run free, even if we fear crossing the line into lust. Some people make the mistake of believing that because they have been burned by their passion, the antidote is to completely cut it off. They do to sex what an anorexic does to food: "I don't want to overeat and become fat, so I won't eat at all." This is a demented attitude, not a healthy one.

The healthy life says both yes and no at appropriate times. I travel quite a bit, so my wife and I often fast from sexual expression. Couples with young kids, particularly babies, soon learn that they cannot express themselves sexually whenever they get the inclination. At other seasons, our spouse may be ill or worn-out, and it would be unkind to place sexual expectations on them. In such situations, sexual fasting is appropriate and necessary.

But times of feasting also are necessary. In fact, every no we say to sex should be placed in the context of a corresponding yes. To fast from sexual contact because we think *eros* is evil is not a Christian idea, but an unholy and unhealthy flight from God's good creation.

Abstinence is not a cul-de-sac or dead end; it is a long on-ramp. Rather than being a denial, it is a channeling of desire into the proper place. The bottom line is this: Passion and engagement are both extremely important. We should cultivate them in marriage and bring them to bear on all of life.

Sacred Marriage, 222–23

SEX AND PRAYER

God views my life as a seamless garment. I'm not divided into "holy Gary" and "secular Gary." There's no "Gary the husband" versus "Gary the Christian." It's not a compromise for me, for example, to desire to grow in prayer *and* to express my sexuality.

Does this sound odd? In fact, the apostle Paul sees sexual abstinence in marriage as dangerous, and so he suggests, "Do not deprive each other except by mutual consent and for a time, so that you may devote yourselves to prayer" (1 Corinthians 7:5). In essence, Paul is saying, "Use marriage the way God intended it. Meet your sexual needs by making love to your spouse. Then your mind and soul will be more open to prayer."

Paul is a practical pastor. He recognizes that the sex drive is a biological reality. By engaging in sexual relations within a lifelong relationship, a major temptation and distraction are removed and our souls are placed at rest. This is especially important for contemplative prayer, a type of prayer in which the mind must be unusually free of distractions. While it may sound bizarre to some, Paul is telling Christian husbands and wives that they can serve their partner and at the same time create the climate for an enriching prayer life by serving each other sexually.

Our evangelical culture may have difficulty embracing this explanation. I've never read a book on prayer that included the step, "If you're married, have sex on a regular basis," but it seems clear that this is what Paul intends here!

God made me and you complete human beings. I can give myself unabashedly and enthusiastically to my wife and still give myself unreservedly to God. I can express sexual desires in a marital context, and I can still be passionate about prayer. The two go together. Even stronger than that, the two *complement* each other. Not only are my sexual desires and my spiritual needs not competitive; they are mutually supportive. Both marital sex and prayer bear God's enthusiastic imprimatur.

Sacred Marriage, 79–80

EMBRACE LIFE

Christians, born of the creator God and redeemed in his image, have the great privilege of embracing life in all of its fullness. We are to give God praise for his glorious work—the life of family and business and achievement, the abundant life that he lavishes on us in many delightful ways.

Christianity will always sing the song of self-denial, but we can also teach redeemed Christians to view feelings of love, pleasure, and achievement as pointing them *to* God instead of competing *with* God. I love the way C. S. Lewis treated a young reader who worried that she loved the Narnia character Aslan more than she loved Jesus. Lewis replied that she loved the Jesus in Aslan; everything that drew her to Aslan was the spirit and character of Jesus. Aslan merely demonstrated the beauty of Jesus in a way she could understand.

When a mother loves her baby, she loves maternity as created and celebrated by her heavenly Father. When God our Parent allows us to become parents, we get a glimpse of him. When we love our spouse, we love the way our divine King relates to his people. When we love music, we love God's creativity. When we love eating, we love our Lord's generosity and inventiveness. To the redeemed, everything we love about such pure desires reflects on God. Let's use these desires to focus our worship and praise rather than see them as competitors.

During one of our vacations, I tried to help my kids do just this. As we sat around the table, I said, "Everything you like about your life is from God. The fact that your parents are still married—that's our Creator's work. The fact that we have money to go on this vacation—that's his provision. The fact that I'm able to do what I enjoy for a living, and have an attitude of joy about it—that's God's gifting. Literally every aspect of your life that you find pleasing and satisfying ultimately has its roots in God's goodness."

Spend some time today glorifying God for the good things of this earth—beauty and pleasure and intimacy, everything that points us back to the genius of his creative work.

Pure Pleasure, 63–64

BLIND TO THE BLESSING?

The routine of family life can hide the daily miracle we enjoy. Just a simple, quiet Saturday morning sounds like a slice of heaven to a man who has lost everything, but to those of us who still wake up in the same house next to the same spouse with the same kids, we can become blind to what a blessing it really is.

When we're surrounded by this blessing, it's easy to look at the downside —our spouse's wrinkles or morning breath, the fact that one of the kids left the milk out or the refrigerator door open, a teen waking up at noon—but if suddenly everything was taken away, our highest wish would be to restore things just the way they were, spilled milk and all.

In the heat of a newfound and misplaced affection, it's easy to grow bored with or even to despise the wonder of a quiet morning in a stable home with a long history. Every routine Saturday morning is a blessing, a quiet miracle, a little slice of heaven. Enjoy it. Protect it. Thank God for it. And certainly don't even *think* about throwing it away. Its familiarity may have masked the wonder, but its absence would tear out your heart.

This morning, I walked upstairs and saw my family getting around to eating breakfast. Graham was home from cross-country practice, eagerly evaluating his high school team's chances in the coming season. Allison was her quiet self, reading the newspaper and wearing her favorite pajamas. Kelsey was lamenting how a bagel had fallen into the pancake batter. Lisa was outside in the sun, moving the sprinkler to a different spot.

Just an ordinary morning in the eyes of most people, but because I had been crafting these words, my appreciation had grown, and I thought, "You know, it really doesn't get much better than this." I went around the kitchen and touched each child. I tried to take a mental picture, preserving this moment—and I thanked God for this little slice of heaven here on earth.

Devotions for Sacred Parenting, 151

November 9

A Look in the Mirror

Parenting demands of us patience, perseverance, and long-suffering—but what our children ask of us pales in comparison to what we ask of God. In our struggles and our weariness, we may forget that God has forgiven us, is patient with us, and endures our own failings to a far greater extent than we do with our children.

Most kids live with us for two or two and a half decades; God puts up with us for the full breadth of our lives. While our children may occasionally provoke us with offensive words, God sees every offensive inclination of our hearts. For every offense for which we forgive our children, God forgives us many times over. He remains patient with us much longer than we exercise patience with our children. He doesn't ask anything of us as parents that he hasn't delivered a hundred times over himself.

We need to use the most wearisome aspects of parenting as the occasion for thanking God for putting up with us. When we look through this lens, we find that raising a demanding child can become motivation for worshiping and adoring God. No spiritually aware parent can at the same time become self-righteous. Only the most forgetful and most blind among us can act arrogantly before God, as though he gave us a heavier burden than we had given him. Sacred parenting reminds us that no matter how difficult a child may be, we still play in the minor leagues compared to God's great sacrifice.

Consider how many times you have broken your promises once offered earnestly to God. Consider on how many occasions you've said or thought or done vile things in full sight of a holy and perfect God. Consider God's eagerness to forgive you, the persistence of his grace, the limitless supply of understanding, patience, and mercy—all offered without condition in your behalf.

Without difficult children, we might take this patience and mercy and forgiveness for granted. Difficult children become a rare gift, showing us a side of God we might otherwise miss.

Sacred Parenting, 149–50

CHRIST IN YOU

Some time ago, I caught myself stewing in some destructive attitudes. For instance, I displayed constant irritation at people over petty things, like getting bad customer service in stores or being cut off by thoughtless drivers. One time I was singing a worship chorus to myself in a store, and my behavior made me feel like a hypocrite. I was going to have to either lose the attitude or lose the chorus.

I opted to lose the attitude.

The route I took to change was a gradual one. I thought, "What if I adopted another mind-set?" I didn't want to become a Christian Pollyanna: "Gee, Lord, I'm so amazingly grateful that traffic was heavy and I missed my plane today. I really *love* this character growth stuff." That would have been playacting, and it was doomed to failure. But I did need to face up to the gap between my surliness and the spirit and character of Christ.

So I began by offering up to the Lord the inner stresses I felt. Each time I set out, I chose an attitude of acceptance. I accepted the fact that I might get caught by every red light, that the people serving me might have their own limitations and hassles. I dropped the unrealistic view that this is an easy world where everything should go right ("right" according to *my* plan, that is). Instead, I relaxed in the biblical view that this is a fallen world where unnerving things happen. When I began my day, I forced my mind off myself, my demands, and my goals. I began to think a little about giving God a place in my demanding schedule: How could I make other people's experiences more pleasant, perhaps with a smile, an offer of assistance, or patience at the check-out line? Instead of scowling at slow-moving checkers, I started commending efficient ones.

That day I made an important commitment to my own spiritual growth. I chose to make a place in my life for the virtues that would cause the character of Jesus to become, little by little, real in me.

Large character is forged from consistently making the right small decisions.

The Glorious Pursuit, 28–29

KEEP THE LIGHTS ON

When I became the holder of a mortgage and the father of three kids, I began to understand the concern about high electric bills. I found myself coming home from work and being able to spot my house a mile away—it was the one with every light on.

One day, Lisa found me going from room to room, muttering under my breath. "What's wrong?" she asked.

"Nothing," I said. "I'm just trying to find a lightbulb that's not turned on. I don't want it to feel left out."

One winter evening some time later, I drove up to the house—and saw not a single light on. At first I thought there must be a power outage, but our neighbors' homes were lit up.

I walked into an empty house. The silence overwhelmed me. It looked like an alien place, so I did something I thought I'd never do. I turned on most of the lights to welcome home Lisa and the kids.

That incident became one of those "lightning" moments when God impressed a truth on my heart. I realized that every blessing comes with a burden.

If God were to take my wife and children home, I would have a much smaller electric bill—and a hole in my heart the size of Texas. I soon realized that in just about every complaint lies the foundation of thanksgiving. The fact that a rainy day upsets you is due in part to the fact that you can go outside and enjoy the weather. The fact that you're busy assumes you have a job or children. The fact that there's a load of laundry means someone is alive to get it dirty.

It comes down to how we choose to look at it. God could remove the burden, but if he did, he would also take away the blessing.

Whenever you are tempted to complain because your kids are being kids, ask God to remind you of the blessing behind the burden. And give thanks that your dirty house, big electric bill, and messy car mean you are blessed with relationships of love.

Devotions for Sacred Parenting, 61–63

TAKEN FOR GRANTED

As a child grows up, he or she will surely pass through a season when parents have to pitch in and remove as much stress and time demands as possible. Maybe it will be a difficult semester at school. Maybe they are having a challenge with some social adjustment. Maybe their hormones are boiling inside and they just need some extra space. When such seasons arise, you know that *now* is the time to lessen the load on their shoulders at home so they can marshal their resources to face the challenge before them.

Many times, this effort goes unnoticed and unappreciated. I remember a mom in Kansas commenting about her daughter, "She has no idea how much I'm doing for her," she said. "I'm happy to do it, but she really has no clue."

It struck me that this is exactly how God must feel. Think about it: How many times do we drive down the road, about to carelessly slip into an accident, when God's providence spares us a potentially fatal encounter? We proceed on our way with only a glance backward, not realizing that God has miraculously intervened.

How many times has God opened the door vocationally, relationally, and otherwise, yet we fail to notice his handiwork? Maybe we pass it off as "networking" or our amazing ability to build friends, not realizing the divine hand that moved human hearts on our behalf.

God is a busy God. He is pervasively present in our lives, showering us with his goodness and mercy and favor. But how frequently do we specifically recognize what he does for us and thank him for it?

Not nearly often enough.

The next time you become aware that your kids aren't noticing how much you do for them, remind yourself of how much God does for you. Let's use our children's taking us for granted as a call to worship the God we often forget to thank.

Devotions for Sacred Parenting, 114–16

THE LATTE FACTOR

During the second week of November, Starbucks switches from its ubiquitous white cups and ushers in the Christmas season with festive red cups. Our family is weird enough that we talk about this day before it comes, and then we usually toast it after it arrives. Just this year, as I poured a little cinnamon into my chai tea, I got a text message on my phone: "The Christmas cups are here!"

I smiled and typed back, "I know. I'm holding one."

Graham replied, "They make me happy."

You can't read my books without coming across Starbucks references. Once, while I was traveling, the conscientious couple chauffeuring me noticed the Starbucks cup in my hand. The woman said, "Have you ever thought of giving up Starbucks and giving the money to missions?" Now, the car they drove exceeded the cost of my Ford Focus by at least $20,000. I could have said, "Have you ever thought of trading in your vehicle for a Ford and giving the money to missions?" But of course I didn't.

Financial planners love to use the "latte factor" to show how a daily cup of luxury coffee can decimate retirement planning. And I do think we should be willing to part with any luxury to sacrificially support the advancement of God's kingdom here on earth.

Even so, consider an intriguing, albeit counterintuitive bit of wisdom from the book of Ecclesiastes: "Do not be overrighteous, neither be overwise—why destroy yourself? . . . The man who fears God will avoid all extremes" (7:16, 18).

An extreme fussiness can wear us out. Worse, it can set us up for failure after we run ourselves into the ground and, weakened by exhaustion, collapse into a foolish act of sin. Here's what I have found: Too little pleasure can lead us into the same place that Christians fear too much pleasure will take us. The road may be different, but the destination is the same.

Pure Pleasure, 168–69

A PLATFORM FOR PRAISE

Are you bold enough to believe that God created this world not to tempt us but to reveal himself to us? Even this fallen world provides windows through which we may glimpse the one who created it, prompting our heartfelt praise.

One writer took stinging aim at a worldview that reduces this world to mechanical chance, devoid of God's mysterious and delightful touch: "The birds sing much more than Darwin permits." Birds chirp and twitter and trill and coo because God made them that way—much to his and our delight.

In her wonderful book *Cold Tangerines*, Shauna Niequist describes how becoming pregnant made her almost mystically alive to the world's truest and purest pleasures:

> One of the best things about being pregnant, I think, is how vividly I taste and feel and smell things. A soft chair can truly make me believe that all is right with the world, and sweet corn and ripe peaches just annihilate me with their flavor. Lavender soap can make me almost pass out with happiness. I have never been so easily and deeply satisfied.[2]

God's design displays utter brilliance. I can't imagine a more intelligent thing for the Creator to do than to make a pregnant mother—who is literally repopulating the world—intoxicated with the beauty of life. If she's going to prepare the way, why not make her an enthusiastic fan?

The heart of every healthy believer gravitates toward worship, singing, and thanksgiving. All of these good things bring great joy and pleasure. God made us and this world. So when we participate in this world as he made it, we celebrate him every bit as much as we honor him when we do things that reflect his redeeming work. He invites us to truly enjoy him and all that he has made, no longer using God merely to enjoy the world (as he sets us free from addictions, helps us reclaim our finances, restores our health), but also using the world to enjoy God.

Our planet is a platform for praise. How can you use the earth to enjoy God today?

Pure Pleasure, 53–54

THE CONNECTION BETWEEN
PRAISE AND DELIGHT

Watch a young mom play with her baby. Most mothers become enthralled when they get their babies to laugh. They'll spend a half hour trying to elicit one last giggle, because the sound of a child learning to giggle feels intoxicating.

It's life with a capital *L*.

All of this merely reflects our heavenly Parent. As our true and perfect Father, God delights in our delight. Isaiah 62:4–5 reads, "The LORD will take delight [i.e., *pleasure*] in you ...; as a bridegroom rejoices over his bride, so will your God rejoice over you." Those close to God's heart embraced this delightful truth with unparalleled exuberance and praise. Despite the serious troubles he passed through, King David never lost the sense that God always sought his best, and therefore he praised his Lord for it: "The LORD be exalted, who delights in the well-being of his servant" (Psalm 35:27). Note the close connection between our *praise* of God and his *delight* in us.

The psalms proclaim a generous God who loves to give his creatures things that bring delight: "He makes grass grow for the cattle, and plants for man to cultivate—bringing forth food from the earth: wine that gladdens the heart of man, oil to make his face shine, and bread that sustains his heart ... When you give it to them, they gather it up; when you open your hand, they are satisfied with good things" (Psalm 104:14–15, 28).

The Bible insists, "The LORD takes pleasure in those who fear him, in those who hope in his steadfast love" (Psalm 147:11 ESV). When we enjoy God and what he has created, we bring great pleasure to God. In fact, it is the pathway to worship and praise and robust thanksgiving and increases our own spiritual vigor: "[The LORD] satisfies your desires with good things so that your youth is renewed like the eagle's" (Psalm 103:5).

Who knew? Pure pleasure can be a pathway to worship, a heart of thanksgiving, and spiritual strength! How can you embrace the godly qualities of pure pleasure today?

Pure Pleasure, 33–35

INSTRUMENTS OF PRAISE

In her classic work *To Kill a Mockingbird*, author Harper Lee recounts how "foot-washing Baptists" condemned Miss Maudie for spending too much time with her flowers. Miss Maudie explained to Scout:

> "Foot-washers believe anything that's pleasure is a sin. Did you know some of 'em came out of the woods one Saturday and passed by this place and told me me and my flowers were going to hell?"
>
> "Your flowers too?"
>
> "Yes, ma'am. They'd burn right with me. They thought I spent too much time in God's outdoors and not enough time inside the house reading the Bible."[3]

When Jesus said he came to give us an abundant life (John 10:10), he spoke not so much about *length* of life as about *quality* of life. Eugene Peterson in *The Message* renders John 10:10, "I came so they can have real and eternal life, more and better life than they ever dreamed of."

The church has gotten off track when we fail to make the distinction that Paul makes: "To the pure, all things are pure, but to those who are corrupted and do not believe, nothing is pure. In fact, both their minds and consciences are corrupted" (Titus 1:15). In other words, *redemption*—becoming a believer, being born again—*means something*. Paul is arguing against teachers who want to enslave Christians to the old belief that if a defiled person touches something (food, drink, or even another person), this something also becomes defiled. Paul cleverly turns this around, stating that if someone is pure, then whatever she touches becomes pure!

We need to look at pleasure and the good gifts of this earth through the eyes of redemption. The good things of this earth, created by God to be received with thanksgiving and praise, can be redeemed to season our life and faith in many positive ways. God can even give us the power to take what we formerly misused and transform it into an instrument of praise.

Pure Pleasure, 21

FORTIFIED BY SATISFACTION

Recently I had a very good day. It began with a rich time of Bible reading, prayer, and study, followed by a productive session of writing. Then my wife treated me to a glorious time of physical intimacy (the first time we had been alone in the house for quite some time). I followed that up with a meeting with a local pastor at Starbucks.

We talked about life, about running, about theology, about church. I returned home and set out on a beautiful early autumn run, leaving in time so I would return by the time the kids got home from school.

By late afternoon, my heart was overflowing with joy. Mental stimulation, vocational fulfillment, sexual intimacy, rich Christian fellowship, a well-made chai tea, physical exercise — I felt like the most blessed person on the face of the earth. With my heart so full, what could sin offer me? Any evil would be a step back.

My intimacy with God in the morning gave me infinitely more fulfillment than watching an inane television program. Sex with my wife helped maintain our relationship, strengthened my family's bond, and helped secure stability for my children — why would I allow illicit sex to undo all this? The conversation with the pastor inspired both of us; it honored God and served each other. Why would I ever want to gossip when I can encourage and be encouraged?

And since I believe that a direct connection exists between physical fitness and spiritual fitness, the training run helped feed my spirit and fight off any number of spiritual ills. Because I've experienced the benefits of keeping in shape firsthand, a life of sloth holds little appeal.

I don't want to overstate the power of pleasure. Because of the residual sin nature within me, I will never face a life of no temptation. Because of my weakness, I will never, this side of heaven, reach moral perfection. I won't even smell it. But I can begin to develop a taste for it. True God-honoring pleasure can help me do just that, and it can do the same for you.

Pure Pleasure, 25–27

SOUL REST

Contentment is nothing more than soul rest. It is satisfaction, peace, assurance, and a sense of well-being, cultivated through pursuing the right things. Instead of more power, money, pleasure, and control, we seek an abundance of grace and peace (see 1 Peter 1:2). Contentment is the opposite of striving, aching, restlessness, and worry.

Ask yourself, "Which life would I rather live?"

Contentment	Discontentment
Soul rest	Agitated spirit
Satisfaction	Continual disappointment
Peace	Frustration
Assurance	Anxiety
Sense of well-being	Bitterness

One writer of Scripture surveyed the situation and prayed this prayer: "Two things I ask of you, O LORD; do not refuse me before I die. Keep falsehood and lies far from me; give me neither poverty nor riches, but give me only my daily bread. Otherwise, I may have too much and disown you and say, 'Who is the LORD?' Or I may become poor and steal, and so dishonor the name of my God" (Proverbs 30:7–9).

Solomon understood how much better it is to choose inner tranquility over vain striving: "Better one handful with tranquility than two handfuls with toil and chasing after the wind" (Ecclesiastes 4:6). Solomon warns that once the lust for more captivates us, we will be wretched prisoners indeed: "Whoever loves money never has money enough; whoever loves wealth is never satisfied with his income. This too is meaningless" (Ecclesiastes 5:10).

Externally based Christians will never enjoy the profound tranquility of spirit exhibited by Paul, who wrote these poignant words: "I have learned to be content whatever the circumstances. I know what it is to be in need, and I know what it is to have plenty. I have learned the secret of being content in any and every situation, whether well fed or hungry, whether living in plenty or in want. I can do everything through him who gives me strength" (Philippians 4:11–13).

Authentic Faith, 169–70

November 19

ARE YOU THANKFUL OR TOLERANT?

Did you know that the brain is wired toward discontentment? Neurologists explain how our brain becomes accustomed to whatever is happening within and without. The phenomenon can perhaps be best understood by considering substance addiction.

If a man puts chemicals into his body, eventually the chemical makeup of his brain learns to tolerate the drugs by achieving a chemical balance that depends on the drug's introduction. Withdrawal, therefore, becomes exceedingly difficult, because withholding the substance upsets the new balance.

Many brain researchers believe the same process takes place with non-substance addictions, although the contention is more controversial. We are physically wired, they say, to become comfortable with what we have. Our brain gets used to it.

All of this means, neurologically, that no matter how much money we make, our mind will function in such a way that even vast wealth eventually will feel "normal." Our brain becomes accustomed to a certain standard of living, and once we become accustomed to something, it's only a matter of time until we become bored with it.

It is vital to understand this process if we are ever to rid ourselves of this spiritual sickness. Spiritually speaking, we become sick when we start *tolerating* God's blessings instead of being *thankful* for them. The Bible prescribes thankfulness as the way to counteract growing accustomed to our affluence.

Every time we sit down for a meal, instead of taking the food for granted, we are encouraged to remember God, who provided it and to thank him for its provision. Every time we enter our houses, it is good to thank God for providing shelter. We should be thankful every time we adjust the thermostat, bringing either refreshing cool air or comforting warmth. Gratitude should cover us every time we put on a shirt or cover our feet with shoes. The discipline of thankfulness keeps God's goodness fresh.

Authentic Faith, 174–75

THE PROBLEM OF POSSESSIONS

When I drove a ten-year-old van, I was never concerned about where I would park it. I didn't worry about someone bumping the side with their car door. I didn't look out at it and wonder if I had remembered to lock it. When a friend or a neighbor kid slammed the sliding door a little too hard, I couldn't care less. But when we bought a new van, suddenly I thought twice about where to park it at church or at the mall. Maintenance demands started dominating my thoughts. When a kid slammed the side door a little too hard, I winced. Upgrading our van, at least initially, took its toll on my psyche. It was embarrassing to admit, but I was attached to a piece of metal.

I've found that greater abundance often invites *more* anxiety rather than less. Put in new carpet or a new wood floor, and see if you have the same attitude the next time people walk into your house.

Jesus got at this when he said we can't serve two masters (Matthew 6:24). Notice that Jesus didn't say it is *hard* to serve both God and money, but that it is *impossible*. We will inevitably hate one and love the other. We are instructed not to worry about physical provisions. Although pagans run after these things, we are called to seek first the kingdom of God and his righteousness (Matthew 6:33).

Paul's words to Timothy put the contentment bar quite high. Paul thought that if we have food and clothing—which seems to imply shelter—"we will be content with that" (1 Timothy 6:8). The real "getting," in Paul's mind, is spiritual: "But godliness with contentment is great gain" (1 Timothy 6:6).

Throughout Christian history, a number of saints have taken these words at face value. Ambrose wrote, "It is not property which makes rich, but the spirit … For the more a man has gained the more he thirsts for gain, and burns as it were with a kind of intoxication from his lusts." He then adds, "Why do you seek for a heap of riches as though it were necessary? Nothing is so necessary as to know that this is not necessary."[4]

Authentic Faith, 176–77

WHEREVER I AM . . .

The Primitive Benedictines are known for their vow to a geographical location, meaning they agree to stay in one place for their entire lifetime. This profound contentment with and appreciation for where you are provides an antidote to the wanderlust of "I've got to get out of here." It is taking to heart the words of Scripture: "Like a bird that strays from its nest is a man who strays from his home" (Proverbs 27:8).

On the flip side, many may experience what Woody Allen confesses to in the documentary *Wild Man Blues*: "I've got the kind of personality where when I'm here in Europe I miss New York, and when I'm in New York I miss Europe. I just don't want to be where I am at any given moment. I would rather be somewhere else. There's no way to beat that problem because no matter where you are, it's chronic dissatisfaction."

This is a devastating and soul-destroying attitude for a believer. Francis de Sales warns, "As long as your spirit looks elsewhere than where you are, it will never apply itself rightly to profiting from where you are."

Contentment is a conscious decision to rest in the providence of God, a humble embracing of the fact that we can learn lessons wherever we are. It doesn't entirely preclude working toward something "better," but it cultivates a spirit of thankfulness even in less-than-ideal situations.

Once we start on the cycle of "if only . . . ," there is no stopping. We pray for a new job, but then imagine life would be much more pleasant if we got a promotion. Two weeks after the promotion, we realize the new boss is a bit of a jerk and think how much better it would be if we had a new supervisor. This obsessive rewriting of our desires and expectations can drive us crazy.

There is a place called contentment where ambitious strivings are replaced by firm resolution; daydreams of glory-filled service give way to patient and humble obedience; and restlessness transforms itself into peace.

Let's choose contentment.

Authentic Faith, 183

THE HEART OF CONTENTMENT

Discontentment is most often born out of comparison. We look at someone else (almost always at someone who has it just a bit better than we do), and feel cheated. Rarely do we look at someone who has it worse and wonder why God has been so good to us.

Spiritually immature people don't believe thanksgiving is born out of a change of heart; they think it requires a change of circumstances and frequently idealize their desired change in a way that makes them even spiritually sicker than they already are. When we seek change, we often forget that every change brings its own trials as well as blessings.

Francis de Sales warns about this:

> We must consider that there is no vocation that has not its irksome aspects, its bitternesses, and disgusts. And what is more, except for those who are fully resigned to the will of God, each one would willingly change his condition for that of others: those who are bishops would like not to be; those who are married would like not to be, and those who are not married would like to be. Whence comes this general disquietude of souls, if not from a certain dislike of constraint and a perversity of spirit that makes us think that each one is better off than we?[5]

A discontented person won't find contentment through any outward change. Put her in a new and bigger house, and she'll still complain about the color of the walls or the entrance to the street. A discontented man can change wives, but if he doesn't address his own failings, he'll soon grow just as weary with the new one. Trying to find contentment in this world without addressing the inner person is like changing cubicles while continuing to work for the same company. Your location may change, but the overall environment stays exactly the same.

We can't always change our circumstances, but we can address our hearts —and our hearts are the ultimate guardians of contentment. For Jesus' sake, and for your own, work to find contentment even within current frustration. This is the way of authentic faith.

Authentic Faith, 186–87

THE SAFE HARBOR OF CONTENTMENT

Imagine you are a realtor. You've just become a member of the "million dollar club" and feel great about it—until you realize that a woman who got her license the same time you did has just hired two more staff people and bought a huge billboard on the busiest street in town. You think you have the ability to catch her, but your daughter has been asking you to coach her soccer team this spring. You know you make enough money for your family's needs, but the fire of competition still burns.

Or maybe you're facing your twentieth high school reunion with a sense of regret. Everyone thought of you as "most likely to succeed," and, in fact, you did go on to graduate with honors from college. Then you started a family, and you've been a stay-at-home mom ever since. You greet former classmates who were less skilled than you but who now have their own corner offices, and their IRAs are worth more than your house.

Or let's say you are a pastor. God has been moving in your community. Several marriages have been saved; many individuals have made decisions for Christ over the past months. But you realize you'll never be able to compete with that church just ten miles away that has more staff people than your entire congregation has members. You'll never be asked to speak at your denominational convention, even though you know you have a lot to say.

Social situations often assault our spiritual integrity. They can take our eyes off of obedience to God and focus them on what brings praise from other people. Until we value obedience over human affirmation, integrity over achievement, and relationships over success, our souls are in peril.

Contentment is a safe harbor, a true shelter, from the desires that would destroy all that we hold as most precious.

Authentic Faith, 189

PROFOUNDLY THANKFUL, UNCOMMONLY GENEROUS

John Wesley was a wealthy man in his day. His writings brought in about 1,400 pounds annually, but he lived on just thirty pounds a year and gave away the rest. Wesley surrendered to God about 98 percent of his income.

Wesley believed that anything beyond the "plain necessaries of life" should be given to the poor or for the propagation of the faith. The fact that most believers didn't act this way merely proved to Wesley that many professed believers are "living men but dead Christians."

"Any 'Christian' who takes for himself anything more than the plain necessaries of life," Wesley wrote, "lives in open, habitual denial of the Lord." Such a person has "gained riches and hell-fire!" When Wesley died, he left behind virtually nothing, a goal he had long set out to achieve. "If I leave behind me ten pounds," he wrote, "you and all mankind bear witness against me that I lived and died a thief and a robber."[6]

Let's be honest. Few of us will ever achieve such a spirit, much less such a self-sacrificial lifestyle. A biblical argument could even be made that it is wise and responsible to prepare for emergencies and for retirement with savings accounts, IRAs, and the like. Otherwise we would become financial liabilities in our old age.

But all of us are obligated—perhaps better to say, invited—to be freed from the endless pursuit of accumulation and become instead profoundly thankful and uncommonly generous people. Ultimately, it is to our own advantage to receive this spirit from God. "A heart at peace gives life to the body, but envy rots the bones" (Proverbs 14:30).

Do we really believe Jesus when he says, "Watch out! Be on your guard against all kinds of greed; a man's life does not consist in the abundance of his possessions" (Luke 12:15)? Do we really trust him when he says, "It is more blessed to give than to receive" (Acts 20:35)? And if we do, then how is our belief reflected in our decisions and lifestyle?

Authentic Faith, 177–78

An Undeserved Gift

Though South Bend, Indiana, had descended into the throes of November, the weather hovered in the low sixties. "Touchdown Jesus"—the gigantic artwork of Christ emblazoned on Notre Dame's library overlooking the football stadium—loomed large to my right, while the Navy Midshipmen bounced up and down to my left. Rick Callahan, a friend and pastor at nearby River Valley Community Church, sat next to me. Notre Dame Stadium doesn't have a bad seat, but we were doubly blessed, sitting near the forty-yard line.

My mind wandered back to a testimony I heard while leading a Sacred Marriage conference. A pastoral couple offered a moving account of God's grace and healing in their marriage. They recounted the words of a counselor who reminded them that, apart from Christ's work, we all deserve hell. "So if it's true that we all deserve hell," Randy's counselor had said, "then isn't it also true that anything less than that is a pretty good day?"

I remember sitting in Notre Dame Stadium—with the sun keeping me warm but not making me hot, with the energy of the students providing more than enough enthusiasm for everyone within ten miles of the stadium, with the beauty of Notre Dame's campus satisfying my soul, with the drama of the football game below me—and thinking, "I deserve hell, and I get to experience a day like this?"

When we look at life through God's eyes, we become lost in wonder and convinced of God's astounding generosity, marvelous mercy, and gigantic grace. Sin causes us to look at life through the lens of entitlement—that we deserve salvation without repentance, wealth without work, accolades without self-denial, health without personal discipline, pleasure without sacrifice. Biblical truth reminds us that, in reality, we deserve hell.

Every small laugh, each tiny expression of joy, a simple meal—indeed, every single moment lived outside of the agony of hell—truly is an undeserved gift. When we add the assurance that the completed work of Christ guards our eternal destiny, our lives should radiate not merely joy but wonder and astonishment at how good God truly is.

Holy Available, 57–58

A PURE PARTY

A marvelous passage in 1 Kings describes Solomon's dedication of God's temple. The king offered thousands of fellowship offerings to the Lord, which were eaten and enjoyed by the people. Now notice this:

> They celebrated it [the Feast of Tabernacles] before the Lord our God for seven days and seven days more, fourteen days in all. On the following day he [Solomon] sent the people away. They blessed the king and then went home, joyful and glad in heart for all the good things the Lord had done for his servant David and his people Israel. (1 Kings 8:65–66)

Did you catch that? *Fourteen days of celebration!* In many Christian churches, people feel guilty for celebrating for fourteen *minutes*. If you throw one feast, at least one somber saint will complain, "Shouldn't we fast and give all this to the poor?" If a church decides to spend a little money to do a fun activity, someone will piously confront the pastor: "Wouldn't it be better to stay home and pray for our missionaries and send this money to them?"

Somehow, we seem to have lost the concept of creating inviting communities in which people get built up with joy and strengthened in celebration. We must not, we cannot, neglect the poor or lose our zeal for mission outreach, but for the sake of honoring God, we must not and cannot neglect celebrating God's goodness and thanking him for his generous faithfulness.

There is a time to sacrifice and fast, and there is a time to celebrate and feast. The wise Christian is as comfortable in one as in the other, and over the course of his or her life, you will see an abundance of both.

Pure Pleasure, 28

THE GOD-CENTERED SPOUSE

Pastor Greg Nettle was walking to his car after a golf tournament when he realized the remote trunk opener wouldn't work. Or the automatic door locks. When he finally got in the car, he saw the fuel gauge reading empty, even though he had filled up on gas less than twenty-four hours before. More frustrating yet, the car would turn over, but then immediately die.

After a tow truck delivered the disabled vehicle to the dealership, a mechanic came out to Greg and told him the problem: a bad BCM.

"What's a BCM?"

"The basic control module. It's essentially the car's brain, and once it goes bad, everything starts malfunctioning."

Greg could have insisted that they fix the trunk, the door locks, the gas gauge, and any number of problems—but those were merely the symptoms of an overall malfunction.

How often do we do the same with marriage? We can spend a lifetime focusing on the symptoms (communication, conflict, sexual issues, and so forth) or we can replace the BCM—the basic control module. I believe the BCM for marriage is our spiritual motivation.

It all comes down to this: Are you a God-centered spouse or a spouse-centered spouse? A spouse-centered spouse acts nicely toward her husband when he acts nicely toward her. She is accommodating, as long as her husband pays her attention. A spouse-centered husband will go out of his way for his wife, as long as she remains agreeable and affectionate. He'll romance her, as long as he feels rewarded for doing so.

But Paul tells us we are to perfect holiness out of reverence for God (2 Corinthians 7:1). Since God is always worthy to be revered, we are always called to holiness; we are always called to love. A God-centered spouse feels more motivated by his or her commitment to God than by whatever response a spouse may give.

In one sense, what my spouse says or does or doesn't do is almost irrelevant. Every decision I make, every word I utter, every thought I think, every movement I perform, is to flow out of one holy motivation: reverence for God.

Are you a God-centered spouse?

Devotions for a Sacred Marriage, 11–12

A THANKFUL SPIRIT

I recently talked to a godly young man named Brian who suffered severe burns in an industrial accident more than a decade ago. He lost 90 percent of the skin on his body, lost his eyesight, and had two arms and a leg amputated. As we spoke, I was astonished at his utter lack of self-pity; on the contrary, he expressed great thanks for how God used the injury to cement his faith. He has become a tower of strength, and as he described his relationship with his wife, I marveled at the obvious intimacy of their relationship on all levels, even in the face of such a debilitating injury.

I compared his Christlike, thankful spirit with my own whining when I suffered a running injury and had to take a few weeks off—and I just sighed. In a fallen world we can develop a radically unrealistic perspective. One severely disabled man said, "When you're a quadriplegic, you look at a paraplegic and think, 'Man, they've got it made!'"

When we feel sorry for ourselves, we work against finding positive solutions. Brian can't see his wife, and he'll never be able to hug her, but he can talk to her, pray with her and for her, and comfort her with wise words of love, care, and concern. Through the Internet, he has even discovered ways to buy her presents without her knowing about it ahead of time.

Sometimes, in God's providence, certain pleasures may be closed to us, as they have been to Brian. God says, in effect, "This is not for you, at least not now." We have to trust him to provide alternate pleasures—perhaps of an entirely different sort—that will sustain us in our trials. Feelings of entitlement feed anger; feelings of thankfulness swell our souls and can make us tear up with overflowing gratitude. Thanking God helps us recognize what pleasures we have while at the same time *increasing* our pleasure. Only when we stop focusing on what we've lost and instead become grateful for what we do have, or what we might work toward, do we find true joy.

Pure Pleasure, 206–7

JESUS-STYLE

In the Gospels, Jesus stresses God's generosity and our obligation to show generosity. Social mercy begins with the freedom we have because God is so generous: "Do not be afraid, little flock, for your Father has been pleased to give you the kingdom," followed by the invitation, "Sell your possessions and give to the poor. Provide purses for yourselves that will not wear out, a treasure in heaven that will not be exhausted, where no thief comes near and no moth destroys. For where your treasure is, there your heart will be also" (Luke 12:32–34).

This verse follows the well-known "don't worry about what you will eat or wear" passage. Jesus wants his followers to know that God's kingdom is theirs. We are going to inherit unimaginable wealth. We should respond not by putting on airs but by giving away what we have, knowing that abundance awaits us.

If we fail to live up to this ethic, we can expect severe punishment. Jesus' teaching about the sheep and the goats has one clear strain: The sheep are rewarded for their good deeds—feeding the poor, visiting the sick and imprisoned, clothing the naked. And the goats are punished for what they left undone—ignoring those already mentioned. All judgment is based on what individuals did or didn't do for hurting human beings (Matthew 25:31–46).

Because of this truth, Jesus stresses that the parties we throw need to be the kind that reap heavenly rewards. He tells his disciples that when they have a banquet, they shouldn't invite the rich or their own relatives. Otherwise, they'll be repaid and lose any reward. Instead, they should invite the poor, the crippled, the lame, and the blind (Luke 14:12–14). Think about this when you plan activities. When you take in a movie, is there a lonely person you can invite to tag along? When you invite friends to a meal, is there someone who is typically left out that you can invite?

This isn't about theory or feeling or study; it's about action. Ask God to put someone on your heart today, and then reach out to them in Jesus' name.

Authentic Faith, 109–10

GOD-DEPENDENT MINISTRY

God-dependence liberates us from our weaknesses, saves us from hiding behind our strengths, and delivers us from selfish preoccupation.

Perhaps you find yourself coming into work early to catch up on some work. You notice a new coworker in a corner cubicle, bent over her desk, clutching a tissue to her face. Her shoulders shake violently — but you're *really* busy. You came in early to get work done, not to play counselor.

What will you do?

Wherever we go — whether the golf course, a church conference room, a restaurant, or the local mall — we have the opportunity to open our eyes to what's happening around us, to think thoughts bigger than those that concern only us, and to be used by God even when we least expect it and especially when it is least convenient.

God-dependence frees us up in other ways too — in large part by no longer allowing us to use personal limitations as an excuse. Let's say your pastor notices a gift you haven't been using or presents an opportunity for service that sounds inviting and that fits with what you believe God has called you to do, but you're bothered with the nagging question, "Am I qualified to do that?" Christians who let their weaknesses and inadequacies hold them back are just as sinfully self-focused as believers who misuse their strengths to build self-glorifying kingdoms.

When will we learn that it's not about us? God is not impressed by our gifts, nor is he frightened by our inadequacies. God-dependence means that we will slow down in the midst of our ministry, making way for God's still, small voice, his gentle whisper, to guide us. The next time you're listening to someone pour out her heart or voice a complaint or ask for advice, what well are you going to draw from? Whose shoulder will you lean on? As we take to the front lines of ministry, let's check our hurry and our agendas at the door, be fully present in the moment, and invite God to take the lead.

Authentic Faith, 32–33

DECEMBER

December means a time of joyful celebration and anticipation. We take great joy in God's beauty and marvelous gifts, remembering not only the coming of the Messiah but also our promised eternal home with him. What a grand privilege we have to leave behind a legacy of joy-filled faith.

CELEBRATE!

Since I tend to be overly serious in my faith, I was challenged when I came across Elton Trueblood's titled *The Humor of Christ*. He writes, "Any alleged Christianity which fails to express itself in gaiety, at some point, is clearly spurious."[1]

He has plenty of biblical support to back up his claim. The Old Testament prescribed at least three major feasts — Passover, Weeks, and Tabernacles — as well as many other religious celebrations (Leviticus 23; Numbers 28, 29). These could be elaborate affairs. The Feast of Tabernacles, for example, involved a seven-day feast in which the Israelites were commanded to rejoice and forbidden to mourn.

The fact is, God is worthy of infinite celebration. Jesus said at one point that if the crowds had not broken forth in praise, the very stones would have cried out (see Luke 19:40). God forbid that we would get shown up by a bunch of rocks!

I have to constantly break out of my "serious" rut. I tend to view celebration as "flighty" or less reverent — but this is a personal prejudice I'm trying to overcome. It's easy to take this same attitude toward God — all business, no celebration — into our marriages, and it is just as destructive. Perhaps to counteract this, God has created a marital experience that calls us back to pleasure and rejoicing.

Marital sexuality provides a unique context for celebration. Naked in each other's arms, it doesn't matter if you have a portfolio worth a million dollars or if you're struggling with the realities of negative net worth. You could be delighting in a honeymoon as you celebrate life in your twenties or thirties, or renewing your passion as you celebrate life in your sixties or seventies. Regardless of station or status, you are celebrating a deeply human dance, a transcendent experience created by no less a preeminent mind than that of Almighty God himself.

Some of us need to be reminded to celebrate with zeal. Marriage makes available a full, responsive, and responsible human experience, the opportunity to relish the real and earthy pleasure of sexual activity, an intense celebration that gently reminds us of the heavenly existence that awaits all God's children.

Sacred Marriage, 224–25

IF NOT US, WHO?

Besides the prescribed celebrations detailed in the Old Testament, believers often erupted in individual, spontaneous celebration. David, the man after God's own heart, danced enthusiastically before the ark of the covenant, and when his wife despised him for it, he replied that the Lord had chosen him, and in response he would celebrate and "become even more undignified than this" (2 Samuel 6:22).

David also appointed singers and musicians, that they might worship and "sing joyful songs" (1 Chronicles 15:16). A musical, celebratory style of worship was one of the hallmarks of David's era: "David and all the Israelites were celebrating with all their might before God, with songs and with harps, lyres, tambourines, cymbals and trumpets" (1 Chronicles 13:8). Many years later, Israel was still using the instruments commissioned by David.

Jesus also encouraged celebratory styles of worship. Not only did he and his disciples participate in hymn singing, but when religious leaders complained about the people's loud celebration of Christ's entrance into Jerusalem, Jesus said, "I tell you, ... if [the people] keep quiet, the stones will cry out" (Luke 19:40).

This celebratory style is carried over into apostolic, New Testament worship. Paul and Silas sing hymns while in prison, and Paul exhorts the Ephesians to use psalms, hymns, and spiritual songs in their worship.

The act of celebration reminds us that we have much to be thankful for. God is worthy of great praise, and who else will sing that praise if not those who believe? A group of fifth-century Greek monks were known as the "non-sleepers" because they frequently spent an entire day and night in uninterrupted praise of God.

Even more than it is an obligation, celebration is a privilege. Celebrative worship leads to joy, which is a foundational virtue leading to spiritual strength.

As we enter the Advent season, let's renew our resolve to celebrate the goodness of God, beginning with the gift of his Son.

Sacred Pathways, 177–79

December 3

THE GIFT OF FEAR

If I could preach only one sermon to the church today, it wouldn't be faith—we hear more about faith today than ever in the history of the church. It would be about fear.

Moses was motivated by a godly fear of a holy God: "I feared the anger and wrath of the LORD" (Deuteronomy 9:19). According to the book of Isaiah, Jesus had more than mere wisdom and understanding and knowledge. He also lived with a healthy fear of the Lord (Isaiah 11:2–3).

Biblical fear is more complex and profound than what we usually think of when we use the English word *fear*. It isn't defined fully by the words *terror* and *dread*. Although it encompasses these emotions, it also carries the ideas of a passionate love, the positive desire to please God, and a worshipful awe.[2]

God is gracious—yes! God is merciful—absolutely! God is kind, good, loving, and caring—no doubt! But it is still a fearful thing to offend God, to fall into his holy hands, for he is a just God with the power and will to carry out judgments and discipline against those who offend him. Our Lord used this godly fear to root the early church in a proper attitude toward him. Ananias and Sapphira lost their lives when they tried to deceive the apostolic leaders. The surviving community responded just as God intended: "Great fear seized the whole church and all who heard about these events" (Acts 5:11). Keep in mind, this is the church *after* Pentecost, filled with the Holy Spirit yet needing an appropriate fear to help its members live godly lives.

I realize that talking about the fear of God seems outdated. Recently a pastor told me outright that he didn't believe he should fear God, but rather love him. And yet the Bible is clear that "[the church] was strengthened; and encouraged by the Holy Spirit, it grew in numbers, living in the fear of the Lord" (Acts 9:31).

I adore God. I feel safe with him. But I also fear him. I've come to view the fear of God as a shelter, a covering, a mighty force. I know I'm sinful. I know my own good intentions are far too weak in the face of way too many temptations. But I've also found that my fear of God is growing greater than my rebellion; it reins in my baser instincts and helps me to make choices that lead me to become the type of man I want to be rather than the type of man I despise.

Faith isn't fueled by sentiment alone; biblical faith needs an appropriate reverence, a proper fear of God.

Devotions for a Sacred Marriage, 23–24

GOD IS SETTING YOU UP!

One evening I stood on the edge of a new frontier. The next day, *Focus on the Family* would air my first interview with them, creating a platform I had never had. As I went to bed and prayed, I sensed God saying, "I have waited forty-two years for this day."

I cried at the impact of those words.

For years, people had asked, "Why haven't you been on *Focus on the Family*? Your stuff on Sacred Marriage is the best I've heard." What was I supposed to say? It's not like I didn't want to be on the program, but I could hardly call Dr. Dobson, introduce myself, ask him to join me for a cup of coffee, and then start talking broadcast dates.

Finally, about three years after *Sacred Marriage* came out, the producers contacted us to set up the interview that would reach millions of listeners. As I thought about the absurdity of it all, it dawned on me that I might have been their most unlikely guest. What do *I* know about marriage? I'm not a trained therapist, and at one point I practically destroyed my own marriage with my selfishness. Nor am I a particularly gifted writer. Early on, I went through *eight years* of rejection from publishers and magazine editors. Experts in the business told me either I had nothing to say or couldn't say it well enough.

And yet, as I lay in that bed, it dawned on me that only God can create a platform like this. Through it all, God knew. He had a plan, and he worked it out. When I cried about typing out words that never made it into print, God knew what lay ahead. When I thought I was wasting my time, God had marked this day on the calendar, and somehow—through all my tantrums, doubts, and accusations—had brought me to it. It took him forty-two years, but he made it happen.

And doing so brought him great joy.

Have you ever thought that God is taking his time to set you up as well, in a good way? He may not explain the delay or even narrate your passage through the detours, but he is an active God, an all-powerful God, who is more than capable of accomplishing his good purposes in his good timing.

Holy Available, 122–23

DEFIANT BEAUTY

Years ago on a trip through southwestern Washington, I traveled through miles and miles of tree farms. Each farm had a sign announcing, "These trees were planted in 1988." "These trees were planted in 1992." "These trees were planted in 1996."

Interspersed among the tree farms were occasional stretches of clear-cut logging projects. They looked devastated, broken, and abused. Even knowing that, after planting, the land will come back, it's still a bit sad to see such brutal scarring of a forest.

As I passed yet another clear-cut stretch, my eye caught something that almost made me pull off the road. There, in a devastated patch of land, stood a startlingly beautiful maple tree, in full autumn colors. Somehow, the loggers had missed it.

The contrast could not have been more stark—or more beautiful. Beauty surrounded by beauty begins, after a time, to seem mediocre. But beauty in the midst of chaos or ugliness stuns us. It seizes our attention. In a barren, broken stretch of land, this tree captured my imagination and told another story. Had it stood in the midst of New Hampshire's White Mountains during autumn, it likely would have been missed—one stunning tree in a forest of stunning trees. Here, however, in a broken, hurting land, this glorious tree proclaimed a transcendent truth.

In the deepest part of us, we truly yearn for such "defiant beauty." In a world where people choose self-centered lives, where ugly things happen, where sin seems to spread unchecked, where daily assaults take their toll, we can point to the defiant beauty of a selfless life, seeking first the kingdom of God, putting others first, and even sacrificing, if need be—all to proclaim a transcendent truth greater than ourselves.

I invite you to develop a defiant beauty this Christmas season, the kind that has shone through all generations of the church. At your office, in your home, during walks through the malls and visits to friend's houses, let's carry the defiant beauty of our Savior's love and hope to a sin-stained world.

Authentic Faith, 15

December 6

DON'T LOOK BACK

A relationship from my teen years still makes me wince whenever the girl's name comes to mind and I think about the hurt I caused her. One day I was praying about looking her up to tell her how sorry I felt for how I acted twenty-five years ago.

One of my best friends—a marriage and family therapist from San Diego—adamantly opposed the idea. "Gary," Steve said, "I'm thinking this is more about *you* than it is about *her*." In his experience from counseling, Steve has discovered that looking up someone after two and a half decades can be dangerous. You don't know where they're coming from or what's happening in their life. The potential for hurt is just as great as the potential for healing.

But the clincher came when he said, "Look, why don't you take all the energy you're using thinking about this and spend it planning on how you can love your wife *today*?

That's when it dawned on me that guilt attacks us by using a dead relationship to distract us from a living one. When guilt comes knocking on your door about a failed relationship from the past, start praying about how to love your spouse *today*. Don't let a dead relationship pollute or weigh down a living one.

For some people, the dead relationship isn't about guilt, but fantasy. They allow a relationship that never worked out to steal the energy they should be pouring into their marriage. "If only I had married him instead!" they think, or, "I wonder what so-and-so is doing right now?" So instead of praying about how to love their spouse, they daydream about being married to this other person.

Few things are as destructive as giving way to such fantasies. Those fantasies can't be fulfilled biblically. It is simply wasted time taken from what could be used to make our current marriage more meaningful. Besides, our memories tend to be highly selective. We forget the negative and fixate on the positive, and every such fantasy robs our spouse of energy and thought that should be expended on them.

Don't look back. You're cheating your spouse—and ultimately yourself—when you do. Pour all your energy into something current and real.

Devotions for a Sacred Marriage, 26–27

December 7

JOYS THAT LAST

While incessant laughter and joking can speak of shallowness, it can also reveal a profound depth. In his classic work *Orthodoxy*, G. K. Chesterton argues that Christianity fits humankind's deepest needs because it makes us concentrate on joys that do not pass away rather than on inevitable but transitory grief. Instead of getting buried by the seriousness of a fallen world, faith in Jesus Christ offers us the ability to laugh and enjoy ourselves, resting in God's promised eternal joys and pleasures.

Throughout history, even the most devout Christians have lived with exuberance. Saint Francis of Assisi and his followers got rebuked in church for being so happy as they worshiped God. The first generation of Methodists received constant criticism for being "too enthusiastic." And the early leaders of the Salvation Army knew such joy that they could scarcely contain themselves. When someone told a drummer not to hit his drums quite so hard, he said, "Oh, sir, I'm so happy I could burst the blessed drum!"[3]

One of my favorite writers, Elton Trueblood, goes so far as to make this declaration:

The Christian is [joyful] not because he is blind to injustice and suffering, but because he is convinced that these, in the light of the divine sovereignty, are never *ultimate* ... Though he can be sad, and often is perplexed, he is never really worried. The well-known humor of the Christian is not a way of denying the tears, but rather a way of affirming something which is deeper than tears.[4]

From first to last, the gospel is joy-producing good news. The New Testament commands us (no less than *seventy* times) to rejoice! Joyless Christians have lost sight of the good news of the gospel: that God created us, loves us, redeems us from our sins, and is preparing a place of unimaginable glory for us to enjoy throughout eternity. Children can help to awaken in us this God-given penchant toward joy. Particularly in the difficult times of life, children can be a source of profound encouragement.

Sacred Parenting, 79–80

HOLY SELF-FORGETFULNESS

To experience Christ's joy, passion, and fulfillment, we must adopt an entirely new mind-set and motivation. Jesus invites us to join him in living for the glory of the Father instead of for our own reputation. He calls us to give ourselves to the salvation and sanctification of Christ's bride, the church, rather than to be consumed by our own welfare. This holy self-forgetfulness is the most genuine mark of true faith, the evidence of God's merciful grace in our lives.

The Christlike life is not simply about practicing impeccable morality, overcoming temptation, and faithfully performing a few spiritual disciplines. The Pharisees did all of these far more faithfully than any of us ever will, and yet Jesus himself said these religious zealots had missed God's intention.

Paul defiantly took his passion for God several steps further than modern society believes is healthy. He didn't just love Christ; his commitment to his Savior and to the church nearly consumed him. He clearly laid out his goal and motivation: "And [Christ] died for all, that those who live should no longer live for themselves but for him who died for them and was raised again" (2 Corinthians 5:15).

Everything in Paul's life went through this grid. He even learned to rejoice in suffering, because by suffering "I fill up in my flesh what is still lacking in regard to Christ's afflictions, for the sake of his body, which is the church" (Colossians 1:24).

Paul didn't look at what hardship did to him; he focused on what his suffering accomplished for God's church. While imprisoned, Paul took heart that "because of my chains, most of the brothers in the Lord have been encouraged to speak the word of God more courageously and fearlessly" (Philippians 1:14).

The key to experiencing Paul's joy is adopting Paul's mission — to become a champion of God's work on this earth — which, ironically, creates a fountain of joy: "A generous man will prosper; he who refreshes others will himself be refreshed" (Proverbs 11:25). Selflessness seasons our faith with meaning and applies purpose to our pain.

Authentic Faith, 23–24

BRINGING JOY TO OUR HEAVENLY FATHER

At an end-of-the-season sports banquet, my son and his teammates slipped out of the restaurant and went next door to a video store to scope out the newest games. About five minutes later, Graham returned to the restaurant, alone. We thought it odd that Graham came back early, but we didn't say anything.

When we returned home, we found out what had happened. After checking out the video games, one boy said, "Hey, let's go look for dirty covers on the movies." The rest of the team fell into line; Graham said no and slipped out of the store.

I felt my heart swell with affection for Graham when I heard the story. We had been having a series of lunches discussing a hundred-year-old book, J. C. Ryle's *Thoughts for Young Men*, in which Ryle warns of a young man's temptations. It encouraged me greatly to see Graham take this teaching to heart. I felt far more proud of him for this than for his outstanding play in the championship game.

The next day, I had to leave for a cross-country trip. As I prayed in the early morning hours on my drive to the airport, God brought back to my mind the affection I had felt for Graham. I believe he was suggesting that that's how he feels when we adults walk away from temptation. Our temptations may differ from those of our children, but the spiritual pressure is just as real and the consequences just as severe. When God sees an adult son or daughter face temptation and walk away, his heart swells with affection.

The apostle John wrote that nothing gave him more pleasure than to hear that his children were walking in the truth; in this, he modeled the father-heart of God.

Today, you will have opportunities to bring pleasure to God. What a way to look at the day! You can make God smile. You can make God proud. You can bring God great joy!

So let's put that smile on God's face. Let's bring him great happiness. Let's choose obedience.

Devotions for Sacred Parenting, 19–20

THE BIG MAN

As a young boy, I felt great joy growing up with a father I could look up to. My dad worked in management at a public utility, and he regularly helped some of our friends get summer jobs there. When a girlfriend of mine got hired, everybody kept asking her if she had met "the big man" yet—referring not to his size but to the fact that he ran the whole office.

"No," she replied, "I don't think so."

"You will," they told her, "but don't worry. He's a really nice guy."

When the time came for the grand introduction, my girlfriend laughed as she realized she *had* met "the big man"—and my dad gave her a hug. When she told me about this, I can't tell you how much my heart swelled that others looked up to my dad as I did. I knew my dad wouldn't scandalize our family. He had a respectable job, and he was a man of character and integrity. I felt proud to be his son and took great joy in my connection to him.

Part of the discipline of parenthood is to be a person my children can feel proud of and take great joy in. *My* reputation will affect *theirs;* I don't want them to have to feel embarrassed to admit that, yes, they are related to me. I've invited a few key people to keep me accountable for this very reason. I don't want to do anything that would make my kids ashamed. And since I know the heart is deceitful beyond understanding, I want other men to warn me when I get too close to the boundaries.

Luke tells us that Elizabeth, the mother of John the Baptist, attracted God's attention in part because she was "upright in the sight of God." She observed "all the Lord's commandments and regulations blamelessly" (Luke 1:6). Like Elizabeth, we must consecrate ourselves for the purpose of raising one of God's image bearers. There is great joy in such a calling—for both parents and children.

Devotions for Sacred Parenting, 43

December 11

A TREMENDOUS BLESSING

I want my children to think of me as their chief encourager, next in line only to the Holy Spirit. Regardless of how the world receives them, I hope they will know that at least two people—their mother and father—will always delight in them. I pray that they believe without a single doubt that raising them has been one of the greatest blessings God could ever have given to us.

I learned this attitude from the apostle Paul, who experienced tremendous joy while loving followers who could be very difficult (even though our children have been particularly easy to love). These may have been his "spiritual children," but his love for them was as intense as anyone could feel for his own flesh and blood. Listen to the way Paul spoke to his sons and daughters in the Lord:

> "I am full of joy over you" (Romans 16:19).
>
> "I have great confidence in you; I take great pride in you. I am greatly encouraged; in all our troubles my joy knows no bounds" (2 Corinthians 7:4).
>
> "I thank my God every time I remember you. In all my prayers for all of you, I always pray with joy" (Philippians 1:3–4).
>
> "Indeed, you are our glory and joy" (1 Thessalonians 2:20).
>
> "Your love has given me great joy" (Philemon 7).

If someone were to interview our kids and ask them, "Do your parents find great joy in loving you?" what would they say? Would our kids have the sense of cherished affection that Paul's spiritual children felt, or would they feel more like a burden than a blessing?

One of the greatest gifts we parents can give to our children is to enjoy them, to cherish them, to laugh with them, to give them the satisfaction that we are thankful to walk this life with them.

Sacred Parenting, 77–78

AN EXUBERANT GOD OF GLORY

Biblical accounts of the glory of God in heaven are elaborate and sense-exploding affairs. Consider, for example, the experience recounted by Ezekiel. He *feels* a wind. He *sees* flashing lightning surrounded by brilliant light, fantastic creatures, and a magnificent and stunning throne of sapphire (Ezekiel 1:4, 5–14, 26–27). He *hears* the sound of wings like the roar of rushing waters, and a loud rumbling (1:24; 3:12–13). Ezekiel is then asked to *eat* a scroll that tastes sweet (3:1–3). After it is all over, Ezekiel feels so overwhelmed—perhaps the sensory onslaught is so great—that he sits down, stunned, for seven days (3:15).

A similar appearance occurs in Ezekiel 10 where the prophet experiences burning coals, great radiance, a loud sound, clouds filling the temple, and fantastic sights and movements—wheels that sparkled like chrysolite, and cherubim with four faces.

When the glory of the Lord returns to the temple, we again read that God's voice is like the "roar of rushing waters" (Ezekiel 43:2), and the land becomes radiant with his glory. The sight is so great that Ezekiel falls facedown.

When Jesus appears to John in the book of Revelation, the experience is also a sensuous one. When Jesus proclaims his name, John describes it as a "loud voice like a trumpet." Jesus' head and hair were "white like wool ... and his eyes were like blazing fire." Jesus' voice was "like the sound of rushing waters." Jesus' face "was like the sun shining in all its brilliance." As anybody who tries to look into the sun knows, such brilliance forces you to turn away, and this is what happened to John. "I fell at his feet as though dead" (Revelation 1:10, 14–17).

These pictures of God in his glory contrast greatly with the calm, quiet, "greeting-card" Jesus often depicted today. And they bear no resemblance to a bruised and bleeding Jesus suffering on a cross. Those who think only silence is reverent may be a bit uncomfortable in heaven! Something within each of us is awed by the presence of beauty. I believe it is a flashing glimpse of our desire for the transcendence of heaven.

Sacred Pathways, 62–63

Blessed Encouragers

A friend of mine wept at the altar of a conference, knowing that God was calling her to release her fears for her children and hand them over to him. As she was praying, an anxious pastor, who had no earthly way of knowing what was going on, walked up and said, "I'm really nervous about saying this, but I believe God wants you to hear this Scripture." The pastor turned to the passage where Hannah gives up Samuel. My friend was overwhelmed, knowing God had read her heart and was giving her direction.

Scripture and church history are full of accounts where God moves mysteriously and powerfully, sometimes confronting entire nations, at other times reaching just one individual.

Years ago, wanting to become a writer, I spoke with a published author about a book idea. He gave me all the doom and gloom about the publishing business and basically told me I was wasting my time. A pastor overheard our conversation. I'll always remember his words: "Don't give up. If God is calling you to do this, it will happen."

I don't remember who that pastor was and I can't even begin to recall what he looks like, much less what his name is, but how I wish I could send him a couple copies of my books only to say, "Thank you for your role in making that dream a reality."

In a cynical, hurting, and depressed world, encouragers point toward faith, mystery, and expectancy. When the situation seems impossible, encouragers say, "Now God's *really* going to move."

Will you allow God the opportunity to give you hope when hope seems almost foolish? Will you make yourself available to encourage someone whose faith is being shaken? Sometimes God *does* move in strange and powerful ways. Will you open yourself up to such movements of God today?

Sacred Pathways, 184–85

DELIGHTING IN OTHERS

Being a professional athlete makes you an object of either love or hate. When you play well, the fans love you; during a bad season, the fans think you're an overpaid bum.

The precariousness of such a livelihood tempts many athletes to become extremely self-centered, but Major League pitcher Orel Hershiser found a better way. In the late 1980s and '90s, Orel was about as accomplished as a pitcher can get. During one stretch, he pitched a Major-League-record fifty-nine consecutive scoreless innings—almost seven straight games—an astonishing run by any measure. In 1988, he won the National League Cy Young Award (given annually to the league's outstanding pitcher) and was voted the World Series Most Valuable Player.

In short, Hershiser had a lot of "stock." Young players looked up to him as the model of what they wanted to achieve. Players can use this cache either to lord it over others or to serve them. Orel took the latter approach.

After the Los Angeles Dodgers spring training camp ended in 1992, a young, skinny pitcher felt devastated after being demoted to the minor leagues. When the young pitcher turned his head, Orel quietly slipped a ball into his bag. On the ball, Orel had written, "From one big leaguer to another. See you back here soon."

Imagine being that discouraged pitcher, wondering if you'll ever get another chance—and then reaching into your bag once you get home and having the most accomplished pitcher of your day write, "From one big leaguer to another." Even more encouraging, Orel showed his confidence in the young man when he added, "See you back here soon."

Orel's words proved prophetic. The skinny pitcher's name was Pedro Martinez, in his prime considered by many to be the best pitcher in baseball.

Encouragement is such a blessed, joy-producing ministry. When our happiness depends on what happens to us, our joy shrinks to what can be contained in one solitary life. But when we learn to delight in the welfare of others and rejoice in what God is doing in their lives, the potential for joy is limitless.

Authentic Faith, 27–28

A SACRED CALLING

In the early 1990s, I commuted to work on the highways outside of Washington, D.C. I had to leave the house by 5:30 a.m. at the latest. If I left at 5:45, it took an extra thirty minutes to get to the office; if I didn't leave until 6:00, I might not get to work before lunch.

One morning I paused for a few moments before I left for the day. Usually I rushed out the door, but this day I had a feeling that something miraculous was taking place. I went upstairs and checked the kids' rooms; two of them had left their beds. I returned to the master bedroom and saw Lisa fast asleep, her arm around little Kelsey, whose tiny nostrils (she was just a baby back then) flared gently with every breath. Three-year-old Graham had wedged himself in by the foot of the bed, making the three of them look like pieces of a jigsaw puzzle. They slept peacefully, contentedly. Allison, knocked out to the world, lay tangled up in her bedsheets and blankets, as is her custom.

The quiet hours of the morning bring a certain holiness, when a simple house —even a town house or an apartment—becomes a sanctuary. The silence brings to my mind God's joyful peace and presence. While laughter may roar throughout the day—and sometimes tears too—nothing speaks as loudly as the quiet of the early morning.

Finally I stepped outside into the dark, unusually satisfied. My soul felt completely full. I sat in my little Honda Civic as I drove toward Route 66, enjoying the peaceful sensation that the Lord provided me, but wouldn't have been any happier in a Mercedes Benz. My riches were behind me—in a small townhouse filled with love.

We don't have to make family life sacred; it already is. The only question is: Will we treat it as such?

Sacred Parenting, 222–23

THINKING OF HEAVEN

Christians who try to obey God without keeping heaven firmly in their sights will have spotty obedience at best. Meditating on the afterlife is an enormously effective spiritual exercise. It strengthens us like few other spiritual disciplines. Knowing our future hope helps us persevere in our faith and endure current trials and temptations.

Cynics will say this is falling into Marx's trap. Yet when Marx called religion "an opiate" for the people, he had it exactly backward, at least in regard to Christianity. Opium deadens the senses; Christ makes them come alive. Our faith can infuse a deadened or crippled marriage with meaning, purpose, and—in what we graciously receive from God—fulfillment. Christianity doesn't leave us in an apathetic stupor; it raises us and our relationships from the dead. It pours zest, strength, and purpose into an otherwise wasted life.

God never promises to remove all our trials this side of heaven—quite the contrary!—but he does promise there is meaning in each difficulty. Our character is being perfected; our faith is being built; our heavenly reward is being increased—and so we keep on keeping on.

One scene from *Star Wars* still tears me up inside (I say this with some shame). After Luke Skywalker and Han Solo save the rebel forces, they receive great honor as they enter a great hall. They walk down a long aisle, with everyone standing at attention, and then climb several high steps until the leader of the rebel forces honors them in front of everybody.

I think this hits me hard because it echoes a heavenly truth. Jesus never told us to erase our ambition. Jesus never said to shun all thought of rewards. He told us to turn from *earthly* ambition and to shun *earthly* rewards. He said, in effect, "Put yourself last here on earth, and in heaven you'll be first." That's a trade, not a renunciation! That thirst for glory you feel in your heart is part of what makes you human. Jesus just wants you to focus it on heaven, to look for your rewards there.

Heavenly hope gives feet to our obedience, and endurance in the midst of trials. Let us live now so that what we do on earth will be rewarded and even celebrated in heaven.

Sacred Marriage, 150–51

AN EXTRAORDINARY, ORDINARY DAY

When our son, Graham, was about five years old, he astonished me by blurting out, "This has been the best day of my entire life."

Until that moment, I had considered the day a downer. A couple of weeks before, I had sent a children's book manuscript to an agent but received only silence, the biggest insult a writer can get. Like a narcissistic fool, I colored the day with my own disappointment. Meanwhile, my son filled it with promise.

The best day in his entire life? The day had begun with Graham and me visiting the athletic fields in Manassas, Virginia, to sign him up for fall soccer and to watch a game. When we came home, I laid down with Graham as he took his nap. When he woke up, I held him for a few minutes before we ate lunch. Then we went to a video store and rented a Speed Racer cartoon.

Because of my discouragement and vocational frustration, I might have given the day a C-, and yet Graham graded it an A+. "What is so special," I mused, "about running errands, receiving no news on the new book project, and getting ordinary stuff done around the house?" Graham looked at the soccer sign-up as a future promise, nap time next to his dad as a sacred moment, and spreading ant crystals as "a whole lot of fun."

He taught me that a gentle but firm hug between a father and a son as they walked out of a video store means more than all the full post office boxes in the world. His ears could hear a song that I had grown too busy to hear—until I truly listened to this joy-filled assessment of what once seemed just an ordinary day.

Let's allow our children to bring the wonder and awe of intimacy and relationship back into our lives, lest we fixate on what doesn't really matter.

Sacred Parenting, 66–68

A PLACE OF EXTRAVAGANCE

As a high school student, I read the words of a popular Christian teacher who questioned why teens would want to do anything other than pray, worship, study the Bible, or share their faith.

"If you don't like doing those things and only those things all day long," this teacher said, "you're going to be very miserable in heaven."

Unfortunately, many believers, like this teacher, define godly pleasure so narrowly that they reduce it to religion-oriented worship. Not only do I think this teacher is wrong about the place and use of pleasure in this life; I think he is entirely wrong about the place and use of pleasure in what we commonly call "the afterlife." Heaven goes far beyond singing worship songs.

In a great gift to God's church, Randy Alcorn blew away many erroneous assumptions about heaven in his marvelous book titled *Heaven*. Randy forcefully challenges the view that all we'll be doing in heaven is praying, singing, and reading the Bible; he calls this error "Christoplatonism," a distortion of the faith that assumes the spiritual is all good and the physical is all bad. Indeed, Randy talks of heaven as having room for pets and even—brace yourself—coffee.[5]

In that glorious place, we will enjoy feasting, play, and the arts, including "the best of meats and the finest of wines" (Isaiah 25:6). There will be choice fruits (Revelation 22:2) and laughter (Luke 6:21). Some faithful believers will live with what Jesus describes as "treasures" (Matthew 6:19–21). Heaven seems, quite clearly, to be a place of extravagance.

Without question the best, richest, and most rewarding part of heaven will be living in the presence of God—looking on his face, reveling in the light of his glory. This is what he made us for, and this is what will bring us the highest joy. God's presence will set us free to truly enjoy all that he has made for our benefit. This also means we can train our hearts for heaven in part by learning to enjoy all that God has created on earth, recognizing his role as Master Artist as we receive merely a taste of the even better pleasures that await us in heaven.

Pure Pleasure, 77, 79

ANOTHER WORLD OF LOVE

Jonathan Edwards has often been called the last of the Puritans and America's greatest intellect. In his book *Heaven: A World of Love*, Edwards writes, "There are none but lovely objects in heaven ... And there is nothing ... with any natural or moral deformity; but everything is beautiful to behold and amiable and excellent in itself."[6]

This gives great hope to parents who have "less than normal" kids. My friend, Alan, has a developmentally challenged son named Robby. "The day is coming," Alan told me, "when Robby's disabilities will fall away. He'll laugh right on cue instead of three minutes after everybody else has moved on from the joke. For the first time, the beauty of his glorified heavenly body will lead others to admire him instead of to look at him like he's weird while they try to figure out what's wrong with him."

"Now get this," Alan gushed, reading from another chapter in Edwards's book: "Love in heaven is always mutual. It is always met with appropriate returns of love ... No inhabitants of that blessed world will ever be grieved with the thought that they are slighted by those that they love, or that their love is not fully and fondly returned."[7]

He paused. "Do you have any idea how many times my and Lindsey's hearts have been broken as we've watched Robby call a friend? We've winced through an insecure, hard-to-understand phone call and then were crushed to see the hurt look on Robby's face as he sensed his former friends pulling away. In heaven, all that will be over. Robby will never be slighted; his love will always be fondly returned."

The hope of heaven reminds us that while everything won't be put right on this earth, eventually everything *will* be put right in heaven. Neglected kids won't just be mainstreamed; they'll be celebrated. Their glorified bodies will shine through eternity, testifying to a God who not only created this earth but is preparing a new heaven and a new earth. Today's world is just a temporary dwelling place in comparison.

Devotions for Sacred Parenting, 70–72

IMMORTALS IN OUR HOUSE

For centuries, Jewish mothers eagerly anticipated the birth of a child, asking one of two questions: "Will this boy grow up to become the Messiah?" or, "Will this daughter become the mother of the Anointed One?"

Christians believe these questions have been answered, but every birth is still filled with enormous promise. A schoolmaster in Britain became well-known for his practice of doffing his hat to his students. "I never know which boy may grow up to be prime minister," he explained.

Of course, my son isn't the Messiah. Neither of my daughters will give birth to the Anointed One. But according to the Messiah, all three can do even greater things than he did, because he has sent his Holy Spirit to guide and empower them (John 14:12).

When you look at a drooling baby, a toddler with spaghetti sauce on her shirt, a preteen who hasn't changed his socks for five days, or a teen with enough pimples on her face to play "connect the dots," it's easy to forget we are raising immortals—men and women who will live forever in unimaginable glory and beauty.

There are no ordinary babies, no ordinary toddlers, no ordinary grade schoolers, and no ordinary teens. You live with a young person who, when inspired and empowered by the Holy Spirit, can do things even greater than what the Messiah himself did! And when this Messiah returns and your son or daughter assumes the immortal body, he or she will shine like the brightest and purest star you have ever seen.

If we really believe in eternity, can we ever look at our children in the same way again? We are raising a future king or queen, an immortal regent, a being of amazing, almost unimaginable potential and worth. How much would our homes change if instead of doffing our hats when we entered our kids' rooms, we took off our shoes, remembering that we are standing on holy ground? Your home is more than a house; it is a temple of immortals, a holy and sacred place in heaven's sight.

Devotions for Sacred Parenting, 128–29

December 21

TELL YOUR STORY

In the late 1950s, Ruth Bell Graham published a children's book titled *Our Christmas Story*. In the foreword, her husband, the evangelist Billy Graham, wrote:

> When it was suggested that Ruth tell the Christmas story for children everywhere, we were delighted. But we had to warn the publisher that "our" Christmas story would be different from the traditional manger scene that spells Christmas for many people. Of course, the manger scene is an important part of Christmas in our home—the joyous and beloved climax to the story. But it is only a part of the story. For Christmas does not begin in the stable of Bethlehem. It does not begin in the Gospel of Luke, but in the Book of Genesis.[8]

Christmas Eve and Christmas morning are merely chapters in a long-running story set in motion centuries before. It's a fascinating tale, one that God follows with all the passion of a husband, the hurt of a betrayed friend, the frustration of a wise parent, and the perspective of an aggrieved Lord and King. It would not be fair to judge that history at any one point, for it is the history of God and his people Israel—his bride and his spouse—taken together over the long run, that completes the tale.

Learning to cherish my sacred history with Lisa has been one of the most spiritually meaningful practices of my life. We have an unusual story, going back to two weeks of being "junior high sweethearts." We have created a history together that is enriching, meaningful, and laden with passion. Yes, we have had to travel through a few valleys to get to where we are, but the sights along the way and our destination have been well worth it. Author Jerry Jenkins encourages us to revel in our own marital story: "Tell your [marital] story. Tell it to your kids, your friends, your brothers and sisters, but especially to each other. The more your story is implanted in your brain, the more it serves as a hedge against the myriad forces that seek to destroy your marriage."[9]

Sacred Marriage, 124–25

POINTING TOWARD THE STABLE

A Christmas program moved me to tears when dance after dance centered the audience's attention on the newly born Christ child. These dancers (my two daughters among them) were beautiful and gifted and graceful, but their most significant act occurred at the end, when they turned all eyes away from themselves and toward the feeding trough — symbolically, toward Jesus.

Though Christmas comes just once a year, its penetrating truth should pierce our hearts every second of every day. We live to point others to Jesus.

Living to point others to Jesus is essential to the notion of sacred parenting. When parenting is about *me* — my comfort, fulfillment, happiness, joy in life — I'll regularly compare the cost with the personal benefit. But when I live to point others to Jesus, personal sacrifice becomes a red carpet leading them to the place I desire them to go above all else.

The glorious day will come when nothing will matter but him. Forgiving and being forgiven — over! Measuring our wants against faithful stewardship — past! Paying bills, scheduling doctor visits, attending sporting events and school programs — history! In one incredible, all-consuming moment, every eye will be riveted by the splendor of God's glory.

When we consider our children's activities and friendships, their use of free time, how to educate them, the root issue is how each decision will affect their relationship with the child born in Bethlehem two thousand years ago.

This day, let's turn our heads, hearts, minds, souls — our entire being — toward that baby who grew up to reveal himself as Savior and King. *Our* story is built on *his* story. Our family life should point to the "First Family" — Mary and Joseph and Jesus. In the ultimate scheme of things, *we* don't matter. Jesus is *all*. He is the focal point of eternity, and our calling is to take whatever little light he has given us and point it straight into his overwhelming glory.

Devotions for Sacred Parenting, 126–27

SECRET ACTS OF DEVOTION

On a cold December night — the next day would bring Christmas Eve — I snuck out of my house, put on a coat, grabbed my bag, and headed outside. A youth outside in the dead of night usually means trouble, but this time I had a different intention. I wanted to give a present to Jesus.

Earlier that day, I had picked out a ham from a local grocery store. I wrote "Merry Christmas" on the bag and now left it on the front porch of a financially strapped family who had lost their father just a few months earlier. I was practicing my first secret act of devotion. (Now I guess I've lost one!)

I like to encourage all Christians to engage in "secret acts of devotion." A secret act of devotion is something you do without letting anyone, even the person who benefits, know you had anything to do with it.

The importance of secrecy is that it ensures you are doing it for the love of God, and the love of God only. Any intimate relationship has its secrets; a husband and wife share things with each other that they will never share with anyone else. In our relationship with God, part of the intimacy is to share secrets with him.

Some secret acts of devotion may include: an anonymous gift of cash to someone in need; a poem or letter written to God but never revealed to anyone else; a song sung only in the presence of God; working behind the scenes to help an unemployed person get a job; sending an anonymous note of encouragement to a pastor or friend; planting a tree or sowing wildflower seeds in a field to celebrate God the Creator.

Why not give such a gift to God this Christmas?

Sacred Pathways, 195–96

GOD'S CATHEDRAL

One Christmas Eve afternoon, I walked through a favorite part in the woods on the outskirts of Manassas, Virginia. The quiet, motionless world was a welcome change from the butting and clawing of the department stores and malls. The stillness created a sense of expectancy of the birth of Jesus, far removed from the hurry and worry of the artificial hoopla of the malls and stores.

The woods opened into a clearing and I pulled my coat tighter as the cold wind licked at my neck. The gusts blew around me, picking up momentum, and then suddenly burst forth into snow. I turned my back to the biting wind, pulled my hood up to cover my neck, and watched the wind carry the snow parallel to the ground, making it travel some distance before it could rest. My heart nearly stopped as I witnessed the sheer beauty of a heavenly show. The snow lasted only a few minutes, but those few priceless moments did more to draw me into a remembrance of the Christ child than did weeks in shopping malls, post offices, and gaudily decorated rooms.

This experience helped me to begin looking at creation as God's cathedral, as perhaps the premier place to meet with God. Francis of Assisi's famous poem "The Canticle to Brother Sun" is perhaps *the* Christian classic on the beauty and glory of creation and its ability to draw us into the presence of God. As a young man, the great eighteenth-century revivalist Jonathan Edwards wrote a monograph on the flying spiders of the North American forests. A number of years later, in one of the most famous sermons ever preached on American soil, Edwards used the analogy of a spider hanging by a thin web to depict an unrepentant sinner's dilemma in the hands of an angry God. Edwards is just one of many Christians who learned to use God's creation to understand God the Creator and his ways with men and women.

Those who allow winter's cold to keep them inside; those who become more familiar with the stores of a mall than a forest's trees, are missing out on a great opportunity to experience a new kind of Christmas.

Sacred Pathways, 43–44

ONE LAST CHRISTMAS

In 1918, a doctor told Billy Miske, a professional heavyweight boxer, that life had handed him a knockout blow called Bright's disease. Billy's severely damaged kidneys made it unlikely that he would reach thirty. The doctor urged him to hang up his boxing gloves and retire to a softer job.

This physician didn't realize the mound of debt that buried Billy. Billy knew only one way of putting bread on the table: win it with his fists. So the sick man kept fighting. In fact, he entered the ring thirty more times after his diagnosis. And he didn't fight marshmallows — three of the bouts were against the legendary Jack Dempsey, whose fists felt like wrecking balls.

Eventually the disease took its toll. Billy fought his second-to-last fight in January 1923. By autumn he had become a shrunken caricature of his former self. Billy hoped to have one last Christmas with his family. He couldn't bear the thought of his wife and three children celebrating Jesus' birth in a house without gifts, so he decided to do the only thing he knew how to do. He went to his manager and asked him to arrange one last fight.

The manager laid it out straight: "Billy, I don't like to say this, but if you went into the ring now, in your condition you might get killed."

"What's the difference? It's better than waiting for it in a rocking chair."

Knowing Billy's desperation, the manager said he'd consider it if Billy got himself in shape. "Can't do the workouts," Billy admitted, "but I've got one more fight left in me. You've got to help me."

The manager gave in and found a decent opponent. The fight was scheduled for November 7. As expected, the fight lasted just four rounds, but Billy took home a check for $2,400 — a small fortune in the 1920s.

On Christmas morning, Billy Jr., Douglas, Donna, and their mom, Marie, woke up to a storybook Christmas. Around a wall of presents, a toy train clanged around the tracks. Marie couldn't believe her eyes when she saw the baby grand piano of her dreams in the living room. They ate like kings and queens, laughing, singing, celebrating. The kids couldn't wipe the smiles off their faces, but one man's smile outshone them all — Billy Miske knew the fight had been worth it.

The day after Christmas, Billy called his trainer. "Come and get me, Jack. I'm dying." The trainer rushed Billy to the hospital, but they could do nothing. His kidneys failed, and he left this life, at age twenty-nine, on New Year's Day 1924.

Oh, one more thing. Do you know why the November 7 fight lasted just four rounds? The emaciated, deathly ill Billy Miske knocked out his opponent.

Never bet against a dad determined to give his family one last Christmas memory.

Sacred Parenting, 195–97

A Delayed Greeting

In the early 1970s, few places on this earth endured more human misery than Calcutta, India. Franklin Graham, now president of Samaritan's Purse, once told me about his first visit there. He knew he was visiting a place where hygiene is an afterthought when he saw a man urinating in the gutter; half a block away, downstream, another man was using the "water" in that same gutter to brush his teeth.

Franklin was traveling with Bob Pierce, founder of World Vision and Samaritan's Purse. They stopped off to visit Mother Teresa, a Macedonian-born nun who left her home to live and work in the slums of Calcutta.

Place yourself in Mother Teresa's position. You're being visited by Bob Pierce, founder of one of the most influential Christian development and relief ministries in the history of Christianity. Along with him is Franklin Graham, who one day would become head of Samaritan's Purse, and who, as the son of Billy Graham, represented the doorway to millions of dollars' worth of aid. When you run a charity dependent on others' good favor, you need money to continue your work, and here were two of the most influential gatekeepers in the world.

Yet when Franklin and Bob stopped in to announce their arrival, one of the sisters returned to say that Mother Teresa would be happy to greet them just as soon as the dying man she was caring for had breathed his last.

Today, nobody knows the identity of the dying man. His name has been forgotten, lost among the thousands of seemingly insignificant casualties that take place each day in Calcutta. Yet for a few hours, that man was more important to Mother Teresa than two men representing some of the biggest religious influencers from the United States.

Throughout history, an authentic faith has sparked a compassionate response toward those the world tends to forget. Whether these persons are poor, imprisoned, disabled, sick, or mentally challenged, God calls us to dignify them by caring about their condition and, whenever possible, reaching out to them on God's behalf.

Authentic Faith, 102–3

AN ETERNAL PERSPECTIVE

I suffer from keratoconus in my left eye, which has left me essentially with just one functioning eye. The doctor gave me information about "keratoconus support groups," but I thought that was overreaching. Just about everyone over forty I know has some physical malady—a bad back, severe allergies, migraine headaches, arthritis, or much worse.

The same is true of marriage. All of us see certain things in our spouses that may be difficult to accept. There isn't a single marriage that doesn't have some irksome aspects for either partner. It simply is not possible to be married to a fallen human being without being occasionally annoyed or legitimately frustrated. Yet I talk to people all the time who think they can solve or cure any part of their marriage that is less than pleasant. They think they need to join a support group for their particularly difficult situation, when in reality, they're in a normal marriage with a normally imperfect spouse.

Common experience has taught me that the expectation of complete health is unrealistic. Even though I function with just one eye, I'm grateful my right eye is still pretty strong. I hate the fact that I'm losing all my hair, but I love the fact my body can endure marathons. I can obsess over a shiny forehead and a blurry eye, or I can be grateful for strong knees and a healthy heart.

In the same way, you can choose to obsess over every marital disappointment, even legitimate ones, or you can praise your spouse's strengths. Don't let the fact that you're not married to a perfect spouse blind you to the fact that you're married to a good spouse. You'll be much happier that way.

Sacred Marriage, 149–50

A HERITAGE OF FAITH

As a member of the Authors Guild, I get a quarterly bulletin that usually includes about two pages of names of recently deceased members. One issue mentioned that Frank Slaughter, a hugely successful writer in the mid-twentieth century (today's equivalent of a John Grisham), died at the age of ninety-three. You think Slaughter stole the headline? Nope. You think he got at least a picture? After all, this is a *writer's* publication, and Frank Slaughter was one of the most popular writers of his day. No way. He got *one paragraph*. Frank was a physician whose novels became instant bestsellers in the 1940s and 1950s—but this was many decades ago. Few people read his books today, and even fewer will read them tomorrow. In another fifty years or so, probably no one will read him, but he made headline material for a few glorious decades.

Who was the senior vice president of General Motors in 1975? Who were the two senators from Virginia in 1910? Who was the top fashion designer in 1954? Few people could answer even one of these questions. And does anybody honestly think that people will be talking about Tom Cruise or Paris Hilton a hundred years from now?

What popular society values most grows irrelevant at a shockingly rapid pace. Our empty ambitions are almost comical when confronted by the inexorable weight of history that buries us in anonymity.

What often gets the least attention—passing on a heritage of faith to our children—in our desperate pursuit to achieve significance is actually the most lasting thing we can do. If you have some downtime before the new year starts, spend a few moments considering your priorities. Let's step off the treadmill of desperate striving and focus on the only things we can actually leave behind—our children and a heritage of faith.

Sacred Parenting, 158–59

"WE WILL SEE THEM IN HEAVEN"

As a college pastor in the Pacific Northwest for more than thirty years, Brady Bobbink has attended more regional conferences than he can count, but he enjoyed something special in September 1995 — the first time that he, his wife, Shirley, and all four of their children attended together. Their youngest son, three-year-old Seth, had left diapers behind, making traveling easier. And their oldest daughter was engaged to be married the following summer, making this conference one of the final family vacations with just the kids. Brady couldn't wait.

He soon found, however, that traveling with the whole family provided a very different experience than going by himself — and delightfully so. After concluding his lecture on worship, Brady was informed by his son Micah that they were going down to the river to throw rocks, then to play miniature golf, then to lunch, after which they were going swimming.

"Who decided all this?" Brady asked.

"Mom, Seth, and me voted on it," Micah explained. "Even if you vote differently, it's going to be three to one."

"Whatever happened to patriarchal rule, Micah?" "You know, where the dad actually makes the decisions?"

"Come on, Dad," Micah said. "That was the seventies."

Brady had a lot of fun that day with his boys, but it was his daughters who brought him to tears later in the week when they helped lead a worship service. Surrounded by the people he loved most, worshiping the God he loved above all, Brady's heart practically burst. Does life get any better than this?

Not for a gospel-centered dad, it doesn't.

Overwhelmed with joy that his little girls had grown up into godly women, Brady turned to Shirley, pointed at the girls, and said with a choked-up voice, "We will see them in heaven."

Shirley began to cry.

Isn't that what matters most?

Sacred Parenting, 86–87

A QUIET FUNERAL

C. S. Lewis, died on the day United States president John F. Kennedy was assassinated. With the world focused on the shocking events in Dallas, Texas, only a few people attended Lewis's funeral at Holy Trinity Church in Headington Quarry, England.

According to George Sayer, Lewis's close friend for three decades, those who came were nearly all personal friends. Sayer's description of the funeral is both moving and a little sad: "A lighted church candle was placed on the coffin, and its flame did not flicker. For more than one of us, that clear, bright candle flame seemed to symbolize Jack. He had been the light of our lives, ever steadfast in friendship. Yet, most of all, the candle symbolized his unflagging pursuit of illumination."[10]

Lewis's estate was valued at just 37,772 pounds. He had given away most of his literary earnings and never owned a house. Consequently, he left just a small legacy of 100 pounds to his caretaker, Paxford.

When asked about the paltry gift, Paxford said, "Werl, it won't take me far, wull it? Mr. Jack, 'e never 'ad no idea of money. 'Is mind was always set on 'igher things."[11]

That such an influential man should die so humbly and so quietly, with such little fanfare, is almost disturbing. Yet it also seems appropriate, considering everything Lewis stood for. Because he didn't live solely for this world, he had to look to a new world in which to receive his full reward.

What we do as Christians today will have value chiefly in another time. To some, our accomplishments won't be worth the gasoline spent in transporting us from place to place. But in another context, according to Scripture, these heavenly works, performed with the right motivation, will be eternally golden. We are reminded to expect our rewards in another age. Ambrose tells us, "Do not ... as a child claim those things now which belong to a future time. The crown belongs to the perfect. Wait till that which is perfect is come."[12]

Authentic Faith, 235–36

Transcendent Times

My eighteen-year-old son and I slipped out into the desert air for a late-December run. We had spent a week with my wife's parents in Southern California. On our last full day in Palm Desert, we wanted to take advantage of running under a blue sky without rain gear before we returned to the ever-wet Pacific Northwest.

We decided on a nine-mile course, uphill for the first four and a half miles. Running with a high school cross-country athlete is like trying to keep up with a cheetah. Graham's relaxed pace equals my speed workout. A dad can feel old — really old — when he runs with his teenage son, but I had reached marathon shape and thought I might as well give it a try.

At the three-mile mark, my son suggested taking a side trail that I never would have considered. I obsessively stick to main routes, but I wanted to hang with Graham, so I followed him. Eventually we came to a wide-open desert space, intoxicating in its breadth. We felt like we were running on the tops of clouds.

Grinning now, Graham kept going, skittering up and around a small hill, running like a sure-footed billy goat while I poked around the edge like a cow. We eventually reached an even larger expanse and just about fell over at the beauty of the desert.

As our heart rates climbed and the sun beat down, we both got lost at the same time in that famous runner's high. Even better, we turned around and began running *downhill*. When I checked my watch at the last mile, we had a 6:45-per-mile pace — which, for me, approaches the miraculous.

What an adrenaline rush!

I worshiped hard and long that morning. I was unspeakably grateful to God that Graham and I could share that moment. We've had meaningful talks, difficult talks, and occasionally even embarrassing talks — all the normal father-son stuff that any family experiences — but what a blessing that we could enjoy such an exquisite time together.

On this last day of the year, let us cherish those memories from the previous twelve months that make life worth living.

Pure Pleasure, 182–83

ACKNOWLEDGMENTS

Many thanks to Steve Halliday, who waded through my books to pull out many of these devotions; Sarah Johnson and Beth Shagene, who made the interior look so spectacular; and Lori VandenBosch and Dirk Buursma, who provided expert editorial assistance. I also want to thank the twelve readers who read through many entries to help us choose the strongest ones: Charlotte Skadal, Kevin Hicks, Edy DeGood, Thomas Feller, Mary Wilhelm, Eva Wilson, Chris Castle, Lynn McCallum, Steve Ruggerio, Baron Miller, Peter Sim, and Becky Henderson.

NOTES

January

1. Evelyn Eaton Whitehead and James D. Whitehead, *Marrying Well: Stages on the Journey of Christian Marriage* (New York: Doubleday, 1983), 187.
2. Brother Lawrence, *The Practice of the Presence of God*, trans. John J. Delaney (New York: Doubleday, 1977).
3. Martin Luther, "Sermons on the Gospel of John," cited in H. Paul Santmire, *The Travail of Nature* (Philadelphia: Fortress, 1985), 131.
4. Andrew Murray, *The Holiest of All* (New Kensington, Pa.: Whitaker House, 1996), 39.
5. M. Basil Pennington, *Daily We Touch Him* (Garden City, N.Y.: Doubleday, 1977), 51–52.
6. John Calvin, *Genesis*, trans. John King (1554; repr., Grand Rapids: Baker, 1984), 376.
7. Ibid., 484.
8. Ibid., 104–5.
9. J. I. Packer, "Sin," *Systematic Theology B*, Tape Series 2645 (Vancouver, B.C.: Regent College, 1996).
10. R. Somerset Ward, *To Jerusalem: Devotional Studies in Mystical Religion* (1931; repr., Harrisburg, Pa.: Morehouse, 1994), 131.
11. Eberhard Bethge, ed., *Letters and Papers from Prison* (New York: Macmillan, 1972), 203.

February

1. William Bennett, "Teaching the Virtues," *Imprimis* (February 2003), 4.
2. Katherine Anne Porter, "The Necessary Enemy," in *The Collected Essays and Occasional Writings of Katherine Anne Porter* (New York: Delacorte, 1970), 184.
3. John Wesley, *The Heart of John Wesley's Journal*, ed. Percy Livingstone Parker (New York: Revell, 1903), 265 (entry for 16 January 1760).
4. Andrew Murray, *Raising Your Children for Christ* (New Kensington, Pa.: Whitaker House, 1984), 250.
5. Ibid., 276.
6. Charles Spurgeon, *Spiritual Parenting* (New Kensington, Pa.: Whitaker House, 1995), 35–36.
7. Philip E. Hughes, *Paul's Second Epistle to the Corinthians* (Grand Rapids: Eerdmans, 1962, 1982), 178.
8. Austin Farrer, *Saving Belief* (Harrisburg, Pa.: Morehouse, 1994), 124.
9. A Monk of the Eastern Church, *Orthodox Spirituality* (Crestwood, N.Y.: St. Vladimir's Seminary Press, 1978), 74.
10. Charles Spurgeon, *Joy in Christ's Presence* (New Kensington, Pa.: Whitaker House, 1997), 103.
11. Ibid.
12. Ibid., 111–12.
13. Gerrit Scott Dawson, *Jesus Ascended: The Meaning of Christ's Continuing Incarnation* (Philipsburg, N.J.: P & R, 2004), 168.
14. C. S. Lewis, "Christian Apologetics," in *God in the Dock: Essays on Theology and Ethics*, ed. Walter Hooper (Grand Rapids: Eerdmans, 1970), 103.

15. John Lennon, "Whatever Gets You Thru the Night," from *Walls and Bridges* (Apple Records, released October 1974).

16. J.N.D. Kelly, *A Commentary on the Epistles of Peter and Jude* (Grand Rapids: Baker, 1969), 302.

March

1. Gary Hook, "Everest Is Crowning Glory of Woman's Seven-Peak Dream," *USA Today*, December 19, 2006, 8C, emphasis added.

2. C. E. B. Cranfield, *The Epistle to the Romans* (Edinburgh: T&T Clark, 1979), 606.

3. Quoted in James Gilchrist Lawson, *Deeper Experiences of Famous Christians* (1911; repr., Anderson, Ind.: Warner, 1970), 224.

4. Ibid., 227.

5. Ibid., 228.

6. Cited in *The Paris Review Interviews, 1* (New York: Picador, 2006). From a Hemingway interview with George Plimpton in *The Paris Review* 18 (Spring 1958).

7. J. P. Moreland, *Love Your God with All Your Mind: The Role of Reason in the Life of the Soul* (Colorado Springs: NavPress, 1997), 39.

8. I was introduced to the Tabors through an unsigned article in *Psychology for Living* (July/August 2000), 17.

9. Jonathan Edwards, *Religious Affections* (Minneapolis: Bethany, 1996), 144.

10. John Calvin, *Hebrews and 1 and 2 Peter* (1549, 1551; repr., Grand Rapids: Eerdmans, 1994), 234.

11. C. J. Mahaney, "God's Purpose and Pattern for Marriage," *According to Plan* audiotape series (Gaithersburg, Md.: PDI Communications, 1994).

12. Calvin, *Calvin's Commentaries: The Gospels*, 395.

13. Ibid.

14. Ken Garfield, "The Season of Forgiveness," *Sports Illustrated* (March 27, 2000), 32.

15. Philip Yancey, *What's So Amazing About Grace?* (Grand Rapids: Zondervan, 1997), 263.

April

1. Quoted in Jim Corbett, "Palmer, Donor Family Bond," *USA Today* (December 6, 2006), 9C.

2. John Piper, *Future Grace* (Sisters, Ore.: Multnomah, 1995), 386.

3. John Calvin, *Calvin's Commentaries: The Gospels* (1555; repr., Grand Rapids: Associate Publishers and Authors, Inc., n.d.), 515.

4. Ibid.

5. William Shakespeare, *Twelfth Night, or What You Will*, act 1, scene 5.

6. *The Little Flowers of Saint Francis*, trans. Raphael Brown (New York: Doubleday, 1958), 285.

7. Merrell Noden, "Marty Liquori, Dream Miler," *Sports Illustrated* (June 5, 2000), 18.

8. Iris Krasnow, *Surrendering to Motherhood: Losing Your Mind, Finding Your Soul* (New York: Hyperion, 1997), 86–67.

9. Donald R. Harvey, *The Spiritually Intimate Marriage* (Old Tappan, N.J.: Revell, 1991), 84.

May

1. Thomas Chalmers, "The Expulsive Power of a New Affection," in *The Protestant Pulpit*, comp. Andrew Blackwood (1947; repr., Grand Rapids: Baker, 1977), 50.

2. G. K. Chesterton, *Heretics* (1905; repr., Nashville: Nelson, 2000), 10.

3. Charles Francis Adams, *Familiar Letters of John Adams and His Wife Abi-*

gail Adams (1875; repr., New York: Kessinger, 2007), 411

4. Gerrit Scott Dawson, *Jesus Ascended: The Meaning of Christ's Continuing Incarnation* (Philipsburg, N.J.: P & R, 2004), 53.

5. Ibid.

6. Dawson, *Jesus Ascended*, 54.

7. Ibid.

8. Ibid., 181–82.

9. Ibid., 182.

10. Ibid., 281.

11. John Climacus, *The Ladder of Divine Ascent*, trans. Colm Luibheid and Norman Russell (New York: Paulist, 1982), 136.

12. Kim Painter, "Life's Little Pleasures Can Relieve Illness, Stress," *USA Today* (May 11, 2008), D4.

13. Susan Power Bratton, *Christianity, Wilderness, and Wildlife: The Original Desert Solitaire* (Scranton, Pa.: University of Scranton Press, 1993), 90–91.

14. See Duane Miller, *Out of the Silence: A Personal Testimony of God's Healing Power* (Nashville: Nelson, 1996).

15. Patrick Carnes, *Out of the Shadows: Understanding Sexual Addiction* (Center City, Minn.: Hazelden, 2001), 5.

16. Ibid., xviii.

17. Henry Drummond, *The Greatest Thing in the World* (London: Collins, 1930), 54–55.

18. Ibid.

19. Gary and Betsy Ricucci, *Love That Lasts: Making a Magnificent Marriage* (Gaithersburg, Md.: PDI Communications, 1993), 70.

June

1. Shauna Niequist, *Cold Tangerines: Celebrating the Extraordinary Nature of Everyday Life* (Grand Rapids: Zondervan, 2007), 84.

2. This quote and the following quotes are taken from Phyllis Alsdurf's article "McCartney on the Rebound," *Christianity Today* (May 18, 1998).

3. Ibid., 138.

4. Ibid.

5. John Calvin, *Calvin's Commentaries: The Gospels* (1555; repr., Grand Rapids: Associate Publishers and Authors, Inc., n.d.), 532.

6. Augustine, "Enchiridion," ch. 74, in St. Augustine: On the Holy Trinity, Doctrinal Treatises, Moral Treatises, vol. 3, *A Select Library of Nicene and Post-Nicene Fathers of the Christian Church*, ed. Philip Schaff (1887; repr., Grand Rapids: Eerdmans, 1998), 261.

7. François Fénelon, *Christian Perfection* (Minneapolis: Bethany House, 1975), xxx.

8. William Law, *A Serious Call to a Devout and Holy Life* (New York: Paulist, 1978), 294.

9. Fénelon, *Christian Perfection*, 90.

10. Told in Richard Wurmbrand, *Tortured for Christ*, 30th anniversary ed. (Bartlesville, Okla.: Living Sacrifice, 1998), 33–34.

11. John Climacus, *The Ladder of Divine Ascent*, trans. Colm Luibheid and Norman Russell (New York: Paulist, 1982), 209.

12. Jonathan Edwards, *Religious Affections* (Minneapolis: Bethany, 1996), 109.

13. Johannes Tauler, *Sermons*, trans. Maria Shrady (New York: Paulist, 1985), 122.

14. Ignatius Loyola, *The Text of the Spiritual Exercises of Saint Ignatius* (Westminster, Md.: Newman Bookshop, 1943, 34.

15. Anonymous, The Cloud of Unknowing, XXIII:4.

16. Jonathan Edwards, *A Treatise Concerning Religious Affection*, ed. James

Houston (Minneapolis: Bethany House, 1984), 132.

17. Andrew Murray, *Raising Your Children for Christ* (New Kensington, Pa.: Whitaker House, 1984), 121.

July

1. This quote and the next four quotes are taken from Terry Glaspey, *Pathway to the Heart of God* (Eugene, Ore.: Harvest House, 1998), 16, 24–25.

2. The story is told in *The Jerusalem Post* (May 15, 1998).

3. Yancey, *What's So Amazing About Grace?* 84.

4. Cited in *The Little Flowers of St. Francis*, trans. Raphael Brown (New York: Doubleday, 1958), 92–93.

5. Ibid., 18–19.

6. Omer Englebert, *St. Francis of Assisi: A Biography*, trans. By Eve Marie Cooper (Cincinnati, Ohio: Servant, 1979), 32.

7. C. S. Lewis, *Mere Christianity* (1943; repr., New York: Macmillan, 1981), 191.

8. J. I. Packer, "Sin," *Systematic Theology B*, Tape Series 2645 (Vancouver, B.C.: Regent College, 1996)

9. Ralph Venning, *The Sinfulness of Sin* (1669; repr., Carlisle, Pa.: Banner of Truth, 193), 276.

10. John Wesley, *The Heart of John Wesley's Journal*, ed. Percy Livingstone Parker (New York: Revell, 1903), 144 (entry for 26 October 1745).

11. Aaron Milavec, *The Didache: Text, Translation, Analysis, and Commentary* (Collegeville, Minn.: Liturgical, 2003), 40.

12. Elton Trueblood, *Incendiary Fellowship* (New York: Harper, 1967), 31.

13. "CT Talks to Kathleen Norris," *Christianity Today* (November 22, 1993), 36.

14. Philip Whitfield and Mike Stoddart, *Hearing, Taste and Smell: Pathways of Perception* (New York: Torstar, 1985), 63.

August

1. John of the Cross, "The Ascent of Mount Carmel," in *John of the Cross: Selected Writings*, ed. Kieran Kavanaugh (New York: Paulist, 1987, II:7–8.

2. Henry Drummond, *The Greatest Thing in the World: and 21 Other Addresses* (London: Collins, 1953), 236.

3. Ibid., 237–38.

4. Klaus Bockmuehl, *Listening to the God Who Speaks* (Colorado Springs: Helmers & Howard, 1990), 81.

5. Elton Trueblood, *The Life We Prize* (New York: Harper & Brothers, 1951), 49.

6. Ibid., 48–49.

7. Ibid., 49.

8. Ibid., 50.

9. Ibid., 51.

10. Francis Schaeffer, *The Mark of the Christian: The Complete Works of Francis Schaeffer* (Westchester, Ill.: Crossway, 1982).

11. Quoted in Charles Colson, *Loving God* (Grand Rapids: Zondervan, 1996), 96.

12. See "Spending Time with Tyson," *Sports Illustrated* (May 20, 2002), 38.

13. Iris Krasnow, *Surrendering to Motherhood: Losing Your Mind, Finding Your Soul* (New York: Hyperion, 1997), 166–67.

14. Rachel Cusk, *A Life's Work: On Becoming a Mother* (New York: Picador, 2002), 107–8.

15. Lance Armstrong with Sally Jenkins, *It's Not About the Bike: My Journey*

Back to Life (New York: Putnam, 2000), 191.

16. Ibid., 193.

17. See Lance Armstrong, "Back in the Saddle," *Forbes ASAP* (December 3, 2001), www.forbes.com/asap/2001/1203/064.html.

18. Thomas à Kempis, *The Imitation of Christ*, ed. Paul Bechtel (Chicago: Moody, 1980), III:17:1–2.

19. William Law, A Serious Call to a Devout and Holy Life (New York: Paulist, 1978), 66.

September

1. Joseph Jungmann, *Christian Prayer Through the Centuries*, trans. John Coyne (New York: Paulist, 1978), 30.

2. Lorenzo Scupoli, *Spiritual Combat* (Manchester, N.H.: Sophia Institute Press, 2002), 76.

3. Saint Augustine, *Confessions* (Philadelphia: Westminster, 1955), 10.26.37.

4. Ibid., 12.16.23.

5. Quoted in Klaus Bockmuehl, *Listening to the God Who Speaks* (Colorado Springs: Helmers & Howard, 1990), 8.

6. Bockmuehl, *Listening to the God Who Speaks*, 49.

7. Quoted in Bockmuehl, *Listening to the God Who Speaks*, 8.

8. Ibid., 106.

9. Jerry Sittser, *When God Doesn't Answer Your Prayer* (Grand Rapids: Zondervan, 2003), 163.

10. Frank Buchman, *The Revolutionary Path* (London: Grosvenor, 1975), 2–3.

11. Ibid., 5.

12. Gordon Smith, *On the Way: A Guide to Christian Spirituality* (Colorado Springs: NavPress, 2001), 72.

13. M. Basil Pennington, *A Place Apart: Monastic Prayer and Practice for Everyone* (New York: Doubleday, 1983), 26.

14. Peter Howard, *Frank Buchman's Secret* (London: William Heinemann, 1961), 13.

15. François Fénelon, *Christian Perfection*, trans. Mildred Whitney Stillman (Minneapolis: Bethany House, 1975), 40.

16. Thomas à Kempis, *The Imitation of Christ*, ed. Paul Bechtel (Chicago: Moody, 1980), II:3:1.

17. Quoted in Brother Ugolino di Santa Maria, *The Little Flowers of Saint Francis* (trans. Raphael Brown (New York: Image, 1958), 62–63.

October

1. Marco R. della Cava, "The Price of Speed," *USA Today* (August 3, 2000), 10D.

2. R. Somerset Ward, *To Jerusalem: Devotional Studies in Mystical Religion* (Harrisburg, Pa.: Morehouse, 1994), 178.

3. Basil, "Letter CCXXXVI," para. 3, in St. Basil: Letters and Select Works, vol. 8, *A Select Library of Nicene and Post-Nicene Fathers of the Christian Church*, 2d series, ed. Philip Schaff and Henry Wace (1887; repr., Grand Rapids: Eerdmans, 1989), 279.

4. Quoted in Joseph Paul Kozlowski, *Spiritual Direction and Spiritual Directors* (Santa Barbara, Calif.: Queenship, 1998), 187.

5. Ibid., 253.

6. Ibid., 298.

7. George B. Sayer, *Jack: C. S. Lewis and His Times*, 187.

8. Ibid., 194.

9. Ibid., 203.

10. Ibid., 160.

11. Ibid., 200.

12. Ibid., 225.

13. Ibid.

14. Dan Allender and Tremper Longman

III, *Intimate Allies* (Wheaton, Ill.: Tyndale House, 1995), 287.

15. Ibid., 281.

16. Elton Trueblood and Pauline Trueblood, *The Recovery of Family Life* (New York: Harper, 1953), 50–51.

November

1. Otto Piper, *The Biblical View of Sex and Marriage* (New York: Scribner's, 1960), 215

2. Shauna Niequist, *Cold Tangerines: Celebrating the Extraordinary Nature of Everyday Life* (Grand Rapids: Zondervan 2007), 84.

3. Harper Lee, *To Kill a Mockingbird* (1960; repr., New York: HarperCollins, 1999), 49.

4. Ambrose, "Letter LXIII," para. 89–91, in Ambrose: Select Works and Letters, vol. 10, *A Select Library of Nicene and Post-Nicene Fathers of the Christian Church*, 2d series, ed. Philip Schaff and Henry Wace (1887; repr., Grand Rapids: Eerdmans, 1989), 470.

5. Francis de Sales, *Thy Will Be Done: Letters to Persons in the World* (Manchester, N.H.: Sophia Institute Press, 1995), 9–10.

6. Ron Sider, *Rich Christians in an Age of Hunger*, 20th anniversary revision (1977; repr., Nashville: Word, 1997), 190.

December

1. Elton Trueblood, *The Humor of Christ* (New York: Harper, 1964), 32.

2. I discuss this more fully in *Authentic Faith* (Grand Rapids: Zondervan, 2002), 228–34.

3. John and Susan Yates, *What Really Matters at Home: Eight Crucial Elements for Building Character in Your Family* (Dallas: Word, 1992), 141.

4. Elton Trueblood, *The Humor of Christ*, 32.

5. Randy Alcorn, *Heaven* (Wheaton, Ill.: Tyndale, 2004), 297–98; 373–90. Randy's comments about Christoplatonism are sprinkled throughout the book. Appendix A includes a helpful section that addresses the assumptions of Christoplatonism more fully.

6. Ibid., 15.

7. Ibid., 27.

8. Ruth Bell Graham, *Our Christmas Story* (Minneapolis: World Wide Publications, 1959).

9. Jerry Jenkins, *Hedges: Loving Your Marriage Enough to Protect It* (Brentwood, Tenn.: Wolgemuth and Hyatt, 1989), 142.

10. George Sayer, Jack: *C. S. Lewis and His Times*, 252.

11. Ibid.

12. Ambrose, "On the Duties of the Clergy," bk. 1, chap. 16, para. 62, in Ambrose: Select Works and Letters, vol. 10, *A Select Library of Nicene and Post-Nicene Fathers of the Christian Church*, 2d series, ed. Philip Schaff and Henry Wace (1887; repr., Grand Rapids: Eerdmans, 1989), 11.

SELECTIONS BY SOURCE

Authentic Faith

January 18, 19, 23, 25, 28
February 6
March 4, 5, 6, 18, 21, 22, 23, 25, 26, 27, 28
April 11, 13, 17, 19
May 12, 13, 20
June 5, 8, 14, 16
July 13, 14, 15, 16, 19, 20, 21, 29, 30
August 5, 27, 28, 29, 30
October 1, 2, 3, 4, 5, 6, 7, 9, 11, 12, 13, 14, 15, 16, 18, 19, 20, 21, 31
November 18, 19, 20, 21, 22, 23, 24, 29, 30
December 5, 8, 14, 26, 30

Devotions for a Sacred Marriage

February 29
June 3, 17, 27
July 7, 22
September 15
November 27
December 3, 6

Devotions for Sacred Parenting

January 13, 15, 16, 26
February 1, 2, 10, 11, 12, 14, 18
April 5, 23, 24
May 28
June 21, 28
July 18
August 19
September 14, 18, 25
November 8, 11, 12
December 9, 10, 19, 20, 22

The Glorious Pursuit

March 20
June 18, 19, 20, 22, 23
November 1, 2, 4, 10

Holy Available

January 1, 7, 8, 10, 14, 24, 29
February 5, 9, 16, 17, 19, 20, 22, 23, 25, 26, 28
March 1, 2, 3, 7, 8, 9, 13, 15, 16, 17
April 6, 7, 14, 22, 29, 30
May 4, 5, 6, 7, 8, 9, 21, 22, 23
July 10, 23, 24, 25
August 3, 4, 6, 7, 10, 11, 12
September 1, 2, 5, 6, 7, 8, 9, 10, 11, 12, 13, 16
October 8
November 25
December 4

Pure Pleasure

February 21
March 14, 30
April 8, 10, 18, 20
May 1, 3, 16
June 1, 6
November 7, 13, 14, 15, 16, 17, 26, 28
December 18, 31

Sacred Influence

January 11
June 10

Sacred Marriage

January 3, 6, 9, 20
February 3, 7, 8, 13, 15, 24, 27

March 10, 11, 19, 24, 31
April 1, 9, 28
May 2, 10, 11, 26, 29, 30, 31
June 4, 15
July 1, 3, 5, 12, 17
August 17, 18, 26
October 17, 22, 23, 24, 26, 27, 28
November 3, 5, 6
December 1, 16, 21, 27

Sacred Parenting

January 2, 4, 12
February 4, 24
March 12, 29
April 3, 4, 16, 21, 25, 26, 27
May 14, 15, 19, 27
June 9, 11, 12
July 4, 28, 31
August 2, 20, 21, 22, 23, 24, 25
September 17, 20, 23, 24, 26, 27, 30

October 10, 30
November 9
December 7, 11, 15, 17, 25, 28, 29

Sacred Pathways

January 5, 17, 21, 22, 30, 31
April 2, 12, 15
May 17, 18, 24, 25
June 2, 7, 13
July 2, 6, 8, 9, 11, 26, 27
August 8, 9, 13, 14, 15, 16
September 3, 19, 21, 22
December 2, 12, 13, 23, 24

Thirsting for God

January 27
June 24, 25, 26, 29, 30
August 1, 31
September 4, 28, 29
October 25, 29

CREDITS

The author thanks the following publishers for permission to excerpt passages from their books:

Harvest House: *Thirsting for God* (copyright © 1999/2011 by Gary Thomas). Used by permission.

NavPress: *The Glorious Pursuit* (copyright © 1998 by Gary Thomas). Used by permission.

Zondervan: *Authentic Faith* (copyright © 2002 by Gary L. Thomas), *Devotions for a Sacred Marriage* (copyright © 2005 by Gary L. Thomas), *Devotions for Sacred Parenting* (copyright © 2005 by Gary L. Thomas), *Holy Available* (copyright © 2007/2009 by Gary L. Thomas), *Pure Pleasure* (copyright © 2009 by Gary Thomas), *Sacred Influence* (copyright © 2006 by Gary L. Thomas), *Sacred Marriage* (copyright © 2006 by Gary L. Thomas), *Sacred Parenting* (copyright © 2004 by Gary L. Thomas), *Sacred Pathways* (copyright © 1996/2010 by Gary L. Thomas). Used by permission.

GARY THOMAS

Feel free to contact Gary at glt3@aol.com. Though he cannot respond personally to all correspondence, he would love to get your feedback. Please understand, however, that he is neither qualified nor able to provide counsel via e-mail.

For information about Gary's speaking schedule, visit his website (www .garythomas.com). Follow him on Twitter (garyLthomas) or connect with him on Facebook. To inquire about inviting Gary to your church, please e-mail his assistant: laura@garythomas.com.